P9-DGU-660

ESSAYS ON OLD TESTAMENT
HISTORY AND RELIGION

ESSAYS ON OLD TESTAMENT HISTORY AND RELIGION

ALBRECHT ALT

Translated by R. A. Wilson

Doubleday & Company, Inc.
Garden City, New York
1967

The versions of the essays here translated were published in a collection of Alt's essays on the history of Israel, *Kleine Schriften zur Geschichte des Volkes Israel*, I, II, III, München, 1953, 1959, 1964, and are printed by arrangement with C. H. Beck'sche Verlagsbuchhandlung. This volume was first published by Basil Blackwell in England.

Library of Congress Catalog Card Number 67-10372

Printed in the United States of America
First Edition in the United States of America

BIOGRAPHICAL NOTE

ALBRECHT ALT

The work of Albrecht Alt (1883–1956) must be reckoned among the most far-reaching and fruitful influences in European Old Testament scholarship in the twentieth century. As a University teacher he served in the Universities of Greifswald, Basel, Halle, and finally (from 1922 onwards) Leipzig. For a time he was Director of the German Evangelical *Institut für Altertumswissenschaft des Heiligen Landes* in Jerusalem, and for several years leader of its annual study course. From 1925 onwards he was President of the German *Verein zur Erforschung des Heiligen Landes.* These latter appointments indicate the principal spheres of Alt's interests and achievements in both teaching and research. He combined a mastery of the archaeology and historical geography of the Holy Land with a profound knowledge of the extra-biblical records relevant to the history and institutions of Israel. Until almost the end of his life, his publications in these fields of study remained for the most part dispersed in learned journals, *Festschriften,* and the like. When he reached the age of seventy, however, many of the most important were collected in two volumes of *Kleine Schriften.* A third volume appeared after Alt's death. It is from these collections that the essays translated in this book have been selected.

G. W. Anderson
Department of Old Testament
Literature and Theology,
University of Edinburgh.

CONTENTS

ABBREVIATIONS

The abbreviations used in the appendix to 'The God of the Fathers' are given at the end of the appendix.

AASOR	The Annual of the American Schools of Oriental Research.
AfO	Archiv für Orientforschung.
AJSL	The American Journal of Semitic Languages and Literatures.
AO	Der Alte Orient.
ARW	Archiv für Religionswissenschaft.
ASAE	Annales du Service des Antiquités de l'Égypte.
Ath. Mitt.	Mitteilungen des Kaiserlich Deutschen Archäologischen Instituts. Athenische Abteilung.
ÄZ	Zeitschrift für Ägyptische Sprache und Altertumskunde.
BASOR	Bulletin of the American School of Oriental Research.
BBLAK	Beiträge zur biblischen Landes- und Altertumskunde.
BJRL	Bulletin of the John Rylands Library.
BWAT	Beiträge zur Wissenschaft vom Alten Testament.
BZAW	Beihefte zur Zeitschrift für die Alttestamentliche Wissenschaft.
EAO	*Clermont-Ganneau,* Études d'archéologie orientale.
FuF	Forschungen und Fortschritte.
HUCA	The Hebrew Union College Annual.

JBL	Journal of Biblical Literature.
JEA	The Journal of Egyptian Archaeology.
JPOS	The Journal of the Palestine Oriental Society.
K.S., I; *K.S.*, II	*Alt*, Kleine Schriften zur Geschichte des Volkes Israels, Vols. I and II.
MVAG	Mitteilungen der vorderasiatisch-aegyptischen Gesellschaft.
OLZ	Orientalische Literaturzeitung.
PAES	Syria. Publications of the Princeton University Archaeological Expeditions to Syria in 1904–5 and 1909.
PEF Quart. Stat.	Palestine Exploration Fund. Quarterly Statement.
PJB	Palästina Jahrbuch des Deutschen evangelischen Instituts für Altertumswissenschaft des Heiligen Landes in Jerusalem.
RAO	*Clermont-Ganneau*, Recueil d'archéologie orientale.
RAss	Revue d'assyriologie et d'archéologie orientale.
RHR	Revue de l'histoire des religions.
RB	Revue biblique.
T.B.	Theologische Blätter.
ThLZ	Theologische Literaturzeitung.
VT	Vetus Testamentum.
WZKM	Wiener Zeitschrift für die Kunde des Morgenlandes.
ZAW	Zeitschrift für die alttestamentliche Wissenschaft.
ZDMG	Zeitschrift der Deutschen Morgenländischen Gesellschaft.
ZDPV	Zeitschrift des Deutschen Palästina–Vereins.
ZTK	Zeitschrift für Theologie und Kirche.
ZS	Zeitschrift für Semitistik.

THE GOD OF THE FATHERS

DER GOTT DER VÄTER
Beiträge zur Wissenschaft vom Alten und Neuen Testament, herausgeben von Rudolf Kittel, III Folge, Heft 12 (1929). W. Kohlhammer, Stuttgart

INTRODUCTION

Historically, the people of Israel came into existence because their tribes united in the worship of the god Yahweh. The tribes, or at least particular groups of them, may very well have considered themselves to be related even earlier than this, but not until they were so united were they all conscious of being one people. This awareness provided the indispensable spiritual foundation for their history as a nation. We know of no all-embracing political organization, nor of any common cultural influence, that might have played a creative role at the very beginning, and the later history of the nation shows that the consciousness of national unity was hampered rather than strengthened by political and cultural developments. We can hardly suggest, therefore, even as a hypothesis, that such factors were at work in the earlier period. Even much later, however, the fact that all the tribes worshipped a god who held this special relationship with no one else, proved to be the strongest force in preserving Israel's distinct characteristics and in restoring order in her life when outside influences had disturbed it. If we are in any way justified, then, in arguing back from the later history of the Israelite nation to its origins, we can only conclude that the event on which all further development was based took place when the tribes united in the worship of Yahweh.

Can we go on to describe this decisive process in historical detail? The condition and the nature of the tradition that has come down to us make it very difficult. For no foreign nation observed the growth of Israel or left any account of it; and as far as Israel's own literature is concerned, not only are there absolutely no records, in the strict sense, of the very early period, but it also lies far beyond the time which was fresh in the memory of the first true historians, writing during the foundation of the monarchy. We are dependent on a collection of sagas which were transmitted orally for a long time before they were put into literary form. The process by which the Israelite tribes were united in the worship of Yahweh was undoubtedly very complicated, and from the very nature of these sagas we cannot expect them to provide a complete picture. They isolate incidents that can only be properly evaluated in the context of the events leading up to and following them, and they weave together what in reality ought to remain separate. They collect round the figure of one hero what came about by the combined efforts of many, and they speak of the whole nation where only parts of it were involved. One would expect the history of the adoption by the tribes of the worship of Yahweh to have been recorded principally in the traditions of Moses and Joshua, but in their extant form these traditions are clearly dominated by the double tendency to reduce everything to the personal triumph of the hero, and at the same time to expand it into something that happened to the whole nation. At no point is it certain that their original form can be reconstructed.[1] One thing that may to some extent be faithfully reflected in them is the part played by the great national leaders; this, however, is only one factor, though an important one, in the course of events.[2] But the external history of the peoples who took part in these events is still largely obscure, and their inner development completely so; while no one who is acquainted with the matter would deny that the actual result, the bond between the tribes and God, and between themselves, can be explained

[1] A thorough analysis of the sagas of Moses and Joshua has recently been carried out by GRESSMANN and NOTH. But even their studies leave much still to be done.

[2] The historical relationship between what the tradition attributes to Moses and what it claims for Joshua raises special problems. This has been rightly stressed by SELLIN (*Mose* [1922]; *Geschichte der isr.-jüd. Volkes,* I [1924], pp. 97 ff.; *Oriental Studies Paul Haupt* [1926], pp. 125 ff.) and BIN GORION (*Sinai und Garizim* [1926]). An attempted solution is found in NOTH, *Das System der zwölf Stämme Israels* (1930), pp. 65 ff.

only when the inner and spiritual part of the process has been made clear.[3]

Of the many questions which the historian has to face in this connection, only one will be dealt with here. Was there anything in the existing religious inheritance of the tribes that paved the way for what was to come, so that what happened did not appear as a radical break with the past, destroying what already existed, but, in part at least, continued and developed it? Anyone who knows the considerable powers of assimilation displayed by the religion of Yahweh during its later history will immediately be inclined to suppose that this force must have been at work at the very beginning, perhaps to an extraordinary degree, to win for Yahweh not only single leaders, but a wide cross-section of the people. It is because of this possibility that the previous history of the tribes must be brought into our investigation; and this obliges us to examine all that the Israelites were conscious of as memories preserved from the time of their earliest ancestors. On this subject the sagas of Moses and Joshua yield very little information; they attribute everything to the establishment of the bond with Yahweh as the God of Israel. But is it not possible that reminiscences of the earlier stages in the religion of the tribes were preserved in the sagas of the Book of Genesis, from Abraham to the sons of Jacob, which are far less dominated by Yahwist tendencies?

The relatively recent date of the stories of the patriarchs in their literary formulation was recognized during the course of the last century. It seemed at once that the only possible result was the complete abandonment of any attempt to obtain information from them about the nature of the religion

[3] Of course no student of religious phenomena will be so misguided as to study Moses' personal experience of God without relating it to the experiences of the people as a whole. Cf. e.g. STAERK, *ZTK*, N.F. iv (1924), pp. 289 ff. But if the historian concludes that this experience led to a genuine innovation in religion, he is immediately obliged to consider what it was that enabled the people to accept the innovation, even, as perhaps was the case at first, with certain reservations, as the basic foundation of their national religious consciousness.

of the Israelite tribes before the adoption of Yahwism. How could any genuine memories of such an early period be preserved in them, when they were first put into literary form after the settlement and the formation of the kingdoms in Palestine? Would not every really ancient feature that they may have displayed in their earliest form now have faded to almost nothing, or even have disappeared completely, under the influence of the changes that had taken place in the meantime in the cultural and religious institutions of Israel? If this was so then the only remaining method of research into the nature of the religion that preceded Yahwism was the indirect one of working back from the fragments of non-Yahwist religion and superstition that can be observed here and there in the life of Israel during the later period. The results obtained from this method by Robertson Smith, Wellhausen, Stade and others after them are too well known for me to have to describe them in detail here.[4]

But surely the ideas and practices disclosed by this procedure, which were similar to those found underlying every ancient religion, go back too far into prehistory for us to suppose that they constituted the whole of the religion of the Israelite tribes, immediately before they united in the worship of Yahweh.[5] The religion of this whole region was already on a much higher plane. The more that was learnt during the last hundred years of the general religious characteristics of the second millennium B.C., the less one could be content with the picture presented by simply working backwards in this way. In addition to this, there was a development in the scientific method employed: the approach from the point of view of literary criticism alone, dealing principally with the more recent and written forms of the tradition, was supple-

[4] More recent studies along these lines may be found in HÖLSCHER, *Geschichte der isr. und jüd. Religion* (1922), pp. 3 ff., and BEER, *Welches war die älteste Religion Israels?* (1927).

[5] We must at least mention that this method is not altogether reliable, in that many of the elements on which its conclusions are based were first adopted by the Israelites, after their settlement in Palestine, from the original inhabitants.

mented by research into the growth of the sagas, the purpose of which was to separate the originally independent single saga from the secondary complexes in which it now appears, and to establish its earliest form and its primary meaning. It was Gunkel's work above all which brought about this change in direction. The natural result was that attention was drawn once more to the possible traces of earlier stages of religion in the sagas of Moses and Joshua, but particularly in those of Abraham and his sons; the prehistory of Israel now seemed as a whole to grow more important and easier to understand than in the research of the previous generations.

A basis for the reconstruction of the religious *status quo ante* was sought from the sagas in two directions. The first concerned the worship of Yahweh himself. Had his cult already been of considerable importance among the Israelite tribes for a long time, so that when they based their union on it, this was only to crown and consolidate their traditional inheritance? No certain proof of this has yet been given. The well-known restriction of the name of Yahweh to the period from Moses on, in the Elohist and priestly treatment of the sagas, can hardly be explained as simply the result of later theories about Israel's prehistory without any basis in the tradition, although there is no doubt that it was quite consciously seized on by the authors of these narratives in order to mark off different eras in the past. And while the Yahwist consistently calls Yahweh by this name from the very earliest times, this expresses his dominating conviction that Yahweh has always been God not only over Israel, but over the whole of history as well. It is therefore neither an unsophisticated customary usage, nor is it something taken over as it stood from an older form of the tradition. So it can hardly be claimed as a genuine reminiscence of the existence of the worship of Yahweh among the Israelite tribes before they united. The names of the tribes and their forefathers do not give a single reliable indication of its existence;[6] this does

[6] The view of PROCKSCH (*Kommentar zur Genesis,* 2nd and 3rd ed. [1924], p. 178, on Gen. xxix. 35), that Yahweh formed the first element in the name of the tribe Jehuda (Juda) depends on a very

not tell us a great deal, since they are comparatively few in number, but it is worth noticing nevertheless. A more important consideration, to my mind, is that the creative power in the bond of unity between the tribes forged by their worship of Yahweh can hardly be explained if this form of worship had already played an important part among them previously. It seems unlikely, then, that the Israelite tribes—some or all of them—had for a long time practised the worship of Yahweh at sanctuaries of their own in the regions from which they came.[7]

This view is supported by the fact that the oldest tradition, as has for long been recognized, contains several indications that the worship of Yahweh was not originally peculiar to Israel, but was located at a mountain sanctuary in the desert, visited and used—perhaps exclusively at first—by other tribes besides the Israelites. The best example known of such a place of pilgrimage, attracting worshippers from a very wide area, is provided by the so-called Sinai inscriptions of the first centuries A.D., according to Moritz's interpretation of them as the memorial inscriptions of Nabataean pilgrims at the foot of the holy mountains in the Sinai peninsula;[8] and I consider it perfectly possible not merely that this is an exact analogy to the mountain of God in Israelite tradition, but that the Nabataean cult in the high ranges of the Sinai peninsula is actually the successor, in the same place, of the oldest form known to us of the worship of Yahweh.[9] Be this as it may,

---

unusual phonetic formation and is thus improbable. I consider Jehuda to be a place-name like Jogbeha, etc.; cf. also ALBRIGHT, *JBL*, xlvi (1927), pp. 168 ff., and NOTH, *Die isr. Personnennamen* (1928), p. iii, n. 4.

[7] A recent presentation of the contrary view can be found in ELLIGER, *T.B.*, ix (1930), cols. 97 ff.

[8] MORITZ, *Der Sinaikult in heidnischer Zeit* (1916); cf. in particular, GRESSMANN, *ThLZ*, xlii (1917), cols. 153 ff.

[9] Most recent studies place the biblical mountain of God in Midian in N.W. Arabia. (This is argued, and the literature given, in GRESSMANN, *Mose und seine Zeit* (1913), pp. 409 ff.; cf. also MUSIL, *The Northern Ḥeğâz* [1926], pp. 296 ff.). This is usually based on the details of the description of Yahweh's appearance on the mountain of God (Exod. xix. etc.) which fits the volcanic

the enduring effect on the Israelite mind of the original localization of Yahweh on the holy mountain in the desert (and nothing suggests to us that Israelite tribes ever lived in its immediate neighbourhood) warns us against supposing that Yahweh had always been the particular god of these tribes. We may presume no more than that a close connection existed between them and the purely local numen of this mountain sanctuary, which other peoples visited besides themselves.[10] However important such a connection may have been in preparing the Israelites for a unity centred on Yahweh, which later separated them from his other worshippers, yet if it really existed during the period before they united, it did not imply any bond which prevented the tribes from practising other cults, especially those more peculiarly their own.[11]

---

mountains of Midian but cannot easily be explained from the geological features of the Sinai peninsula. It becomes unnecessary, if in accordance with the saga of Moses (Exod. ii. f. 18) we accept that the Midianites took part in the cult of this distant mountain sanctuary and that they attributed to the numen they worshipped there the volcanic phenomena of their own country. But cf. also DALMAN, *Arbeit und Sitte in Palästina,* I, i (1928), pp. 216 ff.; NOTH, *PJB*, xxxvi (1940), pp. 5 ff.

[10] This limited purpose provides the strongest reason why BEER's view (*Welches . . . älteste Religion,* pp. 10 ff.) that the Israelite tribes worshipped Yahweh as a 'High God' even before the time of Moses is open to objection. I shall not discuss here the evidence, in most cases very doubtful, which has been alleged from cuneiform documents to show that the worship of Yahweh existed outside Israel (cf. in particular the recent discussion in DRIVER, *ZAW*, N.F. v [1928], pp. 7 ff.; NOTH, op. cit., pp. 101 ff.). I refer only to LIDZBARSKI's observation, usually overlooked, that in the proper name עבדאהיו found several times in the Sinaitic inscriptions mentioned above, there is contained a divine name אהיו, presumably pre-Nabataean, which is philologically identical with the Hebrew אהיה, as the name of Yahweh is transcribed in Exod. iii. 14 (*Ephem. f. semit. Epigr.*, III [1912], p. 270, n. 1; but cf. also *Nachr. d. Gött. Ges. d. Wiss.*, phil.-hist. Kl., 1916, pp. 91 ff.)

[11] There is nothing to prove the theory that at this early period the cult of Yahweh had already been introduced in sanctuaries in the area inhabited by Israelite tribes, or as one might easily suppose in Kadesh, which plays so important a part in the saga of Moses. The saga of Kadesh could just as easily consist of reminiscences of the actual introduction there of the worship of Yahweh.

From this angle, then, there is no difficulty in supposing that the Israelite tribes took part at the same time in the worship of the gods whose titles appear here and there in the sagas of the patriarchs in Genesis, and which we may take with Gressmann and others to be originally quite distinct numina, even though in the more recent forms of the tradition, which are all we possess, they are throughout identified with Yahweh as the God of Israel.[12] This identification was made easier by the fact that in common with so many other deities in Palestine and Syria, they had no proper names, but were called by compound expressions, whose first element is regularly the appellative *'Ēl*, 'God', while the second element, usually subordinated to the first in the genitive, marks the individual characteristics of the numen in question; thus the whole expression serves at least as a substitute for a personal name. This made possible the secondary understanding of these titles as mere epithets of Yahweh. Of these gods, the following are mentioned in the sagas of the patriarchs in Genesis: *'Ēl Bēt'ēl* of Bethel,[13], *'Ēl 'Ōlam* of Beersheba,[14] *'Ēl Ro'i* at a sanctuary even farther south,[15] and, in addition, without any localization, *'Ēl 'Ēlyōn*[16] and *'Ēl Šaddai*.[17] The

[12] GRESSMANN, *ZAW*, xxx (1910), pp. 8, 23; *Mose und seine Zeit*, pp. 426 ff. KITTEL makes considerable use of the theory based on this type of religion in another context: *Geschichte des Volkes Israel* (5th and 6th ed.), I (1928), pp. 258 *et passim; Die Religion des Volkes Israel*, 2nd ed. (1929), pp. 9 ff., 27 ff.

[13] Gen. xxxi. 13; xxxv. 7. Cf. DUSSAUD, *Les origines cananéennes du sacrifice israélite* (1921), pp. 231 ff.; JIRKU, *ZAW*, xxxix (1921), pp. 158 f.; BAUDISSIN, 'Vom Alten Testament' (*Marti-Festschrift*, 1925), pp. 1 ff.; KITTEL, *JBL*, xxxxiv (1925), pp. 123 ff.; GRESSMANN, *ZAW*, N.F. ii (1925), pp. 281 ff.; KITTEL, ibid., N.F. iii (1926), pp. 170 ff.; EISSFELDT, *ARW*, xxviii (1930), pp. 1 ff.

[14] Gen. xxi. 33. Cf. SÖDERBLOM, *Das Werden des Gottesglaubens* (1916), pp. 302 ff.; BROCKELMANN, *ARW*, xxi (1922), pp. 120 f.; KITTEL, *Die Hellenistische Mysterienreligion und das Alte Testament* (1924), pp. 76 ff.

[15] Gen. xvi. 13.

[16] Gen. xiv. 18 ff., etc. Cf. SCHWALLY, *ARW*, xix (1919), p. 356.

[17] Gen. xvii. 1, etc. Cf. TORCZYNER, *Die Bundeslade und die Anfänge der Religion Israels* (1922), pp. 282 ff.; ALBRIGHT, *JBL*, liv (1935), pp. 180 ff.

Book of Judges adds *'Ēl Berīt* or *Ba'al Berīt* of Shechem.[18] No one need doubt, in view of the available analogies from outside the Bible, that all this belongs to a very ancient type of religious practice.

But what can we say about the participation of the Israelite tribes in the worship of these numina? For example, can we say, with some scholars, that this *'El*-religion was the normal cult of the tribes before they united, as opposed to the later religion of Yahweh and the *Ba'al* cult of the Canaanites? The religion of *'El* is obviously to be distinguished from that of Yahweh. But we cannot very well make a distinction between *'Ēl* and *Ba'al* when both are used as alternatives in the title of the numen of Shechem mentioned above; the absence of compounds with *Ba'al* in Genesis is presumably the result of the artificial unity obtained later by eliminating from the titles the part that had become offensive. Apart from this, the only important characteristic of these *'El*-deities, whose nature does not appear clearly in the brief mention that is made of them, is their localization at a holy place in Palestine. As a rule, the original purpose of the sagas in which they appear is the legitimation of these sanctuaries. In these circumstances we cannot exclude the pre-Israelite population of the country from those who took part in their worship, and suppose that it was the Israelites who used them, even before entering Palestine.[19] Much more likely would seem the older theory that they were local deities, and that the Israelites were first numbered among their worshippers during and after their settlement in the area where they were acknowledged.[20] In this

[18] Judges ix. 4, 46.

[19] It was a mistake on GRESSMANN's part to begin his investigation of the *El*-religion from the question 'What was the religion of the Hebrews?' (*Mose und seine Zeit*, p. 472, n. 1), instead of trying to find out by whom these gods were worshipped, quite independently of the other problem. It was also a mistake to accept the oldest Israelite proper names, compounded with *'Ēl* (such as Israel itself) as a proof of the existence of this particular form of the religion of *'Ēl* amongst the tribes.

[20] Recent arguments in favour of this can be found in BAUDISSIN, '*Vom Alten Testament*' (*Marti-Festschrift*), p. 11; *Kyrios*, III (1927), pp. 128 ff.; WEISER, *Religion und Sittlichkeit der Genesis* (1928), pp. 13 f., n. 9 f.

case, these cults could not be taken into account in inquiring into the nature of the religion of the Israelite tribes before the establishment of their bond with Yahweh. And if one supposes that the relations Israel had with Palestine in general extended to these sanctuaries, this would amount to no more than what was involved when the tribes took part in the worship of Yahweh at the holy mountain in the desert: a loose association with the religious practice of other peoples and not the characteristic religion of the forefathers of Israel.

Scholars cannot rest content with this, especially since a further consideration, to which we have so far given no attention, shows that the above conclusions are unsatisfactory. This is the question of the relation of the Israelites' religion to the oldest forms of communal organization among them, i.e. to the formation of the tribes and the smaller groups of which they were composed. Was the religious element altogether lacking in their ideal constitution? And if not, can we accept that their inmost bond of unity was the connection with Yahweh, the god of the holy mountain in the desert, or with the numen of some sanctuary in Palestine? It is generally accepted as axiomatic that in the semi-nomadic life led by the ancestors of Israel before they united in the worship of Yahweh, they were divided according to their tribes in their religious belief and practice.[21] But the sagas that have been handed down, and other records from later times, so far do not seem to contain sufficient material for us to reconstruct the actual religious belief and practice of a whole tribe or group.[22] Considering the tenacity with which the Israelites retained their ancient tribal divisions after they had adopted the culture of Palestine, this apparent deficiency is surprising. Did the process of uniting in the worship of Yahweh, or the adoption of the cults they found established in Palestine supplant the tribes' own religion so completely that not a single

[21] Cf. BAUDISSIN, *Kyrios*, III, pp. 163 f. *et passim*.

[22] BAUDISSIN, *Kyrios*, III, pp. 169 ff., deals in full with the failure of recent attempts to deduce the names of Israelite tribal gods from the names of tribes and figures in the sagas.

trace of it could survive, not even in the form of a saga or a term used in the cult? Or have scholars simply made the mistake of not paying sufficient attention to the forms of tradition that deal with this religion?

I am inclined to believe the latter. For the Israelite tradition in fact contains a distinctive religious element of which the peculiar characteristics have not yet been recognized and which, if I judge aright, goes back to the original religious forms used by individual tribes and groups. This is the tradition of the God of Abraham, the Fear of Isaac, and the Mighty One of Jacob, or in short, of the God of the Fathers.

THE TRADITION

The Theory of the Elohist

To get to the roots of the tradition about the God of the Fathers, we cannot start from the passages in the later literature that call Yahweh by the liturgical title of the God of Abraham, Isaac and Jacob.[23] For although the persistence of this formula is very remarkable, it has been so rubbed smooth by time that it no longer betrays anything of its origin. If it were all we possessed we could only pose the question, and have no hope of deciding, whether either the identification of the God of the Fathers with Yahweh, taken for granted in this expression, or the definite linking up of the names of the patriarchs, were altogether original.

We can come a great deal closer to the origins if we turn to the narrative works woven together in the Hexateuch. Here there is at least one place where the connection between Yahweh and the God of the Fathers is presented as fundamental to the fullest extent possible within the bounds of a story. I refer to the Elohist version of Yahweh's first ap-

[23] The passages are collected and an attempt made to interpret them in STAERK, *Studien zur Religions- und Sprachgeschichte des Alten Testaments,* I (1889), pp. 21 ff.

pearance to Moses in Exodus iii.[24] It is true that even here the names of the three patriarchs have already been linked together in the formula 'the God of Abraham, Isaac and Jacob'; this is the title by which God, appearing to Moses, immediately makes himself known to him (vs. 6). On the other hand the identification of Yahweh with the God of the Fathers is not simply presupposed, but is as it were solemnly ratified before the eyes of the reader as the story proceeds and God reveals himself, in answer to Moses' question, by pronouncing his name Yahweh with his own lips (vs. 14).[25] The specific function of this story in the plan of the whole Elohist narrative is, on the one hand, to make the reader conscious of the complete contrast in the sight of God between the time of the patriarchs and that of Moses, and on the other hand to compose the difference again in a higher unity by presenting the same God as bearer of the old and new divine names. The story thus becomes the link by which the Elohist sagas of the patriarchs and of Moses can be kept distinct and yet brought into a very close relationship with one another.

No other narrative work in the Hexateuch contains an exact parallel to this, and the Yahwist, who shows Yahweh in intercourse with men, and especially with the ancestors of Israel, from the very beginning, obviously cannot be expected to provide one. He cannot present the new element that comes into the picture with Moses as the revelation of the name Yahweh, and so he describes even the actual call of Moses without the slightest suggestion of anything similar.[26] The priestly narrative is different again. Its version is like that of the Elohist, in that it combines the revelation of the name Yahweh with the call of Moses in a single act, and thereby contrasts the new name uttered by Yahweh himself with the title revealed to the patriarchs. The more sophisticated style

[24] The Elohist version consists of vss. 1, 4b, 6 (a lacuna), 9–14, 18–23*.

[25] In vs. 15 (an addition) the two divine names are immediately combined.

[26] Exod. iii. 2–3, 4a, 5, 7–8a.

of this writer enables him to express the underlying significance of the distinction between past and present even more clearly than the Elohist. But in the priestly narrative the title of the God of the Fathers, which is now superseded by the name of Yahweh, is not 'the God of Abraham, Isaac and Jacob', as in the Elohist, but *'Ēl Šaddai,* one of the ancient forms discussed in the introduction.[27] This divergence between the Elohist and the priestly writer at the crucial point of a story which they tell otherwise in the same way, and which has the same important function to fulfil in both narratives, as well as the complete lack of any parallel in the Yahwist, is of fundamental importance for our study of what they tell us about the tradition behind them. For it follows that the writers could not have possessed at this point any fixed and unified tradition that they felt bound to follow. They may owe the form their narrative takes to earlier writings and traditions, which can neither be proved nor disproved, but in any case they each order their material in their own way, and the real reason for the different pictures they give is that the traditional material in each is adapted to a different dominant theme. Later theories about the theology of history are here in conflict, and anyone who wishes to sift out the genuine ancient traditions must set these secondary elements aside altogether.

Gressmann and Galling have recently and rightly emphasized that the Elohist account in Exodus iii, in particular, can only have reached its present complicated state by the conscious intervention of the writer.[28] As it stands, it contains obvious tensions, which can hardly be conceived of within the simple original saga. The revelation of Yahweh's name and the call of Moses could each in themselves have provided the substance of a single complete story, and the Yahwist shows us moreover that the two themes were by no means invariably linked together in Israel. But this tension is bearable, and is probably not noticed by the reader in most cases,

[27] Exod. vi, 2–8.

[28] GRESSMANN, *Mose und seine Zeit,* pp. 31 ff.; GALLING, *Die Erwählungstraditionen Israels* (1928), pp. 56 ff.

since the writer skilfully makes one theme develop organically out of the other. Moses, called to save his people out of Egypt (vs. 9), desires to know, as proof that his call is legitimate, the name of the god who is sending him (vs. 13); and he receives from the mouth of Yahweh a barely concealed answer (vs. 14). Whether the Elohist is the first to weave the material together in this way can hardly be determined; it is quite possible that he was following older versions of the whole saga of Moses. All this, however, does not affect the element in the story which matters most for us here, the identification of Yahweh with the God of the Fathers. For if the god who appears to Moses announces himself in his very first words as the God of Abraham, Isaac and Jacob (vs. 6), there is no need for him to be given a new name. That Moses should expect that his people would ask him the name of the god who commissioned him when he came to them with the message 'the God of your Fathers has sent me to you' (vs. 13) is self-contradictory.[29] Nothing occurs in the story to resolve this tension; the naming of the God of Abraham, Isaac and Jacob at the beginning of the whole scene develops no further, and a clear sign that this element is foreign to the story is found in the fact that if it is completely removed a coherent narrative can still be constructed from the remainder of the text.[30] The analysis of the passage confirms the result we have ob-

[29] This was first clearly recognized by GALLING (op. cit., p. 57). GRESSMANN presumed that for God to announce himself as the 'God of Abraham, Isaac and Jacob' was not sufficient to remove every doubt in the minds of Moses and his fellow Israelites as to which numen it was who had appeared (p. 34). He was thus prevented from making this decisive observation.

[30] The passage is constructed so as to imply that at first Moses does not realize which God is calling him (vss. 2, 4b) and commissioning him to lead the Israelites out of Egypt (vss. 9–12). This makes it easier to understand why he asks the name of the god (vs. 13), especially when one considers that the scene takes place at the mountain of God in the desert, where perhaps several different gods were worshipped and where in any case different gods could reveal themselves. The secret of Yahweh is thus kept right up to the last moment, and the conclusion becomes the climax of the whole.

tained above by comparing this Elohist presentation with the other narrative works in the Pentateuch: the writer was the first to bring the naming of the God of the Fathers into the story, and his intention in adding this was to reveal to the reader, at the very point where the age of the Fathers passes into the age of Moses, the close connection which according to his view of the theology of history exists between these two periods.

But if it is the case that the purely theoretical purposes of the Elohist led him to place the figure of the God of the Fathers in a position of such emphasis, then the question arises whether the distinctive title God is given here was coined by him in the first place, merely in order to contrast it with the name Yahweh, thus effectively demonstrating the difference between the two main eras in the past. It is not very likely that he invented so freely. For it is not usual for Israelite historians to develop their theories without any reference to factors supplied by tradition; their procedure is normally to isolate from the traditional material current at the time the single features that seem particularly important to them, at the expense of others, and to make these chosen elements express their own views. This is the case, for example, with the use of the divine title *'Ēl Šaddai,* which the priestly writer introduces with the very first revelation to Abraham and then repeats several times in his very brief sketch of the time of the Fathers, finally contrasting it with the name of Yahweh, first revealed at the call of Moses.[31] That this is not a newly-invented title for God is nowadays admitted by everybody, and the contribution of the priestly writer is seen to be simply that he ignored the other names and expressions that occurred in the tradition in order to lay all the stress on this one title. Is the preference of the Elohist for 'the God of the Fathers' an example of the same procedure, and does this mean we have in it another ancient element out of the common tradition of Israel, used for the quite secondary purpose of expressing a particular theory?

[31] Gen. xvii. 1; xxviii. 3; xxxv. 11; xliii. 14; xlviii. 3; Exod. vi. 3.

We can only accept this if we can show not only that the Elohist gives the name of the God of Abraham, Isaac and Jacob in Exodus iii, and by way of preparation for this, in his version of the sagas of the patriarchs, but also that the other forms of the ancient tradition, unaffected by the theories of the Elohist, are likewise acquainted with it.

The Material in the Sagas of the Patriarchs

Once the principles of the bond between the tribes and Yahweh have been introduced through the call of Moses, however the latter may be presented in the different narratives, there is naturally no further place in the tradition concerning the period immediately following for the God of Abraham, Isaac and Jacob: Yahweh and his name dominate the whole scene from this point on.[32] The position of this title in the developed tradition is therefore the same as that of the *'Ēlīm* of the sanctuaries in Palestine. We can only expect further traces of the cult of the God of the Fathers, if we are looking for genuine ancient tradition, in the sagas of the patriarchs themselves. There is in fact no lack of such traces there. Some of these are to be found in the Elohist version of the tradition in Genesis, and gradually introduce the reader, almost without his noticing, to the writer's version of the course of history, which is consummated theoretically, as we know, in Exodus iii.[33] But references to the God of Abraham, Isaac and Jacob in Genesis are by no means restricted to the Elohist, but are even more frequent in the Yahwist narrative, and the substance of the reference is essentially the same at

[32] The fact that in Deuteronomy the expression 'the God of thy (your) Fathers' is often found in apposition to the name of Yahweh, has no connection with the narrative tradition, and need not be taken into account in this context.

[33] There is thus no reason to follow STAERK (*Studien*, I, p. 32) in excluding the expression 'the God of Abraham, Isaac and Jacob' in Exod. iii. 6 as a later addition. For there would still remain the expression 'the God of thy father' (vs. 13 'the God of your fathers'), which in the Elohist would mean exactly the same.

both sources. We have evidence to work on, therefore, from the whole tradition, and not merely from its later literary ramifications.[34] The priestly writing provides no further material; the little that the writer thought fit to add from the tradition of the patriarchs, he linked so consistently with *'Ēl Šaddai* that it seemed impossible for him to use other divine titles as well. But because we know the reasons for what he did, his omission of any reference to the God of the Fathers is no longer remarkable, and cannot reduce in the slightest the value of the other earlier tradition preserved by the Yahwist and the Elohist.

In the whole context of the patriarchal sagas each element of the expression 'the God of Abraham, Isaac and Jacob' naturally occurs apart from the others in historical sequence. We shall consider later whether this breaking down of the single formula of Exodus iii and subsequent passages is secondary, or whether it represents the original formulation, the history of which must be investigated in its turn. We must also leave open for the moment the question whether the identification of Yahweh with the God of Abraham, Isaac and Jacob, which is naturally only asserted openly by the Yahwist, but is taken for granted, as we saw above, in the theory of the Elohist, accords with the original meaning of these divine titles; or whether, as in the case of the *'Ēlīm* of the Palestine sanctuaries, there was an earlier stage where the numina were regarded as quite distinct from each other. First of all we must look at the relevant passages in Genesis.

The Yahwist prehistory must be excluded at once, because it goes back beyond the time of the patriarchs. The phrase

[34] The so-called 'Laienquelle' which EISSFELDT isolates from the other ancient traditions (*Ḥexateuchsynopse* [1922]) and which according to him is the oldest of all, does not mention the God of the Fathers at all in Genesis, but in its account of the calling of Moses, introduces it without any previous preparation in a very full and formal expression (Exod. iv. 5). This is a very remarkable fact, which provides little support for Eissfeldt's analysis. I should hesitate to follow Galling (*Die Erwählungstraditionen Israels*), pp. 57 and 64 f., in drawing further conclusions from it.

'Yahweh the God of Shem', in a blessing spoken by Noah, stands quite alone and, if it belongs to the original text at all, can only be useful for our purpose later on, in connection with the similar expressions given by this writer in the patriarchal sagas.[35] But of course the Yahwist and Elohist versions of the story of Abraham do not refer to the God of Abraham by this name; it begins to occur, fairly frequently, in the sagas of Isaac and Jacob. There is however one exception; during Abraham's lifetime the Yahwist makes his chief slave, on a journey to seek a wife from among the Aramaeans for Isaac, call on and praise Yahweh as 'the God of my lord Abraham'.[36] But the expression occurs in such a special connection that any generalization can be ruled out automatically. Because the slave belongs to his master's *familia*, he worships his god, and when he is far from his master and appeals to this god concerning his master's affairs, he very properly expresses his right to do so by mentioning in his prayer the relationship that exists between God, master and servant. This reference to the God of Abraham is likewise valuable only in connection with the passages we have yet to consider.

More seems to be implied by the Yahwist when he begins Yahweh's words in a theophany to Isaac with the declaration 'I am the God of your father Abraham', the name Yahweh not being included.[37] The following words show why, when at the beginning of the theophany God reveals his identity, he refers to Abraham: it is for Abraham's sake that Isaac is to be blessed; the special concern of God for the destiny of Isaac's descendants results from the special relationship between him and their forefather. The conclusion of this very bare account is the erection of an altar by Isaac—to the God of Abraham, we should have thought from the introduction; but the Yahwist puts in the name of Yahweh again. The whole story does not give the

[35] Gen. ix. 26 J.

[36] Gen. xxiv. 12, 27, 42, 48 J. The author of this long and detailed story obviously intends to differentiate between the title each person gives to God: He makes Abraham use the expression 'Yahweh the God of Heaven (and of the earth)' (vss. 3, 7); the Aramaean invariably uses the name 'Yahweh' by itself (vss. 31, 50 f.).

[37] Gen. xxvi. 24 J.

impression that it goes back to an older, independent saga. In all probability it was simply made up by the Yahwist himself.[38] What this passage does make very clear is the value this writer set on the expression 'the God of Abraham'; it seemed to him particularly suitable for making his readers aware of the inner connection between Abraham and Isaac.

The Yahwist introduces the God of Isaac with like solemnity, in the revelation made to Jacob at Bethel as he fled from Esau.[39] Here are Yahweh's first words: 'I am Yahweh, the God of your father Abraham and the God of Isaac.'[40] Jacob represents the next generation, and so God's title acquires one more clause, but the meaning remains unaltered, as is shown by what God goes on to say to Jacob in the course of this appearance. In the overall plan of the Yahwist history of the patriarchs this scene obviously has the same function as the appearance to Isaac discussed above: it links Jacob with Isaac as the appearance to Isaac links him with Abraham. It must also have been composed by the Yahwist, especially since the Elohist version of Jacob's experience at Bethel, which shows quite clearly its origin in an old and independent saga, contains no parallels at all with the speech in which God reveals himself in the Yahwist version. It does not mention the God of Abraham and Isaac.

But even the Elohist begins to speak of the God of the Fathers in the saga of Jacob. At first he does so only in a general sense; when Jacob proclaims to his wives 'The God of my fathers has been with me'[41] and in the important confession of Laban: 'The God of your father has spoken to me

[38] Like PROCKSCH, ad. loc., GUNKEL takes this as a later addition, but he probably underestimates the extent to which the Yahwist was prepared, here as elsewhere, to alter and adapt his traditional material.

[39] The Yahwist has already shown Jacob speaking deceitfully to Isaac of 'Yahweh thy God' (Gen. xxvii. 20). This is certainly not meant as a preparation for this scene.

[40] Gen. xxviii. 13 J; 'of thy father' might be an interpolation (cf. SIEVERS and PROCKSCH, ad loc.).

[41] Gen. xxxi. 5b.

this night.'[42] He uses more specific terms—if this saying is rightly assigned to the Elohist—in the course of Jacob's quarrel with Laban: 'If the God of my father, the God of Abraham and the Fear of Isaac, had not been by my side.'[43] We shall have to return later to the peculiar and distinctive title 'the Fear of Isaac'. But all the passages we have just given act simply as a preparation for the conclusion of the story: when Jacob and Laban make peace with one another, in accordance with the custom of the ancient world, each names his θεὸς πατρῷος as his surety for the treaty they have concluded: 'Let the God of Abraham and the God of Nahor be judges between us.'[44] 'So Jacob swore by the fear of his father Isaac', says the other source.[45]

The conclusion of this story gave rise to considerable misgivings later on. Was it not plain paganism for the ancestor of Israel and one of his relations to swear by two different gods? This dangerous sentence had to be rendered harmless by an addition or alteration. When the text was amended to this end, the result was not always the same. The easiest solution appears in the Greek translation, which changes the predicate into the singular: 'The God of Abraham and the God of Nahor shall be a judge between us', so that the reader would naturally conclude that the two subjects were identical. The Jewish Massoretic tradition went about it differently, not daring to alter the original plural of the predicate, but attempting to put a singular sense on the two subjects by the apposi-

[42] Gen. xxxi. 29b; 'your' is perhaps a later alteration replacing 'thy' on account of Laban's words immediately preceding, which are in the plural.

[43] Gen. xxxi. 42a. Opinions differ as to which source this verse comes from. The reference to the God of the Fathers shortly afterwards in vs. 53 must obviously be divided between two sources, i.e. the Yahwist and the Elohist, and one might suppose that both are involved in this verse also. Since the Yahwist up to now has spoken simply of 'the God of Isaac', the distinctive expression 'the Fear of Isaac' is more likely to come from the Elohist. I do not feel that I can give a certain decision.

[44] Gen. xxxi, 53a—presumably from the Yahwist; see the previous note.

[45] Gen. xxxi. 53b E?

tion 'the God of their fathers'; the weakness is simply that the addition fits clumsily into the sentence, does not agree with the plural predicate, and above all does not fit the idea in the speech of judging 'between us'.[46] The Samaritan Massoretic version goes the furthest, following the subjects by both the singular predicate and the singular apposition, and altering the latter as well: 'Let the God of Abraham and the God of Nahor be a judge between us, the God of Abraham.' Obviously this version is equally unsatisfactory.

All these abortive attempts to improve the text only show the great antiquity of what is revealed by the original form: like Jacob, Laban also had a θεὸς πατρῷος, referred to by the name of his ancestor, and for both parties these numina were their own gods, apart from whom no other could serve to bind permanently by an oath the men belonging to the leaders. It is most improbable that the writer should have introduced this feature voluntarily, as a secondary element, into the story of the pact between Jacob and Laban, which, it can hardly be denied, has the characteristics of a genuinely ancient and independent saga; the occurrence of the θεὸς πατρῷος in *both* the literary versions in which the story is given is a decisive argument against such a possibility. The choice of two different titles for the god from among the various ancient forms available seems to have been the responsibility of the writers—it is due to them that in one source we hear of the 'God of Nahor' and in the other of the 'Fear of Isaac'.[47] Unless the whole picture is false, then, this story brings us considerably closer to the origins of the tradition than the

[46] One may doubt whether König, ad. loc., has given the correct meaning of the words in apposition with his translation 'the God of each of their tribes'. What could have been the purpose of the addition if this is what it means? Ehrlich's correction (ad. loc.): אבותינו for אביהם was anticipated hundreds of years ago (cf. the MS. o of the LXX in Brooke-Maclean).

[47] The inconsistency that in one version the oath is taken by the gods of both parties, whereas in the other, only the god by whom Jacob swears is mentioned, must also be attributed to the literary redactors (cf. below pp. 35–36).

artificially constructed scenes of the Yahwist in the stories of Isaac and Jacob.

The rest of the saga of Jacob contains only one further mention of the God of the Fathers, at the beginning of a prayer which the Yahwist puts into the mouth of Jacob before his meeting with Esau: 'O God of my father Abraham and God of my father Isaac, Yahweh . . .'[48] This is clearly reminiscent of the Yahwist theophany at Bethel and also of the similar revelation to Isaac, which we regarded as being composed by the writer himself. Our verdict must be the same here: the whole prayer obviously has no older tradition behind it.[49]

This is probably also the case with certain passages in the story of Joseph, such as when Joseph, in Egypt, before he has made himself known, speaks to his brothers about 'your God and the God of your fathers';[50] when Jacob, at the blessing of the sons of Joseph, calls on the God 'before whom my fathers walked, Abraham and Isaac';[51] and finally when, after the death of Jacob, the brothers of Joseph refer to themselves before him as 'the slaves of the God of thy father' —by pointing to the religion they share with him they hope to dispose him towards an ultimate reconciliation.[52] All these passages, especially the last, are fresh evidence about what the literary redactors of the older stories and sagas, both the Yahwist and the Elohist, considered to be the distinctive element in the religion of their nation's ancestors. In these passages also, however, the form in which they now appear is

[48] Gen. xxxii. 10.

[49] Here again GUNKEL suspects a later addition; cf. above, n. 38.

[50] Gen. xliii. 23 J.

[51] Gen. xlviii. 15 E. The names of the patriarchs fit awkwardly into the picture; they were added later. GUNKEL's proposal to alter the relative clause so that 'God' becomes the subject: 'God, who walked before my fathers' is worthy of consideration, but cannot be shown to be necessary. One must notice here that the reference to the patriarchs is only one element among several in the title which God is given; the hand of the literary redactor can be seen unmistakably in the whole passage.

[52] Gen. l. 17 E.

the work of the redactors; it is not possible to decide whether the pre-literary tradition of the story of Joseph already contained these features.

Only one episode of the story of Joseph is perhaps rather different. On the way to Egypt Jacob offers a sacrifice at Beersheba to 'the God of his father Isaac',[53] and there he is granted a revelation, which begins 'I am God, the God of your father'.[54] For the first and only time, then, we hear of the cult of a θεὸς πατρῷος offered in a particular place. Gunkel has rightly emphasized that this does not mean that the episode is the legend of the founding of a cult, such as we often find for the *'Ēlīm* of the sanctuaries of Palestine. It takes for granted the cult of the God of the Fathers, and significantly this cult is situated in Beersheba, where according to the sagas Jacob's father Isaac had lived. It is therefore conceivable that even though this episode may not itself belong to the oldest stratum of the tradition, it may go back to a no longer extant saga about Isaac.[55]

Quite distinct from what we have dealt with so far, and outside the saga traditions, is the reference to the God of the Fathers in the oracle concerning Joseph in the Blessing of Jacob, which must be considered as an independent document, even though it comes to us as part of the whole Yahwist history.[56] The poet is speaking here of the God who keeps Joseph, and certainly means none other than Yahweh; but he intentionally avoids the name Yahweh, and replaces it by a series of ancient divine titles, which it is clear are not applied to Yahweh for the first time in this period, but had been transferred to him long before. It is very important for our purpose that amongst the consciously archaic forms in this list 'the God of your father' is named, in parallel with the

[53] Gen. xlvi. 1 J or E.

[54] Gen. xlvi. 3 E.

[55] GUNKEL suspects accordingly that behind this lies a lost Elohist parallel to the Yahwist saga of Isaac in Gen. xxvi, which takes place around and in Beersheba.

[56] Gen. xlix. 25.

completely different *'Ēl Šaddai*[57] and 'the Mighty One of Jacob'. We shall have to consider whether the last title may not have had a close connection with the God of the Fathers from its very origin. The poet must presumably consider the θεὸς πατρῷος to be part of the earliest form of the religion of Israel, otherwise it is difficult to understand why he should ever have mentioned him in this context. We have here, therefore, completely independent evidence, which brings us just as close to the origins of Israelite religion as the oldest material found in the historical strata of Genesis.

What judgment can we pass on this material as a whole? It does not need to be shown that the tradition of the God of the Fathers has been developed and elaborated in a completely different way from that, for example, of the *'Ēlīm* of the Palestine sanctuaries. The latter always appear on the scene for a brief moment only, and never seem to have any permanent effect on the group of stories they occur in.[58] On the other hand, the God of the Fathers is mentioned again and again both in the Yahwist and Elohist works, and not only occurs more often, but has a much greater influence on the content of the works as a whole than all the *'Ēlīm* put together: speeches of revelation, prayers, blessings, oaths, confessions of faith, sacrifices, in short virtually every form of religious activity that could occur in historical writings is found somewhere or other applied to the θεὸς πατρῷος. To the superficial reader there seems to be no doubt which is the more important: the God of the Fathers is a living element in these stories, whereas the *'Ēlīm* are merely relics.

Nevertheless, the extent to which the tradition of the God of the Fathers has developed has its disadvantages as well. For when an *'Ēl* occurs, it is practically always in the context of an individual saga, with clear traces of its origin in the pre-

[57] This is the correct reading.

[58] The only exception to this is the *'Ēl Bēt'ēl*, who is first mentioned in Gen. xxxi. 13 and who reappears in Gen. xxxv. 7; but this later reference is very unimportant. We are not of course concerned with the status of *'Ēl Šaddai* in the priestly narrative, for that is the result of a much later development.

literary tradition, and the *'Ēlīm* can therefore be assigned automatically to the original matter of the sagas. On the other hand, in many cases where the God of the Fathers is mentioned, we noticed that this was due to the literary editor of the traditional material composing the account himself. The editors included the *'Ēl* sagas in their histories but developed them no further, while they seem to have been the first to widen and exalt the significance of the God of the Fathers to its present extent. Was the God of the Fathers in fact an entirely new figure introduced into the tradition by the literary editors? The few passages where we thought we saw the effect of a previous tradition of the God of Jacob's covenant with Laban and the oracle concerning Joseph in the Blessing of Jacob, would make so complete an elimination of the figure from the pre-literary tradition extremely difficult, but perhaps not entirely impossible, for we can only make a hypothetical reconstruction of its earlier development. We must look more closely if we wish to ascertain how old the figure of the God of the Fathers really is.

The great difference in the way the *'Ēlīm* on the one hand, and the God of the Fathers on the other, were treated in the historical works, is at any rate not a sufficient reason for accepting only the former as an ancient element in the tradition, and taking the latter as a completely new invention of the writers. Their preference for the latter is much easier to explain if its essential features were supplied by the tradition. It was obviously they who took the step of emphasizing the connection between each of Israel's ancestors, apart from their family tree, by tracing their religion in an unbroken line from Abraham, through Isaac to Jacob and his sons. This could not be so easily achieved with the *'Ēlīm;* for the sagas concerning them were tied to the one place, the particular sanctuary of each in Palestine, while the history of the patriarchs as a whole, built up from individual sagas set in many different places, could only be made coherent by accepting frequent changes of place as a basic element in the story. The writers would have had to take from the *'Ēlīm* the most characteristic feature they possess in the tradition, if they were to move from place to place, to wherever the history of the patriarchs was set; but this they would have to do if they were to be the kind of god who was always close to the ancestors of Israel throughout their wanderings. And the disorderly variety of the *'Ēlīm,* the result of their function as local numina, would have had to be disguised; for so long as it continued, it would have hindered the presentation of a religious unity in the patriarchal history. The author of the priestly narrative provides the best proof of this whole argument by the way he handles one of the *'Ēlīm,* the *'Ēl Šaddai:* he actually bases the continuity in the religion of the patriarchs on this one numen, but in such a way that the original connection of *'Ēl Šaddai* with a particular place is completely lost, and the other deities of the same type disappear altogether. The Yahwist and the Elohist could not employ such a radical procedure: they were still far too close to the living tradition of the sagas. That is why we find from time to time in their works, for a brief moment, an *'Ēl* of the kind described, still of the same nature as in the old independent saga, tied to its sanctuary and restricted in its sphere of action; but nothing more is made of these, and there can be no question of any indispensable function accorded to these numina within the overall plan of the Yahwist and Elohist histories of the patriarchs.

The God of the Fathers is of a quite different nature. There is no connection with a specific sanctuary,[59] and particular preference is shown for this god when the scene of action lies far from the normal dwelling-place of the ancestors of Israel, be it in the land of the Aramaeans on the Euphrates, or amongst the Egyptians on the Nile. This absence of any local connection in the picture given of the God of the Fathers can hardly result from the writer's own presentations, neither in the sense that the authors deliberately excluded from a divinity created by themselves any link with particular places, in order to be able to introduce it at any time or place

[59] The only exception is the sanctuary at Beersheba, where Jacob sacrifices to the God of Isaac, but this is not a fact which throws any light on the character of that numen.

in the story, nor by their being the first to separate the God of the Fathers, supposedly drawn by them from the earlier tradition, from its original local connections. The real reason for the quite different treatment this figure receives must lie in the fact that from the very beginning it represents a quite different type of religion from that of the *'Ēlīm*, characterized not by a firm link with one place, but by a continuous connection with one group of people. A certain sign of the particular nature of this form of religion is that the θεὸς πατρῷος always takes its name from a person and never from a place. But if this is correct, then the preference of the Yahwist and the Elohist for the God of the Fathers is adequately explained even on the supposition that they found this figure in the pre-literary tradition in just the same way as the *'Ēlīm*. For the possibility of unrestricted changes of locality lay in the very nature of a θεὸς πατρῷος—that is to say, such a god is present wherever the group moves whose god he is; and this is presumably what was important for the writers, if they were to show a unity, *sub specie Dei*, behind the profusion of their stories of the patriarchs. They did not make such consistent use of this fact for their purpose as the priestly writer, with the exclusive prominence he gives to *'Ēl Šaddai*, and although they gave the God of the Fathers much greater importance than he has in the ancient tradition, by introducing scenes of their own composition, they did not completely exclude the *'Ēlīm* on this account. But they customarily show a similar respect for the often heterogeneous material of the sagas.

This approach, therefore, provides no decisive objection to the view that the God of the Fathers was a figure already present in the pre-literary tradition, which for easily understandable reasons the writers simply brought further into the foreground of their picture of the whole patriarchal period. I am of the opinion, however, that other aspects of the way these traditions have been developed make the case for this view considerably stronger. In the Yahwist and Elohist histories the God of the Fathers not only appears side by side with the *'Ēlīm;* he is also largely overshadowed by the constant use of God's name Yahweh in the one, and the general term for God, *'Elōhīm,* in the other. There is naturally a difference between the two. The reader easily gets used to the change from a general term for God to the special title of the God of the Fathers, and is scarcely conscious of the discrepancy in the content of the two forms.[60] But when the name Yahweh occurs, and then the God of the Fathers appears again without it being made obvious on every occasion why the transition takes place, or whether the two are to be identified, the inconsistency is clearly felt. This unevenness is particularly remarkable in the Yahwist history, in that neither in the prehistory of Genesis i–xi, nor afterwards in the story of Moses, does the author give any other name but Yahweh, so that this name obviously provided the easiest and most effective means of treating the whole patriarchal history from a single coherent viewpoint. Why then does he introduce the God of the Fathers here, composing whole new passages for this purpose alone? There can hardly be any other reason for this inconsistency than that the Yahwist already possessed a tradition of the God of the Fathers, by which he felt himself bound, and which was of so much importance for him that he not only retained the name this tradition used for God, but gave it even greater prominence by himself composing new variations on its theme. This tradition in no way weakens his conviction that Yahweh is at work in the whole of history, since he presents the God of the Fathers and Yahweh as expressly or implicitly one and the same. But the theory and language peculiar to the Yahwist scarcely conceal the older strata that lie behind them, in which the God of the Fathers is clearly visible as a distinct figure. We are more than ever forced to the conclusion that this figure was not created by the Yahwist himself, but must have had a place in the pre-literary tradition.

The same is true of the Elohist. The general term for God, *'Elōhīm,* is an even more transparent device for glossing over

[60] They are made even easier to identify in the Elohist narrative, because it begins with the history of the Patriarchs, so that from this point on the reader is faced with numerous titles for God.

the older materials. But a further sign of his dependence on older traditions seems to be provided by his own peculiar theory of the relationship between the God of the Fathers and Yahweh. The special revelation at the beginning of the story of Moses is the first time he affirms the identity of the historical God of the people of Israel with the God of their ancestors, worshipped before the nation's history began. This of course makes it unnecessary for him to combine the two within the sagas of the patriarchs as does the Yahwist, and there, as a result, he could let the tradition speak for itself without constraint or special emphasis. This explains why he gives no parallels to the speeches of revelation by the God of the Fathers to Isaac and Jacob, intentionally composed by the author of the Yahwist history. He had no need for them, for the scene in which the same God first identifies himself as the God of the Fathers and then makes known his name Yahweh to Moses, seemed to provide a sufficient substitute. The tradition he records is therefore far less subjected to adaptation in his version of the patriarchal history.

But if the identification of the God of the Fathers with Yahweh can be made both by the Yahwist and the Elohist, with a noticeable difference in the point of their narrative at which they make it, it follows that in this respect they had no fixed tradition behind them. Both were apparently guided by their own opinion, and the most we can ask is whether the theories of particular schools of thought in different circles within Israel had already worked out the basis for these opinions. But this would only concern the more recent stages of the pre-literary development, and at an earlier period Yahweh and the God of the Fathers must have been much more clearly distinguished from one another. When we look at the material we are still able to distinguish quite clearly the different elements in a process of assimilation only gradually completed, and it becomes all the more necessary to examine the type of religion in which the God of the Fathers is worshipped as an entity in himself.

The Titles of the God of the Fathers

One particular feature of the tradition that remains to be evaluated is the variety of the titles under which the God of the Fathers appears in the literature. Though lacking the form of proper names, they fulfil this function, so we may expect them to be set expressions, which would not easily be altered even when their context in the various forms taken by the developing tradition did not remain the same. This is all the more likely in this case, since they are names of gods, originating in the invariably conservative and often archaic language of the cult, and able within the cult to survive far-reaching changes in religion, even though their own significance might be altered in the process. We may use these names, therefore, to judge whether or not in fact the God of the Fathers represents an ancient and distinctive type of religion.

It is the rarest of the titles of the God of the Fathers that give the impression of the greatest antiquity. We came across one of them in the saga tradition, פַּחַד יִצְחָק, the 'Fear of Isaac', by whom Jacob swears an oath, to confirm his treaty with Laban; the other is given by the oracle for Joseph in the Blessing of Jacob: אֲבִיר יַעֲקֹב, the 'Mighty One of Jacob'. The former is not attested anywhere else, and therefore seems to have soon become obsolete; we meet the second occasionally in the later religious poetry of Israel.[61] Everyone admits nowadays that both are ancient terms from the language of the cult, but differences of opinion still exist as to their original meaning. The dispute about the meaning of אביר יעקב does not seriously concern us in the present investigation; for one translates 'the Mighty One of Jacob' as above, or as 'the

[61] Isa. xlix. 26; lx. 16; Ps. cxxxii. 2, 5. The retention of the expression in the worship of Yahweh in historic times was facilitated by the fact that 'Jacob' could be taken as the equivalent of Israel, as so often occurred in poetry, and accordingly 'the Mighty One of Jacob' could be seen as a title of the God of Israel. In Isaiah i. 24, in fact, the expression is altered to אביר ישראל.

Bull(-god) of Jacob' (as the mania amongst modern scholars for seeing bulls everywhere has led several of them to suggest without very convincing reasons),[62] in any case אביר is there as the real, albeit very unusual title of the god, and the word יעקב, dependent on it, is an addition which serves to establish the individuality of the numen in question by naming a man particularly connected with him. The whole expression, therefore, in its linguistic form and its content corresponds to the 'God of Abraham', etc., and we can thus include it with confidence amongst the titles of the God of the Fathers. But it presumably goes back to the pre-literary tradition; אביר for 'god' is too far removed from later usage to justify one in taking it as a neologism produced in the literary period. The same is true of פחד יצחק. The expression has of course been seen as designating, in accordance with the normal usage of later literature, the 'Fear that proceeds from Isaac', so that Isaac himself would be the *numen tremendum.*[63] It would then have no connection with the idea of the God of the Fathers. But can we base our explanation so straightforwardly on a later meaning of פחד when it leads to an interpretation of the expression that clearly does not fit in with its function in the few places where it occurs? For there can be no doubt that in the story of Jacob's treaty with Laban it is not פחד on its own, but the whole expression פחד יצחק which is understood as the divine title. It is therefore much more likely that we have here the last traces of an older usage no longer found elsewhere, in which פחד may be used for God, in poetry at least if perhaps not in prose. According to this, פחד יצחק would be an archaic title of the numen whose appearance terrified Isaac and thereby bound him to himself for ever. If it is understood in this way, as an expression

[62] For the latest attempt cf. TORCZYNER, ZAW, xxxix (1921), pp. 296 ff. (he translates 'the Lord of Jacob'); CASPARI, ZS, vi (1928), pp. 71 ff. ('God-centred supernatural power'—originally meaning magical apotropaic power).

[63] See especially STAERK, *Studien,* I, pp. 59 ff.; LUTHER, ZAW, xii (1901), pp. 73 f.; MEYER, *Die Israeliten und ihre Nachbarstämme* (1906), pp. 254 ff.

forming a parallel to אביר יעקב above, we can probably use the analogy as a secondary argument for our interpretation.[64] But then we would be obliged to say that this also is an ancient divine name, distinguished by the unusual use of פחד for God, but providing another example of a numen characterized by a particular connection with a man.[65]

In spite of their close formal likeness, however, we must not forget how independent the two expressions are of one another. If we did not find them connected in their present literary context[66] we should hardly have found it so easy to guess that both stand for the same god. In the *'Ēlīm* of Palestine we came across gods whose titles were formed in similar ways and yet without doubt were originally quite distinct. We could quote many more examples if we included the *Ba'alim*. But what is true of the *'Ēl 'Olām* of Beersheba and the *'Ēl Berīt* of Shechem must presumably also apply to the Fear of Isaac and the Mighty One of Jacob. We are faced with the question whether the Israelite tradition may preserve traces of several divinities of the same type as the God of the Fathers, all identified of course with Yahweh, but still recognizable from their titles.

This question is provoked by the titles that are really the principal form in the sagas of Genesis: אֱלֹהֵי אַבְרָהָם, אֱלֹהֵי יִצְחָק, אֱלֹהֵי יַעֲקֹב. We first meet them in Exodus iii, united in a single formula, and at least two parts occur linked together several times in Genesis in the phrase אֱלֹהֵי אַבְרָהָם וֵאלֹהֵי יִצְחָק.[67] But normally the individual titles are used

[64] There is therefore no reason to follow GRESSMANN in turning פחד יצחק into an אל פחד (*ZAW*, xxx [1910], p. 8; *Mose und seine Zeit*, p. 426).

[65] ALBRIGHT refers to the meaning 'family, clan' which the word פחד has in Palmyrene and Arabic and translates this title 'Kinsman of Isaac'. This proposal deserves consideration (*From the Stone Age to Christianity*, 2nd ed. [1946], pp. 188 f., 327, n. 71).

[66] As a matter of fact they occur in the same context as a result of the later redaction of the Hexateuch. It appears that only the Elohist gives the term פחד יצחק, while אביר יעקב only occurs in the Yahwist Blessing of Jacob.

[67] Gen. xxviii. 13; xxxi. 42; xxxii. 10; cf. xlviii. 15.

separately, the 'God of Abraham' in the stories of Isaac, the 'God of Isaac' in the case of Jacob, and the 'God of Jacob' in the case of his sons.[68] But in the original form of the tradition the titles could neither have been apportioned in this way, nor all found together. Only when the heroes of the saga had been put into a fixed genealogical order could the appropriate title be used by each;[69] only when you had a family tree of the patriarchs could you have as it were a family tree of their religion. But the reason they can be linked together in this way clearly lies in the belief that every one of these divine titles referred to Yahweh himself; there is a natural growth from the 'God of Abraham' through the 'God of Abraham and Isaac' to the 'God of Abraham, Isaac and Jacob', the final synthesis on which the Elohist bases the theory in Exodus iii. Both the use of appropriate titles by different generations, therefore, and their incorporation into a single formula, are part of the process of reducing the various elements of the tradition to a preconceived unity, and accordingly they must both be set aside if we wish to get back to the original material. The consequence of this is the same as in the case of the 'Fear of Isaac' and the 'Mighty One of Jacob': behind each of these three divine titles we must suppose that there was originally an entirely distinct numen.

This supposition is strengthened by the only scene in the patriarchal sagas which resisted the tendency to unification in the later tradition, and preserved its distinguishing features for a comparatively long time—the story of Jacob's treaty with Laban. For if at least one of the settings in which these titles have come down to us, the אֱלֹהֵי נָחוֹר, is contrasted with the אֱלֹהֵי אַבְרָהָם without any special preparation, the

[68] The 'God of Jacob' is consequently of little importance in the patriarchal sagas, and indeed is not mentioned in them under this title. But this of course is the god who is meant when Joseph is held by his brothers to an oath by 'the God of thy Father'.

[69] The secondary character of this genealogical connection has recently been discussed by WEISER, *Religion und Sittlichkeit der Genesis,* p. 11, with n. 7.

author who gave the scene this form must have expected his readers to understand that the 'God of X' is not the same as the 'God of Y'. Here the traditional material contradicts the intention observable in the passage, of identifying the two titles, if the writer was to avoid the natural impression that here two different gods were being named as sureties for a treaty between two groups of people, then he would have had to omit Laban's oath by his θεὸς πατρῷος altogether. In fact the second writer who worked on the story seems to have chosen the latter course, and to have spoken only of Jacob's oath by the 'Fear of his father Isaac'. The inconsistency of the other writer is all the more valuable, preserving as it does a trace of the original words, and so showing for a brief moment what all these divine titles stood for, before the later tradition and authors took hold of them and attached a new meaning to them. The type of religion was always the same, but it was expressed through a number of individual gods. The consequences for the God of Abraham, etc., are obvious.

One final effect of this process of assimilation carried out in the later stages of the tradition is to be seen in the greater frequency of divine names taking the colourless אֱלֹהִים, as opposed to old and striking expressions like פחד and אָבִיר. Naturally פַּחַד יִצְחָק, for example, can from the earliest times also be called אֱלֹהֵי יִצְחָק; but it is worth noting that only one of the authors, probably the Elohist, uses the ancient formula, and that with complete inconsistency, whereas everywhere else the less colourful expression is the rule. Even more characteristic is the position of אֲבִיר יַעֲקֹב and אֱלֹהֵי יַעֲקֹב; if the former title did not occur in several places outside the literary versions of the patriarchal sagas, we should never have known of it. In this case the older title of an individual god has been totally suppressed from the history of the patriarchs. Similarly, the God of Abraham is never called anything in the sagas except אַבְרָהָם אֱלֹהֵי –the analogy would suggest that this is the result of a secondary transformation. We have established, therefore, that the schematization of the divine titles was carried through almost to completion, and we may presume that the process was carried out consciously. In so far as it aided the imposition of a unity upon the tradition, and made easier the assimilation of the θεὸς πατρῷος to Yahweh, it was in accordance with plans of the editors of the sagas. This can be tested by replacing the monotonous 'God of Abraham, God of Isaac, God of Jacob' in the revelation of Exodus iii with the older, distinctive titles 'I am the . . . of Abraham, the Fear of Isaac, the Mighty One of Jacob'; how much less natural it sounds that these names should all refer to the same God, the very God, moreover, who bears the name Yahweh!

The examination of the titles of the numina, therefore, leads us to the same conclusion as does our study of the course taken by the development of the whole tradition: a body of very ancient material can still be dimly perceived behind the present literary redaction of the patriarchal sagas; the concern of the more recent authors to present a unified picture of the past has considerably obscured it. But the transformation has not been carried so far as to remove entirely the distinction between the θεὸς πατρῷος and the *'Ēlīm* of the Palestine sanctuaries. In fact the titles of the divinities are just where this distinction is most clear. For whereas in the case of the θεὸς πατρῷος the writers use almost invariably compounds with אֱלֹהִים,[70] for the numina of Palestine they use forms with אֵל, without exception. We have already mentioned in the introduction that the latter usage only became general as the result of a secondary unifying process at the expense of the title בַּעַל, which for a long time had remained in use alongside אֵל.[71] There is schematization here as well! It is significant that for each kind of divinity a different expression was as it were canonized, and that the specifically Israelite word for God, אֱלֹהִים, unknown in Canaanite, was

[70] The only exception: אֵל אָבִיךָ, in the blessing of Jacob lies outside the sagas, is a poetic expression, and is perhaps occasioned only by the parallelism with אֵל שַׁדַּי (an emended reading) in the same verse.

[71] See above p. 11.

retained for the θεὸς πατρῷος.[72] This distinction between the terms used can scarcely have been made without any support from the older tradition; it perhaps suggests that the early history of the θεὸς πατρῷος took place in a different setting from that of the *'Ēlīm*. But even if the writers were entirely responsible for it, it would not be without significance; for we should still be able to conclude from it that these authors were fully aware of the difference between the two types of religion, and that they believed they ought to apply the normal Israelite designation of God only to the θεὸς πατρῷος.

COMPARISON

The further we go with our examination of the tradition of the God of the Fathers, the stronger the impression becomes that we have in it a genuine recollection of a very ancient and distinctive body of religious belief and practice. Admittedly it exists hardly anywhere in the Old Testament in a form corresponding to its original nature, but its content is always such that it cannot be satisfactorily explained as an invention of the literary editors. It seemed that originally several distinct gods of this type must have existed side by side, before they were combined in the figure of the God of the Fathers and identified with the God worshipped by Israel in historic times; and we believed that there was evidence that the authors of the great compilations of sagas saw in this type of religion the characteristic and distinctive religion of their people's ancestors, in which only tribes closely related to them took part, and not the inhabitants of Palestine, or other nations. We must try to discover whether this tradition reflects any historical reality.

This is often denied out of hand, and the God of the Fa-

[72] Corresponding forms to אלהים are not found in Phoenician, but do occur in Aramaic and Arabic. Cf. BAUDISSIN, *Kyrios*, III, pp. 6 ff.; and for אל, NOTH, *Die isr. Personnennamen*, pp. 82 ff. and p. xvi.

thers explained simply as an 'image of the national God of historical times', 'transformed into a family god'.[73] Of course no one suggests why it was necessary to create such an image at all, and to give it so much space in the patriarchal history. But it must be understood that anyone who starts from the later religion of Israel and tries to understand the saga tradition from that point of view alone, is bound to find in the God of the Fathers only a reflection of Yahweh as the national God. He sees no more in a divine title like 'the Fear of Isaac' than, for example, in Elisha's words: 'Where is Yahweh, the God of Elijah?'[74] or the cry of Nebuchadnezzar, 'Blessed be the God of Shadrach, Meshach and Abednego';[75] the titles in Genesis are taken in the same sense as these, as epithets applied to Yahweh on a particular occasion and then abandoned.[76] But the fundamental question remains, whether justice is done to the historical content of the titles when they are interpreted solely from the point of view of the later religion of the Israelites: in fact it is clear from the start that such a procedure is bound to miss the original meaning if genuinely pre-Yahwist material has been retained in the later tradition, where everything is attributed to Yahweh. The strategy required by the problem is exactly the same as in the case of the *'Ēlim* of the patriarchal history, whose true nature can only be recognized when one disregards their subsequent identification with Yahweh.

If the later development in Israel cannot be expected to provide any information about the type of religion which we meet in the God of the Fathers and the individual numina which we presumed lay behind this figure, nothing remains but to attempt a comparison with other religions and see if gods of the same type are found there. We can use in this comparison only the few details we have so far discovered

[73] The words are those of BAUDISSIN, *Kyrios*, III, p. 152.
[74] 2 Kings ii. 14.
[75] Dan. iii. 28.
[76] Similar titles attributed to God on one occasion only are still being found afresh in the language of early Christian acclamations, etc. Cf. PETERSON, Εἷς Θεός (1926), esp. pp. 210 ff.

from the Israelite tradition to be characteristic of this type of religion. Principally, there is the fact that the numina are known not by proper names, but by compound expressions which distinguish an individual god by the exclusive emphasis laid on his connection with a human individual. Secondly, the local connection of the god is of minor importance, as opposed to his connection with a group of people. Finally, there is the fact that this particular form of religion is limited to tribes still living outside the sphere of the ancient civilizations. Each of these three points, particularly the last, restricts considerably the field of comparison; but it will be all the more significant if we can find parallels which fulfil all these conditions.

We need not travel far either in time or place from the oldest dwelling-place of Israel to find the desired parallels; we need look no further than the remains left by the tribes which in the same way as the Israelites abandoned a nomadic life in the Arabian desert for the civilization of Palestine and Syria. The family of tribes ranging from the Aramaeans to the Edomites, to which Israel itself belonged, and which before and at the beginning of the second millennium B.C. came to settle in Palestine and Syria, cannot however be taken into account; the few records discovered date from the early period of their recorded history, after their settlement, and unfortunately give us no help.[77] The next group, which travelled the same road scarcely a thousand years later, is therefore all the more important. We can trace its progress in particular in the records left by the Nabataeans and the Palmyrenes. Even there the monuments, and in particular

[77] Both the inscriptions set up by the Moabite king Mesa and the Old Aramaic inscriptions of Northern Syria occur in the territories where the tribes concerned had settled. J. LEWY (*RHR*, 110 [1934], pp. 50 ff.) compares Old Assyrian records from Cappadocia, in which not only the god Assur, but also 'thy God' or 'the God of thy (our, your) father' is invoked as the witness to a contract. These also occur in a settled civilization and as far as I know the title 'the God of X' is not found, and there is no evidence that the cult of individual gods of this type was carried on there permanently.

the inscriptions, do not begin to give any information until long after the tribes had settled, and much of what they say is obviously either taken over from the ancient culture of the country they entered or has reached them from outside, that is from Hellenism. But besides this a good deal remains that we can easily see has come from the previous period when the tribes lived as nomads, and has maintained itself very tenaciously in a completely altered setting. This is particularly to be seen in the case of the Nabataeans. We also know of them, from other sources, that they had no intention of giving up their traditional way of life immediately they adopted a settled existence.[78] But even the Palmyrenes present certain traces of their previous existence in the desert, and the same occurs even as far away as the north of Syria. Elsewhere, along the outermost edge of the settled area, among scarcely civilized Arabian tribes, the old customs were naturally carried on almost unaltered.

Among the thousands of Semitic and Greek inscriptions of this vast region, dating from the time before it became Christian, there appear from time to time the names of gods, which in the way they are formed are strongly reminiscent of the Israelite God of the Fathers. This similarity has not gone unnoticed;[79] but I do not know that anyone has yet drawn any further conclusions from it. The fault may lie in the scattering of the relevant texts in a large number of greater and lesser and often extremely inaccessible publications, and partly in the lack of interest in these frequently very unlikely-looking records, whose historical value can naturally only be seen when the entire corpus, with all the various types of material it contains, can be considered as a whole. I have tried to remedy this evil by collecting the inscriptions that are important for our comparison in as full a

[78] Cf. Hieronymus of Cardia in Diodorus xix. 94 and the comment of Ed. Meyer, *Die Israeliten und ihre Nachbarstämme*, p. 84.

[79] Observed a long time ago by Nöldeke in Euting, *Nabatäische Inschriften aus Arabien* (1885), pp. 62 f.; for a more recent discussion, see Littman and Magie, *PAES*, iii, A (1911), p. 407, and Sourdel, *Les cultes du Hauran à l'époque romaine* (1952), pp. 95 f.

form as possible in an appendix to this essay, which must be referred to continuously in the following exposition; the figures in my references indicate the numbering of individual texts.

In the case of the Semitic and Greek inscriptions of the type we are discussing, it was not recognized until some time after the first discoveries had been made that they contained divine titles formed, like אֱלֹהֵי אַבְרָהָם, etc., of the *status constructus* of a noun meaning 'god' governing in the genitive the proper name of a human individual. De Vogüé, who found in אלה קציו the first trace in a Semitic language of this group of numina (Appendix, no. 13), was of the opinion that it referred to a god who himself was called קציו; and the same happened with the discovery of similar divine names. Nöldeke was the first to make the undoubtedly correct observation that by the rules of the Aramaic language אלה קציו could not mean 'the God קציו', which would be written: קציו אלהא; whereas both the word order and above all the *status constructus* אלה made the translation 'the god of (the man) קציו' the only possible one.[80] The larger number of examples that have appeared since then have given no cause to doubt that this interpretation is correct; most of the names compounded with אלה are known from other inscriptions as human personal names, and all are conceivable as such.[81] The same is true of the recently discovered forms with גד instead of אלה.

The right interpretation of the analogous divine names in Greek inscriptions was likewise not reached straight away, which is less remarkable, in that the first example known was one in which the genitive relation between the noun θεὸς and the following proper name was doubtful: Ἥλιον Θεὸν Αὖμον, according to Waddington's reading.[82] Yet at the

[80] In EUTING, loc. cit.; also in *ZDMG*, xlii (1888), p. 475.

[81] Only nos. 3 and 12 are uncertain because they could possibly be place names. (The numbers in this and the following notes refer to the Appendix, p. 87.)

[82] No. 41. Unfortunately no one hitherto seems to have checked WADDINGTON's reading against the original.

same time forms like Θεῷ Αὔμου began to come to light,[83] and could only point to Θεὸς Αὔμου as the nominative, not to Θεὸς Αὖμος as in the case of Θεὸν Αὖμον. The question was, how the two forms could be reconciled. Waddington and others who followed him had recourse to the idea that Αὔμον was the original undeclinable form of the name with an Aramaic ending, and Αὖμος a declinable form derived from it with a Greek ending, while both forms referred to the god himself. But as the parallels to Θεὸς Αὔμου grew more and more common, while not a single counterpart was found to Θεὸς Αὖμος, and when to crown all there appeared a Θεὸς Ἀρκεσιλάου, where there could be no question of an Aramaic ending,[84] it was inevitable that this explanation should be abandoned altogether. In the meantime the real content of the divine titles in the Semitic inscriptions had become known, as shown above, and this led to the right solution: Θεὸς Αὔμου can likewise only mean 'the God of (the man) Αὖμος'.[85] In fact the proper names in the genitive in these titles are either attested as the names of human individuals or can be explained as such by every analogy, and it only remains to see in the alleged Θεὸν Αὖμον a mistaken text or reading, which must be corrected to Θεὸν Αὔμου.[86] It would naturally be very pleasant if, as in the case of no. 25, not quite a normal one, there were more references to the same

[83] Nos. 35, 36. Cases where both words are in the genitive (Θεοῦ Αὔμου nos. 43, 44) were naturally of no use in deciding this point.

[84] No. 32.

[85] CLERMONT-GANNEAU was particularly responsible for the acceptance of this interpretation; cf. *RAO*, ii (1896), p. 110; *EAO*, ii (1897), p. 33, etc. The inquiry into the meaning of divine names constructed in the same way, in Greek inscriptions from Maeonia (Μὴν Τιάμον, etc.) took a very similar course; cf. KEIL and VON PREMERSTEIN, *Bericht über einer zweiten Reise in Lydien* (1911), p. 104.

[86] I cannot understand how BAUDISSIN, in his latest work (*Kyrios*, III, p. 205, n. 1) contrived to reject these conclusions. (In the case of the Θεὸς Αὔμου he still held WADDINGTON's view and took the other gods with names in this form as deified men!).

god both in Semitic and Greek inscriptions, to confirm the equivalence of the formulae.[87]

But even though the texts in the two languages are outwardly distinct from one another, inwardly they unite to give a completely unanimous testimony. Only the outward appearance distinguishes the θεὸς Αὔμου from the אלה קציו, but their nature is the same, and what is true of these is true of the others also, whether we meet them in inscriptions from the first century B.C.[88] or from the fourth century A.D.[89] In every case there is a god without a proper name, designated only by the addition of a human personal name in the genitive to the general word for a god. In the most westerly regions of Palestine and Syria, which were not reached by these very early waves of Arab tribes, for example, on the Philistine or Phoenician coast, there are no parallels to this phenomenon whatsoever, and this makes it certain that they were introduced by the new element in the population which had come out of Arabia. Further confirmation is provided by the explicitly Arabic character of the personal names used to form the particular title of each god, with the exception of the Θεὸς 'Αρκεσιλάου already mentioned.[90] There can no longer be any doubt that this type of religion originated in the nomadic life of the desert.

There is nevertheless one group in the inscriptions contained in the appendix which can be introduced into this context only with great caution. These are the Nabataean texts that speak of a 'God of our lord', whether it be King Aretas

[87] Unfortunately one cannot hope for very much material of this kind, since in general (except among the Palmyrenes) Semitic inscriptions cease where Greek inscriptions begin.

[88] Nos. 3 and 13; none of the inscriptions from this area go back further than this.

[89] Nos. 32 and 41 ff. About this period the whole area was beginning to be converted to Christianity.

[90] Even in the case of this one exception the name does not come from a different Semitic language from the Arabic, but is a Greek name, so that it is possible that the man from whose name the god's title is formed was a hellenized Arab. No. 49 is uncertain.

IV or King Rabilos II.[91] What we have here is clearly a distinct form of royal and state religion, which is not without analogies elsewhere in the Semitic sphere.[92] The 'God of our lord' is in reality the great imperial god Dusares,[93] and this name is always given to him in addition, so that his particular connection with the reigning king is only expressed by an apposition to his main proper name. Inscriptions giving the form 'the God of our lord' cease very quickly as soon as the king in question is dead, so that no permanent cult seems to have arisen in this case at all.[94] These two divine figures obviously do not lend themselves to a comparison with the Israelite God of the Fathers, and I should therefore have omitted them entirely from my collection of texts, had it not seemed worth noting that amongst a people whose religious traditions provide so many gods of the type 'the God of X', even the state religion can be included in one division of this type. The peculiar problems that the occurrence of the 'God of our lord' raises for the student of the history of the Nabataean kingdom[95] need not be gone into here.

On the other hand, the remaining gods of this type have nothing to do with the state religion. It thus becomes important to examine more closely the locality and period in which their circle of worshippers lived, and the group of people to which they belonged. One cannot go very far in this direction when there is only a single piece of evidence for the cult of a particular god, often without a date and naming only individual worshippers. But even such isolated inscriptions are not altogether worthless. They help us to determine how far the

[91] Nos. 5–8, 9–11.

[92] Even in the Old Testament Yahweh can be referred to as the god of the reigning king (1 Kings i. 36).

[93] He appears under Rabilos II in a form peculiar to this locality: די אערא דושרא בבצרא

[94] Of the inscriptions which refer to 'the God of our Lord' Aretas IV, none provide any evidence for a cult, since they are all funerary inscriptions.

[95] The first question that needs to be answered, is why 'the God of our Lord' only appears in two reigns, with an interval between them.

area extended where this type of religion was practised, and reveal by their frequency in particular districts, especially in the Ḥaurān and the Leja, how densely grouped together the sanctuaries of these gods could be in places where the invading tribes had settled in a relatively compact area. They also show, in the names of those who gave altars and other objects for the use of the sanctuaries, that it was in fact among the invaders that this type of religion continued to flourish.[96] But the character of the god that was worshipped naturally remains indefinite in them and no light is cast as a rule on the relationship between the person dedicating the gift and the man by whose name the god is known.

But there are a few exceptions, which deserve careful consideration. These are the inscriptions in which the person dedicating the gift calls the god his θεὸς πατρῷος, and thus stresses the participation of his family in that cult for several generations past;[97] they do not go so far, admittedly, as to say that the man after whom the god is called belonged to the same family. But one case exists where the personal name that characterizes the god also appears in the genealogy of the offerer[98] and this would suggest that this was the private cult of that family.[99] If this is so, then Littmann's combination of an inscription in which an individual offers a gift to the אלה קציו with another in which the אל קציו, that is the whole family group that called itself after a real or fictitious ancestor קציו, does the same for 'their God'[100] does not seem too bold; and it is likewise a valid supposition that the frequently-attested גד תימי at Palmyra should be taken as the special god of the בני תימי who also appear in the same place in other inscriptions, and the גד עוך at Safa as that of

[96] During the later centuries, however, Semitic names were largely replaced by Greek and Latin names, and this makes the whole picture much less clear.

[97] Nos. 25, 32, 48, 54.

[98] No. 2.

[99] It is doubtful whether the title 'Lord of the house' given to a god in no. 16 is to be interpreted in this way.

[100] Nos. 13, 14.

the tribe of the 'Aουιδηνοί.[101] The next step would seem to be to extend these conclusions by analogy to the rest of the gods; the strength of the idea of genealogy among the Semitic peoples makes it perfectly easy to understand that in designating the god by the name of a human individual the principal thought was of a permanent and unique relationship between the numen and the whole of the particular group of people who rightly or wrongly regarded themselves as descended from the individual in question. Unfortunately the isolated inscriptions, in which a large number of persons are named without any reason being given for their joining together in a common offering, can only probably and not certainly be connected with such family groups.[102]

We possess, however, at least one group of texts which shows clearly the extent of the area from which the worshippers of a single god were drawn: the inscriptions in honour of the Θεὸς Αὔμου.[103] Particularly useful is the fact that they are distributed over a number of places in the same area and, as far as can be made out, over a period of a century and a half.[104] Offerings were of course also made to this god by individuals, which tell us no more than the similar texts relating to other gods.[105] But besides this we find whole communities (κοινά) taking part as such in his cult; some-

[101] Nos. 17–24, 25–29. (References to the literature in the Appendix.)

[102] No. 1 and 2 while perhaps no. 50 is also relevant.

[103] Nos. 33–45.

[104] It is true that in the oldest inscription which can be dated, written as late as the second century A.D. (no. 33) the name of the god can be filled in only by conjecture; but this conjecture provides the right number of letters to fill in the gap in the inscription, and is made more probable by the fact that the cult of the Θεὸς Αὔμου is attested with certainty in another dedication in the same place (no. 34). Next comes a group of inscriptions in another place, from the first half of the third century (nos. 35–37), and finally at a third place a group from the very end of the heathen period (*c.* 320; nos. 41–44).

[105] Nos. 33, 34, 37, 44 and the inscriptions in the Appendix from the same place, which refer to dedications, but do not give the name of the god.

times each village possesses a sanctuary with priests and temple treasurers,[106] and in other cases several neighbouring settlements, whose inhabitants do not even belong to the same tribe, unite in setting up and caring for a larger sanctuary dedicated to him.[107] His cult can be traced almost from place to place in the south-east of the Leja, right up to the foot of the mountain of the Ḥaurān, and there is no other god in this district who can be called a serious rival to him. In short, the Θεὸς Αὔμου, attested nowhere else, has become the divine lord of this whole region, and this actually took place in the final period before the coming of Christianity brought the cult to an end.

For the cult of a god of this kind to spread over a considerable area was not the normal course of development, and far less ought we to see in it the result of a distinctive tendency of this type of religion. Normally we found that even where such a god, designated by the name of a human individual, is mentioned in more than one inscription, the inscriptions are either in a single place[108] or in a few places close together.[109] Usually, therefore, there would be only a limited number of worshippers, which made it very easy for these cults to die out. We cannot even take it for granted that the whole population of a given place took part in a particular cult; we have in one inscription in honour of the Θεὸς Μαλειχάθου a clear reference to the later participation of the whole village community in a cult that had been carried out until then by a much smaller body of worshippers.[110] Simi-

[106] Nos. 35, 36, 39, 40. No. 38, where the actual person responsible for the creation of the shrine is not named, should certainly also be included with these. For the village κοινά as quasi-municipal organizations on lands which belonged to royal estates cf. Rostovzeff, *Jahreshefte d.Österr. Arch. Instituts,* IV (1901), Beiblatt, cols. 39 ff.

[107] Nos. 41–43. Waddington, No. 2396, shows a third place taking part in the worship of the same sanctuary. Similarly no. 45.

[108] No. 53 f.

[109] No. 13 f. (cf. above p. 46). 51 f. See also nn. 30 f. Cf. *PJB,* xxxvi (1940), p. 102.

[110] No. 52: the κοινόν is associated in the same construction at the sanctuary μετὰ τῶν θρησκευόντων. Note that no. 51 shows the same cult in a neighbouring village half a century earlier.

larly, the cult of the Θεὸς Αὔμου must have spread quite slowly over the region where it finally predominated, and it almost seems as if we can still trace its advance in stages from its place of origin in the east of the Leja to the foot of the Ḥaurān in the north, by looking at the date and place of the inscriptions that mention the god.[111] The final result of the development in this particular case is an unusual one and consequently ought not to determine our picture of this type of religion as a whole. There is no question here of regional gods, whose principal feature would have been their local and territorial connections. The connection described between these gods and groups founded on a genealogical relationship, that is, families and tribes, has a much stronger claim to be taken as the determining factor in their nature.

With regard to the latter point, we must take special note in the case of the inscriptions from the Leja, which form the great majority of our Greek texts, of the fact that this region, the ancient Trachonitis, was settled relatively late, and not by a uniform population. We know from Josephus how little it had been penetrated even as late as Herod's reign, and that until then there was no serious attempt to civilize it by introducing suitable elements from outside.[112] The development under the Romans can be thought of in the same way: groups of different origin were settled here alongside and in between each other. This was particularly true of what was certainly the most numerous section of the population, the Arabs, as the inscriptions show when they occasionally mention a variety of tribes,[113] and we must take into account the fact that their formerly united groups often broke up during and as a result of the settlement. This change in their circumstances could hardly be without effect on the gods worshipped by the tribes as nomads. Thus a good many such groups,

[111] The inscriptions which can be dated occur in chronological order; they begin with 'Āhire (no. 33), continue with Lubbēn (no. 35) and end with Dēr el-Leben (no. 41). Of course one must not forget that the cult at each of these places is certainly older than the inscription in which it is attested.

[112] Ant. XVI 9, 2 § 285; cf. XVII 2, 1 ff. §§ 23 ff. NIESE.

[113] Cf. nos. 30, 33, 41.

settling apart from the main body of their tribe, may have given up their hereditary cult, which in other places was preserved and took root in or around the place they settled.[114] So far as the gods of the type we are considering go back into the nomadic period, the inscriptions which only show a body of worshippers coming from a particular area cannot give us an accurate picture of the earlier stages, but only show the surviving remnants. Under the quite different conditions of civilized community life, however, and in isolated cases, such as that of the Θεὸς Αὔμου, a new process of expansion took place, reaching far beyond the former limits of the tribe. We must be content with being able to reconstruct the final chapters of the story in at least one part of the area under discussion.[115]

It is not until these later stages that another phenomenon appears, which is observable in both Semitic and Greek texts —the identification of the original and quite unpretentious numina with other greater gods. Three steps in this process can be traced in the case of the Θεὸς Αὔμου: until well into the third century the god was known only by the simple title he had originally; then the presumptuous title ἀνίκητος is inserted; and finally, in the fourth century, conglomeration of titles states openly what was implied by that adjective:[116] Ζεὺς 'Ανίκητος Ἥλιος Θεὸς Αὔμου—the solar henotheism, which was the final point reached by heathen religion and theology, particularly in Syria,[117] is seen here depriving the lesser god of his individual personality by seemingly exalting him to undreamt of heights. We can hardly have any doubt

[114] The most recently built or restored sanctuary of the Θεὸς Αὔμου, that of Dēr el-Leben, seems to have been some distance from the village (cf. BUTLER, *PAES*, ii, A, p. 359); this would have made it easier for it to serve as a common sanctuary for several villages belonging to different tribes.

[115] This type of religion seems to have died out much earlier in the original home of the Nabataeans.

[116] For ἀνίκητος as an epithet applied particularly to sun gods cf. WEINREICH, *Ath. Mitt.*, xxxvii (1912), p. 29, n. 1.

[117] Cf. especially CUMONT, *La théologie solaire du paganisme romain* (1919).

what the next step in this development must have been, if it had not been halted at this point by the conversion of the region to Christianity: the merging and swallowing up of the Θεὸς Αὔμου in the all-inclusive figure of Ζεὺς Ἥλιος. That the entire process was brought about by the more powerful influence of the dominant religious tendencies in the settled regions, and is thus of no significance for the original nature of the Θεὸς Αὔμου, is in fact confirmed in this particular case by the dates of the inscriptions.

This is, however, by no means an isolated case, but has parallels in considerably older Semitic and Greek inscriptions. In Petra we find an identification made with the principal local god דושרא;[118] several times with the true regional god of the Ḥaurān, בעלשמן;[119] and once with the otherwise unknown אשדו;[120] in Palmyra with מלכבל,[121] a god much worshipped there. From Greek texts we can add one identification with Ζεὺς Μέγιστος Ὕψιστος[122] and one with Θεάνδριος, a form only attested in the Ḥaurān, and explained by some writers as specifically Arabic.[123] In these cases it is still clear that assimilations have taken place of a sort that could not have come about except after the tribes had settled in civilized districts. They show once more how the fusion of one god with another led the original titles to lose their significance and disappear. They no longer satisfy the religious needs of the worshippers who used them, in their altered situation; so first of all compromises are made between the tribal and regional gods, and the final result of the compromises is the absorption of the tribal god by the other. We seem to be justified in concluding that the former originates

[118] No. 3. For the peculiarities of nos. 5–8, 9–11 see above p. 45.

[119] Nos. 12, 15.

[120] No. 4 (uncertain). Cf. ALBRIGHT, *JBL*, liv (1935), p. 182, n. 27; *JPOS*, lvii (1936), p. 319.

[121] Nos. 25–29.

[122] No. 55 (uncertain).

[123] No. 54 (a secondary formation by comparison with no. 53!). For this god cf. HÖFER in ROSCHER's *Lexicon der griech. u. röm. Mythologie*, s.v.

in the religion of the tribes before they settled, and we are obliged once more, in elucidating the original nature of gods whose titles were formed from the names of human individuals, to disregard all secondary identifications.

The titles themselves, then, are all that remain of the original cult. How are we to interpret them? The inscriptions naturally tell us nothing, since they do not go back to the time when the names of the gods were coined; they only show how persistently these substitutes for the nonexistent proper name remained in being, so long as the cult of these gods was carried on, and how far it was from the intention of the later worshippers ever to make any alteration in the titles once they had been formed.[124] We should only expect the titles to be so persistent if they characterized the numina by representing an unvarying relationship to an unchanging object in the terrestrial sphere, as for example when a god is named from the place where his sanctuary is. With the gods of the type we are considering this is only true when the human names used in their titles are either the names of tribes or become such in the course of time. We have already referred to the few cases where this is likely to be so;[125] but they are too few for us to make a generalization. Most of the names that occur in these composite divine titles must in fact have been simply the names of individuals at the time the expressions were coined. This means that they must have been taken from persons who were alive at the time the cults came into being, and this leads us to ask what gave these individuals such great importance in connection with the numina known after them that their names were incorporated for ever into the title of the god, and were so used long after they were dead. The later worshippers are certain to have had a tradition about this, especially if they regarded them-

[124] The identification with the names of other gods, mentioned above, forms no exception to this rule; it does not cause the alteration or abandonment of the original name of the god.

[125] See above pp. 46 ff. Even in these uses it must remain an open question whether the names had always been the name of a tribe.

selves as the descendants of these men. But in their inscriptions they let slip not one word of this, so that we are forced to seek an explanation of this characteristic in the titles themselves.

We begin with the linguistic form of the divine titles, and with the fact that the genitive phrase 'the God of X' always bears the meaning 'the God worshipped by X'.[126] But when we consider that these expressions must have been coined at the very time that the cult came into being, we can give an even more precise interpretation: 'the God of X' becomes 'the God first worshipped by X', and the man whose name remained linked for ever with the title of the god is shown by this to be the founder of the particular cult.[127] Dussaud tries to establish an even more exact interpretation, that X was the head of the priestly family who were always responsible for the cult, and believed that he had actually discovered in the case of the Θεὸς Αὔμου evidence in an inscription for the priest Αὖμος, attempting to propagate the cult of his god in Trachonitis.[128] But on chronological grounds alone the last suggestion is untenable,[129] and as for the theory that in general the title of the god was taken from the ancestor of the priestly family, it is uncertain even for the period after the settlement, and highly improbable for the previous nomadic stage, that the cult of these gods was conducted by a hereditary professional priesthood.[130] Be this as it may, we are cer-

[126] This interpretation was first given by CLERMONT-GANNEAU, *EAO*, ii (1897), p. 33.

[127] The same conclusion was reached for the gods in Asia Minor whose names were formed in a similar way; cf. KEIL and VON PREMERSTEIN, *Bericht . . . Reise in Lydien*, p. 92.

[128] DUSSAUD, *Mission* (1903), p. 64 (466); *Les Arabes en Syrie* (1907), p. 148; *Topographie historique de la Syrie antique et mediévale* (1927), p. 351.

[129] The priest Αὖμος from whom DUSSAUD seeks to derive the title of the Θεὸς Αὔμου first occurs in an inscription of the year 320 A.D. coupled with another priest (no. 41): the cult of the god, however, is already attested more than a century earlier (nos. 33, 35, 36). How this discrepancy in time is to be explained remains a mystery.

[130] Even DUSSAUD concedes this point for the nomadic period, and thus, in fact, removes the basis of his own theory; for no

tainly justified in seeing the man after whom the numen was named as the originator of the cult.

But even this affirmation does not solve the problem of the ultimate origin of the type of religion we are studying. We must go on to ask what could have led an individual, either privately or with the immediate concurrence of a body of others, to adopt the worship of a god that was so completely new that a name of his own had to be found for him then and there. In the light of religious psychology and history there can be only one answer. The founder of this cult must have experienced a revelation from a hitherto unknown god, and been compelled by it to worship him.[131] Anyone to whom it was vouchsafed before all others to receive such a new revelation surely deserved to have the god who appeared to him called *his* god, and to have his name perpetuated in the title; no experience of a second or third person was of the same importance as this primary one. And obviously it was the personal element in the original event, the relationship desired and brought about by the god between himself and a human being, which became the essential feature of his character. The place and time and accompanying circumstances of the first theophany had by comparison little or no influence on the way those who first gave the god his title conceived of him. All this implies that the seeds of a completely different development from that of local and nature gods were implanted at the very inception of the cult: the god was not tied to a greater or lesser piece of earth, but to human lives,

---

difference can be shown between the meaning of the divine names before and after the settlement. Moreover, we must take into account the possibility that the members of the worshipping community exercised the priestly functions in turn (in the same way as the Athenians took on the responsibility of the λειτουργία for one year); this hypothesis provides a particularly good explanation of why the inscriptions commemorating important events in the history of the sanctuary contain the names of the officiating priests (nos. 38, 41, 54) or alternatively, of those who were εροταμεῖς at the time (nos. 30, 35) or πιστοὶ (no. 41 ὑπερετήσαντες τὸν ἑαυτῶν χρόνον, also nos. 42 f., 45).

[131] Peterson, Εἷς Θεός, p. 211, already suspected the truth.

first that of an individual, and then through him to those of a whole group. There are good grounds for recognizing these gods as typical tutelary deities and the question is only whether this describes their whole character.[132] In any case, this approach explains how the basic relationship between these numina and individual men could grow into a permanent association between them and larger groups of men. Such a group might consist of the descendants of the particular individual who remained faithful to the cult founded by their ancestor, or it may be a larger body, either a whole tribe or, after the tribe had settled, a group of neighbouring villages which had associated themselves with the cult. Whatever happened in individual cases naturally depended on the historical circumstances, and can consequently be worked out only for the most recent stages of the development, where the evidence of inscriptions is available. But more important than what we find out about individual instances is the principle that from the very beginning these gods were distinguished by a peculiar faculty of adaptation to changing circumstances in the lives of their worshippers, precisely because their association with certain men outweighed all other connections. The gods of this type of religion show a concern with social and historical events which most other primitive numina either lack altogether or possess only to a much more limited degree. This makes it even more appropriate to the way of life of nomadic tribes, and explains why their migration and settlement did not involve its rapid disappearance.

A single inscription—and significantly the very one that lies farthest in time and place from the origins of the cult—provides an opportunity of checking the view set out above of the nature of this form of religion. This is the long inscription on the tomb of Abedrapsas, written in the year A.D. 324, a real תּוֹדָה, and as such able to show an individual example of what the worshippers of such gods, even as late as this, ex-

[132] The examples of 'the God of our Lord' as the divine protector of the Nabataean king (nos. 5–8, 9–11), dealt with on their own above, are particularly instructive when seen in this context.

pected to receive from them.[133] The title of his θεὸς πατρῷος comes from a man with a Greek name: Θεὸς Αρκεσιλάου, while Abedrapsas himself bears an unmistakably Semitic name. This reflects the conditions in the area the tribes had settled, where they retained in part their traditional names and in part adopted names from the Greek (and Roman) upper classes. Since Abedrapsas' god takes his title from a man with a Greek name, his cult must have arisen after the settlement. But his nature is that of the gods from the desert. Just as he appeared to Arkesilaos, so Abedrapsas claims to have seen him in bodily form; whether once or more often is uncertain. But the important thing for him is something else, for which the appearance of the god was only a preparation —the benefits he received from the god in his private life. Looking back over his whole life he mentions two in particular: his god enabled him while he was still a young man to learn in a short time a τέχνη—we do not learn which—and gave him in due time the inspiration to buy a property in the country, through which he was able to retire from his profession in the town. When we look at this, we see that Abedrapsas is really only describing the events of an ordinary, average life; but he quite consciously traces back every decisive step in his modest but prosperous existence to his god's special care for him, and goes out of his way to emphasize at the end how in the way he had spent his life his own 'righteousness' and that of his god had gone side by side. Here, carried over into the conditions of a much more advanced culture and revealed in the experience of an individual with his limited outlook, is what we know was characteristic of all these gods from their origin, and we can only regret that no more of such confessions by devout worshippers have been preserved.

When one looks at the Israelite tradition of the God of the Fathers in the light of these facts, there can be no doubt that a comparison is justified. In both cases we have a type of god, appearing in a number of separate figures, which arises in

[133] No. 32.

the way of life of nomadic tribes in the desert and maintains itself long after they have settled in a civilized area. Its most striking feature is the absence of proper names and the substitution of others formed from the names of the men to whom these divinities first appeared, and who thereupon became their first worshippers. The relationship between the god and the man, and in the further development between the god and a group of men, is conceived of as a special care on the part of the god for the fortunes of his worshippers in their earthly concerns, and dominates the whole picture in this form of religion. On the other hand, a connection with a place is in principle of no importance, and only becomes necessary afterwards, because the way of life of the tribes after their adoption of a settled culture demanded that the cult also be regulated with regard to particular places. The more civilized conditions under which they lived could in certain circumstances lead to a considerable increase in the number of worshippers, if the sanctuary of one of these gods attracted other groups of men. More often, perhaps, they represented a danger, either of the breaking up of the previous worshipping communities or of the swallowing up of the older and lesser gods by new and greater ones. Outwardly this was to the greater glory of the lesser gods, but in reality it meant that the greater overcame them, for by virtue of having actually originated and developed within the civilized regions they were able to convert the assimilation of the characters of different gods into a complete absorption into themselves.

It naturally cannot be expected that an analogy between the God of the Fathers, as far as one can still recognize the figure from the Israelite tradition, and these Arabic-Aramaic numina can be worked out to the last detail. The material we have to work with is on both sides much too recent for this, and too much influenced by certain peculiar later developments, which I shall discuss in the next section. But we can safely say that Old Testament scholars are neglecting a duty if they continue to pass over the tradition of the God of the Fathers without making serious use of the opportunity for comparison offered by this material, which has been lying ready for use for some decades.

CONCLUSION

There is a limit to what can be proved scientifically by even the most successful comparison, and we must not forget it. The inscriptions we have used make it impossible to doubt that the Israelite tradition of the God of the Fathers presents us with a type of religion that was a living force among other Semitic tribes both in the desert and for centuries after their settlement; and this justifies us in concluding that the analogous Israelite tradition may likewise rest on historical facts in the nation's early history. It does not yet make it certain that this *must* be the case. But even to show that this is historically possible brings us a good deal nearer to the solution of the problem. What the Israelite authors said about the God of Abraham, etc., is usually dismissed as a purely literary artifice without a solid basis in the tradition that lay behind them. This was largely due to the fact that up to the present no one has seen any reason for asking whether anything different could be possible. People will not be able to be so careless in future: the comparative material now available is too weighty for that. Our study of the way the tradition has developed suggested that we are dealing with the elements of the Israelite tradition which go back long before the literary editors, and which they took up and adapted to their own purposes. The comparison we have made goes far to confirm this; but we have not yet achieved a decisive proof. We must look for further indications which either make the matter certain, or completely rule out the possibility. In this frontier region between history and prehistory there is no alternative to the patient weighing of evidence for and against our hypothesis.

Since we have already examined the direct tradition of the Old Testament about the God of the Fathers, without coming to an entirely satisfactory conclusion, we can obviously obtain other evidence of whether this tradition is primary or secondary only by extending the investigation over a larger field of Israelite tradition and history. First of all we must look at the patriarchal sagas as a whole, and secondly at the form Israelite religion took later. Which gives the more satisfactory explanation of the general picture of the patriarchal period given by the tradition: the view that in the religion of the Israelite tribes, before they united in the worship of Yahweh, there was one or more gods of this sort, or the prevailing view that this element was produced in its entirety by the literary editors or the tradition immediately preceding them? Work already done on the interpretation of the patriarchal sagas is far from having resolved all the difficulties there. But the unsolved problems themselves can serve as criteria for the question in hand; for they can show us whether or not what has hitherto been merely a hypothesis is of any positive value for the understanding of the tradition. But in view of the profuse variety of the patriarchal sagas, we obviously shall not expect it to give us the key to every hidden treasure in them.

We can take as a starting-point the different titles for the God of the Fathers or, as we suspect, for the several numina which were eventually combined in that figure. Since they always contain the names Abraham, Isaac and Jacob, they involve the problem of the God of the Fathers in that of the patriarchs themselves. What are we to make of these names? The repeated attempts to prove that they were originally divine names have been as unsuccessful as the efforts to take them as referring to tribes rather than individuals. It is accepted nowadays by practically everyone that they were always personal names.[134] But this is not sufficient to explain their origin. Are they to be reckoned among the historical or the legendary elements in the sagas? To my mind no one has given a reliable answer to this. It is obvious how important this is for the conclusions we reach about the patriarchal sagas as a whole. If Abraham, Isaac and Jacob are originally

[134] For this and the following cf. especially GRESSMANN, *ZAW*, xxx (1910), pp. 1 ff.

only legendary names, then all the historical material of the sagas that have taken shape around them is naturally secondary, and *a fortiori* the problem of the God of the Fathers disappears completely. But even if the patriarchs are not legendary—and there is no necessity for thinking so—but are historical personages from Israel's early history, it is not easy to say precisely what part these persons actually played and why their memory was so well preserved that a genealogical link was created between the three of them and between them and the system of the twelve tribes of Israel. There is a whole complex of problems here, none of which has been satisfactorily resolved.

Now let us see what can be done by starting from the hypothesis that there existed among the Israelite tribes at an early period the cult of the God of Abraham, the Fear of Isaac, and the Mighty One of Jacob. The whole complexion of the problem is altered. The tradition of the God of the Fathers is no longer a mere appendage to that of the patriarchs themselves which remains unexplained, but becomes of great importance and can be discussed separately. And since the tradition finds its own sufficient explanation in what we know to have been regular religious institutions before the historical period, it contains as it were a ready-made solution to the problem of who the patriarchs were. For just as Αὖμος is the man to whom the Θεὸς Αὔμου first appeared and who became as a result the founder of the cult of this god, so Abraham, Isaac and Jacob must be understood as those who received revelations from, and founded the cult of, each particular numen; and this brings us at once to the origin of the tradition concerning them. The great advantage of such a view seems to me to be that it places the figures of the patriarchs from the very first in an organic relationship to the whole religious and cultic practice of the Israelite tribes, and allows it a proper part both in the constant and in the developing features of their religious history. This explains one thing which is otherwise difficult to understand—the fact that these individuals were remembered from the earliest times on. As long as the God of Abraham was regularly worshipped under this formal title, and even after his cult had died out completely, as long as his title was used in the worship of Yahweh, to whom it had been transferred, men were always reminded of Abraham. And as we said, the later worshippers of the Θεὸς Αὔμου would certainly have possessed and handed on their own traditions about Αὖμος. We can see how in the same way every kind of tradition gathered round the figures of Abraham, Isaac and Jacob, even material which had nothing to do with the cult of the numen in question. But the suspicion often voiced above, that just as we are dealing with three individual persons, so there are three distinct numina, becomes irrefutable.

The conclusion to be drawn from this, that the part played by Abraham, Isaac and Jacob in the tradition of the Israelite sagas is principally due to their receiving a revelation from a god and founding his cult, fully accords with the picture given by the sagas as a whole. They continually appear in this role, even though not everything that is recorded about them quite fits it. When looked at more closely, this latter fact seems to constitute a serious objection to our theory, for the stories of revelations and the founding of cults in the patriarchal history usually have no connection with the God of the Fathers, but refer on the contrary to the *'Ēlīm* of the Palestine sanctuaries. The Yahwist accounts of revelations by the God of Abraham to Isaac, and by the God of Isaac to Jacob, which at a superficial glance may seem to be the counterparts of the genuine ancient ἱεροὶ λόγοι, are in fact not so at all. We saw instead that they were simply composed by the literary editors to express the theory of an inner unity among the patriarchs, which was presented schematically by the god of each patriarch appearing first of all to his son. It looks in fact as if the type of religion we are dealing with lacked the kind of saga that is the normal form in which the recollection of religious origins is preserved. Or may we perhaps take the story of Genesis xv, which speaks of a revelation made to Abraham, and is neither attributed to any special place nor mentions the name of a particular numen, as the tradition of the first appearance of the god of Abraham? I shall return to this question later in another connection. But even if this is the case, the existence of this one saga is far from satisfying the need for genuine ancient ἱεροὶ λόγοι for the cults of this type of religion. If the God of the Fathers is taken to be a purely artificial figure, this deficiency is not surprising; if we wish to argue that it is really ancient, it forms a serious problem.

Moreover this problem is not an isolated one but leads at once to further questions. How has it come about that the traditional sagas of the patriarchs are almost all situated in Palestine, where the Israelites settled, and yet always refer to the period before the Israelite occupation took place? Secular history provides no grounds for believing that the ancestors of Israel lived for a time in Palestine, then went away, and finally returned to establish themselves. A way out has been sought by ignoring the coming and going and connecting the stories of the patriarchs with the earliest thrust of the advancing Israelite tribes, which more recent studies have quite properly distinguished from the later stages of the occupation. But this explanation is not satisfactory, especially as regards the sagas of Abraham and Jacob;[135] for they are mostly set in parts of Palestine which only came into Israelite possession with the entry of the last group, the House of Joseph, or as a result of further territorial expansion.[136] The only other possible conclusion seems to be that none of these sagas came into being until after the settlement, and the tradition perpetrated a grave anachronism by dating the patriarchs long before Joshua and Moses.

Although what has been shown from secular history about

[135] The situation is naturally much simpler in the case of Isaac, whose saga is restricted to the southern border, between Gerar and Beersheba, of the territory west of the Jordan settled by the Israelites. On similar grounds we can eliminate the sagas which concern only the tribes of Simeon and Levi (Gen. xxiv) and Judah (Gen. xxxviii).

[136] West of the Jordan this is true of Bethel (Judges i. 22) and even more of Shechem (Judges ix), and east of the Jordan of all the sites connected with the saga of Jacob: Mahanaim, Pnuel and Succoth (Judges viii. 5 ff., 14 ff.).

the relation of the patriarchal sagas to the course of the Israelite migration into Palestine may be of great importance, it is not decisive for the present question. For the places in Palestine where the sagas are enacted are always sanctuaries, and as a rule the sagas themselves are concerned with theophanies and rites carried out at these places. We must first formulate more exactly the chronological problem of the connection between Abraham, Isaac and Jacob, who are presented as living in pre-Mosaic times, and the sanctuaries of Palestine which first came into Israelite possession during or after the settlement. We can only hope to solve this problem by reconstructing the religious development that took place during the movement of Israelite tribes from the desert into the civilized regions. It seems to me that the view advanced above, that the reason the names of the patriarchs first acquired a central place in Israelite tradition was their connection with the cult of their gods, provides a very easy way of resolving the discrepancy between the dates given for the entry and the complete certainty with which the tradition places the patriarchs in a much earlier period. For these cults, and therefore the names of their founders, originate right back in the period of Israelite history before the entry. The chronology of the tradition is basically correct in insisting that Abraham, Isaac and Jacob came before Moses and Joshua. But when the worshippers brought these cults with them into Palestine and took possession of the sanctuaries they found already there, they had to relate the tradition about the patriarchs themselves to the new places of worship, and adapt them to new conditions. Thus the figures of the patriarchs now appear in an area to which they cannot have belonged before the tribes settled in Palestine. We can presume that the development of the corresponding cults on the edge of the Arabian and Aramaean territories was similar. It is to be regretted that this cannot be verified in a specific case from any of the inscriptions found there.

Once it is realized that the process by which the patriarchal sagas grew and were handed down in the tradition can be divided into two distinct stages, the first in the wilderness before the entry and the second in Palestine itself, several consequences can be seen. It is now clear why no sagas are preserved about the founding of the cult of these gods. Such sagas could have arisen only in the stage before the entry, in which the cult came into being and its earliest development took place; they must certainly have been in existence then. But the tradition obviously did not attain the form in which the Yahwist and the Elohist preserve it for us, giving it literary expression, until after the Israelites had established themselves in Palestine. For it was then that these cults became attached to sanctuaries in Palestine, and the figures of the patriarchs, going back to the period before the entry, were given a place in the ἱεροὶ λόγοι that had always been recounted at the sanctuaries the Israelites took over. In this completely different setting, the new life taken on by the figures of the patriarchs made its own demands on them—everything that was no longer of use died out. From the period before the entry, only the cults of the gods themselves remained, and with them the names of the founders of the cult. But the ancient aetiological sagas of the cult, which had no connection with the places where it was now practised, no longer had any significance and were forgotten. Most of the traditional stories that were retained from the period in the wilderness found their way into the cycle of sagas about Moses, a different type of tradition with a different history. It is easy to understand, therefore, why when the literary editors afterwards sought to fit the memories that were still alive of the God of Abraham, etc., to a new purpose within the framework of the patriarchal sagas, they found very few individual stories available among the existing material. In most cases they had to compose their own, as for example the Yahwist did in the case of the theophanies before Isaac and Jacob. What actually happened, then, seems to be much more complicated than the current view supposes; but this involved process answers exactly to the changes which the tribes of Israel had to undergo in their way of life and thought as they moved out of the wilderness into Palestine. In no way does it make less probable the view we are developing here.

In the tradition, the taking over of the sanctuaries of Palestine was expressed by bringing the ancestors of Israel into the ἱεροὶ λόγοι of each place and representing them as receiving revelations from the numina who had always been worshipped there, and as the founders of their cult. It is this type of cultic saga which is predominant in the patriarchal history of Genesis. The Yahwist was not able to alter this, the Elohist still less. But when these writers wished to reintroduce the tradition of the God of Abraham, etc., into the cult sagas, the result is that the two different kinds of god and divine title are simply placed side by side without being in any way related. Compare for example the Yahwist and Elohist accounts of Jacob's vision in the night at Bethel.[137] Only the first treats it as a revelation of the God of Abraham and Isaac, and consequently makes the speech of the god who appears the climax of the whole story. As a result, his version lacks almost all the characteristic features of the old cultic saga of the *'Ēl Bēt'ēl*, which the Elohist preserves almost intact.[138] Or again, at Beersheba, first Abraham appears as the founder of the cult of *'Ēl 'Ōlām* and then Jacob sacrifices to the God of Isaac.[139] There is hardly any attempt formally to equate the two.[140] Moreover, the one story in which the solemn naming of the θεὸς πατρῷος belonged to the original form, that of Jacob's treaty with Laban, does not take place at a great sanctuary and can in no way be considered a cultic saga. So there is no question of a local numen coming into the story as well. This peculiarity of the tradition seems to reflect something of the decline in the cults practised by the Israelites before the entry, once they had settled in Palestine. These

[137] Gen. xxviii. 13–16, 21 (?), 19 J; xxviii, 11–12, 17–18, 20, 22, E.

[138] Admittedly the Elohist introduces the old title of the god not here, but later on, in xxxi. 13; xxxv. 7; but these passages clearly look back to the first appearance.

[139] Gen. xxi. 33 J; xlvi. 1 ff. JE.

[140] The only place where one might suspect an attempt to harmonize here is where in xlvi. 3 the Elohist makes the numen who speaks to Jacob introduce himself with the words: 'I am הָאֵל, the god of thy father.' Cf. with this xxxi. 13.

cults certainly gained a foothold in the sanctuaries there—according to our view this explains the association of the patriarchs with the sites. But the cults that already existed there, with their sagas, proved stronger, and brought the tradition of the patriarchs under their influence. This is why it is not obvious, in the present state of the tradition, in what way the cults which were carried in from the period in the wilderness continued to exist after the entry.

Yet even in their present form the sagas provide a solution indirectly, if we remember that it follows from our view that the incorporation into the traditions of the Palestine sanctuaries of the *names* of the patriarchs results from the transplanting thither of the cult of their gods. For we can then go on to take the places where the cult is associated with the figures of individual patriarchs as the sites of sanctuaries where the gods named after them were worshipped. When we come to examine the distribution of these sanctuaries, certain inferences can be drawn about the worshippers there. In the case of Jacob and his god, a very clear picture emerges: all the sites east and west of the Jordan, in which the sagas connect him with a sanctuary, lie in the area settled by the House of Joseph.[141] We are forced to the conclusion that the whole of this particularly powerful group of tribes either worshipped the God of Jacob from the beginning, or began to do so during and after the settlement.[142] In any case, the diffusion of this cult over the whole area in which the sagas of Jacob are found took a considerable time.[143] This shows

[141] West of the Jordan this includes Bethel (Gen. xxviii. 11 ff.; xxxi. 13; xxxv. 7, 14), Shechem (xxxiii. 18 ff.; xxxv. 2 ff.), and perhaps also Dothan (xxxvii. 17 ff.), and east of the Jordan, Mahanaim (xxxii, 2 f.), Pnuel (xxxii. 25 ff.) and probably also Succoth (xxxiii. 17). Note that almost all these sanctuaries lie on or near sites which are known to have existed in pre-Israelite times. The cult sagas, therefore, also help to show that none of these sanctuaries were newly founded by the invading Israelites.

[142] It is presumably no coincidence, then, that the 'Mighty One of Jacob' is referred to in the Blessing of Jacob in the oracle concerning Joseph (Gen. xlix. 24).

[143] This is particularly true of its extension east of the Jordan. There is no convincing basis for the widely-held view that the sagas

that this cult was strong enough, even after the first sanctuaries had been taken over, to move forward in step with the tribes as they increased their territory and took over one sanctuary after another.[144] The spread of the cult of the Θεὸς Αὔμου in Trachonitis, it will be remembered, took a similar course; but there is a difference not only in the greater area in which the God of Jacob was worshipped, but also in the fact that the cult was everywhere carried on by the same group of tribes, and not as in the case of the Θεὸς Αὔμου by neighbouring communities belonging to different tribes.

In the case of Isaac the picture is quite different. Both the cultic and secular elements in the sagas concerning him are restricted to Beersheba and its immediate neighbourhood.[145] This suggests that only a single sanctuary maintained the cult of the 'Fear of Isaac';[146] its isolation at the southernmost limit of Palestinian civilization may have prevented the cult from spreading. But we know that even after the formation of the Israelite states this sanctuary was not only frequented by the inhabitants of the immediate neighbourhood, the tribe of Simeon,[147] but was also visited by worshippers from as far away as the kingdom of Israel[148]—presumably at the great annual feasts. And we may suppose that the other settlers in the Negeb, the tribe of Judah and other groups,[149]

---

of Jacob located east of the Jordan preserve reminiscences of an earlier period when the Israelite tribes lived there.

144 Thus the history of the House of Joseph, both religious and secular, makes clear why their relations with the Aramaic tribes on their borders form such an important theme in the sagas of Jacob.

145 Gen. xxvi. Cf. with the rest of the paragraph ZIMMERLI, *Geschichte und Tradition von Beersheba im Alten Testament* (Diss. Göttingen, 1932).

146 Thus the only scene in the saga tradition concerning the God of Isaac takes place at this sanctuary (Gen. xlvi. 1 ff.).

147 Joshua xix. 2 ff. (xv. 21 ff.).

148 Amos v. 5; viii. 14. Cf. also 1 Kings xix. 3. Does this cultic relationship perhaps arise from the fact that part of the tribe of Simeon remained in the Samaritan mountains after the unsuccessful attempt to settle in the region of Shechem (Gen. xxxiv), and were later absorbed by the House of Joseph?

149 Cf. 1 Sam. xxvii. 10; xxx. 26 ff.

also took part in this cult. Instead of the spread of the cult from one sanctuary to another, which we believe happened in the case of the God of Jacob, the picture seems to be that of a cult restricted to a single site, but extending the circle of its worshippers far beyond the borders of the local tribes. This is a different kind of expansion, and without it Isaac and his god would hardly have found their way into the tradition of the whole of the people of Israel. Here again the history of the cult explains the content of the tradition. It is difficult to decide whether the cult of the God of Isaac was brought to Beersheba from elsewhere, or originated there, and who were the first to practise it.[150]

Abraham is associated with the sanctuary at the tree of Mamre, at least in the Yahwist version.[151] This seems to be where the cult of the God of Abraham should be localized, if it is true that in every case the sites at which the sacral elements in the patriarchal history are set correspond to the sanctuaries where their gods are worshipped after the entry. Now the sanctuary of Mamre lies in lands belonging to Hebron,[152] and therefore in the territory of an ancient city which did not belong to an Israelite tribe, but to a group of Calebites originally distinct from them.[153] Can we infer that Abraham and his god originated among the Calebites? If so,

[150] The saga of Isaac in Gen. xxvi J, belonging to secular history (and transferred to Abraham in Gen. xx ff. E), is concerned apparently only with the territorial circumstances of the tribe of Simeon in the Negeb, and naturally provides no solution for the problem of the history of the cult.

[151] Gen. xviii J. But perhaps a cultic saga concerning Mamre lies behind the Elohist narrative of the sacrifice of Isaac (Gen. xxii). The frequently recurring play of words in this story on forms of the verb ראה may be based on the foreign-sounding name ממרא.

[152] The results of MADER's excavations in Ḥaram Rāmet el-Chalīl (1 km. south of the northern border of the territory of Hebron, towards that of Ḥalḥūl) remove all grounds for supposing that the connection of the Mamre tradition with this site is secondary. (Cf. especially *Oriens Christianus,* 3, Ser. ii [1928], pp. 374 ff.)

[153] Cf. Num. xiii. 22; Judges i. 20, etc.

it would be difficult to see what caused the tradition of the whole of Israel to include him in the genealogy of the patriarchs, actually placing him at the very beginning. But here again it is most improbable that the worshippers at the sanctuary of Mamre were anciently drawn from Calebite territory alone. This sanctuary was destined by its position on the border between two territories to become the centre of a much more widespread body of worshippers, and that it in fact performed this function is adequately attested from later periods.[154] The people to the north of the border, the tribe of Judah, can be included among the worshippers at Mamre at an early period[155] and this sacral union of the men of Judah with the Calebites (and presumably also with their neighbours to the south) helped to make it possible, about 1000 B.C., for the neighbouring tribes to unite in one political unit, a kingdom called Judah, with the seat of its king in the Calebite capital Hebron.[156] This gives a similar picture to that at Beersheba, and the only question that remains is which group in the amphictyony of Mamre introduced the cult of the God of Abraham into the common sanctuary. The position of Abraham in the tradition of the whole of Israel implies that it was the one tribe in the area which had a permanent place in the system of the twelve tribes of Israel, that is Judah. How far the beginning of the

[154] Cf. especially SOZOMENOS, *Hist. Eccl.*, II, 4, Hussey. The important role of border sanctuaries in ancient Israel as places where neighbouring tribes could unite in the cult can be seen in several other places, e.g. in Bethel and on Mount Tabor (Deut. xxxiii. 19).

[155] The relation of Mamre to the territories of the neighbouring tribes can be clearly seen from the list of towns in Joshua xv.; even Ḥalḥūl and Beth-sur belong to the territory settled by the original tribe of Judah (v. 58; cf. *PJB*, xxi [1925], pp. 114 ff.).

[156] 2 Sam. ii. 1 ff. This great act of union did not come about suddenly; it must have been prepared for, at least in part, by cultic unions, and the part played by Hebron in the founding of the kingdom, make it likely that a sanctuary in the territory of that town had previously been the most important cultic meeting place of the tribes.

worship of the God of Abraham goes back into its early history, either within or outside Palestine, we cannot tell.

Admittedly Abraham is not absolutely limited to the sanctuary of Mamre in the sagas: the Yahwist shows him coming thither by way of Shechem and Bethel,[157] the Elohist takes him to Beersheba,[158] and the priestly writing only knows of his grave in the cave of Machpelah opposite Hebron.[159] It can scarcely be denied that these are all composed later; they do not bring into question the priority of Mamre. But was the later association of Abraham with these places simply invented by those who transmitted the tradition, or are developments within the history of the cult once more responsible? Thus the transferring of Abraham's grave to a cave very close to Hebron could have been brought about by the setting up in the city of an outpost of the cult at Mamre; the introduction of Abraham into the Beersheba cycle of sagas by the participation, mentioned above, of the groups who had their common sanctuary at Mamre, in the cult at the central shrine of the Negeb; and his much looser connection with the Jacob sanctuaries of Shechem and Bethel by the cultic link with the House of Joseph through Beersheba. It remains to be seen how well established the worship of the God of Abraham in fact was in the latter sanctuaries. A spread of the cult of the sort we believe took place in the case of the God of Jacob, over the whole area settled by the House of Joseph, can hardly be shown to underlie the association of Abraham with Jacob's sanctuaries west of the Jordan.

Thus the figures of the three patriarchs, and the cults connected with them, stood on the whole side by side with each other in separate sites and districts. This is another fact which makes it necessary to treat the God of Abraham, the Fear of Isaac and the Mighty One of Jacob as numina which originally had nothing to do with one another, even though each represented for its worshippers the same type of religion. Looking at the external form from the point of view of

[157] Gen. xii. f.
[158] Gen. xx. ff.
[159] Gen. xxiii.

the history of the cult, we were led to postulate a primary connection between the patriarchal traditions and the cult of the gods of the Fathers, and the same point of view makes possible an understanding of the actual circumstances in which each figure was isolated in a particular place. The analogy of similar cults on the edge of the Arab and Aramaic territories, where there is no case of the overlapping of two cults in one place, can be applied without qualification. But the closer examination of the location of the sanctuaries and of the groups and tribes which participated in the cult there can also show us how it was possible, as the tradition developed, for these figures of the patriarchs to be brought into contact with one another. The attraction of a few great sanctuaries for groups living a considerable distance away gave rise to overlapping between the worshippers at several sanctuaries, and thus permitted the equation, or at least the interchange, of the peculiar religious features of each. The sanctuary of Beersheba seems to have played an essential part in this process. Pilgrims from the House of Joseph, who at home worshipped the Mighty One of Jacob, took part in the cult practised there, and this living contact between North and South had the effect of establishing a connection between their two heroes, Jacob and Isaac;[160] and with the participation of groups from the mountains of Judah, whose own central sanctuary was at Mamre, with Abraham as its ἥρως κτίστης, the same happened between Abraham and Isaac.[161] The incorporation of these figures into a single genealogy was simply the consummation of the whole process. Without it, of course, the patriarchal tradition of all Israel could not have flourished as it did, nor could it have

[160] The connection between the House of Joseph and Beersheba explains the otherwise puzzling fact that the conflict with Esau, i.e. Edom, in the saga is linked with the figure of Jacob, whose other connections are with sites far from the borders of Edom. Did the Edomites also perhaps take part in the cult at Beersheba?

[161] This story of the conflict between Israel and Ishmael, both regarded as sons of Abraham, may first have been told at Beersheba.

attained the proportions we find in the literary versions.[162] Could this not be a primary cause of the ultimate fusion of the gods of Abraham, Isaac and Jacob into one figure, the God of the Fathers, which, as we saw, was to be so important for the literary editors?

If our reasoning has so far been correct, the framework and elaboration of the patriarchal sagas were determined by a few great sanctuaries.[163] Large areas, Galilee in particular, and the southern part of the region east of the Jordan, contribute nothing to the tradition that became common to all Israel, and the cults and cultic sagas of the smaller sanctuaries between Beersheba, Shechem, and Mahanaim are likewise a closed book to us. This implies that we ought not to suppose that the gods of Abraham, Isaac and Jacob were the only gods of this type worshipped during the early stages of Israel's history. They are only three out of many, brought to the fore by the fate of individual cults, after the settlement in Palestine, through the gradual disappearance and extinction of some and the spread of others. There is a particular reason for the mention in one saga of the 'God of Nahor' among the related Aramaean tribes—and he promptly disappears again. The name of one or other of the same type of god from among the Israelites might just as easily have been introduced, had not the importance of their particular cults caused the tradition to restrict itself to the three principal figures. It is not surprising that the comparative material from the Arabic and Aramaic inscriptions provides no parallels. For the actual inscriptions are specifically concerned

[162] Apart from these relationships, there is also on the one hand the connection between Abraham and Lot (Moab and Ammon) which must have had its origin in Mamre—and on the other hand the identification of Jacob with Israel, which of course has its roots in the House of Joseph. But we cannot go further into this here.

[163] We can do no more than mention the fact that many materials of a completely different sort were drawn into this framework. They have originally nothing to do with the gods of the Patriarchs, nor with the Patriarchs themselves, and for the most part are neither cultic in nature nor connected with the history of the tribes.

with a single cult in isolation from the rest; whether or not any links existed between groups who worshipped different numina, the inscriptions would not mention them. If we had any remains of the sagas of these groups, the picture might be somewhat different. But we may be allowed to doubt whether they would present such a closely-knit complex of divine and human figures as we find in the fully-developed tradition of the Israelite patriarchs. For among these peoples a drive towards national unity scarcely existed, while its effect on the process that took place in Israel must always be taken into account.

It cannot be denied that by working out the theory of a relationship between the figures of the patriarchs and the type of religion represented by the gods of the Fathers, we have arrived at a reconstruction of the development of the cult and the tradition during Israel's early history, which provides a tolerable basis for explaining the way the sagas appear in Genesis. Much of what, apart from this hypothesis, looked like a conglomeration of variously assorted material can now be fitted into a process of organic growth. Historical probability is gained rather than lost when the vital connection is shown between the state of affairs before and after the entry, and between the original religious inheritance of each tribe and the evolution it underwent in Palestine. A line can be traced from the names of the patriarchs to their introduction into the cultic sagas of sanctuaries in Palestine, from their separate existence among bodies of worshippers drawn from a single tribe or region to the point where they were brought together and the genealogy was formed. And it must be admitted that the process as described here is consistent with the general course of the early stages of Israelite history, even though allowance must be made for its inevitably hypothetical character.

A conclusion as to the value of this reconstruction of events would be premature, however, if it left unanswered the second of the questions put forward at the beginning of this section: if we accept that the type of religion represented by the gods of the Fathers existed among the Israelite tribes both before and after the settlement in Palestine, how is this connected to the fundamental fact of the history of Israelite religion, the worship of Yahweh by all the tribes? This question has obviously become much more urgent as a result of the conclusions already reached. For we can no longer imagine that when the Israelites had settled in Palestine they allowed the cults they brought with them from their pre-Palestinian period to die out at once, and replaced them by completely different forms of religion. For the application of our fundamental thesis to the sagas of Genesis shows that far from disappearing, some at least of these cults underwent a further evolution of a very special kind after they had been transplanted into Palestine. Where are we to look, as we must, for the point in history at which the tribes united in the worship of Yahweh? Did this decisive act and the development we have described take place at the same time, or can the one only be seen as coming after the other, in which case the adoption of the religion of Yahweh in Israel can only have come about long after the entry into Palestine. The answer obviously depends entirely on how one conceives of the first effects on the whole religious inheritance of tribes of their adoption of the worship of Yahweh, and in particular, the practical effect on their cultic activities. Did this innovation mean that they felt obliged to abandon at once what the tribes had hitherto regarded as sacred? In that case the persistence in Palestine of the religion they had practised before that of Yahweh becomes more and more difficult to explain, the earlier we date the adoption of the worship of Yahweh; and it would be completely impossible if one accepted the view of the Moses saga, that they worshipped Yahweh before the entry. But it is most unlikely that the process should be thought of as being so abrupt. From the very beginning the religion of Yahweh displayed its characteristically exclusive tendency but in the earliest period this plainly relates only to the people as a whole—for it was by this exclusive religion that they were made one nation—and not to individual tribes. Although Yahweh is the God of *Israel*, and will tolerate no other national religion, this does not mean, according to the concepts of the ancient world, that the *tribes*, in their narrower sphere, might not worship other gods. One can compare the cultic practice of a sacral confederation of tribes in Greece, such as the Pylaeic-Delphic amphictyony. They worshipped in common only Demeter at Anthela and the Delphic Apollo—and the carrying out of these cults was in fact the basis of the existence of the amphictyony; but there is no suggestion that on this account members of the confederation, i.e. individual tribes, were forbidden to practise their own tribal cults. This distinction between national and tribal religion must be given more serious consideration in the case of ancient Israel. Even the Israelite tradition as it stands, which goes so far towards eliminating every trace of such a distinction, occasionally reveals something of how the national religion of Yahweh was practised as one cult among many, of which some had existed in Palestine from time immemorial, and others had been introduced by the Israelite tribes. I refer in particular to the sanctuary of Shiloh. There is no doubt of its early importance as the centre of the worship of Yahweh by the whole nation, and yet it has no connections with the patriarchal sagas. The contrast between this sanctuary and those where the tradition of the patriarchs is located is all the greater in that the latter are situated almost without exception within the territory of settlements known to have been established before the entry of the Israelites; whereas the archaeological examination of Shiloh suggests that the settlement and sanctuary were both founded in the early Israelite period.[164] It seems in fact as if the religion of Yahweh was not involved, during the first stages of its existence in Palestine, in the occupation of the older sanctuaries, which according to our view played such a great part in the history of the gods of the Fathers. It was kept separate, and thus established itself at sites unencumbered by any existing sacral tradition. This is in accordance with its distinctive peculiarities.

[164] Cf. KJAER, *PEF Quart. Stat.*, lix (1927), pp. 202 ff.; *JPOS*, x (1930), pp. 87 ff.

Therefore, although in due course the religion of Yahweh put down strong roots in Palestine, this development took place along quite different lines from that by which the cult of the gods of the Fathers was localized in particular districts and ancient sanctuaries. It was carried out by the nation as it came to act more and more as one, and not by tribes and lesser groups, to which the worship of the God of Abraham, etc. was restricted. This means that to date the beginning of the worship of Yahweh by the Israelites in the period immediately before the entry, as is required by the Moses saga, as well as other sources, is not to contradict the view that the cult of the gods of the Fathers, still developing independently of the national religion of Yahweh, established itself in certain localities in Palestine and was there drawn into association with the existing cults. Apart from this, we must take into account, in some cases at least, the likelihood that the tribes in question had already settled in Palestine before the nation united in the worship of Yahweh.[165] Naturally there is an even greater interval here between the time the native tribal cults were localized in the holy places where the tribes had settled, and the introduction of the cult of Yahweh into these sanctuaries. Of course there is no certainty about the details, but basically we are justified in believing that during the first stage in Palestine the worship of the gods of the Fathers was carried on by individual tribes and in single sanctuaries independently of the national religion of Yahweh. Likewise, different strata within the ἱεροὶ λόγοι of the patriarchal sagas can hardly be explained except by postulating such a period, when the religious traditions of each group had not yet been assimilated—just as in the secular sphere, indeed, they were slow to give up their individuality.

This state of affairs obviously did not go on for ever. The

[165] I am thinking in particular of the Leah-tribes of the south, and with them of the sanctuaries of Beersheba and Mamre, and the sagas of Isaac and Abraham which developed there. In the case of the House of Joseph and the sanctuaries in its territory with which the figure of Jacob is connected, the likelihood of this having happened is far less.

patriarchal sagas, like every other tradition, show how the worship of Yahweh spread from the sites where it was first localized in Palestine over the whole country, led to the founding of new sanctuaries, and was even accepted in those which were associated with the tradition of the patriarchs and the cult of their gods. With this, the history of these sanctuaries reaches its final stage: the religion of Yahweh penetrates thither and imposes itself as the newest stratum upon the previous form of worship. When this point was reached at each sanctuary, we do not know. But it is clear that this final development must have been completed before the patriarchal sagas could have taken the form in which we find them in the works of the Yahwist and the Elohist. Take for example the saga of Mamre in the Yahwist version: it still speaks of the three divine beings who had revealed themselves in the sacred grove—this is the pre-Israelite stage. But the man who receives their first revelation has for a long time been Abraham—the first Israelite stage, based on the introduction of the God of Abraham. And out of the trinity of divine beings Yahweh emerges as the one and only God—the second Israelite stage, following the introduction of the cult of Yahweh.[166] The elements coming from the three stages of religious and cultic development can be distinguished almost as easily in the sagas of other ancient sanctuaries. Although the inscriptions from the Arab and Aramaean areas are not lacking in examples of the assimilation of one god to another, the religion of those tribes encountered and had to adapt itself to a different situation, and it is not surprising, therefore, that the records provide no exact parallels to what happened in Israel. Nevertheless a distant analogy can be found in the identification of the Nabataean אלה שעידו in Boṣra with the great regional god בעלשמן [167] and in that of the Θεὸς Αὔμου in the Leja with the even greater Ζεὺς Ἀνίκητος Ἥλιος.[168] The necessary condi-

[166] Gen. xviii.
[167] Appendix, no. 15.
[168] Nos. 41–44.

tions did not exist for the absorption of all other numina by one transcendent deity, as happened with Yahweh in Israel.

The ultimate destiny of the worship of the gods of the Fathers must be understood historically as a result of the encroachment of the *national* cult of Yahweh upon the *local* sanctuaries of the Israelite tribes in Palestine, even where this involved the assimilation of fundamentally different types of religion. An example such as that of the cultic saga of Mamre shows what disparate material, polytheistic in nature very often, underlies this absorption. But we must not overlook the fact that in the case of the God of Abraham, etc., the character of these numina was in one most important respect very well adapted to their identification with Yahweh. For everything that we recognized as truly characteristic of these and similar gods in the Arab and Aramaean areas—their association with particular groups of men, families, clans, or tribes, their providential oversight over the fortunes of their worshippers in the desert, and where they had settled, their concern with social and historical events—all this recurs, only on a higher level and over a much wider field, in the character of Yahweh as the God of Israel. What the gods of the Fathers were to the smaller communities, he was to the whole confederation of the tribes; and this was true from the very beginning, not just in the later stages of the development. In this respect, there is no μετάβασις εἰς ἄλλο γένος when a group in Israel, formerly worshipping the God of Abraham as the guide and maintainer of its individual existence, enters a confederation where Yahweh carried out the same function for the group as a whole, so that they eventually established his cult in their own sanctuary. The same fundamental outlook and practice are simply carried on to a higher plane. The ultimate identification of the gods of the Fathers with Yahweh was the final consequence of their assimilation one to another, which we have already discussed without reference to the religion of Yahweh,[169] and it can

[169] Cf. p. 71. We cannot say to what extent the unifying influence of the religion of Yahweh was already playing its part in this assimilation.

hardly be denied that by following our original hypothesis to its conclusion we have arrived at a reconstruction of the historical process both self-consistent and inherently probable.

We have shown the similarity that exists, in spite of the difference in their relative importance, between the character of the gods of the Fathers and that of the God of Israel. Herein lies the answer to the question asked at the beginning of the introduction, whether or not there was anything in the religious inheritance of the Israelite tribes, before they adopted the worship of Yahweh, which made the people as a whole—and not just a few prominent leaders—ready to unite in a single nation in covenant with Yahweh. The ancient local gods of the regions they settled in Palestine were by their nature unable to fulfil this function, even though the Israelite tribes had been familiar with them for a considerable time before they received the call and the promise of Yahweh. But our contention is that in the God of Abraham and the other gods of the same type the tribes possessed, even in the period when they lived independently of each other, a religion which had one essential mark of the later religion of Yahweh. For it stressed above all the relationship between God and man, and between God and whole groups of men, without any fixed association with one place. This made it all the more adaptable to the changing fortunes of the worshippers. The idea that Yahweh rules over the nation as a whole and over its history, is clear and precise from the beginning, and is the most distinctive characteristic of the religion of Israel. Where does it come from? It can hardly go back to the worship of Yahweh by many different tribes at the mountain of God in the desert. To all appearance it springs up as something quite new, when the Israelite tribes unite, and does not bring them into a closer relationship with the other worshippers of Yahweh—on the contrary, it makes a breach between them and the Israelites. How else could the consciousness of a special relationship to Yahweh have formed the basis of an exclusive Israelite nationalism? If this tendency, peculiar to the religion of Yahweh in Israel, has any previous historical background, it must lie elsewhere. But if, as we suggest, the religion of the gods of the Fathers goes back into the prehistory of the Israelite tribes, then this provides the background we are looking for. It does not of course prefigure what was quite new in the religion of Yahweh, the union of all the tribes under one god. But within the limits of the smaller groups concerned it stands for the same basic relationship between God and men in which the whole nation was placed by the religion of Yahweh. This provides a satisfactory answer to the problem of how it was psychologically possible for the tribes to unite in the worship of Yahweh: the gods of the Fathers were the παιδαγωγοί leading to the greater God, who later replaced them completely.

In the light of this historical connection and the basic similarity of the two forms of religion, it is not surprising that when the Israelite tradition was given literary form, and in fact before this, it speaks both in the story of Moses and in the sagas of the patriarchs of a covenant between God and men, which includes both a call and a promise. This peculiar twofold content of the covenant with the patriarchs and Moses has recently been demonstrated in detail by Galling. In explaining it he asserts that only the idea of the choosing of Israel at the time of Moses forms the hard core of the popular tradition; that of the choosing of the patriarchs, on the other hand, he regards as a secondary elaboration, part of the process of setting Israel's history in a much wider historical context.[170] It is doubtful, however, whether this view really does justice to the literary material on which it is based. In the oracles of the pre-exilic prophets, and in many other places in Israel's religious poetry, Israel's consciousness of being the chosen people seems to be connected exclusively with Yahweh's action at the time of Moses. But this can be an intentional concentration of the tradition which had always been associated with the national religion of Yahweh; the parallel tradition of the choosing of the patriarchs necessarily fell into the background, the more the cult of the gods of the Fathers lost its independence from the worship of Yah-

[170] GALLING, *Die Erwählungstraditionen Israels*, pp. 63 ff.

weh by the whole nation. But if it is possible that the tradition of the patriarchs was overshadowed by the Mosaic tradition, then the extent to which they are reflected in the poetic and prophetic literature of a later period naturally cannot decide the relative age of the two bodies of material or tell us anything about their original nature.[171] In fact the literary version of the traditional sagas in the Yahwist and the Elohist present an essentially different picture, and it is this which ought to be regarded as the real legacy of the pre-prophetic tradition: here the idea of the choosing of the patriarchs exists side by side with that of the choosing of Israel at the time of Moses, no attempt being made to harmonize them. It is clearly this parallel and independent existence of the two traditions which constitutes the real problem. It is understandable that Galling, working on the premiss that both traditions are dealing from the start with the idea of a choosing by Yahweh, is able to accept the Mosaic tradition, the more persistent and influential of the two, as a genuine and ancient popular tradition,[172] while he regards that which is concerned with the patriarchs as an artificial construction of the literary editors. It is certainly true, as we have frequently pointed out in our examination of the tradition about the God of the Fathers, that the literary editors were largely responsible for the final form of these elements. But why should they have taken it on themselves to encumber the conception of the choosing of Israel with a twofold tradition they were unable to harmonize?

Our thesis of a primary relationship between the figures of the patriarchs and the cult of the gods of the Fathers pro-

[171] The emphasis occasionally laid on the tradition of the patriarchs in exilic and post-exilic literature has even less bearing on the question of how the tradition originated (GALLING, pp. 50 ff.). It must be seen as part of the attempt to return to the older and purer national tradition.

[172] The question raised by EISSFELDT (*T.B.*, vii [1928], col. 125) and HEMPEL (*Deutsche Lit.-Ztg.*, N.F. v [1928], cols. 708 f.), whether the tradition concerning Moses was first extended to include the whole of Israel by the literary redactors, need not be raised here.

vides a different explanation of the appearance of the theme of God's choosing of the patriarchs and the tension set up with the theme of the choosing of Israel in the Mosaic tradition: the choosing of Abraham and his descendants has originally nothing to do with Yahweh and his choosing of Israel, but goes back to the religion of the gods of the Fathers. As we have seen, the very names of these numina, the God of Abraham, etc., emphasize the fact that their characteristic feature was the association they entered into, by their own free choice, with certain men, and which they maintained with the groups descended from or owing allegiance to these men. The most important thing about them, of all that could be recounted in story or song, was their first appearance to the men whose names henceforth remained inseparable from their cult. The true ἱεροὶ λόγοι of this type of religion must have consisted of such stories of the choosing of the ancestor of a group by his god. We must postulate such accounts in the case of the gods of the Fathers in Israel, as well as for the numina of the Nabataeans and other nations in the East. There was no need for the idea of God's choosing a man or a people to be transferred artificially from the Mosaic tradition to that of the patriarchs. It has always existed in that tradition, in complete independence from the religion of Yahweh; it was a necessary element in the basic understanding of the relationship of the patriarchs to their gods. The fact that the two traditions of the choice made by God are originally associated with different gods, in one case Yahweh, and in the other the gods of the Fathers, makes it clear at once why they provide such a close parallel to each other and yet show no obvious connection. The result is of course that the literary editors, trying to assert that it was Yahweh who chose the patriarchs, lessen the tension between the two traditions only in appearance, and in reality make it much more acute. In these somewhat special circumstances—its adaptation to a characteristic view of the theology of history—the development of the tradition manifests the same phenomena as we observed in the process by which the gods of the Fathers were identified with one another and then with

Yahweh. I suggest that this approach explains the evidence less artificially, and in a more satisfactory way from the historical point of view, than Galling's construction.

The fact remains, that when the theme of the choosing of the patriarchs is expressed in Genesis by means of a speech containing both a revelation and a promise, the form in which we read it is due as a rule to the literary editor. This is necessarily the case, for these speeches had to be formulated in accordance with the basic principle of these writers, that even the patriarchs were called by Yahweh—whether he appeared under that name or not. But it is noticeable that the names of the gods of the Fathers regularly appear whenever there is any promise made to the patriarchs.[173] The *'Ēlīm* of Palestine are never mentioned in this connection. This distinction is all the more remarkable, in that a constantly recurring theme of the theophanies is the promise that they will possess the land of Palestine in the future. It would have been an easy matter to have linked this with the local deities of Palestine. The procedure of the literary editors seems to have been guided here, as in other instances, by their consciousness that these local numina belonged to a different category from the gods of the Fathers, and that the function of choosing and blessing the ancestors of Israel belonged only to the latter.

From the description given of the type of religion represented by the gods of the Fathers it can be seen that when the Yahwist and the Elohist go out of their way to link the theme of the divine choice and promise with these gods, their tradition reproduces the historical facts. This is what we would expect from the essential character of these gods as the guide and guardian of their group of worshippers. Moreover, the promises are concerned almost exclusively with two matters, the increase of the patriarchs' posterity, and their

[173] The various passages are collected by GALLING, *Die Erwählungstraditionen Israels,* pp. 37 ff. They begin as early as the blessing of Shem by Noah in the name of Yahweh 'the god of Shem' (Gen. ix. 26), although the form of promise in which the god appears is not yet found.

possession of the Promised Land. Here again it almost seems as if two separate sets of ideas have been combined, one originating before the entry, and the other in Palestine itself. On the one hand there is the concern of a nomadic tribe for the maintenance and increase of its numbers, and on the other the claim of settlers to own their land. But it is not men alone who have these aims at heart, but also their god, who assures the earthly prosperity of his worshippers. This providential concern for the basic needs of the tribes, in the desert and in the lands where they settled, is in fact the most important task of the gods in this type of religion. In examining what the patriarchal history promises for the future, we must begin by looking back behind its extension to the national fortunes of Israel, or, as in the Yahwist, to the destiny of mankind as a whole. This wider dimension was obviously introduced by the literary editors when they set out to identify the religion of the patriarchs with the worship of Yahweh. When we go behind this, we find a conception which fits perfectly into the life of small individual groups, each with its own god.

In this connection I should like to refer in particular to the story in Genesis xv, and to the question raised above, as to whether or not it goes back to an aetiological saga concerning the God of Abraham.[174] The Yahwist's account in this chapter of a covenant made by God with Abraham[175] contains cultic and mythological elements which give the impression of great antiquity, and it is very unlike the theophanies composed entirely by this author.[176] A distinct and independent saga almost undoubtedly lies behind this passage.[177] In ac-

[174] See above p. 61.

[175] In the main I follow the literary analysis of PROCKSCH and ascribe to the Yahwist vss. 1a and bα 3–4, 8–11, 17–18a. In my view STAERK's hypothesis of a fundamental difference between vss. 1–6 and the rest of the chapter (*ZAW*, N.F. i [1924], pp. 58 ff.) is only true of the verses taken from the Elohist.

[176] It is particularly unlike Gen. xii. 1–3, where the Yahwist introduces the theme of his whole patriarchal history.

[177] Against STAERK's proposal of a late dating for vss. 7 ff. cf.

cordance with his basic theme, the Yahwist has associated it with Yahweh; but this of course does not show with which god Abraham was originally supposed to have made his covenant. It can hardly be a local Palestinian numen, for in that case we would presumably be told the place where the scene was enacted. This makes it highly probable that it was the God of Abraham, especially since its earliest Yahwist form concludes with the simple promise of a son to Abraham.[178] It would seem to be a genuinely ancient passage, standing first in the series of revelations by the God of the Fathers, which the Yahwist continues through Isaac to Jacob, composing each account himself.[179] We can probably think of all the cultic sagas of the gods of the Fathers as having a similar pattern.

But I shall close, and let the reader search the sagas of Genesis for further effects of the conceptions and outlook found in the religion of the gods of the Fathers. I intend only to show the direct consequences of the view that this type of religion formed one of the characteristic features of the Israelite tribes before they united in the worship of Yahweh, and to indicate whether or not this view leads to a more comprehensible picture of the development of Israel's religion and national traditions. I believe that my view passes this

also GALLING, *Die Erwählungstraditionen Israels*, p. 40. He in his turn, however, makes the mistake of looking for political motives behind the passage.

[178] The limitation of the passage to this theme means that it is parallel to the Mamre sagas of Gen. xviii. and implies that its origin lies elsewhere, perhaps even outside Palestine. I follow PROCKSCH in taking the references to the land Abraham is to possess in the future (Gen. xv. 7, 18 b, 19–20) as later additions.

[179] In fact when the reader of the Yahwist narratives comes to the later appearances of the God of Abraham to Isaac and Jacob, he is intended to look back to Gen. xv as the basis of all that follows. If this passage is really an aetiological saga for the cult of the God of Abraham, one might perhaps suppose from the opening words of the numen: 'I am thy shield' (vs. 1), that the proper name of the God of Abraham (see above p. 37), which is otherwise lost, was: מָגֵן אַבְרָהָם

test, and contains as high a degree of historical probability as is possible in this kind of problem. Abraham, Isaac and Jacob came before Moses; but we can now follow the path which led from their gods to the God of Israel.

APPENDIX: THE INSCRIPTIONS

It would not serve the purpose of this study to arrange the texts in order of time and place. Instead, I have arranged first the Semitic inscriptions, then the Greek, in the alphabetical order of the divine names used in them. The notes accompanying them have been restricted to what is indispensable in the present connection, and refer particularly to uncertain readings and difficulties of interpretation. Further discussions of their meaning can be found in the editions and other literature, to which I have tried to give as full references as possible. At the end is a list of the abbreviations used for the titles of these works.

I. אלה ואלו ?

1. Petra, A.D. 71–106 (Rabilos II),[1] Dalman, No. 92=*RES*, No. 1434, cf. Lidzbarski, *Ephem.* III, pp. 278 f.; Littmann, *ZA*, xxviii (1914), pp. 275 f.; Dalman, *ZDPV*, xxxvii (1914), pp. 147 ff.

[approx. א די א [approx. thirty letters] [ו]ברה [ד]י [מן] קביתא
[approx. ע[ב]דאלגא | בר עבדאלגא די [מ]ן סודי seven letters]
[ו]והבאלהי ורבאל ו[approx. fourteen letters] nine letters]
ובנוהי [approx. ten letters] ו
ווהבאלהי | [ו]בנ[ו]ה[י ל]אלה [וא]לו אלהא [רב]א בנחבתא על
חי[י] | [ר]ב[אל מ]לכא מלך נבטו די אחיי וש[י]זב עמה | [וע]ל חיי

(then come the names of other members of the royal house and the date, which is mutilated).

[1] For the chronology cf. JAUSSEN and SAVIGNAC, *RB, N.S.* viii (1911), pp. 273 ff.; LIDZBARSKI, *Ephem. f. semit. Epigr.*, III, p. 296.

II. אלה חטישו

2. Petra, A.D. 20 (Aretas IV). De Vogüé, *JA*, ix, 10 (1897), p. 200=*CIS*, ii, No. 354. Cf. Clermont-Ganneau, *RAO*, ii (1898), pp. 370 ff.

דנה צלמא די עבדת אלהא די עבדו בני חנינו בר חטישו בר פטמון...| ד.לו.ר.ותרו אלה חטישו די בצהות פטמון עמהם על חיי חרתת מלך נבטו רחם ע[מה ושקילת] | אחתה מלכת נבטו ומלכו ועבדת ורבאל ופצאל ושעודת וחגרו בנוהי וחרתת בר חג[רו ברברה] | [בירח...]שנת xxix לחרתת מלך נבטו רחם עמה.

Note that here the personal name in the god's title occurs in the genealogy of the person who made the dedication. The connection between the two first lines is unfortunately obscure.

III. אלה מנבתו

3. Petra, *c.* 90 (Obodas I) or 62 (Obodas II) B.C. Dalman, No. 90=Savignac, *RB*, *N.S.* x (1913), p. 441=*RES*, No. 1432.

אלך צריחיא וגבא זי עבד אצלח בר אצלח | דנה צריחא די עבד אצלח בר אצלח | לדושרא אלה מנבתו על חיי עבדת מלך | נבטו בר חרתת מלך נבטו שנת ו.

Savignac prefers to take מנבתו as a place-name rather than a personal name; in that case this inscription would be excluded.

IV. אלה מעינו

4. Dēr el-Meshḳūḳ (Ḥaurān), A.D. 124. *PAES*, iv, A, No. 27=*RES*, No. 2053. Cf. Lidzbarski, *Ephem.*, III, p. 292.

דנה חמנא די עבד מעירו בר עקרב | [ב]בת אשדו(?) אלהא אלה מעינו שנת שבע להדרינס קיסר.

V. אלה מראנא (חרתת)

This divine name is only found in formulae threatening a

curse or other punishment, from funerary inscriptions[2] during the reign of Aretas IV (9 B.C. to A.D. 40); it appears as an epithet of the national god Dusares, who is thus claimed as the personal patron of the king. But it is never found in dedication inscriptions, and in particular does not occur in those of a later period. So there is no evidence for the survival of this title after the death of the king.

I give here only the relevant words from one text:

5. Hegra, *c.* A.D. 29–30. Doughty, No. 4=Euting, No. 11 =*CIS*, ii, No. 208=Jaussen, i, No. 28 nab.

ומן די יעבד כעיר די עלא פאיתי | עמה לדושרא אלה (line 5 ff.)
מראנא [כסף סלעין] אלף | חרתי etc.

The other examples are:

6. Hegra, A.D. 31. Doughty, No. 7=Euting, No. 12=*CIS*, ii, No. 209=Lidzbarski, *Handb.*, p. 453, No. 8=Jaussen, i, No. 36 nab.

7. Hegra, 34 B.C. Doughty, No. 9=*CIS*, ii, No. 211= Jaussen, i, No. 11 nab.

8. Petra, not dated, but probably also to be placed in the reign of Aretas IV. *CIS*, ii, No. 350 (further literature given there)=Lidzbarski, *Handb.*, p. 451.

VI. אלה מראנא (רבאל)

9. Hegra, *c.* A.D. 106 (Malichos III). Doughty, No. 1= Euting, No. 21=*CIS*, ii, No. 218=Lidzbarski, *Handb.*, pp. 454 f., No. 12=Jaussen, i, No. 39 nab.

דנה מסגדא די עבד | שכוחו בר תורא לאערא | די בבצרא אלה
רבאל בירח | ניסן שנת חדה למלכו מלכא.

As opposed to nos. 5–8 the worship of a king's tutelary deity is here attested at the beginning of his successor's reign. But the same god also appears during the lifetime of the king whose patron he was, under a similar title.

10. Tell Maʿāz near Imtān (Ḥaurān), A.D. 93 (Rabilos II). Dussaud, Voy. No. 36 nab.=*RES*, No. 83, cf. Clermont-Ganneau, *RAO*, iv (1901), pp. 170 ff.; Lidzbarski, *Ephem.*, I,

[2] For these formulae cf. BR. KEIL, *Hermes,* xliii (1908), pp. 561 ff.

pp. 330 f.; II, p. 262; Jaussen and Savignac, *RB*, *N.S.* viii (1911), p. 273, n. 1.

דנה מסגדא | די קרב | מנעת בר | גדיו ל|דושרא | אערא אלה | מראנא די | בבצרא בשנת | xxiii לרבאל | מלכא מלך | נבטו די | אחיי וש|יזב עמה.

To these Littmann adds:

11. Umm es-Surab near Boṣra, A.D. 72 (Rabilos II). *PAES*, iv, A, No. 2=*RES*, No. 2036. But cf. Clermont-Ganneau, *RHR*, lxxxi (1920), pp. 47 ff.

דנה ארבענא די עבד מחלמו ועדיו וחורו על על[ת דושרא אערא אלה מראנא די בבצרא בשנת] | תרתין לרב]אל מלכא מלך נבטו די אחיי ושיזב עמה]:

It is still doubtful whether *CIS*, ii, 185 (from Ṣalchad in the Ḥaurān) should be taken of this patron of Rabilos II. Cf. Clermont-Ganneau, *RAO*, ii (1898), p. 374, n. 3; iv (1901), p. 181; Dussaud, *Les Arabes en Syrie* (1907), p. 127.

VII. אלה מתנו

12. Ṣalchad, A.D. 70 (Malichos II). *PAES*, iv, A, No. 23 =*RES*, No. 2051.

דא מסגדא | די עבד | עבידו בר | אטיפק | לבעלשמן אלה | מתנו בשנת xxxi למלכ[ו] | מלכא מלך נבט[ו].

Littmann discusses whether or not מתנו may be a place name (perhaps Motha[na], the present-day Imtān near Ṣalchad?) but decides in favour of taking it as a personal name.

VIII. אלה קציו

13. Boṣra, probably *c.* A.D. 40 (Malichos I). De Vogüé, No. 4 nab.=*CIS*, ii, No. 174=Lidzbarski, *Handb.*, p. 450, No. 2.

די קרב נטראל בר | נטראל לאלה קציו | בשנת xi למלכו מלכא.

Littmann considers that the following inscription refers to the same god under another title, but worshipped by a different group.

14. Simj near Boṣra—date unknown. *PAES*, iv, A, No. 11 =*RES*, No. 2042.

דנה עבד אל קציו לאלההם בעל[שמן].

IX. אלה שעידו

15. Boṣra. 1st century B.C.? Levy, *ZDMG*, xxii (1868), pp. 267 ff., No. 2=*CIS*, ii, No. 176.

דא מסגדא | די עבד תימו | בר ולדן לבעלשמן | אלה שעידו.

X. אלה תימו ?

16. Hegra—date unknown. Jaussen, i, No. 59 nab.

אחד שלי למר ביתא אלה ת[ימו].

The restoration of the name of the god (following Lidzbarski's conjecture, *Ephem*, iii, p. 270) is unfortunately uncertain.

XI. גד עוד

17. Ṣafa–date unknown. De Vogüé, No. 110a saf.=Littmann, *Entziff.*, pp. 47 f. (cf. P.V. 14)=*RES*, No. 201 B. Cf. Lidzbarski, *Ephem.*, ii, pp. 39, 42; Dussaud, *Miss.*, pp. 63 f. [465 f.]; *Les Arabes*, pp. 147 f.

למען בן חני בן מלך ודתא וחרץ שנ|א פהאלת דין וגד עוד סלם.

The same God, perhaps named after the eponymous ancestor of the *'Αουιδηνοί* (Waddington, Nos. 2236, 2272) is worked in:

18. De Vogüé, No. 5a saf.=Littmann, *Entziff.*, pp. 44 f. =*RES*, No. 199.

19. De Vogüé, No. 217 saf.=Littmann, *Entziff.*, pp. 52 f. =*RES*, No. 211.

20. De Vogüé, No. 389b saf.=Littmann, *Entziff.*, pp. 61 f.

21. Dussaud, *Miss.*, No. 513 saf.

22. Dussaud, *Miss.*, No. 563 saf.; cf. Lidzbarski, *Ephem.*, II, pp. 34 f.

23. Dussaud, *Miss.*, No. 731 saf.

24. *AAES*, iv, No. 125 saf.

XII. *Τύχη Θαιμεῖος* = גד תימי

25. Palmyra, A.D. 140. Greek text: *CIG*, iii, No. 4480=

Waddington, No. 2588; Palmyrene text: De Vogüé, No. 3 palm.; both texts: Chabot, *Choix d'inscriptions de Palmyre*, Pl. xxi, No. 2 (p. 42). Discussed in Nöldeke, *ZDMG*, xxiv (1870), p. 88, n. 2; Mordtmann sr., *Sitzungber. Bayr. Akad. phil.u.hist. Cl.*, 1875, ii, Suppl. iii, p. 6; Wellhausen, *Reste arab. Heidentums*, p. 61; Reckendorf, *WZKM*, ii (1888), p. 325; Clermont-Ganneau, *RAO*, iii (1899), pp. 244 f.; Lidzbarski, *Ephem.*, I, p. 86; Dussaud, *Notes de mythologie Syrienne* (1905), pp. 73 ff.

Ἡ βουλη|'Αο[φ]αλεὶν Αἱράνου τοῦ Σαβᾶ τοῦ|['Αἱρά]νου τοῦ βωννέους ἐπανγει|[λά]μενον αὐτῇ ἐπίδοσιν αἰωνίαν | [κα]ὶ θυσίαν και ε . . . ἀναθέματα | [Μα]λαχβήλῳ και Τύχῃ Θαιμεῖος και | ['Ατερ]γατει πατρῴοις θεοῖς τειμῆς και | μνήμης Χάριν ἔτους ανυ' Πανήμου.

צלמא דנה די אח[פ]לי בר חירן שבא בר | חירן בונא שבת די עבדת
לה בולא די | מגד לה [מתנא] לעלמא ו[צלותא] ואקם | חר[מא]
ל[מ]לכב[ל ג]ד תימי ולעתרעתה | [א]לה[יא] טב[יא] ... ליקרה בירח |
[קנין? שנו]ת CCCLI.

The name of the god מלכבל גד תימי occurs again in the superscription of certain undated tesserae from Palmyra:

26. Mordtmann sr., loc. cit., No. 68; a better reading in Lidzbarski, *Handb.*, p. 490=*RES*, No. 1730.

27. Mordtmann sr., loc. cit., No. 88=Lidzbarski, *Handb.*, p. 490=*RES*, No. 1731.

28. Ledrain, ii (1891), p. 95, No. 7=*RES*, 1061 C.

29. Ronzevalle, De Vogüé, *CRAI* (1903), pp. 280 f.= *RES*, No. 514=Charbot, *Choix*, Pl. xix, No. 2 (p. 135).

Even if תימי in this title is not to be taken as the name of an individual but of a family or tribe, as has been suspected from the Greek transcription *Θαιμεῖος*, the form גד תימי the particular god of the בני תימי (cf. Mordtmann sr., loc. cit., No. 50), makes it relevant in the present context.

XIII. *θεὸς 'Αμέρου*

30. Tarba (Ḥaurān)—date unknown. Dunand, *RB*, xli (1932), pp. 573 f., No. 115. Cf. Mouterde in Hondius, *Sup-*

plementum Epigraphicum Graecum, VII (1934), p. 141, No. 1069; Alt, *PJB*, xxxvi (1940), p. 102.

..........|..........|*Ἄβγαρος Θα*...|*ου καὶ υ(ἱ)ὸς αὐτο*[*ῦ*], *Χάσετος Μ(ά)νου, Τ* | *άνος ἀδελφός, Σέος* | .... |.......... |*οἱ ἀπὸ φυλῆς Καινῶ*[*ν φ*]|*κοδόμησαν ἐκ τῶν τοῦ κο*[*ι*|*ν*]*οῦ αὐτῶν Θεοῦ Ἀμέρόυ οἶ*|*κιαν τῷ θεῷ διὰ Αἰανοῦ*|*Σαυνάδου και Οὐλπίου Μαΐωρο(ς) Ἀντιόχου και Τάνου Αὔμου ἱεροταμέω*[*ν*].

31. El-Rarīye esh-Sherḳīye (Ḥaurān)—date unknown. Dussaud, *Voy.*, No. 96, Greek. Cf. Lidzbarski, *Ephem.*, I, p. 335.

Γάφα|*λος Χαρ*|*ήτου ἐπό*|*ησεν ἰ*|*ς θεὸν* | [*Ἀ*]*μέρου.*

XIV. *θεὸς Ἀρκεσιλάου.*

32. Frīkya (Jebel Rīḥa, Central Syria), A.D. 324 (cf. *CIG*, iii, No. 4463; *AAES*, iii, No. 240, 241). *CIG*, iii, No. 4464, iv, No. 9899=Waddington, No. 1834=*AAES*, iii, No. 242. Cf. Clermont-Ganneau, *RAO*, viii (1907), pp. 49 f.

Ταῦτα εὐχαρισπῶν λέγι Ἀβεδραψας. Ἐμοῦ ἐφ᾽ἡλικίας | *ὄντος ὁ πατρῷός μου Θεὸς Ἀρκεσιλάου δήλως μοι φ*[*ε*]*νό*| *μενος ἐν πολλοῖς με εὐεργέτησεν· ὡς ἐτῶν γὰρ κε᾽ παρεδό θην εἰς μάθησιν τέχνης καὶ διὰ ὀλίγου χρόνου παρέλα*|-| «*λα*»*βον τὴν αὐτὴν τέχνην· καὶ ἔτι διὰ τῆς αὐτοῦ*[3] *προνοίας* | *ἐπριάμην αὐτῷ χωρίον μηδενὸς γνόντος* | *και ἠλευθέρωσα αὐτὸν μὴ καταβένιν αὐτὸν εἰς* | *τὴν πόλιν· κὲ ἐγὼ δίκεος ἤμην κὲ δικέως ὁδηγήθην.*

XV. *θεὸς Αὔμου.*

33. 'Āhire (Leja), A.D. 180–192. Waddington, No. 2439 =Ewing, No. 93=*IGR*, iii, No. 1180=Brünnow, iii, p. 318.

[*Ἔτους*... *Α*]*ὐτοκράτορος Κομόδου* | [*Ἀντωνείνου*] *Κυρίου Καίσαρος Κλ(αύδιος) Πρεισκ*|[*ιανος?*...]*άθου φ(υ)λ (ῆς) Ὀσαινηνῶν Θε*|[*ῷ Αὔμου? ἐκ*] *τῶν ἰδίων εὐσεβῶν.*

[3] I refer *αὐτοῦ* to the god, of whose providential care for Abedrapsas a second example is given here. *AAES* transcribes *αὐτου* (*ἐμαυτοῦ*) as in the next clause.

34. Ibid.–date unknown. Waddington, No. 2441 + Ewing, No. 88.

Θεῷ Αὔμου | Μοαίε[ϱ]ος Αὔμο|ου ἀνέ[ϑ]ηκεν.

35. Lubbēn (Leja). A.D. 213? Wetzstein, No. 144=Waddington, No. 2455=Ewing, No. 70=*IGR*, iii, No. 1146= Brünnow, iii, p. 324=*PAES*, iii, A, No. 793, cf. Dussaud, *Miss.*, p. 242 [644].

῎Ετους κα' Κυϱίου Μ(άϱκου) Αὐϱ(ηλίου) 'Αντ[ωνείνου Σεβ (αστοῦ)] | τὸ κοινὸν 'Αγϱαίνης ἐποίησεν Θ(ε)ῷ Αὔμου διὰ Αὐϱ (ηλίου) | Πλάτωνος Βαϱβάϱου καὶ Αβούνου Χαιϱάνο(υ)|ἱεϱοταμέων.

36. Ibid., A.D. 233. Wetzstein, No. 116=Waddington, No. 2456=Ewing, No. 69=*IGR*, iii, No. 1147=Brünnow, iii, p. 325=*PAES*, iii, A, No. 793.[1]

῎Ετους ιβ' Κυϱίου Καίσαϱος | 'Αλεξανδϱου τὸ κυνὸν 'Αγϱαίνης ἐπό|ησεν Θεῷ Αὔμου δι(ὰ) Πλάτωνος | καὶ 'Αβούνου.

37. Ibid.—date unknown. Wetzstein, No. 117=Waddington, No. 2457b.

῎Ιδαμος | 'Αμέϱ[ου] | ἀνέϑηκ|εν Θεῷ | [Αὔμου?].

The remaining dedications discovered at Lubbēn (Wetzstein, Nos. 113, 115=Waddington, Nos. 2457, 2457a, 2458= Ewing, Nos. 67, 68=*PAES*, iii, A, No. 793[4.2.5.6.]) probably also came from the sanctuary of the *Θεὸς Αὔμου.*

38. Ḥarrān (Leja)—date unknown. *PAES*, iii, A, No. 794.

Διὰ Τι[βεϱίου] 'Αφι(αν)οῦ Α|ἰανοῦ και Οὐεττίου | ['Ι]ο[ύ]σιου ἐγένετο τὸ ειεϱ|ὸν Θεοῦ Αὔμου 'Ραένϑου (?)| Πϱίσκου Μεν[έ]ου και 'Εμελιανοῦ Οὐετιανο(ῦ) | και Μέωϱ Μαλχίωνευς ειεϱευό(ντων).

39. Dāmet el-'Alya (Leja)—date unknown. *PAES*, iii, A, No. 800[2].

Θεῷ 'Ανικήτῳ Αὔμου ο[ἰ]κο|[δ]όμησεν τὸ κοινὸν κώ[μ(η)] Δαμ|[ά]ϑων διὰ 'Αβχόϱου ῎Ομαϑ κὲ 'Αβ| γάϱου Χασέτου | κὲ Χάσετος | [Ο]ὐαβήλου κὲ Φιλππος Σαα. | . . . εστος(?).

40. Ibid.—date unknown. *PAES*, iii, A, 800[7].

[Θεῷ 'Ανικήτῳ Αὔ]μου οἰκοδόμη[σεν τὸ] | [κοινὸν

κώμ(ης) Δ]αμάθων δι(ὰ) Ἀβχό[ρου . . . other personal names follow]. *PAES*, iii, A, No. 800[5], may also come from this sanctuary of the *Θεὸς Αὔμου*.

41. Dēr el-Leben (border of Leja and Ḥaurān), A.D. 320. Waddington, No. 2393=Dittenberger, ii, No. 619=Brünnow, iii, p. 333.

Ἐπι ὑπάτων τῶν κυρίων ἡμῶν Κονσταντίνου Αὐγ(ούστου) τό ς' καὶ Κ[λ](αυδίου) | Κωνσταντίνου ε[ὐγε]νεστάτου Καίσαρος α[ἰ]ων[ίων] Αὐγούστων | ἡ αὐλὴ και ὁ . . . ε[ἰς] τον δεσπότην [Δία] Ἀνίκητον Ἥλιον | εθὸν Αὔμου Κασσις Μαλίχαθος κώμ(ης) Ῥειμέας φυλ(ῆς) Χασητηνῶν | καὶ Παῦλος Μαξιμῖνος κώμ(ης) Μερδόχωη φυλ(ῆς) Αὐδηνῶν τὸ στ[εγος ἐκ θεμελίων [καὶ] τὸ παν-μέγεθες κτισμα ἀνήγιραν ἀ[φειδῶς] ὑπη|ρετήσαντες τὸν ἑαυτῶν χρόνον προνοίᾳ Αὔμου καὶ Ἀμελάθου [τῶν] ἱερέων.

42. Ibid. Approx. contemporary with No. 41. *CIG*, iii, No. 4590=Waddington, No. 2394=Brünnow, iii, p. 333.

Διὸς Ἀνικήτου Ἡλίου Θεοῦ Αὔμου | ἐκτίσθη τὸ περιβόλεον της αὐλῆς | δια Κασσίου Μαλιχάθου κώμ(ης) Ῥειμέας | και Παύλου Μαξιμίνου κώμ(ης) Μαρ|δόχωη πιστῶν.

43. Ibid. Approx. contemporary with Nos. 41 and 42. Waddington, No. 2395=Brünnow, p. 333.

[Δι]ὸς Ἀνεικήτου Ἡλίου | [Θ]εοῦ Αὔμου ἐκτίσθη | [ὁ] βωμὸς δια Κασσίου | Μαλιχάθου κώμης [Ῥι|μεας και Ῥόδωνος καὶ δι|ὰ Παύλου Μαξιμίνου | Κώμης Μερδόχωη πισ(τῶν).

44. Ibid.—date unknown. Waddington, No. 2392.

Διὸς Ἀνικτή|του Ἡλίου | Θεοῦ Αὔμου.

The inscriptions Waddington, Nos. 2396–2398 probably come from the same sanctuary, cf. also Waddington, No. 2390.

45. Duwēre (Leja), A.D. 326. Dunand, *Le Musée de Soueïda* (1934), pp. 78 ff., No. 163.

Ἐπὶ ὑπάτωη τῶν κυρίων ἡμῶν Κωνσταντι|είνου Αὐγουστου τὸ ζ' και Κωνσταντείου ἐπ|ιφανεστάτου Καίσαρος τὸ α' προνοίᾳ Ἀμελ|άθου ειαρέ(ως) και Χασε|του Ῥουφίνου κώμης | Ἀρράνων | και Σύμμαχος Φ | ιλίππου κώμης

'Α|γρένων|πισιους Θε(ο)ῦ Αὔμου οἰκοδομήθη ἀχυ|ρῶν καὶ τὰ περίβολα.

In contrast to the inscriptions of Dēr el-Leben the older simple form of the god's name is retained here. Cf. Alt, *PJB*, xxxvi (1940), pp. 102 f.

XVI. *Θεὸς Βοάσου*

46. Site unknown (Ḥaurān)—date unknown. Dunand, op. cit., Plate xxiv and p. 58, No. 89.

Θεοῦ Βοάσ|ου τὸ ἄγαλμα.

The inscription is on a bust in relief. For the name, cf. Alt, op. cit., p. 102, n. 1.

XVII. *Ζεὺς Γάλδου?*

47. Sahwet el-Blāt (Ḥaurān)—date unknown. Dunand, *RB*, xlii (1933), Pl. xvi and p. 238, No. 20 (159); Hondius, *Supplementum epigraphicum Graecum*, vii (1934), p. 149, No. 1145.

Κορνήλ|ιος|ὁ κα|ὶ "Αουιδ|ος ἀν[έ|θ]η[κ]εν Διὸς Γάλ.|δου.

Unfortunately the reading of the name at the end of the inscription is uncertain. The title *Ζεύς* for the god would be an unusual one; but cf. below No. 55.

XVIII. *Θεὸς Γεννέα?*

48. Site unknown (Syria), A.D. 196 (Seleucid Era). Heuzey, *CRAI*, 1902, pp. 190 ff.=Dittenberger, ii, No. 637, cf. Clermont-Ganneau, *RAO*, v (1902), pp. 154 ff.; *RHR*, lxxxiv (1921), pp. 124 ff.

Θεῷ Γεννέα Πατρῴῳ Μαζαββάνας|καὶ Μᾶρκος υἱὸς αὐτοῦ ἀνέθηκαν|[ἔτο]υς ζφ' μηνὸς Δύστρου.

Clermont-Ganneau's view, that *Γεννέα* is the genitive of a proper name, is contested by Dittenberger, loc. cit.; Lidzbarski, *Ephem.*, ii, p. 82; Ronzevalle, *MFOB*, v, ii (1912), pp. 200 ff., and Mouterde, ibid., viii (1922), pp. 445 f.

XIX. *Θεὸς Διονυσίου?*

49. Suwēda (Ḥaurān)—date unknown. Dunand, *Le Musée de Soueïda* (1934), p. 19, No. 10.

[Θ]εῷ Δυονυ[σί]ου ἀνέθηκ[εν] εὐσεβία|ς χάρι[ν] | ἐπιμεληθέν|των Θαίμο[υ] | Σάδου Σαγί[ου] | [Ν]εγρίνου π|ρονοητῶ[ν].

If the conjectured restoration is correct, the title of the God is formed, like that of the *Θεὸς Ἀρκεσιλάου* (see above, No. 32), with a Greek proper name. Cf. Alt, *PJB*, xxxvi (1940), p. 101, n. 3.

XX. *Θεὸς Λοαιθέμου?*

50. Msēke (Leja), A.D. 136. *PAES*, iii, A, No. 795[8].

. . . [ἀ]ν[έθ]|[η]καν Θεῷ | [Λο]αιθέ[μου] | ἔτο(υς) | εἰκοστοῦ Κ[υ]|[ρ]ίου Ἁδριανο[ῦ] | [Κ]αίσαρος.

The title of the god has been deduced from an almost contemporary inscription from the same place, in which a certain *Λοαίθεμος Σάδου* dedicates an altar *θεῷ πατρῴῳ* (*PAES*, iii, A, No. 795[7], A.D. 133).

XXI. *Θεὸς Μαλειχάθου*

51. Jedil (Leja), A.D. 106. *PAES*, iii, A, No. 799.

[Ἀγα]θῇ Τύχῃ. Ἔτους θ' Τραιανοῦ Καίσαρο(ς) Σεβαστοῦ Μόκειμος Διογένους . . . βασκησ . . . | Θεῷ Μαλειχάθου εὐσειβῶν ἀνέθηκεν.

52. Sūr (Leja), A.D. 175. Ewing, No. 61=*IGR*, iii, No. 1143=Brünnow, iii, p. 317. Cf. Clermont-Ganneau, *EAO*, ii (1897), p. 33.

Ἔτους ιε' Μ(αρκου) Αὐρηλίου Ἀντονιν|ου Σεβ(αστοῦ) Σαυρόν τὸ κοινὸν οἰκοδό|μασαν μετὰ τῶν θρησκευόντω|ν Θεῷ Μαλειχάθου ἐφεστώτω|ν Γ(αίου) Ἰουλ(ίου) Τερεντιανοῦ Αὔσου κα(ὶ) | Μαλειχάθου Μαίορος και Σεμπρ|ωνίου Ἀδριανοῦ Μαξίμου και Ἀ|σλαμόν Ἀβειβου.

XXII. *Θεὸς Οὐασαιάθου.*

53. ʿAtīl (Ḥaurān)—date unknown, presumably close to that of No. 54. Waddington, No. 2374.

... [κ]αι *Βίδρός υἱοὶ Ἀουεί|δου Χαίρου οἰκοδόμησα|ν την πύλην καὶ τὰ στέγ|η αὐτοῦ Θεῳ Οὐασαιάθου ἐ|κ* [τ]*ῶν ἰδίων τειμῆς χάριν.*

54. Ibid., A.D. 211–12. *CIG*, iii, No. 4609 + Add. p. 1181=Waddington, No. 2374a=*IGR*, iii, No. 1238=Brünnow, iii, pp. 105, 322.

[*Ὑπερ σωτηρίας τῶν*] *Αὐτο*[*κρ*]*α(τόρων) Μ(άρκου) Αὐρηλίου' Αντωνίνου καὶ Π(ουβλίου) Σεπτι*[*μί*]*ου* [*Γέτα Καισάρων*] |*Σεβ(αστῶν) Εὐσεβ(ῶν) Θεῷ Οὐ*[*α*]*στεάθου Πα|τρῴῳ Θεανδρίῳ Ἰούλιος Πρό|κ(λος*] *ἐτε(λ)ίωσε* [*τ*]*ὴ*[*ν*] *πύλη*[*ν*] | ...

XXIII. *Θεὸς Σοαδαοδείου*

55. El-Mismīye (Leja)—date unknown. Dussaud, *Miss.*, No. 2 Greek (cf. Pl. ii, 1).

Διὶ Μεγίστῳ | *Ὑψιστῳ Σοαδο|αδείου τοῦ Καν|καλλου εὐσε|βείας χάριν.*

Clermont-Ganneau, *RAO*, v (1903), pp. 367 f.; vi (1905), pp. 372 f. (cf. Lidzbarski, *Ephem.*, II, p. 326) would read *Σόσδο*[*ς*] |*Ἀδείου* (or *Ἀλείου) τοῦ καὶ* | *Κάλλου.* If this is correct, then the inscription should of course not be included here.

APPENDIX ABBREVIATIONS

AAES	Publication of an American Archaeological Expedition to Syria in 1899–1900.
Ath. Mitt.	Mitteilungen des Kaiserlich Deutschen Archäologischen Instituts. Athenische Abteilung.
Brünnow	R. E. Brünnow und A. v. Domaszewski, *Die Provincia Arabia.* III. Band.

CIG	*Corpus Inscriptionum Graecarum.*
CIS	*Corpus Inscriptionum Semiticarum.*
CRAI	Académie des Inscriptions et Belles-Lettres. *Comptes rendus.*
Dalman	G. Dalman, *Neue Petra-Forschungen und der heilige Felsen von Jerusalem.*
De Vogüé	M. de Vogüé, *Syrie centrale. Inscriptions, sémitiques.*
Dittenberger	W. Dittenberger, *Orientis Graeci inscriptiones selectae.*
Doughty	Ch. Doughty, *Documents épigraphiques recueillis dans le nord de l'Arabie.*
Dussaud, *Miss.*	R. Dussaud et F. Macler, *Mission dans les régions désertiques de la Syrie moyenne.*
Dussaud, *Voy.*	R. Dussaud et F. Macler, *Voyage archéologique au Ṣafā et dans le Djebel ed-Drūz.*
EAO	Ch. Clermont-Ganneau, *Etudes d'archéologie orientale.*
Euting	J. Euting, *Nabatäische Inschriften aus Arabien.*
Ewing	W. Ewing in *PEF Quart. Stat.* (see Abbreviations, p. x), 1895.
IGR	R. Cagnat, *Inscriptiones Graecae ad res Romanas pertinentes.*
JA	*Journal asiatique.*
Jaussen	A. Jaussen et R. Savignac, *Mission archéologique en Arabie.*
Lidzbarski, *Ephem.*	M. Lidzbarski, *Ephemeris für semitische Epigraphik.*
Lidzbarski, *Handb.*	M. Lidzbarski, *Handbuch der nordsemitischen Epigraphik.*
Littmann, *Entziff.*	E. Littmann, *Zur Entzifferung der Ṣafā-Inschriften.*
MFOB	*Mélanges de la Faculté Orientale, Beyrouth.*
PAES	Syria, Publications of the Princeton University Archaeological Expeditions to Ṣyria in 1904–5 and 1909.

RAO	Ch. Clermont-Ganneau, *Recueil d'archéologie orientale.*
RES	*Répertoire d'épigraphie sémitique.*
Waddington	Ph. Le Bas et W. H. Waddington, *Voyage archéologique en Grèce et en Asie Mineure. Inscriptions.*
Wetzstein	J. G. Wetzstein, *Ausgewählte griechische u. lat. Inschriften.*

THE ORIGINS OF ISRAELITE LAW

DIE URSPRÜNGE DES ISRAELITISCHEN RECHTS
Berichte über die Verhandlungen der Sächsischen Akademie der Wissenschaften zu Leipzig. Philologisch-historische Klasse, Band 86, Heft 1 (1934). S. Hirzel, Leipzig

INTRODUCTION

The only tradition we possess of the origins of Israelite law is that of the canonical books of the Old Testament,[1] and the account it contains seems at first sight consistent and unambiguous. According to this tradition, every legal ordinance observed in Israel was laid down by the divine will of Yahweh, and had been revealed by him in the last generation before the tribes came out of the desert to settle in Palestine, at the moment when they united as one people under the guidance of Yahweh in the covenant delivered through Moses. All the laws in the Old Testament, therefore, are given a context in the history of that early period, as it is told in the central section of the Hexateuch, and for the most part are adapted to this context by being presented in the form of speeches by Yahweh or Moses to the people. Later on, anything not found in these books would clearly not have been regarded as obligatory in the same unconditional sense. Legal codes that were obviously of a different or later origin would not have been accorded the same value.[2]

The legal texts as they are actually found in the Hexateuch, however, are far from being as consistent as one might have

[1] Later Jewish Literature contains no further independent tradition, but simply meditates on the canonical account.

[2] This is not of course true of individual ordinances which are set in a period earlier than that of Moses, far back as Abraham or even Noah (Gen. ix. 1 ff., 17 P) and which are regarded as being in force from then on. On the other hand, in the case of a document so preoccupied with legal matters as the so-called 'projected constitution' at the end of the book of Ezekiel (40–48), it follows from the very fact that it appears outside the Hexateuch, that it was never recognized as valid law. That no greater value was set on the law for the king in 1 Sam. viii. 11 ff. is obvious from the context in which it appears.

hoped with the theory of the canonical books, that God gave the whole of the law at one moment at the beginning of Israel's history. For what is found there is not a single comprehensive corpus of law, in which all the relevant material is subdivided according to its contents and dealt with in proper order, but a whole series of smaller collections, down to brief ordinances on single matters separated from one another by narrative passages of various lengths. The contradiction between the fragmentary state of the literary material and the unity demanded by the theory is made tolerable, or indeed escapes the reader's notice altogether, wherever the separation of one of the smaller collections from the others, or the complete isolation of a smaller ordinance, is explained by its association with a particular situation brought about by the events of the story. This is true in particular of the final corpus, the Deuteronomic law, which is presented as a speech by Moses, in which he takes leave of the people and, as it were, makes his will before his death. This distinguishes the Deuteronomic law quite naturally from the codes given in the form of revelations made by Yahweh himself, and directly connected with the covenant in the desert. But this only underlines the complete failure of the passages where Yahweh is the speaker to fit together into a single literary unity. The 'Book of the Covenant' (Exod. xx. 22 – xxiii. 33) and the 'Holiness Code' (Lev. xvii–xxvi), to mention only the two collections which are most important for our purpose, seem on the surface to be distinct and complementary, but their contents belie this. The numerous points at which these two codes and the others repeat and overlap each other would not be found if the whole body of law had been drawn up as a literary unity. Where they do overlap, moreover, we frequently observe important differences and contradictions, which would certainly have been removed if the separate codes had been built up into a single work. They show that the different codes are separate entities and that the theory of a single origin for all Israelite law is not true at least of its literary formulations.

The growth of a scientific literary criticism of the Hexateuch in the latter half of the eighteenth century provided the first opportunity of explaining the existence of parallel and distinct codes of law. Not only the laws but the narrative framework of the books in which they appear was shown to be composite. When other hypotheses had failed, the narrative material of the Hexateuch was seen to consist of several different strata, running through the whole complex. It was then a natural step to work out the literary relationship between the legal codes and one or other of the narrative works, and so to assign them to different periods. Only the Deuteronomic code could not be fitted into this pattern, and had to be recognized as a unique entity, with a literary influence, however, which could be traced far beyond the Hexateuch into the other books of the Old Testament. Deuteronomy was held to have been incorporated into the rest of the material not by the author of one of the single narrative works, but by a redactor of a period when the Hexateuch as a whole was being formed. A more complicated process was proposed in the case of the other legal codes, particularly the Book of the Covenant and the Holiness Code. They could also be distinguished so clearly from their context that they had to be regarded as independently formed literary units. But it seemed clear that each had first been set into one of the narrative works, after which the whole was incorporated into the Hexateuch as it took shape. There is no need to go into these later stages in the history of the legal codes; from the nature of the case every detail cannot be described with equal certainty. But although the argument over the minor issues goes on unabated, the main conclusion reached by the literary critics about the Hexateuch remains unshaken: the canonical picture of the simultaneous origin of the legal codes in the time of Moses has given way to a theory of their origin at various different points in the course of Israel's spiritual history. When the laws are examined in the light of this theory, it is possible to isolate some, if not all, of the particular stages and tendencies in the development of Israelite law.

From this point of view the problem of the origin of Israelite law was naturally different, and apparently much more difficult. For the documents which according to the canonical theory all came down directly from the time of Moses, were now considered to be much later, and were assigned to what could in no way be called creative periods in the history of the law: Deuteronomy to the seventh century B.C., the legal documents in the 'Priestly writing', whether the Holiness Code was included or not, as late as the sixth or fifth century B.C. No one dared to accept even the Book of the Covenant as handed down directly from the time it was originally delivered as law; though as a whole it gives the appearance of being much older, and is as a result much harder to date. Some scholars were prepared to assign the Decalogue to the Mosaic period, and to call it original in the full sense of the word, and indeed it is plainly an independent unit, distinct from other codes;[3] but they were unable to make out a convincing case for this view. In short, the only way to explain the origins of Israelite law lay in working back from the much later formulations available, and it can be understood that scholars hesitated to take up this task as long as the chief duty of the literary critic was considered to be research into the extent, context, and date of the existing codes.

This cautious attitude could not be maintained for ever: even the purely literary approach led on to an inquiry into the earlier stages of the development. In fact, a close analysis of the individual codes of law, in the form in which we have them, showed at once that none of them was composed as a single literary unit; each code, therefore, must have come to its present state by a process of development peculiar to itself. The later and most recent additions were easily distinguished; but even what remained and could be regarded as the work of the actual author himself, did not yet stand out clearly as the unified work of one man. More or less strik-

[3] In Exod. xx. 1 ff. it destroys the coherence of the story in which it is presented, and is separated by this story from the Book of the Covenant. In Deut. v. 6 ff. it forms part of what is clearly a secondary introduction to the Deuteronomic history, which originally began with Deut. vi.

ing inconsistencies of form and content revealed that the authors had worked on older materials, and had to some extent concealed, but hardly ever eliminated completely, their distinctive features. In the oldest code, the Book of the Covenant, this state of affairs is very clearly seen—it consists of passages of different origin set side by side with virtually no formal connection.[4] But even in the more recent Holiness Code, the attempt to harmonize the materials used is so little in evidence that it was recently possible, though without convincing reasons, for a scholar to doubt whether it was complete in itself at all.[5] Deuteronomy has of course been treated somewhat differently. Its author has handled his material much more drastically, presenting all the legal ordinances in the form of a last speech by Moses, and surrounding and elaborating the laws with sermons and exhortations. But even here the original materials on which he worked are clearly recognizable, especially of course where he adapted them to his own style either superficially or not at all.[6] The work of sifting out the older collections of laws from the material as it stands in the Hexateuch is not yet complete, and the tradition as a whole has reached such an advanced stage of development that it is far from certain that this can be done with certainty in every case. This does not alter the basic fact already established, that the existing codes of law, in different ways and to different degrees, are the products of later redactions, and that in consequence we have to look further back for the origins of Israelite law.

It is not surprising that the more recent legal codes in the Hexateuch should be of this derivative kind, when we think of the outlook of the times for which they were composed.

[4] See in particular the following recent studies: JEPSEN, *Untersuchungen zum Bundesbuch* (1927); MORGENSTERN, *The Book of the Covenant, HUCA*, v (1928), pp. 1 ff.; vii (1930), pp. 19 ff.; viii–ix (1932), pp. 1 ff.; PFEIFFER, *Harvard Theol. Review,* xxiv (1931), pp. 99 ff.

[5] KÜCHLER, *Das Heiligkeitsgesetz.* Diss. Königsberg, 1929.

[6] Cf. in particular HEMPEL, *Die Schichten des Deuteronomiums* (1914); HÖLSCHER, *Das Privilegrecht Jahwes* (1930) (includes a bibliography of recent literature).

Deuteronomy, probably compiled in the seventh century B.C.,[7] belongs to a period expressly devoted to a movement of restoration. All the nations whose independent existence had been brought to an end or gravely threatened by the rise of the Assyrian Empire, underwent a period of profound spiritual stock-taking and resolute reassertion of their inherited national characteristics. The general intellectual movement of this period is represented in Israel by the intensive advocacy of Deuteronomy on behalf of the ancient constitution and legal tradition of Israel, presented in a new and revised form, and by the attempt of King Josiah of Judah to introduce them in their new form when he became free from the crumbling power of the Assyrians, as the legal foundation of the whole life of his kingdom. This can be explained in precisely the same way as the conscious returns to ancient and archaic examples in the art and literature of the roughly contemporary 'Renaissance' of Egypt under the Psammetichoi.[8] The following centuries, the period of Babylonian and then of Persian rule, were inspired even more by the spirit of restoration. Under the oppressive rule of the Babylonians, who destroyed Josiah's kingdom after only one generation, this spirit and resolution could be kept alive only in secret. Its sole manifestation was in the theoretical field, and in particular, in the compilation and editing of the literary works which were to form the basis of the restoration of the Old Israel expected in the future.[9] Thanks to the policy of the Persians this hope was gradually realized. The Assyrians and Babylonians had believed that they would ensure the continuance of their rule only by brutally destroying the

[7] This admittedly approximate date for the work is a conclusion drawn from the frequently contested but incontrovertible fact that its visible effects appear from the last quarter of the seventh century on.

[8] HÖLSCHER fails to take into account the nature of the end of the Assyrian domination as a period of restoration, when he dates Deuteronomy a whole century later on account of its peculiar ideology (*Das Privilegrecht Jahwes*, pp. 227 ff.).

[9] A considerable number of the later additions to Deuteronomy belong to this period.

national unity of their subjects. In sharp contrast to this, the Persians clearly carried out a deliberate policy of compensating conquered nations for the loss of their political independence by giving them considerable freedom and even state support in maintaining their national characteristics outside the political sphere, and in particular, therefore, with regard to their religion and their law. According to a Demotic document, Darius I allowed native lawyers to codify the ancient Egyptian law in the years 519–503, so that it could be brought into force again.[10] A few decades later, Artaxerxes I empowered Ezra, a Jewish scribe in his service, to proclaim the law of 'the God of Heaven', that is, Yahweh, in Jerusalem and Judah, and this set the still very precarious Jewish community on a firm legal basis.[11] In both cases it is the same fundamental principle of government which is being applied. The contents of Ezra's proclamation must have been those of the traditional law of Judah and Israel, even though they were presumably given a new form. If this had not been so, the Persian king's intervention would have run contrary, not only to his own policy, but also to the purpose and resolve of the Jews themselves, and would probably have been without any effect. Of course some innovations are bound to have crept in; consciously or unconsciously every restoration imports new ideas into the visionary pictures of the good old days on which it is based. But these newer features must not be allowed to destroy the impression that it is the claims of the old order, the ancient way of life of the nation, which are being advanced once more against every false development of the more recent past. The fact that most of the legal codes in the Hexateuch arose from the special needs of periods of restoration explains the tension

[10] SPIEGELBERG, 'Die sog. Demotische Chronik des Pap. 215 der Bibliothèque Nationale zu Paris', *Demot. Studien*, vii (1914), pp. 30 ff. (verso c., 6–16); see also ED. MEYER, *Sitzungsberichte d. Preuss. Akad.* phil.-hist. Kl., 1915, pp. 308 ff. (repr. in *Kleine Schriften*, II [1924], pp. 95 ff.).

[11] Ezra, vii. 12 ff.; recent studies in R. KITTEL, *Geschichte des Volkes Israel*, III, ii (1929), pp. 575 ff.; H. H. SCHAEDER, *Esra der Schreiber* (1930).

in the literature in its extant form, between the reliance of the codes for almost everything upon older codes, and the frequent overlapping and repetition they display as between each other. Thus history explains and confirms the conclusions reached by literary critics.[12]

But although it is both right and necessary for us to work back from the legal codes we possess to those that lie behind them, we must still ask how near this has brought us to the real origins of Israelite law. The methods of literary criticism alone do not suffice to lead us directly to the oldest forms, for they can only show us older literary versions of the laws, and the oldest written forms which we can isolate with any degree of probability seem bound in any case to be secondary productions, quite distinct from the first promulgation of the laws. The making of law is basically not a literary process at all, but part of the life of a community. This is particularly true of Israel. We can see from the Old Testament that the Israelites only gradually came to give literary expression to their spiritual traditions, and we must give full attention to the possibility that the very oldest written compilations of laws are separated from the real origins of the law by a considerable period in which the law was developed and handed down orally. Now that the purely literary work of sifting out the older compilations of Israelite law from their setting in later redactions seems in the main complete, the progress of further research clearly depends on the discovery of reliable methods leading back to the pre-literary stages, thus bringing us much closer to the origins. The whole course of scholarly research up to the present leads logically to this step, but it has yet to be taken, and it has thus been impossible to write a history of Israelite law from the beginning.

[12] I do no more than mention here the attempts that have recently been made to connect the older legal texts in the Hexateuch, and the Book of the Covenant in particular, with a programme of reform. See MORGENSTERN, *HUCA*, v (1928), pp. 1 ff.; vii (1930), pp. 19 ff.; viii–ix (1932), pp. 1 ff.; MENES, *Die vorexilische Gesetze Israels* (1928); I cannot consider these attempts either as successful or even as suggested by the evidence.

Work carried out in other branches of Old Testament literature, and in particular those of lyric poetry and epic narrative, has shown that the most appropriate method of research into the pre-literary origins of the material embedded in written works is the study of their formal characteristics as related to the circumstances in which they were produced (*Gattungs-* or *Formgeschichte*). Considerable use has been made of the method in these fields. It depends on the observation that in each individual literary form, as long as it remains in use in its own context, the ideas it contains are always connected with certain fixed forms of expression. This characteristic connection is not imposed arbitrarily on the material by the literary redactors of a later period. The inseparable connection between form and content goes back behind the written records to the period of popular oral composition and tradition, where each form of expression was appropriate to some particular circumstance amongst the regularly recurring events and necessities of life. Scholars have already begun to apply this method to the various formulations of Israelite law, considering form and context together, and looking for their roots in daily life. As far as I can see, however, it has not yet been applied as consistently as it ought to be, and has thus failed to cast as much light as it might have done on the history of the material.[13] I feel that it is now time to carry to a conclusion the attempts that have already been made along these lines, and

[13] H. GUNKEL, who introduced the investigation of stylistic forms (*Gattungsgeschichte*) to the study of the Old Testament, has left only a brief discussion of the forms of Israelite legal material (*Kultur der Gegenwart*, I, vii [1906], pp. 74 ff.); the more comprehensive studies of those who have followed his methods will be referred to as occasion arises. The only recent work to treat the whole field (A. JIRKU, *Das weltliche Recht im Alten Testament. Stilgeschichtliche und rechtsvergleichende Studien zu den juristischen Gesetzen des Pentateuchs*) did not carry the method through to its proper conclusion. He began with a schematic investigation of the different stylistic categories, but went no further than to establish certain conclusions of a purely literary nature, neglecting the examination of the origins of the categories in Israelite life.

to go straight to show that the proximity of different forms in the legal codes clearly reveals tensions that were present between the forces at work in the formulation of Israelite law from its very origins. From what I have already said it will be obvious why in trying to do this I have to turn principally to the oldest compilations, the least developed in form and content, and in the first instance, therefore, to the Book of the Covenant. I shall refer to the more recent codes only where it seems necessary in order to complete the picture, and I shall make no attempt to treat them fully. I shall not discuss the forms of the Levitical Torah, that is, the instruction of the laity in the law by the priest, for although written material in these forms makes up a considerable portion of the Hexateuch, they are quite distinct.[14]

LAWS IN CASUISTIC FORM

We can distinguish very clearly from the other forms in which laws are composed in the Hexateuch, that which can be briefly described as 'casuistic'. These laws take up a good half of the Book of the Covenant, and are arranged in unbroken passages and in clear order of subject-matter, apart from a few unimportant dislocations. Except for some passages which can be set aside as later additions, they reveal a complete unity of style.[15] It is generally recognized nowadays both that this part of the Book of the Covenant was originally an independent literary production, and also that it is defective. The beginning has been preserved, for at that point it is provided with a special introduction which separates it from its present context;[16] but it must have been more

[14] J. Begrich, *BZAW*, lxvi (1936), pp. 63 ff., gives a full treatment of these categories.

[15] Exod. xxi. 2–22, 16; cf. Jepsen, *Untersuchungen zum Bundesbuch*, pp. 24 ff., 55 ff.; Morgenstern, *HUCA*, vii (1930), pp. 31 ff.

[16] Exod. xxi. 1. This heading is admittedly phrased, in its present form, as the words of Yahweh addressed to Moses. It is thus adapted to the setting into which the Book of the Covenant was placed

or less severely mutilated at the end, which is missing. Laws in casuistic form, however, are also found outside the Book of the Covenant in more recent codes, especially in Deuteronomy. In some of them one can clearly see, in spite of considerable alterations in their form and context, their direct derivation from the corresponding laws in the Book of the Covenant or in the code that lay behind it.[17] There are others, however, that have no parallel in the Book of the Covenant. A particularly notable example of the latter variety is found in a series of laws concerning marriage in the Book of Deuteronomy, among which a different version is found of the very one with which the Book of the Covenant so abruptly breaks off. It seems here that Deuteronomy preserves what in the original corpus of laws came at the very end, and which was not allowed, as a result, to be completely expunged from the Book of the Covenant.[18] But there is no need here to attempt to reconstruct the former extent of that corpus of law by gathering together all the relevant passages in the later codes. The collection of laws in the Book of the Covenant, casuistic in form and unaffected by later remodelling, is quite extensive, and provides sufficient evidence for us to work out the nature and origin of this form.

Its distinctive formal characteristic is that it is invariably introduced by an objective conditional clause beginning 'If . . .' Throughout, all those who are concerned in the case

---

at some later stage, and from this alone can be seen to be secondary. The only original words—or a part of the original heading—must be 'These are the ordinances.' But even if the whole heading is to be regarded as a later addition, it must still be admitted that whoever put it there realized the difference between the passage that followed (xxi. 2–22, 16) and what preceded it, and knew that this difference must be clearly marked.

[17] The most instructive example of these is the section on the law concerning a man working as a slave to pay a debt, Deut. xv. 12–18. The writer cites in vss. 12 and 16 ff. the fundamental laws from the corresponding section of casuistic laws in the Book of the Covenant (Exod. xxi. 2 and 5 f.) with alterations, and tags his own sermon-like exhortations onto them.

[18] Deut. xxii. 13–29 (somewhat altered); cf. Exod. xxii. 15–16. See Jirku, *Das weltliche Recht*, pp. 49 f.

under discussion are spoken of in the third person—the person who commits the act and his adversary, and also the judge and God himself; wherever the lawgiver uses the subjective 'I . . .' or addresses one of the persons in the case as 'thou', this is a secondary variation in which stylistic elements of other forms have crept in.[19] The syntactical construction of the laws, however, is invariably based on the sequence of the prothesis and apodosis of a conditional sentence, in that order, and the difference between the main cases in question and subsidiary cases is expressed by the use of two different conjunctions for the conditional clause, the stronger 'כִּי', 'granted', or 'supposing that' and the weaker 'אִם', 'if'. One example is sufficient. 'Supposing men quarrel and one strikes the other with a stone or with his . . . , [20] and the man [who was struck] does not die but keeps his bed . . . if then the man rises again and supported on his staff can walk in the street, he that struck him shall be clear, only he shall pay for the loss of his time, and shall have him thoroughly healed.'[21] Here we have the use of the objective conditional clause carried to its fullest extent: there are no less than six conditional clauses, four for the main case and two for the subsidiary case, and then three main clauses, all in the third person. For the Israelite the co-ordination of sentences was the more natural usage, and he would be put to some difficulty to construct such a lengthy period, with its complicated degrees of subordination. But we can understand at once the intention which led to such a forced use of the language. In the conditional clauses the case envisaged by the law had to be exactly described and distinguished

[19] A word of uncertain meaning; LXX: 'fist'.

[20] Exod. xxi. 18–19.

[21] The reason why the consequences of the slightly different cases which are excluded, are not given here, may be either that they were not in fact dealt with in the body of law which lies behind the Book of the Covenant, or were lost in damage to the text either of the earlier work or of the Book of the Covenant itself. In other parts of the casuistic law the judgements on related cases are found in their proper order, all together, e.g. Exod. xxi. 2 ff., 7 ff., 13 ff., 20 ff., 28 ff. and elsewhere.

from similar cases, before the negative and positive consequences laid down by the law could be set out. In our chosen example it was not a case of a premeditated attack of one man upon another 'with a high hand' but only of such an attack as might have arisen without any considered intention from the momentary excitement of a quarrel; it is not a question of an attack with a weapon brought specially for this purpose, but with an object lying within sight and reach of the attacker at the psychological moment; not an attack leading to death, but only such as to confine the victim to his bed. All this, however, merely defines the general features of the case in question. Next, therefore, the conditions of the subsidiary case, for which alone the prescriptions of the main clause are valid, must be set out in two further subordinate clauses: on the one hand the patient must not be confined to his bed permanently, but on the other hand he does not have to regain his previous capacity for work, particularly in the fields, but has only to be sufficiently restored to health to take his full part in the life of the community in the street (and in the gate). Only by the provisions of the two subsidiary clauses is the case given the precise limits intended by the lawgiver: cases that lie on one side or the other outside the lines drawn by him would obviously be judged and dealt with differently by the law.[22]

Once this is done, the necessary details of the penalties to be imposed in this particular case can be summarized in the main clauses. These are also set out with great precision—there is first the negative provision, that the use of capital punishment is expressly excluded, and then the positive provision, that the accused is required to compensate his victim. He must in fact pay a double compensation—first for the time when the injured man could not take part in public life, and secondly for the cost of his restoration to health. This means that each of the nine clauses plays an indispensable part in the structure of the whole law, and that there is not one

[22] This is made particularly clear in the recent study of L. Köhler, *Die Hebräische Rechtsgemeinde* (1931), now printed in *Der hebräische Mensch* (1953).

redundant word in any of them. The apparently pleonastic diction is not so in reality, and the overloaded subordination of conditional clauses to one another is unavoidable. It follows as a necessary result of the complicated nature of the matter that is being dealt with, and especially of the need to make clear distinctions in the application of basic principles. These principles are not stated in the law, but are none the less rigidly applied to the case in question. Many other pieces of casuistic legislation in the Hexateuch are simpler in form, but only because the cases they deal with are less complicated. The fundamental purpose in using the casuistic form remains the same.

This conclusion means that we have reached the end of our search for the sphere of Israelite life in which the casuistic form of law was in use. Such laws can have been used only in the exercise of normal jurisdiction. In their conditional clauses the description and definition of a particular case set the pattern for the trial, while the judgement would be based on the provisions as to the penalty in the main clauses, wherever the same or a closely similar charge was under discussion. In fact as far as I can see there is not a single one of the laws given in casuistic form, either within or without the Book of the Covenant, which could not be used as it stands in the work of the ordinary courts; they were presumably composed, then, to fulfil the needs of these courts. The range of cases covered by the casuistic law corresponds most nearly to the character of ordinary Israelite secular jurisdiction. Numerous passages in the Old Testament show that this lay in the hands of the free men of each separate community, with the elders, that is, the representatives of the leading families, at their head. It was a secular jurisdiction in two senses. In the first place, there was no official judiciary, and secondly, the sanctuary priests were associated with legal procedure only when a case had to be submitted to God for a decision—and then only for this specific purpose.[23] The provisions of

[23] If the expression, פְּלִלִים, occurring only in Exod. xxi. 22, refers in any way to persons giving a judicial decision (the text is uncertain) it would signify persons in authority rather than official

the casuistic law fit without exception into the field of this ordinary local jurisdiction. They know nothing of officially appointed judges, make no reference whatsoever to the priests, and only come into contact with the sacral sphere where they legislate for procedures which had to be carried out before God, such as the transfer of a slave who is serving to pay a debt into the permanent possession of his master, or the oath of innocency.[24] Purely sacral law, which has as its particular object the regulation of dealings with God in the cult, is completely ignored in the casuistic ordinances; the only matters they legislate for are those which we can see at once were within the competence of the local secular jurisdiction: the law of slavery, murder, compensation for bodily injuries, damage to stock and crops, the misappropriation of goods given in trust, and marriage laws. Now we can understand the expression with which Exodus xxi. 1, the heading to the Book of the Covenant, describes the whole corpus of casuistic laws: מִשְׁפָּטִים, i.e. ordinances for the administration of justice by the local secular jurisdiction. These would be read out to the men gathered in the gate to form a court whenever they had to try and give judgement on cases of the particular kind a given law dealt with.

There can scarcely be any doubt, then, about the part played by the casuistic law in the life of the Israelite people. This does not yet tell us what was the ultimate origin of this type of law. The most widely held theory of its origin used to be that each individual ordinance was first formed orally as a result of a crucial legal decision here and there in Israel, and that they then all gradually grew together into a universally accepted customary law, at first transmitted orally, and finally needing only to be given a fixed literary form and to be included in a unified legal corpus; according to this

judges. The restriction of the scope of casuistic law to local matters is never directly expressed in any of the casuistic codes; but neither do they contain any provision which goes beyond the competence of the individual local court.

[24] Exod. xxi. 6; xxii. 7 (xxii. 8 is probably a secondary addition; in xxii. 10 the divine name Yahweh is a correction).

view the entire process took place within Israel.[25] But in the course of the last generation, the legal codes of three other nations of the ancient East, the Babylonians, the Assyrians and the Hittites, have become known, and all these belong to an earlier period than the collections of Israelite law, so that the problem of the origin of the latter now appears much more complicated. In the excitement of the discovery and comparison of the Babylonian Code of Hammurabi some people went so far as to allege the dependence of Israelite law upon it. This was excessive; but since then the material for comparison from outside Israel has been added to considerably, and the methods of comparison have gradually been improved. As a result, much more attention must now be given to the question of whether connections may not in fact exist, to be found not so much in the legal codes of the different nations, but depending rather on a general legal culture in which each nation shared in its own particular way. The casuistic laws raise this question much more urgently than any other Israelite legal form. It is not only the case that this form is almost without exception the only one to be found in the legal codes of non-Israelite nations in the ancient East; from the point of view of their content also, apart from the fact that their ordinances cover almost exactly the same field, they show in matters of detail much more numerous and closer similarities than can be found elsewhere.[26]

The question would be easy to decide if we could show that the casuistic laws, within and outside the Book of the Covenant, were inspired by the specifically Israelite spirit to the same extent as the other forms of which we have yet to

[25] As suggested by Ed. Meyer, *Geschichte des Altertums,* 2nd ed., II, ii (1931), pp. 314 ff.

[26] Cf. the comparisons made recently by Jirku, *Altorientalischer Kommentar zum A.T.* (1923), pp. 90 ff.; Puukko, *Studia Orientalia,* I (1925), pp. 125 ff.; Ring, *Israels Rechtsleben im Lichte der neuentdeckten assyrischen und hethitischen Gesesetzesurkunden* (1926); J. M. P. Smith, *The Origins and History of Hebrew Law* (1931); and also David, *De Codex Hammoerabi en zijn verhouding tot de wetsbespalingen in Exodus* (1939); *Oudtest. Studiën* vii (1950), pp. 149 ff.

speak, or at least to a comparable degree. But we can hardly hope to show this; in fact it is quite obvious that wherever the casuistic law in the Hexateuch is preserved in its original form, it betrays a completely neutral attitude both in outlook and intention to everything that we know to be specifically Israelite. We shall see that the Israelite national consciousness was a very prominent theme in other categories of Israelite law, but its effects are nowhere in evidence here; as in other legal codes of the ancient East outside Israel, so also in these laws, the relationship of man to man is considered and regulated by the law, without reference either to their common allegiance or to distinctions based upon nationality.[27] Of course, the opposite has sometimes been concluded from the words at the beginning of the first ordinance in casuistic form in the Book of the Covenant, that covering the law of slaves sold in payment of a debt, which must originally have read: כִּי יִמָּכֵר אִישׁ עִבְרִי, 'Supposing that a Hebrew man sells himself'.[28] For it was supposed that the

[27] The Hittite law is the only exception in this respect. It grants a privileged position in certain cases to those who belong to particular places and countries.

[28] Neither the Book of the Covenant nor Deuteronomy preserves the original wording. In the first (Exod. xxi. 2) the second person in the sentence כִּי תִקְנֶה עֶבֶד עִבְרִי 'If you buy a hebrew slave' is particularly out of place; it is obviously introduced to follow the preceding passage (not xxi. 1, but xx. 24 ff.) and can be easily seen to be secondary from that fact that it is not carried on at all into the following verses, where there is ample opportunity for its use. The difficulty cannot be removed simply by changing the second into the third person, as JEPSEN (*Untersuchungen zum Bundesbuch,* p. 56) suggests: כִּי יִקְנֶה אִישׁ עֶבֶד עִבְרִי 'Supposing someone buys a Hebrew slave.'; for this would give a very awkward change of subject between this conditional clause and the main clause that follows: 'He shall be a slave for six years', would introduce at the same time a suspicious change of emphasis from the master to the slave, whereas the following verses, up to xxi. 3 inclusive, are so worded that they refer to the slave alone. The damage must go deeper, and this confirmed in a different way by the wording of Deut. xv. 12: כִּי יִמָּכֵר לְךָ אָחִיךָ הָעִבְרִי 'Supposing your brother, a Hebrew, sells himself to you.' The second person comes

word 'Hebrew' should be taken as indicating Israelite nationality, and if this was true, the influence of the Israelite national consciousness on the casuistic law would be demonstrable from this point at least.[29] But a brief glance at the use of the word עִבְרִי, 'a Hebrew', elsewhere in the Old Testament is sufficient to warn us against so far-reaching a conclusion, when it is not supported by the spirit and content of the rest of the casuistic law. For even in the two very late passages which one might allege in support of this meaning[30]

---

naturally to the Deuteronomist, who is presenting his whole work as a speech of Moses to the people; accordingly he uses the second person consistently throughout the passage. This is more appropriate to his purpose, for 'you' means virtually every time the owner of the slave, who from the first is the main object of the Deuteronomist's concern; for it is he who is being warned by a quotation from the ancient law how he is to conduct himself towards his slave. It is all the more remarkable that the writer does not begin, in the quotation itself, by making the owner of the slave, 'you', the subject of the sentence; the version in Exod. xxi. 2: 'Supposing that you buy. . . .' would be much more understandable as a result of particular purpose of the Deuteronomist. But in the first main clause of Deut. xv. 12 he also has the slave as the subject: 'he shall serve you six years,' and here agrees with older version of Exod. xxi. 2, where the second person has not yet appeared. This not only supports the use of the passive in the conditional clause of Deut. xv. 12, but shows that it is the original text. The peculiarly Deuteronomic אָחִיךָ 'your brother', i.e. 'your compatriot', in the subject of the conditional clause, is the first trace of a national and social emphasis in the text, and should be replaced by the colourless אִישׁ 'a man' which is always used in the casuistic law, and it would be to the good to remove also the word עֶבֶד 'a slave', which at best is used proleptically, from Exod. xxi. 2. (Jepsen disagrees, *AfO*, xv [1951], p. 57, n. 9).

[29] Of course we would then have to explain the strange fact that even in the immediately following passage (Exod. xxi. 7) about the legal position of a girl who is sold by her father, the provision it makes is not expressly limited to the people of Israel by the use of the same word.

[30] Gen. xiv. 13; Jonah i. 9. In the latter it is the word used by an Israelite to refer to himself before foreigners and so occurs in basically the same situation as in the sagas of Joseph and Moses and in stories from the time of the Philistines, where it occurs in the plural

it does not carry the full weight of a straightforward description of nationality; no historian, no poet, and no prophet ever uses it in this sense, and in legal language it only occurs as the designation of a man who sells himself to pay his debts.[31] This presumably implies this usage is its proper context, and that it originally referred to the legal and social position in which a man normally placed himself by selling himself into slavery—it was the opposite of the similarly formed word חָפְשִׁי, 'free', which in the casuistic law signifies the status of the slave when he has been released after working off his debt, and which is also used of men who have obtained their release from any special obligations towards others.[32] עִבְרִי, 'a Hebrew', then, tells us as little about

---

both as the word with which the ancestors of Israel refer to themselves before foreigners, and as the term foreigners use to refer to them. In these cases it contains a certain implication of self-effacement, or on the other side of contempt, but never of any national pride. This also explains its use in Gen. xiv. 13. None of these passages give us the basic meaning of the word: we cannot hope to understand its basic meaning till we come across it elsewhere.

[31] Apart from the present context, this meaning occurs in Jer. xxxiv. 9, 14 (dependent on Deut. xv. 12) and 1 Sam. xv. 21, where the 'Hebrews' who belonged to the Philistines, but were presumably Israelite in origin, are contrasted with the free Israelites. I do not completely exclude the idea that in the confused text of Micah ii. 8 we should read מֵעִבְרִים instead of מֵעֹבְרִים בֶּטַח, and give the word the same meaning; the whole prophecy concerns the lot of poverty-stricken peasants in the hands of hard-hearted believers. I do not think our sources justify LANDSBERGER's conjecture, that עִבְרִי could have been the normal substitute for the missing adjective corresponding to 'Israel' (*Kleinasiat. Forschungen*, i [1929], p. 329); 'the Israelite' in the oldest language is אִישׁ יִשְׂרָאֵל 'the man of Israel' (Judges vii. 14) '(every) Israelite' אִישׁ תְּבֵית יִשְׂרָאֵל (אִישׁ) '(every) man from the house of Israel' (Lev. xvii. 3, etc.—that is, in the law itself, even if not in the casuistic law!).

[32] Exod. xxi. 2, 5, 26 f.; Deut. xv. 12 f., 18; Jer. xxxiv. 9 ff.; elsewhere cf. especially 1 Sam. xvii. 25. Both words have in view in the first place the complete ownership of the person referred to and the duties the law imposed on him. עִבְרִי is the man who has such duties and חָפְשִׁי the man who is free from them. That *nisbi*

anyone's nationality, and as much about his legal status, as *ḫabiru* in cuneiform records of the third and second millennia B.C. from Babylon, Mesopotamia, Asia Minor and Palestine; the word not only corresponds in meaning to עִבְרִי, but it is certainly also connected etymologically with it, although no attempt to derive the one from the other has yet been made which is not open to objections.[33] At any rate it is impossible to claim on the strength of this one word that the provisions of the casuistic law do have a specifically Israelite approach; it makes no difference to the man enslaved to pay his debts whether he is an Israelite or belongs to some other

---

forms like these, to signify that a person belonged to a certain legal category, were not otherwise unknown in Hebrew, is shown by the word עֲרִירִי, 'childless', which is always used with the situation in mind of a family that is dying out (Gen. xv. 12; Lev. xx. 20 f.; Jer. xxii, 30). The step from the legal use of the word עִבְרִי, shown here, to its secondary meaning as a substitute for the name of a people which in reality is not respected as a nation in its own right, but is regarded and referred to as an oppressed class, is not a long one, and there can now be no doubt as to the meaning of the passages referred to in note 30 above.

[33] The fullest list of the older examples is given by JIRKU, *Die Wanderungen der Hebräer* (1924); see also LEWY, *OLZ*, xxx (1927), cols. 738 ff.; LANDSBERGER, *Kleinasiat. Forschungen*, i (1929), pp. 321 ff. CHIERA has made available many more cases from documents at Nuri in Mesopotamia (15th century B.C.) (*AJSL*, xlix [1933], pp. 115 ff.); see also SPEISER, *AASOR*, xiii (1933), pp. 34 ff.: SAARISALO, *Studia Orientalia*, V, iii (1934), pp. 61 ff. The particular value of the new documents for the present discussion is that they show the word *ḫabiru* in close connection with the legal procedure for selling oneself into slavery, which we found above with עִבְרִי, and that in addition, by giving the names of the *ḫabiru* they deal with, linguistically very mixed, and naming the different countries they come from, they totally exclude any suggestion that they are of a common nationality. I cannot find a tenable basis in the texts given by CHIERA for his suggestion that *ḫabiru* in the documents from Nuri refers to prisoners of war. We can only mention briefly here that the *'pr* in Egyptian texts from the New Kingdom fit into the same picture; cf. for this WILSON, *AJSL*, xlix (1933), pp. 275 ff. Further examples and references in *PJB*, xxxv (1939), pp. 56 ff.; *K.S.*, I, pp. 168 ff.; and JEPSEN, *AfO*, xv (1951), pp. 55 ff.

nation. The text of the law shows, in addition, that such a slave was not invariably obliged to return to freedom after his years of service, but was expressly permitted to bind himself voluntarily to his lord for the rest of his life, by a new legal contract.[34] These ordinances simply reproduce the character of the casuistic law as a whole, concerned as it is only with achieving a just balance between the claims of one man and another. It does not take into account the overriding demands of loyalty to a larger community, the nation or the state, made in the interest of its preservation against the justifiable desires of its individual members. I know of no provision of casuistic law where this is not the case.

This unqualified conclusion is fully confirmed by the relationship of the casuistic law to another fundamental and distinctive feature of the Israelite people, which is directly connected with their common national consciousness, and on which indeed it is based: the fact that the whole organization of their national life, in its legal as well as its sacral aspect, depended on Yahweh. In so far as it has not been added to, the casuistic law shows not the slightest trace of this relationship neither explicitly, nor if we try to read between the lines; in this point also its attitude is completely neutral. This is not proved conclusively by the mere fact that Yahweh nowhere appears as the source of all laws, uttering them himself. (Where Yahweh is actually presented as speaking in the first person, it is in passages introduced from other formal categories, which can be recognized by this very usage.) We shall see that the strictly Israelite law does not lack formulae where Yahweh is referred to in the third person.[35] But these refer specifically to Yahweh, using his own proper name, and not the general term הָאֱלֹהִים, 'the god', 'the deity', as it regularly occurs in the few passages in question in the casuistic law.[36] It is most unlikely that this term found its way into

[34] Exod. xxi. 5 f.; Deut. xv. 16 f.

[35] Even outside Deuteronomy, where this happens naturally as a result of the convention of making the whole a speech by Moses.

[36] Exod. xxi. 6, 13; xxii. 7 f. (whether xxii. 8, a generalization not strictly casuistic in form, is original, we need not decide here). The name of Yahweh in xxii. 10 is certainly secondary.

the text at a later stage in the development of the tradition by replacing the name Yahweh, as the result of a secondary Elohistic redaction such as we can observe in part of the Psalter.[37] It must be taken as one of the original marks of the law given in casuistic form; this can be said quite categorically, for an exact parallel is found in the laws of the Code of Hammurabi, likewise casuistic in form. But the fact that the same usage occurs there makes it very doubtful whether the more general title for God in the Israelite casuistic law was originally meant to be monotheistic and to refer to the religion of Yahweh, as it was certainly believed to do later. The usage of the general term is presumably intentional, and is much easier to explain if, as in the case of the Code of Hammurabi, it goes back to a polytheistic setting, where in each different case and in each place a legal matter might involve a different god, so that no definite name could be mentioned if the law was to be operative over a wide area. The feeble religious element in the Israelite casuistic law implies therefore that its origins must be sought outside Israel, and its fundamentally secular outlook suggests that where it arose, religion and law were already much more distinct from each other than in Israel—our examination of other legal forms in the Hexateuch will provide most telling evidence that the Israelites were convinced that the two were directly connected.[38]

But if we are obliged to look beyond Israel, scientific caution demands that we look no further afield than necessary. We ought not to try to trace the origin of the casuistic law adopted by Israel among the peoples of far-away Mesopotamia or Asia Minor. By good fortune their legal codes have recently become known to us, but in spite of their many

[37] Even in the form of the theory that the Elohist carried out this alteration as part of the process of incorporating the Book of the Covenant into his historical work.

[38] This secular approach makes the casuistic law of Israel as distinct from the other categories of law as the Corpus of legal ordinances in the Code of Hammurabi is from the religious phrasing of its introduction and conclusion.

similarities they show too many differences both in form and content for them to be the direct ancestor of the casuistic law of Israel. The proposal to derive them from this source is in any case inherently improbable from what we know of the historical situation at the period in question. When the Israelites were in the process of achieving national unity, they had many near neighbours from whom they might, and indeed must, have adopted laws and legal practice. These neighbours were the inhabitants of Palestine before the Israelite settlement. We shall refer to them here, for the sake of brevity, as the Canaanites, without distinguishing between the different elements in the population. The Israelite tribes come into contact with them during the second half of the second millennium B.C., and like every group of tribes to migrate in the same direction, before or since, they had gradually to adapt the semi-nomadic way of life they had known in the desert to the settled and highly developed culture of Palestine. But long before this there had gathered round the economic framework of this culture, with its agriculture and small fortified towns, a fixed religious and political tradition. It would have been strange to find the Israelites adopting its material features only, remaining unaffected by the spiritual. This of course implies the adoption of Canaanite legal procedure, and the casuistic law, which we are discussing here, provides a particularly good example of this. In the first place, its formal characteristics are quite distinct from those of the Israelite legal forms we shall discuss later, but are the same as those of the legal codes in other nations of the ancient East; it can thus be accepted as part of the common legal culture that existed before the appearance of the Israelites, so that it can hardly have been unknown to the previous inhabitants of Palestine. Secondly, and most important, the content of the Israelite casuistic law has as its background throughout the culture first adopted by the people of Israel when they settled in Palestine.[39] Thirdly, it does

[39] It is very odd that SCHMÖKEL should try to derive the casuistic law of the Israelites from the semi-nomadic tribes of the Kenites, from whom, according to him and others, they also received the

not take national or religious considerations into account, and has a secular outlook which is easier to reconcile with polytheistic than with monotheistic thought. These peculiar features of the casuistic law make it most difficult to accept that it is genuinely Israelite in origin, but can easily be explained if it was taken over from the Canaanites; for all the evidence that we have points inevitably to the conclusion that they enjoyed neither national nor religious unity. Finally, a legal institution such as slavery to pay off a debt, or a legal term like עִבְרִי, must surely be seen as elements of the general legal culture of the ancient East, which the Israelites first became acquanted with, and adopted, after their entry into Palestine.[40]

We have at present no original sources for the study of Canaanite law, so that we are unable to follow these indications any further. Its previous history must remain obscure. Even the process by which the Israelites took it over remains unknown, for their own traditions are silent on the matter. Did they become acquainted with this body of law as the peculiar possession of one group among the previous inhabitants, perhaps a single town in Palestine which they conquered, or with which they made an alliance? Or was it a common inheritance of the whole country, which they found everywhere, with perhaps local or regional variations? Most of those who have accepted the view that it was derived from the previous inhabitants of Palestine choose the first alternative.[41] I should prefer to think that it was com-

---

religion of Yahweh (*JBL*, lii [1933], pp. 224 ff.). He is not able to produce serious proof of this theory.

[40] The same seems to be the case with the opposite of עִבְרִי, the word חָפְשִׁי; for it is presumably connected with the expression *amēlūti ḫupši*, with which the prince Rib-Addi of Byblos repeatedly refers in the Amarna letters to his peasants, still free, but threatened by their heavy involvement in debt. (*Am.* 77, 36; 81, 33 ff. KNUDTZON's edition [1907], etc.) See especially PEDERSEN, *JPOS*, vi (1926), pp. 10 ff.

[41] JEPSEN, op. cit., pp. 76 f., who thinks of Shechem or Gibeon, and CASPARI (*ZDMG*, N.F. viii [1929], pp. 107 ff.), who thinks of Hebron. But both involve their argument with premisses that I cannot accept.

mon to all the inhabitants, and that the invading Israelite tribes fell under its influence precisely because they came into contact with it everywhere they went. Admittedly, the centuries immediately preceding the Israelite settlement were scarcely the most propitious time for the development of a unified legal practice in Palestine, for Egyptian records show conclusively that the period was characterized by the fragmentation of the entire country into an incalculable number of tiny states.[42] But this fragmentation was apparently brought about by the collapse of a unified state which consisted in the first half of the second millennium B.C. not only of Palestine but also of the neighbouring countries, and which was ruled by kings whom for the lack of a name in their own language we call Hyksos, the name given them by the Egyptians.[43] So long as they were in power in these countries—and archaeological discoveries are making it more and more clear that the culture of Palestine flourished exceptionally during this period[44]—a more or less complete replacement of the legal traditions of the different elements in the population by a unified system was perfectly possible. This provides the simplest explanation of the remarkable similarity between the casuistic law in the Canaanite form taken over by Israel, and the laws of the nations of the north and east; for the growth of the Hyksos empire must clearly have brought strong northern and eastern influences to bear on Syria and Palestine.[45] The law discovered and adopted by the Israelites in Palestine, therefore, must already have been ancient, not to say archaic, and this is in fact the im-

[42] Cf. ALT, *Die Landnahme der Israeliten in Palästina*, pp. 9 ff.; *K.S.*, I, pp. 97 ff., trans. The Israelite Occupation of Palestine, below pp. 181 ff. It is improbable that the domination of the Pharaohs of the New Kingdom over Palestine and Syria in the second half of the second millennium B.C. had any fundamental influence on the legal system there.

[43] Ibid., pp. 6 ff., *K.S.*, I, pp. 94 ff., below pp. 181 ff.

[44] Cf. WATZINGER, *Denkmäler Palästinas*, I (1933), pp. 29 ff.

[45] The general dissemination of the Babylonian script and literary language should apparently also be dated to the time of the Hyksos. (Cf. JEPSEN, *AfO*, xv [1951], pp. 64 ff.)

pression given by its elaborate periodic technique and its distinctively secular spirit. It was presumably first written down on Canaanite territory in the Babylonian language, and in cuneiform script; but it is not impossible that it had already been transcribed into one or other of the new scripts and languages which appear in the second half of this millennium, before the Israelites came into contact with it.

The process by which the Israelites adopted this body of law is unfortunately also unknown. In particular, we are unable to say whether they took it over as it stood, or whether they shortened or otherwise altered it in the process. While the Israelites were gradually adapting themselves to the culture of Palestine they may not have needed or understood everything that was provided for in these laws—or perhaps they rejected certain parts out of hand, because they could not accept the legal principles underlying them. It is obvious that much that is dealt with very fully in the legal codes of other ancient eastern nations is missing from the Israelite casuistic law as it has been preserved. But much will remain hypothetical as long as we possess neither the pre-Israelite Canaanite law, nor the means wherewith to make a complete reconstruction of its original scope and wording in the Israelite tradition. We must expect abbreviation where the Canaanite law gave special treatment to individual ranks or professions—especially to such as are peculiar to urban life—of which the Israelite tribes, with their much simpler social structure, would know nothing. Laws dealing with trade and manufacturing could be omitted altogether. The most clearly recognizable kind of alteration, especially in the Book of the Covenant, involves the disrupting of the original casuistic formulation to allow for insertions from other, specifically Israelite forms. The Israelite origins of these insertions is not in doubt, and the only problem that remains is whether they were made at the moment the Canaanite law was accepted or were added later, as the laws developed further in their new Israelite context.

The incorporation of the casuistic law into the Book of the Covenant, and its continued use, albeit in a fragmentary condition, in later Israelite works, especially Deuteronomy, allows us to conclude that it was in force throughout Israel. This accords with our view that it was accepted by the whole population of Palestine before the Israelite settlement. But we are still faced with the question of whether it was taken over at once by all the Israelite tribes acting together, or adopted either by a single tribe or by several acting independently, perhaps as a result of their relations with individual Canaanite towns, extending its influence sooner or later to the other tribes. The first alternative would be the most natural if we could suppose that Canaanite law was first accepted as an official act of state during the period of the foundation of the kingdoms at the end of the second and the beginning of the first millennium B.C., or later. But this is most improbable. Until very late in the period of the kings the Israelite state had so little to do with the practical administration of the law that one can scarcely attribute to it any essential part in the actual making of the law; the normal exercise of Israelite jurisdiction, based on this law, had gone on in local courts from a much earlier period and still remained in force.[46] The time of the adoption of Canaanite law must lie in the generations between the entry and the foundation of the Israelite kingdoms in Palestine, when the Israelites first came into close contact with the Canaanites. At this period each tribe lived in comparative isolation from

[46] When the Israelite of the period of the kingdoms speaks of the 'king's law', he is thinking of the military levy, enforced labour, and taxes, in other words of obligations laid by the nation on individual members; and with these the casuistic law has nothing at all to do (cf. 1 Sam. viii. 11 ff.). These are the kind of things that are in question when we hear of an Israelite appearing before the king or his officials on legal matters (2 Sam. xv. 2; 2 Kings iv. 13). The best example of how little any independent royal jurisdiction developed is provided by the case of Naboth, a charge of alleged lèse majesté, which was apparently brought by the king himself, but from beginning to end was conducted before the local court (1 Kings xxi—though this case admittedly did not come within the scope of the casuistic law; cf. Exod. xxii. 27). The altered situation in later times, particularly towards the end of the kingdom of Judah, is not under discussion here.

the others, and there is no doubt that this made it possible for each to adopt Canaanite customs to a different degree, depending on local or regional conditions.[47] But even if the introduction of Canaanite law into Israel began in this way, it is likely that its acceptance by the whole nation took place before the foundation of the kingdoms. In spite of their independence, cultural exchanges certainly took place between the tribes at this stage, and their union in the worship of Yahweh (there is still much to say about the formal character of this union) would provide a particularly good incentive and opportunity for the unifying of their law.[48]

In another part of the Old Testament, admittedly outside the compilations of laws, the memory may have been preserved of an institution found in Israel before the founding of the kingdoms, which was associated if not with the adoption of casuistic law, at least with its later preservation and handing down. I am referring to the unadorned statistics of the lists of 'minor judges', two of which fragments appear in Judges x. 1–5, and xii. 7–15, of which no one so far has made anything. Though they belong to the same early period, they are clearly a different kind of figure from the 'major judges' whose heroic deeds are described in full in the same book. These were charismatic leaders in the struggle of individual Israelite tribes to defend themselves against hostile neighbours; they appear from nowhere and disappear as quickly, and are unrelated to each other either in time or in the work they did.

[47] One could mention in this context 2 Sam. xx. 18 f., where the town Abel Bethmaacah, in the farthest north of Israel, is called 'a mother in Israel', where people used to go to seek advice in legal matters; and the neighbouring town of Dan is possibly also named (cf. the LXX); in the sanctuary there (cf. Judges xviii) divine judgements were given. But it is naturally difficult to decide what was the source of the much-prized legal authority of these distant towns, or how far their influence reached; and it is unlikely that the impulse to adopt the Canaanite law throughout Israel came directly from them.

[48] Cf. NOTH, *Das System der zwölf Stämme Israels* (1930), especially pp. 97 ff. concerning the question of a law for the amphictyony of the twelve tribes gathered at a common sanctuary; (also, NOTH, *Die Gesetze im Pentateuch* [1940], pp. 15 ff.).

The minor judges, on the other hand, have no connections with military functions or authority of this sort. In fact the only thing that is recorded of any of them, apart from his home and the site of his grave, is the stereotyped phrase 'He judged Israel'. If the whole series is taken together, it gives a picture of an uninterrupted succession of members of noble families from different tribes, exercising some form of legal jurisdiction over all Israel. The nearest parallel I can find to this strange fragment of tradition, which if it were preserved in its entirety might perhaps make it possible to work out the chronology of the so-called 'period of the Judges',[49] is in the oldest extant account of Icelandic history, in Ari's *Íslendingabøk* from the twelfth century A.D. Here the basic chronology is likewise provided by an unbroken series of men exercising a similar official legal capacity.[50] The office in question was that of the 'proclaimer of the law' (*lögsögumaðr*) whose peculiar function it was to proclaim from memory to the whole community, gathered every summer at the Althing, a part of the law of the land brought over from Norway in 930 and gradually adopted, and who could also be called upon to provide accurate information about the law in disputed cases.[51] It might seem hazardous to use a parallel so distant in time and space that no connection is possible, to interpret an obscure Israelite tradition. But I think it is permissible, for the two cases are not merely similar in certain details; the parallelism extends to every part of the two

[49] The lengths of time they were in office, which could be added up without more ado, have a completely unartificial appearance.

[50] The brief information about individual holders of the office are likewise on the same scale in the Íslendingabøk as in the case of the minor judges in the Book of Judges. The main difference is simply that in the Israelite document the catalogue of holders of the office is its total content, while in the Icelandic work it is interrupted again and again by stories about other events which have nothing to do with the law-givers, so that it really only provides a framework and serves principally as a chronological device.

[51] For this office, which appears in a similar form elsewhere amongst Germanic peoples, cf. especially K. MAURER, *Vorlesungen über altnordische Rechtsgeschichte*, IV (1909), pp. 263 ff.

traditions, and appears to go back to a similarity between the institutions on which the two traditions rest.[52] In both, we find a people who have no elaborately organized system of government, but desire to live by a unified body of law; in both the law has been taken from outside and is not familiar to the confederate tribes in every detail, and so must be read out to them at regular and not too infrequent intervals, and from memory, because the necessary conditions for its written circulation were not yet present; and finally, in both cases, an official post was created for the preservation and the repeated proclamation of the law, a post which was never allowed to fall vacant, but was not bound by inheritance to a particular family. And a further correspondence may be found in the very fact that the 'proclaimer of the law' is in neither case the supreme judge, for the actual exercise of jurisdiction remained, as it had done long before the appearance of this institution, in the hands of the small local courts. But this is as far as we can take a hypothesis which in the nature of the case cannot be proved conclusively. I have no doubt that it accords perfectly with the theory that the Israelites adopted the Canaanite casuistic law shortly after their entry into Palestine.[53]

[52] For a different purpose, in particular for that of explaining the style of the Deuteronomic legal discourse, AUG. KLOSTERMANN has already made use of a comparison with the Icelandic system; but he thought not so much of the minor judges as of the picture of Samuel in the later stratum of the tradition (1 Sam. vii. f. 12) as the counterpart to the Nordic law-giver. (*Der Pentateuch. Neue Folge* [1907], pp. 348 ff. and especially pp. 419 ff.).

[53] If we were to follow this suggestion up further, we would raise the question of whether Joshua does not belong to this list, perhaps in fact at the head of it. This would not be the Joshua portrayed in the aetiological sagas of Joshua i ff., who is a secondary creation based on the pattern of the charismatic military leader, but the figure of Joshua xxiv, who gives to the whole people, at the very time they unite in the worship of Yahweh in the assembly at Shechem חֹק וּמִשְׁפָּט 'statutes and laws' (vs. 25; cf. also his role in Josh. xvii. 14 ff.). And ought we not to connect with the same office the position of the שֹׁפֵט 'the judge', whose advice, according to Deut. xvii. 8, the local court was as much entitled to

THE APODEICTIC LAW

We can explain the process by which the Israelites took over the Canaanite law if we conceive of it as filling a gap of which they must have become acutely aware as soon as they abandoned their life as nomads in the desert for the civilization of Palestine. But this brief description obviously does not present the full picture. The Israelite tribes did not live without any legal system either in the desert or in the period of their invasion. The Canaanite law did not only deal with matters which had previously been completely foreign to the Israelites, but also with others, which they, like every community, are bound to have regulated, even in the desert, by a fixed code. If the two sets of laws happened not to agree at such a point, then a conflict between them was inevitable. In view of the secondary character of the extant Israelite legal codes, we should not be surprised to find no trace of this conflict between the traditional and the newly adopted laws, and to observe that overlapping between them has been completely eliminated. We might expect groups of material from the two different codes either to be set out side by side without any comment, or to be woven together so completely that they can no longer be distinguished one from another. Fortunately, however, this is not the case, and even in its present form the Book of the Covenant itself provides in a small number of passages clear evidence of the forcible imposition upon the casuistic law of a law different both in form and content, presumably Israelite in origin. It was when I observed this fact that the problem of the origin of Israelite law was first brought to me in its most urgent form. These passages form the best introduction to the under-

---

ask as for that of a divine judgement through the medium of the levitical priest? If, as some scholars have suspected here, the Deuteronomist was thinking of the kings of later times, it would be a blatant anachronism on his part.

standing of that specifically Israelite law and the forms of expression proper to it.[54]

One of these passages appears in the comprehensive section dealing with the legal consequences of bodily injuries. We quoted above, as an example of the genuine casuistic style, the regulation concerning the consequences of the injuries caused to a man in a fight with another, but only temporarily disabling him. This is followed by the case in which a pregnant woman is hurt in a fight between men, and has a miscarriage, but comes to no further harm; and then the contrary is dealt with: 'But if any harm come, thou shalt give life for life, eye for eye, tooth for tooth, hand for hand, foot for foot, burn for burn, wound for wound, stripe for stripe.'[55] Only the conditional clause preserves the casuistic style of the preceding regulation, reproducing the very wording to express as clearly as possible the relation and contrast between the two cases.[56] This shows beyond doubt

[54] I shall disregard all passages where the rearrangement is only noticeable from the content, while the casuistic style has been more or less retained (e.g. the oath by Yahweh, Exod. xxii. 10).

[55] Exod. xxi. 23–25.

[56] In the normal pattern of the casuistic style, the definition of the first case is introduced by כִּי, 'supposing that', while the second begins with the weaker אִם, 'if', and 'if any harm follows' is distinguished from the previous 'if no harm follows' only by the absence of a negative. This formal relationship refutes Budde's suggestion (*ZAW*, xi [1891], pp. 108 ff.) to remove this passage from the place where the tradition sets it and to put it after the ordinance concerning bodily harm in a fight between men, i.e., after xxi. 19, on the grounds that the stern application of the *lex talionis* would be appropriate there, more so in fact than in vs. 23. It would only be possible to work in such a logical way on the assumption made by Budde, but contradicted by the facts, that all the verses in question, including vss. 21, 23 ff., came from one and the same writer. With a secondary interpolation, which is what we actually have in xxi. 23 ff., we have to reckon more with the irrationality of this kind of procedure. To transfer xxi. 23 ff. to a position after xxi. 19 would make no difference to the fact that the *lex talionis* is a foreign and secondary element in the casuistic code. The lacuna after xxi. 19 (or more correctly after xxi. 18, since xxi. 19 is probably the beginning of the second subdivision of this section) can

that it belongs to the old casuistic code. But a most remarkable change of form takes place at the beginning of the main clause; the second person 'thou' appears, and what follows is plainly a formula of a completely different construction. It is related to the casuistic law in so far as in its own way it does deal with cases in law and their consequences, but it is quite distinct in that it makes no attempt to arrange them in the subordinate and main clauses of a conventional sentence, but strings together a number of cases and consequences in a single statement. It is perfectly understandable without being linked to the preceding subordinate clause; it is often enough quoted as it stands even to the present day.[57] We may conclude, then, that it had its own origin, and followed its own peculiar course of development, before it was put into its present position, replacing the main clause of the casuistic law in the process. This can also be seen if it is examined in relation to the whole group of cases in which it has been put to use. For the principle of requital for an injury by an exactly similar injury done to the offender, set out in a long list of examples which goes almost beyond what is practical, was certainly meant, when it was first propounded, to be of general application, and was not limited to the single case to which it is now referred.[58] But the subordinate and main clauses differ not only in form, but in content, and this was the most important issue for whoever introduced the *lex talionis* at this point. The basic principle of exact retaliation for

be tolerated; for whatever legal consequences the casuistic law originally provided for bodily harm after a fight which resulted in death, would have been deliberately omitted and not replaced by anything else, because this case was now dealt within the provisions of the immediately preceding passage concerning murder and manslaughter (xxi. 12 ff.).

[57] Fragmentary quotations already appear in other Israelite legal codes, always in different contexts (Lev. xxiv. 20; Deut. xix. 21). The predicate of the sentence is usually omitted.

[58] A more detailed discussion (though without a full recognition of the tensions of literary form and content that are present) can be found in J. WEISMANN, *Talion und Öffentliche Strafe im mosaischen Rechte* (*Festschrift für Adolf Wach* [1913]), pp. 24 ff.

every injury not only disagrees verbally with the original casuistic ordinance suppressed here, but, much more important, contradicts the legal concept that underlay it. Two laws distinct in every respect, even to their origin, come into direct contact here. We have just demonstrated that one, the casuistic, is to be regarded as of Canaanite provenance; until the contrary is proved, the other, which intrudes itself in the shape of the *lex talionis,* may be regarded as Israelite. From the literary point of view, it seems that the Canaanite law is the older text, and the Israelite a more recent addition; this accords best with our hypothesis of the adoption—and of course adaptation as well—of the Canaanite law by the Israelites. The Israelites felt that in this the Canaanite law needed to be corrected in its basic principle, and we can probably guess the direction in which it differed from the unmitigated application of the *lex talionis* in the Israelite law. It would certainly have been less drastic, and in this case, dealing with the unpremeditated results of an attack made in anger, it would have been content with a sufficient recompense for the loss and damage caused, following the general tendency of the casuistic law in cases of bodily injury.[59] In passing judgement on different cases, the Israelite *lex talionis* never takes into account in this way the subjective guilt of the offender—it only looks at the outward consequences of the deed and exacts accordingly a purely external retribution.[60] We shall see a deeper basis for this principle when we come to look at the ordinances covering murder and manslaughter. From the stylistic point of view the *lex talionis*

[59] This is particularly true of the use of the word אָסוֹן, the 'harm' which could come to a pregnant woman; it apparently only refers to a fatal outcome, and the use of the word elsewhere supports this.

[60] The same attitude is seen in the much more exacting *lex talionis* of a proud nomad tribe in Gen. iv. 23 (which has verbal similarities). Excessive claims for retribution of this sort are resisted from the start by the formula in Exod. xxi. 23 ff., which is much more moderate—a sign of their origin in the outlook of the desert and a proof of the secondary character of their interpolation in quite different laws of civilized Palestine.

is so isolated that we cannot give any precise account of its origin as a literary form.[61]

The more complicated series of laws dealing with murder and manslaughter provide us with further evidence. There also only the conditional clauses of the casuistic law are retained: 'Supposing that a man wilfully attacks another, to kill him treacherously.' 'But if he did not lie in wait for him, but God let him fall into his hand.'[62] Here the weighing of subjective guilt, which, as we have just seen, was characteristic of the casuistic law, is a primary consideration; a clear line is drawn between murder and manslaughter. The legal consequences laid down in the lost main clauses must have been formulated in accordance with this distinction. At least in the case of manslaughter, a sufficient recompense for the loss of a man's life would seem to be what is required, and the only question is whether in the case of murder a similar but obviously heavier indemnity was imposed, or whether because of the deliberate intention of the culprit a punishment was laid down which affected his very existence, that is, punishment by death. In any case, the primitive law of blood vengeance, by which it was left to the family of the victim to exact the reparation due to them, be it a case of murder or only manslaughter, seems here to have been rejected in principle. As everywhere in the casuistic law, it is the business of a court to inquire into a case after a charge has been laid,

[61] Cf. ALT, *Zur Talionsformel*, ZAW, N.F. xi (1934), pp. 303–5; *K.S.*, I, pp. 341 ff.

[62] Exod. xxi. 14, 13. We can tell that the verses came in this order in the casuistic law, not only from order in which the conjunctions come (כִּי in xxi. 14 and אִם, now replaced by אֲשֶׁר in xxi. 13), but also from the fact that only the conditional clause of xxi. 14 mentions the persons concerned in the act, while xxi. 13 takes for granted that they are known, as is also the action with which the law deals. This change of place is occasioned by the later addition of the main clauses that follow them, which make known the right of asylum at Yahweh's sanctuary and must therefore make a positive statement of how far this right extends, before they lay down restrictions. It is astonishing that the casuistic conditional clauses keep their original formulation, which was intended for precisely the reverse order of the two laws.

and to impose a sentence in accordance with the result of the trial.[63]

Here again the form and content change as soon as the main clauses are reached. In the case of manslaughter, 'I will appoint for thee a place to which he may flee'; in the case of murder, 'thou mayest take him thyself from my altar, that he may die'. The second person 'thou', which we have already met in the *lex talionis,* is introduced without warning, and is accompanied here, even more surprisingly, by 'I', referring to someone who has unlimited rights over his altar and over whoever seeks refuge there. The departure from the usage of the casuistic law and the transplanting of foreign material into an Israelite setting are more clearly visible in the form of this law than in the *lex talionis.* Similarly, the legal theory that we considered lay behind the conditional clauses of the casuistic law and the missing main clauses, has disappeared entirely from the provisions that replaced them. It is not a human court, but Yahweh himself who makes the first decision about the fate of someone who has taken another's life, by allowing him to take refuge in his sanctuary. The court can only take action again when Yahweh abandons his protégé to its authority. Here again we have a conflict between two kinds of law based on completely different principles with nothing in common to make their unification a natural process. It is the very nature of the right of sanctuary, which is based on the complete inviolability of a holy place, that originally no relaxation could be made; anyone who was accorded the protection of a god in a particular place would be beyond the reach of secular jurisdiction for ever, whatever judgement happened to be passed on his case.[64] If in spite

[63] With this and the following paragraph cf. WEISMANN, *Talion* . . . , and also MERZ, *Die Blutrache bei den Israeliten* (1916), pp. 93 ff. (although it lacks any thorough-going distinction between literary form and content).

[64] It is not surprising, therefore, that the provisions for the right of asylum occur as corrections which disrupt the pattern of the casuistic law, constructed as it was to answer the needs of purely secular jurisdiction. The casuistic laws of other nations in the ancient East likewise lack any kind of acknowledgement of the exis-

of their contradictory basis the two types of law were drawn into a single code, it could only be done by means of a compromise such as we find in the present case. The scope of each must be so limited as to leave room for the other. It is as though to make this adjustment easier that the provision concerning the right of sanctuary is made not in the form of a legal pronouncement, but as direct statements by Yahweh to the fugitive and to the court. A different provision is made for murder and for manslaughter, a distinction first introduced into the theory of the sacral institution of sanctuary from the realm of the casuistic law.[65] From the literary point of view the position is the same as in the case of the *lex talionis*, in that here again the casuistic law, preserved in a very mutilated condition, provides the basis of the text, while the Israelite law, quite different in form, is interpolated as a secondary element. But whereas the interpolated *lex talionis* was a ready-made formula, the new provisions in this case were obviously composed for this context alone, albeit without thought for the style of the original casuistic text. It cannot be taken without qualification as representing a specifically Israelite legal form.[66]

---

tence of places of religious sanctuary, and it would be false to conclude from their silence that this institution did not exist in the ancient East.

[65] An even more obvious and more involved compromise solution is found in the strongly secularized provisions for sanctuary in Deuteronomy, where the procedure in the case of murder falls into three stages: flight to the sanctuary, handing over to the local court, and delivery by them to the avenger of blood (Deut. xix. 11 ff.). The ancient tribal right of blood-revenge is never mentioned in the provisions of the Book of the Covenant, though it could have been associated without difficulty with the clauses concerning the right of sanctuary, if they had stood alone; but here in Deuteronomy it is given full weight. There is no question in Deuteronomy (xix. 1 ff.) of handing over a man guilty of manslaughter out of sanctuary, say after his case had been tried by the local court as in the casuistic law.

[66] We can do no more than mention the question of whether the manifestly secondary character of the clauses concerning the right of sanctuary may perhaps be connected with the late appearance of this institution amongst the Israelites. It is exceedingly

But we have not yet examined all the provisions of the Book of the Covenant concerning murder and manslaughter. We must go on to examine a law which immediately precedes the one we have just dealt with, thus coming at the beginning of the whole passage. Whoever placed it in this prominent position must have regarded it as the guiding principle for the treatment of the whole matter. 'Whoever strikes a man so that he dies, he shall be put to death.'[67] But this translation cannot help but obscure completely what is not noticeable in the English version; the distinctive form in which the Hebrew is phrased. The translation gives the quite false impression that it is in the usual casuistic form, with the accidental difference that the subordinate clause defining the case is here a relative and not a conditional clause. In fact, the structure of the Hebrew original, מַכֵּה אִישׁ וָמֵת מוֹת יוּמָת, is completely different, and must be taken as a single clause in which both the definition of the case and its legal consequences are compressed into the shortest possible space. The subject, referring to the person who committed the deed, and thereby describing the case, comes at the beginning and takes the form of a participle. By the rules of Hebrew syntax it is possible for it to be followed by a subordinate clause, which expresses the next stage in the action, but is not meant to stand by itself, and does not disturb the compact structure of the main clause. Then the legal consequences are expressed in the verbal predicate, which, since it occurs at the less prominent position at the end of the sentence, is strengthened by the addition of an infinitive absolute in order to preserve the balance of the sentence. The five short words must be spoken very slowly and emphatically,

---

likely that they first came across the right of sanctuary in its developed form during and after their entry into Palestine, at the existing sanctuaries of the people who were already there, and adopted it from them, only transferring it to the newly-founded sanctuaries of Yahweh as these quite gradually came into being and grew more numerous. We cannot tell how widespread it became; Deut. xxix. 1 ff. gives scarcely any help at all.

[67] Exod. xxi. 12.

with a caesura between the subject and the predicate, that is between the third and fourth words, as in the metre of a five-beat Hebrew verse, if the hearer is not to miss any single element of its closely knit construction. Such a heavily weighted style is completely foreign to the casuistic law we have just been examining. Such ponderous and emphatic language would be quite out of place, not to say impossible, in the ordered and uninterrupted flow of its sentences. Formal considerations, therefore, oblige us to find a distinctive term for this new style, which will clearly express the difference between it and the casuistic forms. We shall call it the apodeictic style.

But the content of this apodeictic law is likewise so far and so fundamentally different from the casuistic and other provisions which follow it, that one is forced to ask how it could have occurred to anyone to set it forth, without any explanation or attempt at adaptation, as the guiding principle for the rest of this group of laws; particularly as in fact they do not follow this principle. It refers to homicide; but it makes no distinction between murder and manslaughter, using expressions, indeed, which seem deliberately chosen to leave no doubt that both are included. It treats every killing as a crime punishable by death—and it does not restrict this by any reference to the possibility of allaying one's guilt by paying an indemnity or seeking sanctuary. Its content, then, is as unconditional as its form, and this is what distinguishes it so sharply from what follows. We must ask why it allows of no conditions. The outlook of the whole Old Testament leaves us in no doubt of the answer: it is Yahweh who demands a stern retribution for every drop of blood that is spilt. The blood of a murdered man cries out to him from the earth,[68] and according to a law in Deuteronomy, which certainly goes back to an earlier tradition, the elders of the nearest settlement have to carry out an act of propitiation on behalf of the whole people if a body is found in the common land beyond the fields of the village—that is, if the criminal cannot be

[68] Gen. iv. 10.

found, and regardless of whether it is a case of murder or manslaughter.[69] But normally, of course, the criminal is known, and Yahweh demands his life, without regard to the rights of the injured family for compensation, and without giving the criminal the opportunity to make satisfaction by paying damages. He ignores the difference between murder and manslaughter, and does not even take into account the right to seek refuge in his own sanctuaries.[70] Yahweh's land was profaned and the existence of his people threatened if this demand was not satisfied. We can say of this law, then, as we said of the *lex talionis,* that it rests on a specifically Israelite principle. The tribunal in which this law is accepted as binding consists of the whole people of Israel. We can see at once the characteristic features of true Israelite law, as opposed to that of Canaan. The contrast lies between the implacable will of the national god, and an almost complete divorce of law from religion. This is reflected in the difference between a sentence that says everything in five words without qualification, and the carefully weighed conditions and exceptions of a law built up through long experience. The fundamental difference between the two laws stands out all the more sharply when they occur, as here, in such close juxtaposition, and deal each in their own way with the same cases.

We should hardly be justified in postulating an entire formal category of Israelite law, however, from one sentence in Exodus xxi. 12, were it not that there were a number of exact parallels both within the Book of the Covenant and elsewhere. A group of such laws is found in the next few verses: 'Whoever strikes his father or mother shall be put to death. Whoever steals a man and sells him[71] . . . shall be put to

[69] Deut. xxi. 1 ff.

[70] Without giving further examples, it is sufficient to cite Gen. ix. 6, which is set in the apodeictic style: 'Whoever sheds the blood of man, by man shall his blood be shed.' Lev. xxiv. 17 is directly dependent on this passage.

[71] Exod. xxi. 15–17. In the law against forcible enslavement I consider the words 'or he is found in his possession' as an addition which disrupts the original by its change of subject. The original

death. Whoever curses his father or mother shall be put to death.' The wording of these verses corresponds exactly to that of vs. 12—the subject is once again in the form of a participle in a position of emphasis at the beginning, and is followed by its object, and in one of the clauses the short subordinate clause reoccurs, giving a further definition, while the verbal predicate, with the infinitive absolute to give it extra weight, is exactly the same. The similarity extends even to the number of words used: each clause is meant to be read as a five-beat line of verse. There can be no doubt that they are related to each other and to the clause in Exodus xxi. 12. Indeed, the only explanation of the fact that they occur here at all lies in that verse. The ancient casuistic law proceeds logically from rulings concerning murder and manslaughter to those concerning bodily injury, first such as results in death, and then such as does not. If laws concerning forcible enslavement, or the ill-treatment or cursing of parents, have any place at all in the casuistic law, it is certainly not here. The literary process by which they found their way into the casuistic code must simply have been that they were brought in at the same time as the only clause which treats every act of killing as punishable by death. All these clauses must originally have formed a single unit. This gives us an important new insight into the way in which the style of Israelite apodeictic law took shape. Each concise clause is not handed down and proclaimed as an isolated unity, like the *lex talionis*. They are all grouped together, and when they were read aloud in this form, the inherent force of each would be greatly accentuated by the monotonous repetition of one part of the sentence, the predicate in this case, as each law was read out. This formal device would weld the whole series into a unity, and drive home to the hearer the one sentence laid down for every case. Here is yet another fundamental contrast to the casuistic law. The latter certainly shows a tendency for individual laws to be grouped together, as can

---

law envisaged only the completed act of taking and selling a man into slavery.

be seen in the Book of the Covenant in particular. But it never attempts to create such a formal and sensible unity; its structure is simply what is demanded by its legal system. But if it is true that the clauses in Exodus xxi. 12, 15–17 are parts of a single series, a list of crimes punishable by death, then we must go on to ask whether the whole of the original list is found there. This is inherently improbable and is shown not to be the case by the fact that a considerable number of similarly constructed clauses are to be found in other legal codes in the Hexateuch, although they occur as a rule in widely scattered contexts, among material quite different in style. Two actually occur elsewhere in the Book of the Covenant, outside the ancient casuistic code: 'Whoever lies with a beast shall be put to death'[72] and 'Whoever sacrifices to other gods shall be put to death.'[73] The metrical form, the line of five feet, is clearly visible. Outside the Book of the Covenant we have a law against the profanation of the Sabbath by working, which appears in a double formulation,[74] a law against the sacrifice of children to Melech (Moloch),[75] then a whole series together, in which we find

[72] Exod. xxii. 18. I regard the word כָּל 'whoever' placed before the participle subject as a later addition, foreign to the style, which is intended to emphasize the universal application of the law, but in fact only weakens it.

[73] Exod. xxii. 19 (i.e. immediately after the verse just quoted) I reconstruct the text as: זֹבֵחַ לֵאלֹהִים אֲחֵרִים מוֹת יוּמָת. It has got into its present condition because אֲחֵרִים 'other' was first misread as יָחֳרָם 'shall be utterly destroyed'; and as a result the original predicate מוֹת יוּמָת was felt to be superfluous and was removed, while on the other hand the word לאלהים 'gods' or 'god' was now ambiguous and had to be expanded, which was done by tagging the words 'except to Yahweh alone' onto the end of the sentence. אֲחֵרִים is attested by the Samaritan text and by part of the Greek textual tradition.

[74] Exod. xxxi. 14 f. (Cf. also Num. xv. 35). The original text would have been closest to Exod. xxxi. 15, perhaps מוֹת יוּמָת עֹשֵׂה מְלָאכָה בַּשַּׁבָּת.

[75] Lev. xx. 2. (The beginning is much expanded in a different style, and there is an interpolation at the end.)

a somewhat modified form of the laws already mentioned against bestiality and the cursing of parents, and several others against forbidden forms of sexual intercourse;[76] and finally one against sorcery[77] and one against the abuse of the name of Yahweh.[78] There is perhaps one more, which would form a conclusion to the whole series.[79] Of course the apodeictic style is far from being retained every time in its pure original form. The invariable predicate, strengthened by the use of the infinitive absolute, occurring unchanged at the end of each clause, is the most obvious sign of its presence,[80] but for the most part the subject has lost its participial form and occurs as a relative clause, so that the style is beginning to break down,[81] and there is no lack of what are clearly later additions; we must not forget that we only possess clauses within the framework of later legal codes (most of them are in the Holiness Code). These changes of form, then, can easily be explained from the process of decay which this form underwent like any other. It was natural that the metre should be lost as this happened. Whether this process led to the splitting up of single clauses into two or more, or to the addition of completely new clauses to the original series, is a possibility that cannot be decided with certainty in any given case.[82] The fragments that we possess seem nevertheless to

[76] Lev. xx. 9–13, 15–16 (with many interpolations).

[77] Lev. xx. 27 (with interpolations).

[78] Lev. xxiv. 16 (retained in its original form, but with an interpolation at the end). Next to this in vs. 17 there is an adaptation of the law in Exod. xxi. 12 against killing men.

[79] Lev. xxvii. 29 (with interpolations); the original was perhaps מוֹת יומת כָּל־חֵרֶם מִן־הָאָדָם. Cf. Num. xxxv. 16 ff., 21, 31. It is notable that the Deuteronomist has not retained this clause, written in a style so remote from his own.

[80] The change into the plural in the sexual laws in Lev. xx. 11, 12, 13 is caused by taking into account the woman involved in the action and in any case is secondary; in vs. 10 it is still absent from the Massoretic text.

[81] Jirku (*Die Wanderungen der Hebräer*) overlooks this genetic connection when he compiles his lists purely by distinguishing between 'participle' and 'third person singular' formulations.

[82] Such possibilities must be taken into account in the law

point to the existence of a good twelve clauses in the original.

When this list of crimes punishable by death is completed by fragments found outside the Book of the Covenant, a very significant fact emerges about its content: it shows that the laws in apodeictic form deal to an overwhelming degree with matters which the casuistic law never mentions, and with which from its secular nature it could have no concern. They deal in part with the sacral realm of man's relations with the divine—although the particular form of the laws, a list of crimes and their punishment, restricts this to the exclusion of all actions which treat other gods and spirits on the same level as Yahweh, or imply a misuse of anything that belongs to him, and is thereby holy, such as his name, or the sabbath. For the rest, they deal with sacred areas within the community, and particularly, though not in every case, with the family. Religion, morality and law are all included without any distinction; for everything is referred to the unconditional will of God; so that for every breach of the law only the severest punishment is possible, the personal extermination of the evildoer. The original form of the apodeictic laws naturally tells us nothing about how this was carried out; but its content makes it clear that on principle it must have been the business of the whole Israelite nation, even if in practice it was normally carried out by the individual community that judged the case. This is confirmed by the additions to several of the fragments in the Holiness Code, which undoubtedly conform to the original sense of the formula 'he shall be put to death', when they lay down as the intended means of execution, death by stoning, carried out with the active participation of every member of the community present, as representatives of the whole nation.[83]

---

against offering children to Melech (Lev. xx. 2), when it is compared to the law against offering to any other gods at all (Exod. xxii. 19), though the peculiar nature of the cult of Melech makes the need for a special mention of it understandable. We have also to reckon with it in the case of the sexual laws (Lev. xx. 10 ff.), although one would always have to expect a list of several laws here (cf. Deut. xxvii. 20, 22 ff.).

[83] Lev. xx. 2, 27; xxiv. 16 (cf. also Num. xv. 35 f.). A striking

Closely related to this series of apodeictic laws is the best preserved of all, which we do not have to compile first of all from different parts of the Hexateuch, since it has come down to us in a single passage: the list of crimes laid under a curse in Deut. xxvii. 15–26.[84] It consists of twelve clauses; the last, however, has no specific purpose of its own, but is clearly only meant to be a summary of the others, and to make up the number twelve.[85] The repetition of the same predicate serves here, as before, to make a formal unity of the passage; but the predicate is specially emphasized in this case by being put at the beginning as a noun: אָרוּר, 'cursed'. The subjects which follow it have the same form, a participle with the addition of an object or a qualifying adverb, as in the previous list. Only the first and the last have given way to the modification into a relative clause which we met in the other list and took as a sign of the gradual decay of the apodeictic style.[86] There are some additions, but they are few and unimportant, and can easily be eliminated.[87] It thus appears that the subject again consists of three words, while the invariable predicate is this time only one word, so that the original form was a line of four feet without a caesura. In content, some of the laws are the same, or closely similar

---

example is the setting out of the legal procedure to be taken against a stubborn and rebellious son, which can presumably be taken as an adaptation of the law condemning to death for the cursing of parents (Exod. xxi. 17; Lev. xx. 9): the indictment and condemnation of the wrongdoer by his parents before the local court, and then his stoning by all the men of the city (Deut. xxi. 18 ff.).

[84] We shall discuss the surrounding context below. There are no parallels to the individual clauses elsewhere.

[85] One could regard it as secondary and suppose that it had perhaps displaced or supplanted an original twelfth clause. But cf. note 79 above, on Lev. xxvii. 29 as the concluding clause, in a similar form, to the list of crimes worthy of death.

[86] In the first clause the reconstruction of the participle formulation from the extant text is not difficult—probably it is: פֶּסֶל בַּסָּתֶר אָרוּר שָׂם 'Cursed is he who sets up an image in secret'; a much larger emendation would have to be made to the last clause.

[87] Likewise in vss. 15, 19, 20, 22, 25.

to some of those in the list of crimes punishable by death. The curses against setting up images in secret, moving landmarks, misleading the blind, perverting justice due to those who are underprivileged in law, and accepting bribes, are new. The social aspects of Israelite life are more prominent here. It is significant that the whole passage is concerned with crimes committed in secret, in the hope that they would never appear before a human court. This is the reason why, unlike those of the other list, these laws do not provide for capital punishment to be carried out by the whole community, but carry a curse upon the evildoer, that is, his exclusion from the common life shared by Yahweh and Israel. Accordingly, in any given case the decision to carry out the curse has to be made by Yahweh, who knows even of sins committed in secret. The essential part played by the community is that it should solemnly acknowledge the curse—the people's 'Amen' follows each law—and totally dissociate itself from anyone who should draw one or other of these curses on himself. One might almost say that the two lists are complementary to one another; in crime against the fundamental claims of Yahweh, one deals with the aspect of the deed which is subject to human jurisdiction, the other, that which is reserved to the punishment of God. This shows how far the table of curses is from every connection with the secular law, and how closely linked to religion. A third list of apodeictic laws lends itself to comparison with the other two. It shows the same formal feature, the constant repetition of the same wording in each clause, but in content it is restricted to only one of the themes found in the other two lists. It is a series of at least eleven clauses, heavily interpolated; it occurs in the Holiness Code and deals with degrees of affinity within which sexual intercourse is forbidden.[88] The wording of the verbal predicate which stands at the end of the sentence, and contains the negative particle, is the same throughout; so also, in this case, is the object set in the emphatic position at the

[88] Lev. xviii. 7–17. A twelfth clause of the list could be obtained by rearranging vs. 18.

beginning: 'The nakedness of thy . . . shalt thou not uncover.' The only variable element, then, is the word naming the relationship, which is in the genitive and is governed by the object. In this particular pattern, however, an important formal change of another sort has taken place: the objective style of the lists of crimes punishable by death or a curse has given way to a direct address in the subjective second person: 'thou'—albeit without the appearance of the 'I' of the speaker in association with it. The clauses of this list have thus become direct prohibitions, and can be called apodeictic not only by virtue of their concise and epigrammatic phrasing, but especially because they do not use, in the verbal predicate, the normal form of prohibition in Hebrew, the negative אַל with the jussive imperfect, but the much stronger form of a straightforward statement with the negative לֹא and the indicative of the imperfect. This produces the same categorical and unconditional effect as in the clauses of the other lists we examined, which pronounced certain crimes to be worthy of death or a curse in the same indicative form. The more limited scope of this list is, as we have seen, the only thing which distinguishes it from the others.

The same distinctive features, however, are found elsewhere. The Book of the Covenant contains two other lists, or at least fragments of lists, that consist of categorical prohibitions in the second person, 'thou', and similarly deal only with a single aspect of the apodeictic law. The formal identity of the clauses they contain is limited to the categorical negative לֹא,[89] but both the content and the peculiar sentence structure which occurs in almost all of them—the object and any adverbial qualification replaces the verbal predicate at the beginning—are sufficient evidence that they were thought of and composed as lists.[90] As far as the content is con-

[89] In Exod. xxiii. 1b לֹא is a secondary form, replacing אַל; in Exod. xxiii. 7a the positive תִּרְחַק 'Keep far from . . .' perhaps replaced a word of opposite meaning with a negation.

[90] The last-named clue is missing in Exod. xxiii. 1 f., which could suggest a special origin for these laws.

cerned, the first deals exclusively with the relations of the Israelite to certain persons or categories of persons whom for one reason or another he regards with awe and abhorrence, and towards whom he must accordingly avoid various actions, depending on who it is. God, the representatives of the tribe in the confederacy of all the tribes,[91] the stranger who has sought protection, the widow and the orphan, and the sorceress are all placed in the extant fragments under the same kind of taboo. Scarcely half of the original series can have been preserved.[92] Similarities in content between this and the other lists of apodeictic laws are rare because of its fragmentary condition, and also because of the particular limited sphere to which its prohibitions are directed; the most frequent parallels are found in the other list of the Book of the Covenant, which it resembles closely in form. The latter regulates the behaviour of the Israelite when he is carrying out some function in the local court—it does not lay down an order of legal procedure,[93] but categorically forbids the giving of unfair consideration to persons who have no right to

[91] For this meaning of נָשִׂיא cf. NOTH, *Das System*, pp. 97, 151 ff.

[92] These fragments are plainly in a very confused order. I rearrange them in the same order as I have set the persons named in them above: Exod. xxii. 27a, b, 20 (with interpolations); xxi. 17. There is no clause against breach of respect for parents, such as regularly occurs in the other lists (presumably it has been left out because it is no longer necessary here—especially on account of Exod. xxi. 15, 17). But if the list or persons worthy of special respect extended to five or even (if widows and orphans were originally dealt with separately) to six cases, it is most unlikely that only the sorceress was to be specially regarded in the opposite sense of being avoided; there was no lack in Palestine of other categories of person whom the religion of Yahweh could not tolerate in Israel, because they served foreign religions or even magic (cf. Lev. xx, 27 above). If we accept that the persons to be avoided in the list were covered by as many prohibitions as those to be respected, we come to an original list of ten or twelve clauses. The metrical form seems to be throughout that of a three-foot line (with a stress on the negative).

[93] MERX (*Die Bücher Moses und Josua* [1907], p. 32) wants to describe the list in these terms. I would prefer to see it as a list of penalties.

preferential treatment, and the failure to respect the privileges of those who have a claim to special protection before the law.[94] In the case of the second group, the protected stranger, the widow and the orphan, the connection with the first list is obvious, and it becomes clear that the purpose of the prohibitions is to prevent damage to the life of the community in the exercise of its legal functions.

One final list of prohibitions must be treated here. It is not, however, another mere fragment, but, like the list of crimes punishable by death or a curse, is meant to cover the whole field of apodeictic law, so far as this is possible within so small a compass: the Decalogue.[95] Its formal similarity to the list of apodeictic laws discussed above does not become clear until it is divested of the large number of interpolations with which it is overlaid—they are found largely in the first half but occur also in the final clause, and appear—with variations—in both recensions. This procedure is necessary here, as with all legal material in the Hexateuch, because of the secondary character of the forms in which it has

[94] Exod. xxiii. 1–3, 6–9 (with many interpolations). The metrical form of the original is presumably a four-foot line; but the way it should be reconstructed is not altogether clear. Parts of it reappear in Lev. xix. 15 f.

[95] Exod. xx. 2–17; Deut. v. 6–18. Fragments of the Decalogue occur both in the books of the law (in the Law of Holiness—Lev. xix. 3 f., 11 f.—mingled with elements from other lists of apodeictic law) and also in the prophets (Hosea iv. 2; Jer. vii. 9—in both cases extremely abbreviated) and in a psalm which we will discuss below (lxxxi. 10 f.—recast here in the form of couplets of three-foot lines). I speak of *the* Decalogue and not of *a* Decalogue, because I do not share the opinion first expressed by GOETHE, that in Exod. xxxiv. 10, 14–26 we possess a second Decalogue which is in fact the original from which the second was later adapted. Both from its literary relationship to the Book of the Covenant and from its particular interest, appropriate to its formal structure, the latter text can be seen to be a later and heterogenous compilation, containing priestly ordinances about the cultic duties of lay-people in a greater proportion than apodeictic elements from the Decalogue of Exod. xx. Concerning this passage see the recent comment of PFEIFFER, *JBL*, xliii (1924), pp. 294 ff. MORGENSTERN, *HUCA*, iv (1927); ROWLEY, *BJRL*, xxxiv (1951), pp. 81 ff.

come down to us. It is obviously called for in the case of the Decalogue, where no less than four clauses of the second half have retained their original concise wording, and imply that the other clauses were also originally cast in this form.[96] But the result obtained by simply eliminating the interpolated passages is not entirely satisfactory. Four more clauses turn out to have been framed as categorical prohibitions in the second person singular, 'thou', with the negative לֹא, in addition to the four that have retained this form in the final recension, but two do not fit into this picture at all. These are the commandment to keep the sabbath holy, and to honour parents; even when we go back to what we would expect the original nucleus to have been, it is phrased differently.[97] It hardly seems right simply to exclude them, and to make up the number of clauses from the addition of other clauses.[98] We have already come across the themes they express, in the list of crimes deserving death or a curse, as subject to apodeictic law, and so when they reoccur in the Decalogue we cannot, on principle, suspect them of being alien in origin, or later additions. These parallels, however, lead us to the true solution of the difficulty: in the Decalogue as in the other codes, the two themes were originally not positively phrased, but like the other eight clauses were categorical prohibitions of work on the sabbath and the cursing of parents.[99] Their rewording as positive injunctions must therefore be seen as a stage of their secondary development, which also led to their being laden with interpolations. We cannot proceed with certainty beyond the reconstruction of

[96] It would be avoiding the problem raised by the actual facts, simply to accept the Decalogue in the second, or rather perhaps, the third redaction, in which we possess it, and to try as far as possible to date it from that as MEINHOLD (*Der Dekalog* [1927], pp. 44 ff.) still tries to do.

[97] Cf. the reconstruction in R. KITTEL, *Geschichte des Volkes Israel*, 6th ed., I (1923), pp. 38 f.

[98] As suggested by HANS SCHMIDT, *Eucharisterion* (*Festschrift für Gunkel* [1923]), pp. 78 ff.

[99] SELLIN, *Geschichte des israelitisch-jüdischen Volkes*, I (1924), pp. 83 f.

their original form. The related question, as to whether in the course of the development of the list clauses were not only added to, but were actually omitted, so that perhaps there may have been more than ten, and possibly twelve clauses, as in the list of crimes laid under a curse, must remain unanswered.

Even in the original form as reconstructed, the Decalogue does not show the same regularity of form as the other lists of apodeictic laws. The unexpressed subject 'thou' runs through the whole list, except for the first clause, where the variation does not break up the pattern and occurs in any case for a good reason.[100] Similarly, the categorical negative is the strongest unifying element in the whole list. But the verbal predicates are all very different, and each varies from the next not only in the particular parts of speech, objects, and prepositional expressions used, but even in the number of words they contain. Sometimes an intransitive verb is used, which needs no enlargement: 'Thou shalt not commit adultery' (one word in Hebrew). Sometimes there is a transitive verb, but the object is not expressed: 'Thou shalt not steal.' Sometimes—and this is true in the majority of cases—the verb is transitive and is followed by its object and in appropriate cases with a further qualification: 'Thou shalt not take my name in vain.' The number of words being different in each clause, it seems hardly likely that the Decalogue was intended to be proclaimed in metrical form. It is closer to prose than to verse, in contrast to the form which from the previous example we were led to believe was normal in codes of apodeictic law.[101] Does this peculiarity imply

[100] Since Hebrew possesses no word for 'have', the formula 'there shall be no God for thee except me' in which the second person singular 'thee' is still retained is perfectly acceptable and the transition in the following clauses to 'thou' as the subject is easily made. It would be a different matter, if this clause had stood in the middle of the list.

[101] Since the shortest clauses of the list are lines of two feet, while the longer possess four feet, one is tempted to place each pair together to make a line of four feet, so that such a couplet would be metrically equivalent to one of the longer clauses. But this is

that it was composed much earlier, before the form in verse had become normal—or is it rather the product of a later period, when the close association with the traditional form had grown weaker? From the point of view of the history of literary forms alone, the latter seems most likely.

It would be inadvisable, however, to decide this point purely on the basis of the literary form, without taking its content into account. To all appearances it is the concern for the content, and for the content of individual clauses, which decided the choice of the form, and overcame the tendency towards a regular form throughout. Each clause had to retain to the utmost degree its clarity of expression, and the force of its apodeictic formulation. This was not possible to the same extent in every case, so that when in each clause it was carried out as efficiently as possible, the architectonic of the whole series was bound to suffer. Now as a matter of fact the individual clauses of the Decalogue are so closely related in content to those of other lists of apodeictic laws, that it is not easy at first sight to tell how far it was the emphasis on the content which led to the choice of a different form. Due attention is rarely given to the connection between the contents of different lists.[102] I feel it necessary to present this connection in a statistical table, and shall do so by following, in the main, the arrangement of the Decalogue, ignoring insignificant verbal variations, and listing more serious deviations in a separate column according to the nature of the list in which they are found, but each against the corresponding clause of the Decalogue. Matters only dealt with in other lists I shall leave to the end. (See pp. 156–57)

---

not practicable, unless we accept that there are considerable lacunae in the original text.

[102] It seems to me to be a basic mistake in the latest thorough treatment of the Decalogue (VOLZ, *Mose*, 2nd ed. [1932]), that he completely ignores these connections, and as a result makes no attempt to use the most closely related source material, which would have helped him to avoid severe errors in his total picture and would have provided very many useful details. The same objection must be made to ROWLEY's argument, *BJRL*, xxxiv (1951), pp. 81 ff.

This table shows the internal relationship between the three lists, including the Decalogue, so clearly that its evidence is decisive. Each has been compiled with the express intention of treating in some way the entire field of specific Israelite law. None of them entirely succeeds in this, not even the Decalogue, which ignores the sexual crimes entirely, except for adultery, and includes the special duties towards socially privileged groups at best only implicitly. There can be no doubt why all the lists are incomplete. They could not consist of more than a certain number of clauses, i.e. twelve; and it is probable that they normally consisted of exactly twelve clauses. Whatever the theoretical intention, not everything which was thought worthy of inclusion could be reduced to this narrow framework. In every case, therefore, a selection had to be made from the abundant material available, and it was inevitable that the particular concern at work in each list should determine the choice and cause certain variations from the other lists. The difference between the list of crimes laid under a curse and those judged worthy of death were occasioned, as we saw, by such a shift of emphasis: the former deals with deeds which are known to all, and which it is possible and proper to try and punish before a human court, the other with such deeds as can be reached only by a curse since they are perpetrated in secret and remain unknown. The particular stress laid on social obligations in the list of curses is closely connected with this distinction. The limited and one-sided nature of any given list explains why each had to be supplemented by the others, and so how several came to be found together. The same reason can be given for the occurrence of lists limited to a single field, such as those for dealing with forbidden degrees of affinity or with fair procedure in courts of law. None of the more comprehensive lists could give more than a selection of the individual practical cases for which the special list legislated. Naturally it was always the most flagrant crime which was mentioned. The special lists are intended to make up the unavoidable deficiencies of the general lists. This they do by setting out to treat only a very limited field, but to do so thoroughly,

	The Decalogue	*Crimes punishable by death*	*Crimes laid under a curse*
The worship of strange gods	Exod. xx. 3	Exod. xxii. 19	–
Sacrificing children to Melech	–	Lev. xx. 2	–
Images	Exod. xx. 4	–	Deut. xxvii. 15
Abuse of the name of Yahweh	Exod. xx. 7	Lev. xxiv. 16	–
Work on the Sabbath	Exod. xx. 8	Exod. xxxi. 15	–
Cursing parents	Exod. xx. 12	Exod. xxi. 17	Deut. xxvii. 16
Ill-treating parents	–	Exod. xxi. 15	–
Murder	Exod. xx. 13	Exod. xxi. 12	Deut. xxvii. 24
Adultery	Exod. xx. 14	Lev. xx. 10	–
Sexual intercourse between relatives	–	Lev. xx. 11 ff.	Deut. xxvii. 20, 22 ff.
Bestiality	–	Exod. xxii. 18	Deut. xxvii. 21
Stealing of any sort	Exod. xx. 15	–	–
Stealing a man	–	Exod. xxi. 16	–
False witness before a court	Exod. xx. 16	–	–
Depriving widows and orphans of legal rights	–	–	Deut. xxvii. 19
Taking bribes	–	–	Deut. xxvii. 25
Violation of others' property[103]	Exod. xx. 17	–	–

[103] For this meaning of 'covet' cf. HERRMANN, *Sellin-Festschrift* (1927), pp. 69 ff., and ALT, *Das Verbot des Diebstahls im Dekalog*, *K.S.*, I, p. 333.

	The Decalogue	*Crimes punishable by death*	*Crimes laid under a curse*
Moving landmarks	—	—	Deut. xxvii. 17
Leading the blind astray	—	—	Deut. xxvii. 18
Conjuring up the dead	—	Lev. xx. 27	—

mentioning within the limits of the number of clauses available, every possible case.

The Decalogue provides a sharp contrast to this subdivision of apodcictic law into special lists with a limited purview. It is clearly meant to deal with the whole subject, and comes nearer to achieving its purpose than the lists of deeds deserving death or a curse, in that all its clauses take the form of categorical prohibitions; thus they do not name any punishment, and have no need to take into account whether the misdeed and the criminal will remain unknown, or will be brought to light. The categorical prohibition lays down the law in a much more absolute fashion than the provision of the severest punishment. The tendency towards a much more absolute and unqualified form of expression is reinforced by the fact that the Decalogue, more than the other lists, refrains from naming actual individual cases, but tends rather to lay down principles, without getting lost, however, in abstractions. The rejection of any attempt to make the length and construction of each clause the same, the most remarkable formal feature we observed elsewhere, is of particular value in making this clear, and the desire for such an effect is no doubt what occasioned it. In this respect the clauses which are reduced to the smallest possible compass, a negative particle and a predicate, even where the latter is a transitive verb and implies an object, are particularly instructive. They are so formulated as to avoid any reference to individual cases and include every case that could possibly be covered by the word used.[104] The importance of the Decalogue in world history is undoubtedly due to a large degree to the form in which it is cast, a form which does not occur in any of the other lists we discussed. It keeps the strictly legal purpose of the commandments in the background, thus making their moral import stand out more clearly. With reference to the place of the Decalogue in the life of Israel and in the formal development of apodeictic laws, we have already asked whether the variations in the Decalogue from the norms of form and content found everywhere else imply that it comes from a period before these norms were developed, or whether they are a sign of their incipient decay, and of the obsolescence of this literary form. We have not so far answered this question but it now seems that the latter answer is the true one: the Decalogue deliberately renounces a part of the customary literary form and phraseology in order to fulfil a need which the other lists could not cope with adequately within their stylistic limits, and which indeed they had raised the more urgently by their very incompleteness. But it must be understood that this conclusion does no more than fix the place of the Decalogue within the development of its own literary form. We can only go on to deduce its place in absolute chronology when we have accurately dated the whole course of this development.[105]

[104] The later rephrasing of the prohibition of work on the Sabbath, and of the cursing of one's parents, as positive commands, was a further step in the same direction. The verbs used in the new version for 'keep holy' and 'honour' are much less concrete and much more basic conceptions than the verbs, opposite in meaning, for 'work' and 'curse', which we presume were used in the original form of these clauses.

[105] The argument for the late date of the Decalogue which is commonly given nowadays is not based as a rule on considerations of literary form, but is drawn principally from their supposed dependence on the preaching of the prophets of the 8th century or even later. In my opinion, this is to give too little weight to what was already contained in the law of Israel in the time before the prophets, and too great a weight to the influence of prophecy on the Law. (Cf. M. KÖHLER, *Theol. Rundschau,* N.F. i [1929], pp. 161 ff.)

Now we come to what is for us the more important question, that of the origin of apodeictic law as a whole. We saw that its original form is always a short series of simple clauses, all similarly worded as far as possible. Whatever form they may in fact take, they always express a categorical prohibition; in dealing with the origin of this form we have no need to discuss later elaborations, and the introduction of matter in a different style. These characteristics of apodeictic law clearly distinguish it from the whole body of casuistic law, even—and in fact most markedly—where they touch on the same subject, or overlap. For the most part, however, the apodeictic law deals with matters with which casuistic law is never concerned.[106] We must exclude, therefore, any theory of a common origin for both types of law. The Israelites cannot have adopted the apodeictic law from the Canaanite culture which preceded them in Palestine in the same way as

[106] One might expect that in view of this clear difference between the two kinds of law, there must also have been a special name for the lists of apodeictic law which would distinguish them from the מִשְׁפָּטִים of the casuistic law. But there is no place for such a name normally in the lists themselves; headings and conclusions, in which they might occur, are usually lacking, and other references are naturally not altogether reliable. For example, one could hardly base an argument on Deut. xxvii. 26, where in the last of the twelve curses, the whole list appears to be called הַתּוֹרָה הַזֹּאת דִּבְרֵי 'the words of this law'; for the phrasing of this verse, as we saw above, cannot be held to be original; nor does the much weaker expression כָּל־הַדְּבָרִים הָאֵלֶּה 'all these words' in the introduction to the Decalogue (Exod. xx. 1; cf. Deut. v. 5, 19) and in the story of the making of the covenant in the mountain of God in the desert, which ostensibly looks back to the Book of the Covenant (Exod. xxiv. 3—it occurs side by side with כָּל־הַמִּשְׁפָּטִים v. 4) give the impression of being a technical term for this literary form. A more likely expression is חֻקֹּתַי 'my (Yahweh's) ordinances', which occurs in Lev. xx. 8 at the end of a kind of introduction to a list of clauses taken from the compilation of crimes worthy of death, and presumably refers to these clauses. But even חֻקָּה, חֹק, to judge from their use elsewhere, have a meaning which is not limited to this one literary form.

we concluded they adopted the casuistic law. There is not the slightest indication in the apodeictic codes of a Canaanite origin, neither in the attitudes they reveal nor in the cultural background they presuppose. Everything in them is related exclusively to the Israelite nation and the religion of Yahweh even where their terse wording does not refer directly to either. In any case their origin must be sought within Israel itself; anyone who supposes otherwise will only find them harder to understand. But even within Israel their roots must lie in their own particular context, and this can hardly be the administration of secular justice in each locality, which we discovered to be the setting in which the casuistic law was preserved and handed on from the Canaanites to the Israelites. Of course we must not overlook the fact that a considerable number of the apodeictic laws deal with matters which lay within the competence of the normal judicial procedure in each community—this is particularly true of the list of crimes punishable by death, and in a different way, in the list of prohibitions regulating the personal standing of lay persons before the law.[107] But in the first place, the apodeictic law makes no attempt to treat these matters exhaustively, and secondly, even in the matters it mentions, it does not provide a treatment in any way adequate to the practical needs of secular jurisdiction. It lists only the most serious crimes, and either ignores the whole field of related but less serious offences, or makes no legal provision for them. The very contrast supports the conclusion that the casuistic law alone, with its detailed conditions and exceptions, originates in the day-to-day work of judges and lawyers. It follows that the apodeictic law pronounces on such practical realities from an external point of view, and is not adapted to the details of every issue. Need we add that the passionate intensity, scarcely restrained, of the apodeictic law could never have arisen in ordinary legal practice—who among the laymen

[107] The case of Naboth (1 Kings xxi), already mentioned above, provides an example of the practical application in a local court of the list forbidding a false attitude towards taboo persons.

who had to speak in a secular court[108] could speak like this on his own authority?

Not only this intensity of expression, but the internal construction of the lists of apodeictic laws implies that they were created and maintained in use in a part of Israelite life distinct from that of a single community administering secular justice. A context is required in which the whole people, and through them their God, could adopt the imperative tone towards individuals, and impose on them the absolute prohibitions, or threats of a curse or of death, which we find. We have no need to invent such a context, for it is provided in the tradition itself, wherever a list of apodeictic laws is set in a descriptive framework. A particularly clear instance is the setting of the curses in Deut. xxvii: this list is presented as being delivered orally by the levitical priests to the whole people, assembled in the great natural amphitheatre between Ebal and Gerizim in the Vale of Shechem; the people take each curse upon themselves with a cry of 'Amen'.[109] The apodeictic law provides the central text for a sacral action involving the whole nation, and those who proclaim it are the mouthpiece of Yahweh, the levitical priests, whose task in the assembly of the whole nation was by no means only to conduct the worship of Yahweh, but who also carried out the function, at least equally important, of making his demands known to Israel.[110] Not only this but all the lists of apodeictic law are admirably adapted in form and content to this

[108] If only to avoid misunderstandings, I would remark here that obviously one must not suppose that the priests of the sanctuaries were involved in the local courts. Unlike the lay tribes, they had no land as their own inheritance (cf. Deut. xviii. 1 f.) and therefore lacked the most essential prerequisite to active participation in the normal administration of the law; only when appeal was made to the judgement of God by the court were they required to act. (Deut. xvii. 8 ff.)

[109] The fragmentary condition of the literary context in Deut. xxvii. does not give any cause to doubt these statements. (Cf. on the whole MOWINCKEL, *Psalmenstudien*, V [1924], pp. 74 ff.; *Le Décalogue* [1927], pp. 133 ff.; NOTH, *Das System*, pp. 144 ff.)

[110] Deut. xxxiii. 10.

situation; this is the natural explanation of the brevity of the lists and of each clause, the use of the second person 'thou' in many of them, and especially of the unqualified commands they contain. But if an entire category of Israelite law fits into the scene described in Deut. xxvii this provides strong support for the view that the account is not simply the product of the writer's imagination, bearing no relation to reality, but preserves at least the recollection of a sacral action that actually took place at one time in Israel. The recently established view that this same sanctuary of Yahweh at Shechem was visited and used in common by the whole federation of Israelite tribes, and may perhaps have been their only sanctuary in Palestine,[111] brings the scene in Deut. xxvii quite within the bounds of historical possibility. It naturally does not imply that the rite remained associated with this one place.

We have still to ask whether we should conceive of this scene as taking place on a single occasion, somewhat on the pattern of the account in Joshua xxiv, where in the identical place Joshua gives the Israelite tribes 'statutes and ordinances', חק ומִשְׁפָּט [112] on the occasion of their pledge to worship Yahweh alone; or whether it describes a regular occurrence, at which these lists of curses were just as regularly proclaimed. Only in the latter case can we make full use of the scene in studying the history of apodeictic law as a formal category. Only in relation to constantly recurring situations can such a category take on, as regards both form and content, a clear and consistent shape, without which its further development and constant renewal would be impossible. Like the whole of Deut. xxvii, the section we are discussing is

[111] Cf. NOTH, *Das System*, pp. 65 ff.

[112] Josh. xxiv. 25. As it stands this story purports to represent an event which took place once only, at the time of the occupation of Palestine, but in addition it is intended to serve as an aetiological explanation of a regularly repeated act in the sanctuary of Yahweh at Shechem. (Cf. ALT, *Die Wallfahrt von Sichem nach Bethel*, *Abh. der Herder-Gesellschaft und des Herder-Instituts zu Riga*, VI Band, Nr. 3 [1938], pp. 218–30; *K.S.*, I, pp. 81 ff.; 'Josua', ZAW, Beiheft, lxvi [1936], pp. 13–29; *K.S.*, I, pp. 191 ff.)

presented as an instruction, enjoining the use of the list of curses in a great cultic action. This tends to confirm that it continued in effective and regular use, and formed part of a fixed rite, which as such could provide the basis for the origin and development of the category of apodeictic law. Certain confirmation of this view, however, is provided by another passage, which has not, up to the present, been sufficiently taken into account: not surprisingly, since it has no apparent connection with the matters under consideration. The passage occurs in the later additions to the end of Deuteronomy. Its ostensible and express purpose is to ensure as well as possible the preservation and continued effectiveness of this book of law. The first purpose is represented as being achieved by Moses handing over a written copy of the law to the levitical priests and the elders of Israel,[113] the second by setting up a regular assembly of the whole nation, including not only protected aliens, but also the women and young children, in the common sanctuary of Yahweh at the Feast of Tabernacles, every seventh year, when the solemn reading of Deuteronomy would take place.[114] But it is obvious that this ordinance was most inadequate to the purpose for which in the opinion of the author it was intended. As a matter of fact we do not know whether any attempt was ever made to carry it out. For a book of laws as long and as densely packed as Deuteronomy could certainly not be firmly impressed on the memory of a whole nation, if it was read out to them only once every seven years. This makes it all the more unlikely that he should have made such an attempt with such unsuitable materials on his own initiative. The error into which he fell becomes understandable if we take as a starting-point an older

[113] Deut. xxxi. 9. By mentioning in the same verse the hearers of the priestly and of the lay tradition, the author reveals that he knew perfectly well that he was compiling the Deuteronomic law from elements which originated as a matter of fact in the regular use of one or the other of these categories.

[114] Deut. xxxi. 10–13. Naturally enough the Deuteronomic author does not name any particular sanctuary, but always presupposes the one sanctuary of which Deuteronomy always speaks.

ordinance, either still in force or at the least still remembered, the nucleus of which was the proclamation of the law before the assembly of the whole nation. The Deuteronomist's only mistake, then, was to put the new code of law, in a context to which it was ill-fitted, in place of the older proclamation, shorter, more easily remembered, and therefore much better adapted to this setting.[115] The casuistic law was of its very nature unsuited for such a use, so that the obvious material for the purpose seems to be the short lists of apodeictic laws.[116] This provides the connection with a regularly occurring situation and event in the life of the Israelite people, which we were obliged to postulate in order to understand how this form of law arose. It also justifies us in interpreting Deut. xxvii along these lines, although it does not contain any reference to a particular festival.

Intended as it is to be recited before the assembly of the whole people at the Feast of Tabernacles every seventh year,

[115] I come here to a quite different conclusion from that of MOWINCKEL, who also recognizes in this passage an attempt to adapt very ancient traditional material, but supposes that the original was a proclamation of the law at the Feast of Tabernacles every year, and that the novelty introduced in Deuteronomy was the restriction of the usage to the seventh year, in view of the fact that the Deuteronomic law-book was too long to be read every year (*Psalmenstudien*, V, pp. 108 f.). MOWINCKEL does not appear to have considered that this innovation would defeat the purposes which he ascribes to the Deuteronomist.

[116] This can naturally only be true of the earlier stages, in which we must suppose that the apodeictic law was kept strictly separate from the casuistic law, if we are going to understand how it arose at all. The possibility always remains, that in the later stages of development, after the casuistic law had been adopted, fragments of casuistic law were incorporated with the lists of apodeictic laws in the proclamation of the law, as NOTH, *Das System*, pp. 97 ff., suspects in the case of the law of the amphictyony of all the Israelite tribes gathered in a federation at one sanctuary. This would constitute, at the early stage of oral proclamation, a step in the direction of the heterogeneous compilations of casuistic and apodeictic law, which we possess in a fixed literary form in the Book of the Covenant, and other books of Israelite law. But we cannot be certain about the individual stages of this process.

the formal category of apodeictic law is seen to belong to a set of very characteristic Israelite ideas and institutions, and this gives us a much deeper insight into its nature. The very fact of its connection with the Feast of Tabernacles is significant. This feast, celebrated in the autumn at the end of the agricultural year, was for ancient Israel also the New Year festival, and was filled with the thought of the beginning of a new period in the life and work of both the nation and the individual.[117] But in a special and deeper sense is this true of the Feast of Tabernacles at the end of the seventh year. From the earliest times in Israel this was a year of rest from all agricultural work. The purpose of the fallow year was not economic but religious: while it lasted the right of the Israelite tribes to enjoy the land and territory granted to them by lot was abrogated, and the true and sole ownership of Yahweh is brought once again into prominence.[118] Side by side with this interruption in agricultural work goes the release of the individual from all particular obligations and debts which he has incurred in the course of the previous six years in the cultivation of his land. What a later ordinance enjoined for the end of seven times seven years, the year of Jubilee, certainly held originally for the seventh, the Sabbath

[117] Exod. xxiii. 16; xxxiv. 22; Lev. xxiii. 33 ff.; Deut. xvi. 13 ff. It was VOLZ, in *Das Neujahrsfest Jahwes* (1912), who recognized the character of the Feast of Tabernacles as a New Year festival; cf. MOWINCKEL, *Psalmenstudien*, II (1922), and H. SCHMIDT, *Die Thronfahrt Jahwes* (1927), who based very far-reaching theories on it. The scepticism with which PAP handles the matter (*Das israelitische Neujahrsfest* [1933] appears to me to go beyond the mark.

[118] Exod. xxiii. 10 f.; Lev. xxv. 1 ff. The emergence of this institution only appears credible to me at the time when the Israelite tribes had not yet abandoned the semi-nomadic existence of their earlier period, and had just begun to practise agriculture, but had not yet made it the mainstay of their economy. This stage could have been either immediately before or immediately after their occupation of Palestine; their final transition to an agricultural economy certainly took many generations before it was completed. Cf. ALT, 'Erwägungen über die Landnahme der Israeliten', *PJB*, xxxv (1939), pp. 35 f.; *K.S.*, I, pp. 150 f.

year: 'Each one shall return to his own property and to his own family.'[119] But if the purpose of this unique and peculiarly Israelite institution was the return to normal of the whole national community after the disturbances and false developments of the previous six years, then the proclamation of the apodeictic—the specifically Israelite—law at the Feast of Tabernacles, that is, at the beginning of the seventh year, has a precise and relevant purpose. It signifies the recalling of the people to the ideals on which its existence is based, a renewed pledging of every member of the nation to the will of Yahweh, without which the welding of the tribes into a national unity could not have come about, nor could endure. Hence, although the expression may not be one that is in use, the origin of the proclamation of the apodeictic law, placing an obligation on the whole nation, at the Feast of Tabernacles, is a regular *renewal of the covenant* between

[119] Lev. xxv, 8 ff. (10); the lifting of all debts in the Sabbath year: Deut. xv. 1 ff.; the revision of titles to land and property in the year of Jubilee: Num. xxxvi. 1 ff. The later ordinances for the year of Jubilee were intended to be used to restore the significance of the Sabbath year, since they obviously—although apparently only in theory—were taken from the Sabbath year and transferred to the year which was seven times seven years later, with the intention of preserving it in this way, at least to a restricted degree, after the complete transition of the people to an agricultural economy had made it impossible to carry out the original commandment. One should not try to understand the year of Jubilee apart from the Sabbath year, as Jirku tried to do recently on the basis of a very schematic distinction between the stylistically different strata in Lev. xxv (*Reinhold-Seeberg-Festschrift* [1929], pp. 169 ff.) and as NIKOLSKIJ tried to do in a different way with a very tendentious dating of strata distinguished on different grounds (*ZAW*, N.F. ix, [1932], p. 216). I am inclined to suspect that the removal of previous legal titles to landed property in the seventh year was originally complete, and resulted in a new distribution by lot of agricultural land to individual tribes, which is a procedure often found among semi-nomads (cf. for example, MUSIL, *Arabia Petraea*, III [1908], pp. 293 f.; much material is given without attestation in SCHAEFFER, *Hebrew Tribal Economy and the Jubilee* [1922]); this would provide a particularly attractive explanation for the expectation of a γῆς ἀναδασμός in the future in Judah, in Micah (ii. 4 f.; a corrupt text).

Yahweh and Israel of which they were conscious as the very source of their national life.[120]

In these circumstances it is not surprising that the authors of the Hexateuch chose the lists of apodeictic laws to put into the stories of the first and basic covenant between Yahweh and Israel, on the mountain of God in the desert. They were regularly used in the act of renewing the covenant, and in that context would intentionally and inevitably be conceived of as the fixed expression of the unalterable will of God, which from the very beginning had been the basis of Yahweh's covenant with Israel. It was only natural to presume that they had been uttered in the very same words when the covenant was first made.[121] This explains why the Book of the Covenant is found in its present position—in spite of the fact that its original significance is considerably obscured by the combination of fragmentary lists of apodeictic law with a code of casuistic law, and with other largely cultic ordinances of priestly origin. The function of the Decalogue, both in Exodus xx and Deut. v is explained in the same way. The Decalogue was peculiarly suited to such a use, since its wording reflects much more clearly the actual situation in which Yahweh and Israel entered into a covenant, than do the other lists of apodeictic laws, where it is assumed, but not made explicit. Only the Decalogue precedes its series of prohibitions with a clause of quite a different type, in which Yahweh himself takes the initiative, and speaks in his own person, and

[120] I am in accord here with the view of MOWINCKEL (most recently given in *Le Décalogue,* pp. 114 ff.), but with this difference, that I believe that the sacral act of the proclamation of the law and the renewal of the covenant was limited to the Feast of Tabernacles in the seventh year (and I ignore the so-called Introit-Toroth, such as Ps. xv and xxiv. 3–6, which he uses in this context, but which pre-suppose a different situation. I do no more than mention the fact that even at the time of Ezra the reading of the law and the pledge to obey it takes place at the Feast of Tabernacles (Neh. viii).

[121] Their use in this setting gives the stories of the first covenant the character of aetiological tales for the rite of the later act of renewal at the covenant, and suggests that these stories took their form from that rite (cf. MOWINCKEL, op. cit.).

as the superior party makes on his own behalf the covenant promise, from which proceed the covenant obligations the people make towards him, and which gives them their compulsive force: 'I, Yahweh, am thy God.'[122] The first person, 'I', reoccurs in the first few of the prohibitions that follow. The same form, however, would continue in use later in the regular renewal of the covenant, and the Decalogue must have been used in the proclamation of the law at this event. This we can see not only from the text as we have it at present, overloaded as it is with additions that are presumably the result of prolonged use, but even more clearly from Ps. lxxxi, which is obviously intended, from the hymn with which it opens, for the Feast of Tabernacles and which rapidly reverts to the first person, 'I' of Yahweh, and proclaims the first clause of the Decalogue.[123] We remain, then, with no unassailable proof that the Decalogue was the prototype of the whole literary category of apodeictic law; and the relationship to one another in time and the place of origin of all the extant lists of apodeictic law is still unknown.[124]

This only shows more clearly how deeply the category of apodeictic law, both as regards its formal features, and also

[122] In view of this functional significance of the words for the whole list I cannot accept the opinion of POEBEL, that they are not to be considered as an independent clause at all, but belong syntactically to the first prohibition which follows 'Thou shalt have no other gods but me' (*Das appositionell bestimmte Pronomen der 1. Pers. sing. in den westsemitischen Inschriften und im Alten Testament* [1932], pp. 53 ff.); cf. also BERGSTRASSER, *OLZ*, xxxvii (1934).

[123] Introit-hymn: vss. 2–6a; transition: vss. 6b–9; quotation from the Decalogue: vss. 10–11. Cf. MOWINCKEL, *Psalmenstudien*, II, pp. 152 ff., etc.

[124] Only in the case of the list of curses in Deut. xxvii does the actual context itself lead us to suppose that it originates in the sanctuary of Yahweh at Shechem. As for other sanctuaries, we would think first of those which either earlier or later served in the same way as the sanctuary of Shechem, as the place for the assembly and common cult of the whole people; cf. NOTH, *Das System*, pp. 96 (Shiloh–I would also be inclined to think of Gilgal near Jericho).

as regards all the actual lists of that nature, is rooted in the basic institutions of Israel's early history, and how near it brings us, as a result, to the original characteristics of that nation. We can leave open the question as to whether the Israelite tribes already knew of, or possessed, any such similar legal formulations in the period before they became a nation, that is, before they united in the worship of Yahweh. It seems certain to me, however, on the strength of the above arguments, that the required situation for the appearance of this category was present as soon as the common relationship with Yahweh, and following it, the institution of the sealing and renewing of the covenant between him and Israel, had been established. Thus the creative period in the history of the category would seem in any case to have been the early period of Israel's history, before the founding of the kingdom. Indeed it is a fact that there is hardly a word in the lists of apodeictic law that have been handed down to us, which can be explained only by the later movements in Israelite religion and religious history, and would make necessary a late dating of the series in question. Evidence of dependence on the civilization they adopted in Palestine is only rarely noticeable, a fact that is, of course, closely related to the underlying outlook of apodeictic law and is thus of no value in deciding its date of origin. But since the worship of Yahweh, with which the apodeictic law is inseparably linked, clearly originates from the desert, we can presume the same source for the basis of the apodeictic law, if not for the extant examples in their present form. This would partly explain its severity, and the sharp contrast between it and the Canaanite law. So the assertion of the canonical text, with which our investigation began, that all law in force in Israel came down from the occasion when the covenant was made in the time of Moses, is to some degree confirmed for at least one category of law.

And this newly conceived legislative urge in Israel came into violent conflict in Israel with the ancient and highly developed legal system of Canaan; the apodeictic law clashed with the casuistic. The process is one that is typical of the whole history of Israel, which manifested for centuries a tension that is essentially due to the encounter and conflict between a young people newly come to nationhood and an ancient and alien culture. If the Israelites had brought no enduring characteristics into this situation, they would undoubtedly have been submerged and there would have been no reason for history to have had any further concern with them. But this is not what happened: the Israelites were able to retain their peculiar national characteristics to a considerable degree, and in their encounter with the civilization that preceded them in Palestine, they created something new, which extended far beyond the boundaries of the Ancient East, however deeply it may have been rooted there. The history of Israelite law bears witness to this. The two forms of law that combine therein could not peacefully resolve their conflicting claims to validity in Israel by the device of regulating secular life by casuistic law and leaving religious matters to apodeictic law. For although Canaanite casuistic law remains strictly limited to the secular sphere and showed no tendency to extend its influence, the apodeictic law of Israel displays an unrestrained power of aggression which seeks to subject every aspect of life without exception to the unconditional domination of the will of Yahweh, and can therefore recognize no secular or neutral region. Accordingly, while the lists of apodeictic law are aimed principally at areas of cultic significance, these are never dealt with in isolation, nor, as a result of the prohibitive wording of the apodeictic laws, are they made the subject of positive prescriptions. They are simply fenced off from any alien influence or activity by stern prohibitions.[125] But over and above this, the apodeictic law

[125] It is a fundamental misunderstanding of the nature of the apodeictic law which leads people, as has often happened, to draw conclusions about the character of the religion which lies behind it from the lack of positive injunction to practise the worship of Yahweh in the lists of apodeictic laws, especially in the Decalogue. The Sabbath mentioned in the Decalogue was from its origin characterized only by the prohibition of all work, and at the earliest period of Israelite history, in spite of what VOLZ, *Das Neujahrsfest*

pursues the Israelite out of the sanctuary of Yahweh into his daily life, and inevitably clashed with the carefully itemized instances and exceptions of the casuistic law. If the Israelites were unwilling simply to reject the Canaanite legal culture they discovered on their entry into Palestine—which they could not do, for they brought nothing from the desert to replace it—then the struggle between the two forms of law was unavoidable. This struggle remained a major preoccupation of Israelite law throughout its history, and it will be a task for the future to trace its course step by step through the whole field. We can do no more here than point to the beginning of the struggle, and make clear the original dualism that underlines its later development.

Jahwes, pp. 45 ff. has to say, had nothing to do with the positive cult of Yahweh.

THE SETTLEMENT OF THE ISRAELITES IN PALESTINE

DIE LANDNAHME DER ISRAELITEN IN PALÄSTINA
Reformationsprogramm der Universität Leipzig, 1925

INTRODUCTION

The principal purpose of any examination of the Israelites' entry into Palestine is to illustrate the history of the tribes and people that took part in it. When the Israelites arrived and whence they came, where they settled, what relationship they set up with the people already there, and how this new situation affected people's lives and thoughts are all questions which must be looked into, in detail and as a whole, before an accurate historical picture can be formed of the movement in its entirety. In the last few decades scholars have done their best to satisfy these demands.[1] But the more they go into the material, the clearer it becomes that this approach is insufficient by itself. Israel's own records of the time of the migrations and the settlement are the most important and indeed practically the only sources providing an answer to these questions; but in the Old Testament they are clearly always either too incomplete, or in too late a form, to preserve every important feature of the history of the tribes and of the whole nation. To give a complete picture, what is missing from the tradition must be provided by

[1] Apart from the complete histories of the people of Israel by GUTHE (3rd ed., 1914), KITTEL (5th and 6th ed., I, II, 1923–25), and SELLIN (1st ed., 1924), and more recently NOTH, *Geschichte Israels* (1950, Eng. tr., 2nd ed. revised, 1960), we must mention in particular: LUTHER, 'Die israelitischen Stämme', *ZAW*, xxi (1901), pp. 1 ff.; STEUERNAGEL, *Die Einwanderung der Israelitischen Stämme in Kanaan* (1901); PROCKSCH, *Das nordhebräische Sagenbuch* (1906), pp. 330 ff.; ED. MEYER, *Die Israeliten und ihre Nachbarstämme* (1906); BÖHL, *Kanaanäer und Hebräer* (1911); WEINHEIMER, *Hebräer und Israeliten* (1912); SELLIN, *Gilgal* (1917); BURNEY, *Israel's Settlement in Canaan* (1918); WEILL, *L'installation des Israelites en Palestine* (1924); ROWLEY, *From Joseph to Joshua* (1950); SCHMIDTKE, *Die Einwanderung Israels in Kanaan* (1933).

hypothetical elements: and this is, in fact, what has been done in the more recent accounts. But what is gained by this? The more complete the picture becomes, the less reliable it is: each account proposes a different way of filling in the gaps, so that the results are very dissimilar. As long as research continues to embrace only the history of the tribes and the people of Israel, and is based only on the relevant traditions in the Old Testament, it is extremely doubtful whether the major uncertainties can ever be removed.

In these circumstances it is doubtful whether any further light can be shed on the Israelites' settlement in Palestine, except by putting the question differently, thereby bringing to bear on it information hitherto unused. I think it is both possible and necessary to extend the materials of investigation in this way. It is obvious that in a country where men have dwelt for a long time, settlement by invading tribes will not only have a powerful effect on the way of life of both the former inhabitants and the newcomers, but will also have a substantial effect on the country itself. Now the circumstances of people's lives are easily liable to change: this would be the first effect of the settlement, and when they had been thrown into confusion they would only gradually be brought back to stability. This is why it is necessary to examine very carefully the other much more constant factor, which forms a background that it is difficult to alter. Besides examining the history of the tribes and people, the approach hitherto preferred, it is possible to investigate the history of a country's territorial divisions in complete independence of other aspects of the problem; and this we must do if we are to gain a clear understanding of the settlement, the conditions preceding it, and its effects, from this new point of view. There have been attempts in the past to study the matter in this way, but it is an approach that can bring its proper contribution to our understanding of the history only if it is carried out in full and along its own lines.

In studying the history of the country's territorial divisions, we must employ what seems to be remote and unrelated material from sources hitherto unused. Throughout history territorial divisions, ultimately dependent on the lie of the land, are extremely persistent; even changes of population hardly ever overthrow them completely, but bring about at most, minor alterations.[2] In studying their development, then, it is always best to cover as long a period as possible at once, in order to distinguish the constant features and the gradual variations in the territorial divisions of the area in question, by looking outside any period where the source material is deficient. In the case of the Israelite settlement in Palestine this means that we must examine the history of territorial divisions in the country for a considerable time before and after the entry itself. Only when we have ascertained the state of the territorial divisions that were developed and established before the Israelites appeared, and worked back from the forms they took in the period that followed, in order to find out what remained of the old divisions and what was altered, can we make a true estimate of the effect of the settlement on the political geography of the country. But it no longer matters very much whether the tradition provides us with direct evidence of the details of the settlement; even if there were no evidence at all, it would be possible by comparing the territorial divisions before and after the settlement to say for certain what happened in the obscure period between. We have only to rely on the direct statements of the tradition for exact dates and for the precise details of what took place.

Fortunately we have sufficient material for the study of territorial divisions over this long period, and in almost every case it takes the form of official records. These can almost always be used without the reservations as to their historical worth that have to be made with documents of other kinds. From the period before the entry we have many original Egyptian and cuneiform documents which give us an adequate, if incomplete account of the political geography of

[2] Compare the admittedly one-sided account of what happened at the settlement of German tribes on the territory of the Roman Empire by Dopsch, *Wirtschaftliche und soziale Grundlagen der europäischen Kulturentwicklung*, 2nd ed., I (1923), pp. 94 ff.

Palestine. Unfortunately little has been done to apply them to this purpose; I shall have to examine them more closely in the first section of this essay. The situation after the settlement is shown by a small but very instructive group of records in the Old Testament, which give a clear picture of the extent and the administrative divisions of the two Israelite states in Palestine, the kingdom of Israel and the kingdom of Judah, and frequently lead to reliable conclusions about the earlier situation as well. I can deal with this more briefly in the second section, since I have already dealt at length with part of the material elsewhere.[3] These two pictures will be built up from completely different sources. They must be all the more carefully compared and checked against each other in the third section, which will be devoted to assessing what they tell us of the effect of the settlement of the Israelites on the political geography of Palestine. At the same time, there will be an opportunity of estimating, by comparison with these sources, the value of the tradition of the Old Testament about particular events, and of fitting the events into the final picture of the whole. I do not intend to present more than a preliminary sketch, and in particular, no attempt will be made to discuss the Israelite settlement in the areas east of Jordan, since we have hardly any sources for the history of territorial divisions there comparable to those available to us for the land west of Jordan.[4] But even about the area west of Jordan, many questions that one would like to ask cannot be discussed. For to my mind the time for an exhaustive investigation of every detail can come only when the topographical and archaeological study of Palestine, which has just entered a new stage, has succeeded in providing independent evidence to fill the gaps left by

[3] 'Israels Gaue unter Salomo', *BWAT*, xiii (1913), pp. 1 ff.; *K.S.*, II, pp. 76 ff.; 'Judas Gaue unter Josia', *PJB*, xxi (1925), pp. 100 ff.; *K.S.*, II, pp. 276 ff.

[4] For the country east of Jordan cf. the recent works by Noth, *ZDPV*, lvii (1935), pp. 230 ff.; *PJB*, xxxiv (1938), pp. 23 ff.; xxxvi (1940), pp. 5 ff.; xxxvii (1941), pp. 50 ff.; *ZAW*, N.F. xvii (1942), pp. 161 ff.; xix (1944), pp. 11 ff.; *BBLAK*, lxviii (1949), pp. 1 ff.

various forms of literary tradition. For that reason I touch on questions of topography only when they are of particular importance for determining the exact way in which territorial divisions developed; and even then, where necessary, I simply refer to the existing literature.

I. THE TERRITORIAL DIVISIONS OF PALESTINE BEFORE THE ISRAELITE SETTLEMENT

1. *The Beginnings*

Although there is some even earlier evidence concerning Palestine,[5] the first period where the faint outlines of the political and territorial organization can be made out is the beginning of the second millennium B.C. It is true that the records of the situation in the country at that time were made not by actual inhabitants[6] but by foreigners, the Egyptians of the so-called Middle Kingdom (*c.* 2000–1800 B.C.). But a notable fact in their constant dealings with Asia is that whenever they mention their neighbour, either in inscriptions or in the story of Sinuhe, one of their great literary works, they regularly speak of a monarchical state, to which they give the designation *Rṯnw,* used later in a much wider sense, and which must be in Palestine.

I tried some time ago to show that the later Lod-Lydda (nowadays Lidd), a town on the southern coastal plain of Palestine, was the chief city of the district of *Rṯnw,* and gave it its name, and I have nothing important to add to this view.[7] But in any case, two things are certain; the kingdom

[5] Dealt with in detail by ALBRIGHT, *JPOS,* ii (1922), pp. 110 ff.

[6] The Phoenician seaport of Byblos (*jebel*) whose own princes perpetuated their names in hieroglyphics, I therefore leave out of consideration. Its previous development, which was the result of a very long-established trading connection by sea with Egypt, is too out of the ordinary for us to draw any conclusions from it about conditions in other parts of Palestine.

[7] *ZDPV,* xlvii (1924), pp. 169 ff.; there all the documents from

of *Rṯnw* was not a tiny city-state, such as we find by the dozen in later times in Palestine; nor, on the other hand, did it include all Palestine. Apart from the only moderately trustworthy statements in the story of Sinuhe about grants of land by the princes of *Rṯnw* to the Egyptian heroes,[8] this first conclusion follows from the fact, otherwise almost inexplicable, that in records from the Middle Kingdom *Rṯnw* often appears as the only political representative of Palestine. The restriction of the territory of *Rṯnw*, however, to a part of the country only is shown by a contemporary Egyptian inscription which besides *Rṯnw* mentions other place-names in Palestine, namely the stele on the tomb of *Ḥwjj-Śbk*, an officer of Sesostris III (*c.* 1860 B.C.). According to its unfortunately very brief statements the decisive event in a campaign in Palestine in which he took part was a battle against the 'district of *Śkmm*' and also against 'wretched *Rṯnw*'.[9] This must presumably be understood to mean that the 'district[10] of *Śkmm*', probably the later Sichem (*tell balāṭa*) in the heart of the Samaritan mountains,[11] was a political entity in itself, adjacent to *Rṯnw*, but independent of it.

If we could generalize from what seems to be the case

---

the Middle Kingdom are given. Further details in *PJB*, xxxvii (1941), pp. 25 ff.

[8] Sinuhe B 79 ff.=R 107 ff.; translation in ERMAN, *Die Literatur der Ägypter* (1923), pp. 45 ff., PRITCHARD, *Ancient Near Eastern Texts* (1955), pp. 18–22; cf. *PJB*, xxxvii (1941), pp. 47 ff.

[9] GARSTANG, *El Arábah* (1901), Pl. IV f.; PEET, *The Stela of Sebek-Khu* (1914), Pl. I f., ll. 2 ff.; SETHE, *Ägyptische Lesestücke* (1924), pp. 82 f.; trans. also in BREASTED, *Ancient Records of Egypt*, I (1906), p. 304, para. 680.

[10] Unfortunately the meaning of the word used here is not quite certain. It can mean 'district', 'province', 'town', or 'estate'; cf. GRIFFITH, *Hieratic Papyri from Kahun and Gurob* (1898), pp. 31, 43; VOGELSANG, *Kommentar zu den Klagen des Bauern* (1913), p. 51. But the connection here with *Rṯnw*, a term obviously referring to a whole territory, makes the term 'district' more natural.

[11] This identification is supported by the fact that—taking for granted the identity of *Rṯnw* with Lydda—the battle in which besides *Śkmm*, *Rṯnw* was involved, apparently took place on the return of the Egyptian army from *Śkmm*, that is to the south of it (cf. PEET, *The Stela of Sebek-Khu*, p. 8).

here we should say that at the beginning of the second millennium B.C. Palestine was organized politically into a number of independent territories each centred on a particular town. But we cannot yet decide whether the country was more or less completely settled by that period, and organized throughout into states. When archaeologists have further explored the first stages of town life in Palestine, they may be able to throw more light on the matter; but what has been discovered up to now does not justify any general conclusions. But even if by 2000 B.C. Palestine had a considerable number of towns it is unlikely, from what we have said, that the later system of small independent city-states had already begun.[12]

2. *The effect of the rule of the Hyksos*

After the end of the Middle Kingdom there are no further Egyptian records concerning Palestine for two hundred years. Since no other nation has left written remains to fill in the gaps in our information, this period (roughly 1800–1580 B.C.) looks as if it might remain completely unknown. But in spite of this it cannot be completely passed over, for it is just at this time that those political changes must have taken place in Palestine which affected the later territorial divisions of the country. This being the case, it is essential to deal here with problems involved.

At this period a new power appears on the scene in the shape of the so-called Hyksos, who are clearly recognizable in Egypt and were certainly no less active in Palestine and Syria. For however uncertain the origins of these great conquerors may be, one thing is certain, that their political development originated not in Arabia, as stated in an ancient

[12] Egyptian execration texts discovered since the above was written show the existence of a great many small principalities in Palestine at the beginning of the second millennium B.C., and do make it improbable that there were at that time any larger kingdoms than *Rṯnw*.

opinion quoted by Josephus,[13] but either in Syria or even farther north. For only from there could the Hyksos have introduced the hitherto unknown instrument of war which gave them military and therefore political supremacy, namely horses and chariots. And this is also the only explanation of the presence amongst the names of the Hyksos Pharaohs of Egypt, alongside Egyptian and Semitic names, of some which cannot possibly be either Egyptian or Semitic in derivation.[14] Therefore—and this is important for the present discussion—they must have ruled in Syria and Palestine before they moved against Egypt. If I judge rightly, the story of Sinuhe gives some evidence for their advance upon Palestine at the time of the Egyptian Middle Kingdom.[15]

But even after the conquest of Egypt, which probably did not take place till about 1700 B.C., they seem to have continued to hold sway over Palestine and Syria. This is suggested by the site of their Egyptian capital Avaris (*H·t-w'r·t*) in the eastern part of the Nile delta.[16] Like the later capitals of the Ramessid Pharaohs in the same area[17] it must have been chosen because it was the best place from which to rule Egypt, Palestine and Syria at the same time. But this conclusion seems to follow above all from what the Hyksos did when they were driven out of Egypt. They withdrew first into Palestine and then into Syria, where Kades on the

[13] *Contra Apionem*, I, 14, §82 (NIESE).

[14] Cf. BURCHARDT, *ÄZ*, l (1912), pp. 6 ff.

[15] Sinuhe B 97 ff.; cf. *ÄZ*, lviii (1923), pp. 49 f.; *PJB*, xxxvii (1941), pp. 46 f.

[16] The identification of Avaris with the later Tanis, which has become customary recently (summary in KEES, *Nachrichten der Akad. der Wiss.*, Göttingen, phil.-hist. Kl. [1944], pp. 145 ff.) does not appear to me to be conclusively established; but there is no doubt that it was situated in the eastern Delta.

[17] The prevailing identification of the residence in the Delta of Ramases II and his successors with Tanis (also in KEES, loc. cit.) can hardly include the whole of the establishments they set up. Cf. ALT, *OLZ*, xxviii (1925), cols. 576 ff.; *PJB*, xxxii (1936), p. 27, n. 1; xxxv (1939), p. 50, n. 1; GARDINER, *Ancient Egyptian Onomastica*, II (1947), pp. 171* ff., 278* f.

Orontes (*tell nebi mend*) for long remained their capital,[18] and this plainly shows that they were trying to retain the Asiatic part of their empire when the African part had been lost. Till then they really were 'rulers of the lands' as is shown by their title *ḥḳ3·w-ḫ3ś·wt*, the original form of the word Hyksos.[19]

If Palestine, therefore, was perhaps for two hundred years under the rule of the Hyksos, the question arises whether this had any effect on the territorial divisions of the country. Since there is no direct evidence, it is not easy to answer. The Hyksos could easily have done what the Pharaohs of the New Kingdom were to do after them; they could have restricted themselves to forcing the already established rulers of the country to recognize them as overlords. Such a system of dependencies need have made no difference to the extent of the territories governed by the former princes as vassals of the Hyksos. But that we cannot simply presume that they continued to rule the same areas is shown by the change that took place at this period in the meaning of the name *Rṯnw*. For in Egyptian records of the next few centuries it is a very vague geographical term which can quite easily be extended to cover all Palestine and Syria, and is no longer, as before, the name of a political unity with precise frontiers;[20] while the domain of Lydda, which is considered to be the chief city, giving its name to the whole kingdom, is in future of very limited extent.[21] When the Egyptians in the next period mention the holders of political authority they certainly speak of the 'nobles of *Rṯnw*' (*wr·w nw Rṯnw*), but this has nothing to do with a kingdom of that name; it refers to the great number of petty princes of

[18] SETHE, *ÄZ*, lxvii (1910), pp. 73 ff.

[19] There is some reason, therefore, for the reappearance of this title in the time of the Diadochi, cf. SETHE, op. cit., p. 84, n. 1, and LEFEBVRE, *Le Tombeau de Petosiris*, I (1924), pp. 10 ff., who looks for an explanation in the rule of the Persians over Egypt; and cf. also *ZAW*, N.F. iv (1927), pp. 230 f.

[20] *ZDPV*, xlvii (1924), pp. 169 ff.; GARDINER, *Ancient Egyptian Onomastica*, I (1947), pp. 142* ff.

[21] See below, p. 191.

city-states in the country. This political system does not give the impression of having been created by the Egyptians, so presumably we must see it as a product of the Hyksos domination, unless it be of even earlier origin.[22]

That the rule of the Hyksos should so have disturbed the former political and territorial system of Palestine is not surprising. The characteristic feature of the rise of the Hyksos was, as we saw, the introduction of the horse and chariot. But men who fight from chariots are usually professional soldiers of aristocratic rank. In order to devote their lives to military tasks, they must have a privileged social and economic position. In an economy with little or no money it is normal for rulers who wish to rely on the services of such an equestrian class to invest the appropriate persons with the tenure of large holdings of land, thus ensuring their economic stability, raising them socially and binding them personally to their lords. And at the same time, if this system is extended over the whole area that has been conquered, those who so receive land can strengthen the ruler's authority over the subject population, from whom they are separated by their origin and their personal loyalty to their feudal lord. The hereditary tenure of land need not be intended from the beginning, but the inheritance of military qualities and social claims usually leads to its introduction sooner or later. We must postulate such a feudal system for the period of the Hyksos;[23] and this explains the most peculiar feature of the next period, the existence of a ruling class composed of a mixture of Semitic, Horite and Indo-germanic elements still owing its strength to chariots, and in every fortified town maintaining its rule over a population of serfs. It consisted simply of the military aristocracy set up by the kings of the Hyksos, who, remaining in the country after the decline of

[22] See ALT's previous note, p. 181, n. 12 (Translator).

[23] From the Egyptian part of their dominions, *Ttj* son of *Ppj*, mentioned in the Carnarvon Tablet I, l. 23, as holding the town Nfrwśï in Upper Egypt, seems to be one of these feudal tenants. Cf. GARDINER, *JEA*, iii (1916), pp. 105 f.

their empire, ruled in their own right until the Pharaohs forced them into subjection.[24]

3. *Territorial formations under the domination of the Pharaohs*

It is only when the Egyptians of the New Kingdom, from 1580 B.C. on, reversing the advance of the Hyksos on to the Nile, moved against Palestine and Syria, that their records begin once more to mention these areas, from now on subject to the Pharaohs. During the first hundred years of Egyptian rule, from the conquest of King Amosis up to the incursions of Thutmose III into Asia, their statements are vague and infrequent.[25] But at this point we are given a clear insight into the territorial divisions of the country in the military annals of Thutmose III,[26] and for Palestine in particular in the list of rebel cities which he forced to recognize him as

[24] There is direct proof of the international composition of this aristocracy in the names of the hereditary princes in the cuneiform archives of Amenophis IV. How far these princes are descended from native ruling families, which retained their positions under the Hyksos, cannot be decided.

[25] Collected, and a historical interpretation given by BREASTED, *A New Chapter in the Life of Thutmose III* (1900), pp. 26 ff.

[26] SETHE, *Urkunden des ägyptischen Alterums,* IV (1907), pp. 645 ff.; a full translation in BREASTED, *Ancient Records of Egypt,* II (1906), pp. 175 ff., para. 407 ff. (On the literary construction and value as a source see NOTH, *ZDPV,* lxvi [1943], pp. 1556 ff.; GRAPOW, 'Studien zu den Annalen Thutmosis des Dritten' (*Abh. Akad. der Wiss. Berlin,* phil.-hist. Kl. 1947, no. 2 [1949]). On the course of the first campaign, which is the only one that is relevant here (translation by RANKE in GRESSMANN, *Altorientalische Texte zum Alten Testament,* 2nd ed. [1926], pp. 82 ff.; ALT, *PJB* x [1914], pp. 53 ff.; NELSON, *The Battle of Megiddo* [Diss. Chicago, 1913]; FAULKNER, *JEA,* xxviii [1942], pp. 2 ff.). A further description of the first campaign on a stele of Thutmose III from *gebel barkal* in the Sudan has been published by REISNER, *ÄZ,* lxix (1933), pp. 31 ff.; cf. with this YEIVIN, *JPOS,* xiv (1934), pp. 194 ff.; ALT, *PJB,* xxxii (1936), pp. 10 ff.; NOTH and GRAPOW, loc. cit.

overlord during his first campaign in 1479 B.C.;[27] and less than a century later the cuneiform archives of Amenophis IV from *tell el-'amārna* provide a still richer collection of documents.[28] It is unfortunate for our study of the changes in territorial divisions that detached and trustworthy records such as these are almost entirely lacking for the next two centuries of Egyptian rule in Palestine up to the time of Rameses III.[29] Were they available, the events of the Israelite settlement would be a great deal clearer. But in spite of this grievous lack, we may still attempt to give a complete picture of the political and territorial evolution of the country under Egyptian rule; for the lack of direct records of the second half of the period may be made up in part by deductions from the material of the first half.

[27] SETHE, *Urkunden,* IV, pp. 779 ff.; cf. W. M. MÜLLER, *MVAG,* xii, 1 (1907); SIMONS, *Handbook for the Study of Egyptian Topographical Lists relating to Western Asia* (1937), pp. 27 ff., 109 ff.; NOTH, *ZDPV,* lxi (1938), pp. 26 ff.

[28] A considerable number of these letters come in fact from the time of Amenophis III (from about 1400 B.C. on); cf. RIEDEL, *Untersuchungen zu den Tell-el-Amarna Briefen* (Diss. Tübingen, 1920); STURM, *Klio,* xxvi (1932), pp. 1 ff.; ALBRIGHT, *JEA,* xxiii (1937), pp. 190 ff. I cite these letters by *'Am.'* if they appear in KNUDTZON's edition (1907 ff.) and by *'AO'* if they are amongst those in the Louvre published by THUREAU-DANGIN, *RAss,* xix (1922), pp. 91 ff.

[29] Among the recently discovered accounts of campaigns of Pharaohs later than Thutmose III, the following are very important for Palestine: an account of a campaign under Thutmose III's son and successor Amenophis II in the ninth year of his reign (BADAWI, *ASAE,* xlii [1943], pp. 1 ff.; cf. ALT, *FuF,* xxvi [1950] pp. 85 ff.), and an account of a campaign of Setho I in the first year of his reign (ROWE, *The Topography and History of Beth-Shan* [1930], pp. 26 ff.). Cf. for the latter ALT, *PJB,* xxii (1926), pp. 108 ff. Of the place-lists of later Pharaohs of the New Kingdom those of Setho I are the principal ones relevant to Palestine (W. M. MÜLLER, *Egyptological Researches,* I [1906], pp. 43 ff., Pl. 57 ff.; SIMONS, *Handbook,* pp. 52 ff., 137 ff.; cf. NOTH, *ZDPV,* lx [1937], pp. 210 ff.) The parts of Papyrus Anastasi I (GARDINER, *Egyptian Hieratic Texts,* I [1911]; translated also in ERMAN, *Die Literatur der Ägypter,* pp. 288 ff.) which refer to Palestine have only a limited value for our present purpose, owing to the peculiar literary form of this satire.

Such a procedure is justified by our knowledge of the way the Egyptians generally exercised their rule in Palestine and Syria. The Pharaohs had no intention of making fundamental alterations in the existing political organization and territorial divisions; and where changes appear they are usually brought about not by the Egyptians but by their adversaries. Just as the Egyptian conquest of the country was a direct consequence of their struggle against the Hyksos, so the newly-established domination of the Pharaohs simply removed that of the Hyksos kings; and just as the Hyksos up till now had had vassals in every fortified city, so the Egyptians considered that their authority in the country was assured when this Hyksos aristocracy had sworn allegiance to the Pharaohs. Even a general defection of the hereditary vassal princes, such as Thutmose III had to contend with in 1479 B.C., after he had become sole ruler, made no fundamental difference to the political system. After the rebellious vassals had been defeated at Megiddo and agreed to submit once again to Egyptian domination, the victors did not hesitate to restore them to their inherited privileges.[30] Nor in the letters from the archives of Amenophis IV do we notice any attempt to remedy the state of complete disorder in the province by a thoroughgoing reorganization of the system of government; nor is there any trace of this being eventually carried out under the more powerful Pharaohs of the following centuries. The Pharaohs, therefore, not only continued the old territorial and political system, but in fact were the first really to bring it into its own. The Egyptians lacked the technical ability, if not the power, to develop any different system. Despite every disillusioning experience, they persisted in relying on the doubtful loyalty of the hereditary princes in the conquered areas, and left to them the detailed exercise of the authority that ultimately belonged to Pharaoh himself. We do hear of Egyptian government commissioners, who exercised some kind of control in the province, and of small forces of occupying troops in individual cities,[31] but this did not mean that

[30] SETHE, *Urkunden*, IV, pp. 662 ff.

[31] The best evidence for this is in the archives of Amenophis IV,

there was a rigid system of administration such as the Assyrians erected later.[32] Right through this period the local princes of Palestine were in dependence directly upon the Pharaohs, as is made plain by their dispatches and correspondence with the court.[33]

From all this it is clear that we cannot expect any fundamental changes in the political geography of Palestine under the Pharaohs, so far as government measures are concerned. There is not even any evidence for the division of the land into administrative districts of Egyptian origin. All the more reliable, therefore, is the testimony of the contemporary documents to the native political and territorial system, which can be traced back in part to the rule of the Hyksos, and to even earlier periods, but for the rest must be attributed to new movements distinct from the Egyptian Empire. It is exceedingly fortunate that the Egyptians have left us some account of this system, although they themselves played an extremely passive role in its formation.

A. *City States*

No feature is more obvious in the political scheme in Palestine under the rule of the Pharaohs, than the division of the country into a large number of districts each centred on a city, and possessing its own hereditary prince.[34] Everywhere

---

where the Egyptian commissioners bear the title *rābiṣu* and the occupying troops are called *amēlūti maṣarti.*

[32] A better comparison would be the form taken by the Ptolemies' rule in Palestine a thousand years later: see Rostovzeff, *A Large Estate in Egypt* (1922), p. 26, n. 36.

[33] Apart from the archives of Amenophis IV, the most convincing proof of this is an account-book from the court of Thutmose III, which gives a list of payments in kind from envoys from the princes of numerous city-states in Palestine (*Les Papyrus hiératiques de l'Ermitage à St. Pétersbourg* [1913], Pap. 1116 A Rs.; cf. *ZDPV*, xxxix [1916], pp. 264f.). For a later period, cf. the daily records of a frontier official in Papyrus Anastasi III Rs. and for a comment on it *PJB*, xxxii (1936), pp. 26 ff.

[34] Nevertheless there seem to have been places in which several noble families shared the ruling power. Cities like this appear for example in the account of the campaign of Amenophis II mentioned above, n. 29.

in the texts we hear of these petty princes. It is they who are referred to when Egyptian inscriptions of the New Kingdom speak of the 'nobles of *Rṯnw*', or, to take a particular example, of the 'nobles of *Mkt* (Megiddo)',[35] in the archives of Amenophis IV. 'Regents (*ḫazānūti*)' is apparently the general term for them, while they themselves, in their letters to their overlord, call themselves simply 'man of the city N (*amēlu ali N*)' and normally refrain from the more exalted title 'king (*šarru*)' which was usual amongst themselves.[36] The constant appearance they make in the documents of the time shows how important a part they must have played within the framework of Egyptian policy. The Pharaohs exercised their authority in the country entirely through them, and only with them did they deal directly. The city-princes were personally responsible for everything the subject populace had to pay as tribute in kind or compulsory service,[37] and if, as in the case of an Egyptian campaign against Syria, military service was required, the demand could be made only to the hereditary princes for their small contingents of warriors and chariots.[38] That they sometimes, in letters to the Pharaoh, refer to the inheritance of their office and titles from their father and grandfather,[39] and at other times lay great emphasis on their personal appointment by Pharaoh,[40] gives a true picture of their actual position: they could not exercise the powers inherited by their family if the Pharaoh had not expressly authorized them to do so; but Pharaoh in his turn appointed no one to the post who was not qualified by his descent from the ruling family of the city in question.[41] All this shows that the city-state system in Palestine

[35] E.g. SETHE, *Urkunden*, IV, pp. 662, 8; 663, 15; 664, 4.
[36] It does, however, appear sometimes, e.g. *Am.* 148, 40 f.
[37] *Am.* 294, 18 ff.; *AO* 7018; cf. *PJB*, xx (1924), pp. 34 ff.
[38] *Am.* 141 f.; 195; 201–6.
[39] E.g. *Am.* 253, 11 ff.
[40] So in particular Abdi-Chipa of Jerusalem, *Am.* 285 ff. The expression *wē(ḫ)u*, which is his favourite one for expressing the nature of his dependence on Pharaoh, is the Egyptian technical term for a vassal-soldier (*wʿw*).
[41] This latter principle is expressly emphasized in the annals of Thutmose III: SETHE, *Urkunden*, IV, pp. 690, 2 ff.

under the Pharaohs of the New Kingdom was the direct continuation of the feudalism of the Hyksos period: the descendants of the aristocratic professional soldiers, to whom the kings of the Hyksos had formerly granted the country's fortified towns, were now maintained in their position of authority by the Pharaohs.[42]

The full development of this political system in Palestine naturally resulted in the splitting-up of territorial units to an extraordinary degree. The size of the territorial divisions, where a considerable stretch of country was entirely under the control of city-states, is shown clearly enough, for some parts of the country at least, by the city-list of Thutmose III from the year 1479.[43] This is the case in particular for the coastal plain of Palestine from Carmel to the northern edge of the area of the towns later held by the Philistines.[44] Only a relatively narrow strip of land was fit for cultivation and capable of supporting a dense settlement and an independent

[42] There is presumably no need to point out that a city-state in Palestine of this kind is something essentially different from a fully developed Greek *polis*—cf. MAX WEBER, *Gesammelte Aufsätze zur Religionssoziologie,* III (1921), pp. 16 ff.

[43] According to NOTH's detailed investigation (*ZDPV*, lxi [1938], pp. 26 ff.) this list, like those of later Pharaohs, is based probably on excerpts from the official daily records of the war (cf. NOTH, *ZDPV*, lxvi [1943], pp. 159 ff.; GRAPOW, 'Studien,' pp. 45 ff.) and accordingly gives the names of places visited or conquered by Thutmose III or divisions of his army on the first campaign, and not, as is said in the later headings of two versions of the list, the seats of the princes who finally submitted to him after the siege of Megiddo. Gardiner's objections to this view (*Egyptian Hieratic Texts,* I, pp. 139 f.) are certainly worthy of attention, but not decisive. That a place mentioned in the list of Thutmose III was the seat of a feudal lord or some other kind of ruler can only be proved if other evidence is available, which in the nature of the situation is only possible in a few cases (in particular with the help of the Amarna letters). But even without such proof, one may presume that at least the majority of the places given in the list were the seat of some ruler.

[44] These did not take part in the general rebellion against Egypt that forced Thutmose III to intervene, and could not therefore be included in the catalogue of places recently brought into subjection.

political life. For from the sea coast, hills of calcareous marine sandstone rise towards the east, often as far as 10 km. or more inland. In ancient times, and in part even until quite recently, they were wooded, and so were only fit for grazing.[45] On the east side the coastal plain is bounded by the foothills of the limestone mountains of Western Palestine, which were likewise partly wooded and acted as a defence from the powers in the hinterland. So the only areas left fit for agriculture were the clay lands of the valleys between the calcareous sandstone hills of the west and the limestone mountains of the east; these 'magnificent corn-lands in the plain of Sharon', as a later Phoenician inscription calls them,[46] are widest in the south in the 'plains of Ono'[47] between Jaffa and Lydda, but shrink in the north to a few kilometres in width.[48] It is easy to understand, therefore, why the list of Thutmose III can mention several city-states alongside each other in the southernmost valley (*wādi muṣrāra*), but in the north, usually only a single city:[49]

No. 62: *Jp*, Am. *Japu* (*jāfa*)—11 km. from Ono.
No. 64: *Rṯn*, Lydda (*lidd*)—8 km. from Ono.
No. 65: *in̊*, Ono (*kufr 'āna*)—11 km. from Aphek.
No. 66: *ipḳn*, Aphek (*tell rās el-'ēn*)[50]—22 km. from Socho.
No. 67: *Śk*, Socho (*rās esh-shuwēke*)[51]—4 km. from *Jḥm*.
No. 68: *Jḥm* (*jemma*).[52]

[45] Cf. DALMAN, *PJB*, x (1914), p. 33; xviii–xix (1923), p. 16; *Orte und Wege Jesu* (3rd ed., 1924), pp. 236 f.
[46] *Corpus Inscriptionum Semiticarum*, i, 3, 19 (Eshmunazur).
[47] Neh. vi. 2.
[48] Cf. RANGE, *Die Küstenebene Palästinas* (1922) with a general geological map.
[49] SETHE, *Urkunden*, IV, pp. 783 f.; cf. W. M. MÜLLER, *MVAG*, xii (1907), I, pp. 21 ff.; ALT, *BWAT*, xiii (1913), p. 5, n. 4; NOTH, *ZDPV*, lxi (1938), pp. 46 ff. where places directly preceding and following in the list, by which the line is continued to the south and north, are also identified.
[50] *PJB*, xxi (1925), pp. 51 ff.; xxviii (1932), pp. 19 f.
[51] 1 Kings iv. 10; cf. *BWAT*, xiii (1913), pp. 4 ff.; *PJB*, xxv (1930), p. 33.
[52] This identification should be preferred to that previously sug-

It will be seen that the distance between one city and another in the south is never much more than 10 km., the territory of each independent state extending only about 5 km. around the fortified city. Farther north the distances are sometimes greater. This may have something to do with the smaller amount of arable land there; but it may be that the names of one or two of the towns that ought to appear in this series occur for some reason in a different part of the list where we do not know the true facts. The city-states might be even more closely grouped together in the coastal plain than in the part of the list we have given. But even if no link is missing from the chain this much is clear: the possessions of an average city-state consisted of nothing more than the fields belonging to the city and the few villages round about it.[53]

If we extract from the list of Thutmose III the towns in the plain of Megiddo, we find exactly the same state of affairs. They almost all lie on the south-western edge of the plain, with a line of wooded hills between them and the coast; how far towards the north-east their domains reached, there is unfortunately no way of knowing.[54] I shall list the towns in their geographical order.

---

gested by me, *tell elasāwir,* 13 km. farther north (*PJB,* x [1914], pp. 75 ff.). It is strongly supported by the account of the campaign of Amenophis II mentioned above. Cf. *PJB,* xxv (1930), p. 34; xxviii (1932), p. 34; NOTH, *ZDPV,* lxi (1938), pp. 46, 285 ff.; lxvi (1943), p. 162 with n. 3.

[53] *Jp* (*jāfa*) is the only one of these places where it can be shown to be likely that it was the seat of a hereditary prince at least at the time of Thutmose III; cf. *ZDPV,* lxvii (1944), pp. 10 f.; *K.S.,* I, pp. 223 ff. In particular, the Amarna tablets lack any information; but it is noticeable that for several places in the neighbourhood of Socho and *Jḥm* the account of the campaign of Amenophis II speaks of 'nobles'—in the plural, hence apparently sharing power.

[54] At the time of Amenophis III the land ruled by Megiddo seems to have stretched right to the foot-hills of southern Galilee, according to the Amarna letter *AO* 7098; but this could have been a secondary increase of territory, perhaps only temporary; cf. *PJB,* xx (1924), p. 38.

No. 113: *ʿnḳnʿm,* Jokneam (*tell ḳēmūn*)–11 km. from Megiddo.[55]

No. 2: *Mkt,* Megiddo (*tell el-mutesellim*)–8 km. from Taanach.

No. 42: *Tʿnk,* Taanach (*tell taʿannek*)–11 km. from Jibleam.

No. 43: *Jbrʿm,* Jibleam (*chirbet belʿame*)–14 km. from Shunem.

No. 38: *Šnm,* Shunem (*tell sōlem*)[56]–14 km. from Megiddo.

The possibility of omissions must be taken into account in this case also: but on the whole the list gives the same picture as we saw in the southern coastal plain: the country is parcelled out into the smallest possible political units. One might doubt whether every one of the 117 tiny states in Thutmose III's list was politically autonomous;[57] but a discovery like that of the double list of ambassadors from the towns of Palestine in an account-book from the court of Thutmose III, shows that in fact the princes of the very smallest states maintained their own diplomatic relations with Pharaoh,[58] and it must be admitted that this fragmentation of political units is to be expected from the kind of aristocracy who ruled these city-states.

But it is questionable whether we can generalize from these conclusions and suppose that the mountainous regions of Palestine were broken up into such small units as were the

[55] Between these two places we should probably include No. 114: *Ḳbʿ* (the later Gaba, which is perhaps *el-ḳire;* cf. *ZDPV,* lxii [1939], pp. 3 f.) and No. 116: *Dft* (perhaps *tell abu shūshe;* cf. *PJB,* xxvii [1931], pp. 38 f.).

[56] *PJB,* xxi (1925), p. 40.

[57] Doubts about this were expressed by W. M. Müller, *MVAG,* xii (1907), I, p. 37 (cf. above, n. 43).

[58] *Les Papyrus hiératiques de l'Ermitage Impérial à St. Petersbourg* (1913, Nos. 1115, 1116 A *et* 1116 B); Pap. 1116 A Verso. Of the list above, Megiddo and Taanach are mentioned in this catalogue. For Albright's view that Taanach for the most part belonged to Megiddo (*BASOR,* xciv [1944], p. 27) there is no convincing proof.

plains. The mountains are much less well provided with good arable land than the plains: and this makes it likely that the settlement of the mountains, and the development of an advanced culture there, had not at this stage reached the same level, and that in particular there was not yet the same multiplication of true fortified cities. The distribution of the main trade routes must be noticed in this connection–wherever possible they run through the plains, and only cross the mountains when they have to.[59] This also would give the plains a particular attraction, and might cause the aristocratic families to settle closer together in the plains than in the mountains, thus developing the system of city-states to an even greater degree. Besides this, the mountain terrain gave much less scope for the favourite military technique of the time, chariot warfare. And finally, their overlords, the Hyksos kings and the Pharaohs, would surely have found it desirable that each stage along the main highways should be held by one of their vassals. There is much to be said in theory, therefore, for the view that the tiny city-states were not found in the same proportions in every part of Palestine.

A closer examination of the Egyptian town-lists and the archives of Amenophis IV seems to confirm this view. There is not a single district in the hills of Palestine, either in Galilee, or in Samaria and Judah, let alone in the country east of the Jordan, for which these lists provide any certain evidence of a group of city-states so close together as those we described in the plains. But before any conclusion can be drawn from this discovery, it must be decided whether it can really prove anything at all. For it cannot be disputed that a great many, on my estimation about half, of the Palestinian towns in the lists simply cannot be identified. In many cases it is not even possible to ascertain the approximate positions, for as a rule the town-lists make no attempt to arrange the names in their geographical order[60] and the letters in the archives of

[59] Cf. DALMAN, *PJB*, xii (1916), pp. 15 ff.

[60] The list of towns on the coastal plain south of Carmel (above p. 191) is an exception to the rule (but cf. NOTH, *ZDPB*, lxi [1938], pp. 46 ff.).

Amenophis IV usually give only the name of the place in Palestine where the sender ruled, with no indication of where it lay in relation to other cities. It seems impossible, therefore, to find out which of the unidentified city-states were in the plains and which in the mountains.

Another fact is even more important. There is no reason to suppose that our sources, the list of Thutmose III and the archives of Amenophis IV, include all the city-states of their time in Palestine. The list of Thutmose III, as is expressly stated in its heading, mentions only those cities which had to re-acknowledge Pharaoh as their overlord after the battle of Megiddo in 1479 B.C., which means only those which had placed themselves under the leadership of the king of Kadesh in central Syria, in an attempt to escape from dependence on Egypt.[61] So for example a most conspicuous omission is that of the towns of the southern coastal plain which later belonged to the Philistines. These came without doubt into direct contact with the forces of Thutmose III;[62] for according to Pharaoh's annals the southernmost part of the area in revolt was *Jrḏ* (Am. *Jurṣa*), which plainly lay north of these cities[63] and it is *Jrḏ* again which appears in the list of Thutmose III as the most southerly of the group of city-states on the coastal plain.[64] This list hardly mentions a single city that can be located with certainty in the mountains of Judah and Samaria.[65] The conclusion we must draw is

[61] But cf. above p. 189, n. 41.

[62] This is expressly stated of Gaza in Pharaoh's annals: SETHE, *Urkunden*, IV, pp. 648, 8 ff.

[63] SETHE, *Urkunden*, IV, pp. 648, 2 ff.; cf. SETHE, *ÄZ*, xlvii (1910), pp. 74 ff. (on the site, *PJB*, xxix [1933], p. 13).

[64] This is sufficient to disprove the old proposal to identify the city that occurs as No. 80 on the list, *Krr*, with the biblical Gerar south of Gaza (still made by BURCHARDT, *Die altkanaan. Fremdworte und Eigennamen im Ägyptischen*, II [1910], p. 52, No. 1012); cf. W. M. MÜLLER, *MVAG*, xii (1907), I, pp. 24, 34.

[65] Rightly emphasized, but wrongly interpreted by MÜLLER, op. cit., pp. 33 ff. Even cities like Shechem and Jerusalem, which play a part in the archives of Amenophis IV, do not occur in the list of Thutmose III; nor, for example, do any of the numerous places known to us from the Samaria ostraka.

that in general the mountain regions took no part in the great struggle against Thutmose III. In any case we cannot suppose that the many places that remain unidentified perhaps lay all or even for the most part in the mountains south of the plain of Megiddo; they must be sought rather in the same parts of Palestine as the cities whose locality is already known, that is in the plains, and in the northern hills east and west of the Jordan.

It seems all the more likely that not every part of Palestine was involved in the struggle against Thutmose III, in that the archives of Amenophis IV, barely a hundred years later, likewise show the rulers in different parts of the country ranged politically on opposite sides. This apparently plenteous source of evidence, however, provides no uniform picture of the state of affairs in individual districts. From the very nature of such a collection of letters we would not expect it to be complete in the way that a straightforward catalogue, like the list of Thutmose III, might at least attempt to be. Besides this, in many of the letters, the city of origin if mentioned, cannot be identified. Of the cities we dealt with above, for example, hardly any of those in the southern coastal plain are mentioned, and none of those in the plain of Megiddo;[66] and the same is true for several other areas. But there is another reason for the gaps in the archives: at the time of Amenophis III and IV large areas of Palestine were in open revolt against Egypt, and although the cities and princes of these areas were often spoken of in the letters, certainly no communications from them ever reached Pharaoh's court. The centre of the revolt was no longer the plains, as in the time of Thutmose III, but, with a few limited exceptions, in the mountains, especially those of Judah and Samaria. But the effect of this on the texts is practically the same: the mountain regions are not mentioned in the list of Thutmose III, because they were not involved, or at least

[66] It is difficult to believe that the cities named in this list of Thutmose III, but not appearing in the archives of Amenophis IV, were every one destroyed or deprived of their political rights, even though this happened in some individual cases.

only indirectly, in the political and military events of the time; they are not included in the archives of Amenophis IV, because as a result of the rebellion they had broken off their relations with Egypt.[67] And there are no later Egyptian documents to fill the gaps; for the next two centuries of Egyptian rule in Palestine have left nothing that corresponds to the archives of Amenophis IV,[68] and only feeble imitations of the list of Thutmose III, which alter our picture of Palestine as little as the rest of the texts.[69]

But the fact that the mountains of Palestine took a different political attitude to the plain at the two periods of Egyptian rule best known to us, remains to be explained. Was it perhaps their distance from the great military roads which made possible both their isolation from the wars under Thutmose III,[70] and also their open revolt against Egypt in the time of Amenophis III and IV? Was the cause of the different policies followed there perhaps the personality of individuals amongst their rulers? Or is everything ultimately due to a distinct political and territorial structure? These questions must be fully answered before a complete picture of the period can be constructed.

B. *Larger territorial formations*

At present, only the archives of Amenophis IV throw any light on the political organization of the mountains of Palestine under the rule of the Pharaohs. It can hardly be doubted that small city-states of the type we met in the plains were

[67] Apart from the few vassal princes in the mountains who remained faithful (e.g. Abdi-Chipa in Jerusalem, *Am.* 285 ff.) the other exceptions are the undependable elements that went on sending subservient letters to Egypt, while they pursued an anti-Egyptian policy (e.g. the prince of Hazor, *Am.* 227 f.; 148, 41 ff.).

[68] The extensive archives of the Hittite Empire from Boghazkeui are of no use here, for they simply take for granted the political allegiance of Palestine to Egypt and hence do not refer to the situation there.

[69] See above, n. 29.

[70] Whether before the time of Thutmose III the mountains as a whole had come under effective Egyptian rule is an open question.

not altogether absent. Jerusalem especially, in the letters of its princes[71] and in other sources,[72] gives just the impression of such a tiny state. It appears that Bethlehem, 8 km. to the south, was 'a town of the country of Jerusalem',[73] but this does not imply any greater extent of territory than that of other city-states, and as far as I can see, nothing else suggests that the power of the prince of Jerusalem extended any further.[74] The continual complaints in his letters show rather how hard-pressed and isolated his domain was. Only towards the west are the territories of the cities of the Shephelah, especially Keilah (*Kelti*, now *tell ḳīla*, 29 km. from Jerusalem),[75] Zarah (*Ṣarḫa*, now *ṣar'a*, 24 km. from Jerusalem),[76] Aijalon (*Aialuna*, now *jālō*, 22 km. from Jerusalem),[77] near enough to be accessible; and Jerusalem sometimes received military help from them.[78] But up in the mountains it appears to have stood completely alone, surrounded by hostile powers, which far exceeded the size of a city-state. We must now turn to these.

Since these powers rejected the suzerainty of Egypt, they are mentioned generally only indirectly in the archives of Amenophis IV, in the reports of others, and so are not presented as clearly as we could wish. The nature of the political organization of the mountains south of Jerusalem cannot be deduced with certainty. There is much to be said for the view that the 'cities of the land of *Gari*' which appear in

[71] *Am.* 285–90.

[72] *AO* 7096.

[73] *Am.* 290, 15 ff., according to the reading of the ideographically written place-name suggested by SCHROEDER, *OLZ*, xviii (1915), cols. 294 f.

[74] We have a definite indication of the boundary to the north-west, if Bauer's thesis can be upheld, that the ideograph *UR-MAḪ-MEŠ* gives the name of an independent city, to be identified with Chephirah (Jos. ix. 17, etc.), now *chirbet kefīre*, 14 km. from Jerusalem, *ZDMG*, lxxiv (1920), pp. 210 f.; *Am.* 273 f.

[75] *Am.* 278–84 *et passim;* cf. *PJB*, xxi (1925), pp. 21 f.

[76] *Am.* 273, 21.

[77] *Am.* 273, 20; 287, 57; cf. ALBRIGHT, *BASOR*, xv (1924), p. 10; *PJB*, xxii (1926), pp. 71 f.

[78] *AO* 7069; cf. *PJB*, xx (1924), pp. 27 ff.

one letter[79] are to be found in this area[80] that they should be summed up under this name would show that the whole area formed one territorial unit. But it is scarcely possible to prove this suggestion conclusively,[81] and the only certain thing is that the archives of Amenophis IV do not prove the existence of any city-state in the mountains south of Jerusalem.[82]

On the other hand, the existence of a political unity of considerable extent in the mountains north of Jerusalem is unmistakable. There reigned the notorious Labaya, who actually wrote most submissive letters to Egypt,[83] but in the letters of others appears as the worst enemy of Pharaoh's government in the whole country.[84] His sons tried to carry on the policy he had followed.[85] Shechem (*Šakmi*, now *tell balāṭa*) seems to have been the centre of his dominions,[86] and many of his expressions might be understood to mean that his rule was restricted to this city and its immediate neighbourhood.[87] But although he uses the language of a simple local prince and a faithful vassal, his deeds show that he had pretensions to a much wider authority. A whole series of places suffered under his attacks, and in part succumbed to him; the cities, however, that it was his policy to bring into subjection do not belong to the mountainous region in

[79] *Am.* 256, 22 ff.

[80] STEUERNAGEL, *Einwanderung*, p. 122; DHORME, *RB*, N.S. v (1908), p. 514; WEBER in the notes to KNUDTZON's edition of the letters, p. 1319; ALT, *JPOS*, xii (1932), pp. 126 ff.; NOTH, *JPOS*, xv (1935), pp. 42 ff.

[81] Another identification was proposed by CLAUSS, *ZDPV*, xxx (1907), pp. 20 f.: ALBRIGHT, *BASOR*, lxxxix (1943), pp. 7 ff. (*dschōlān*).

[82] ALBRIGHT latterly takes Hebron to be the seat of government of the prince Šuwardata of *Am.* 278–84 (*BASOR*, lxxxvii [1942], p. 37, n. 31).

[83] *Am.* 252–54.

[84] The references to him have been collected by WEBER in KNUDTZON, pp. 1312 ff.

[85] WEBER, ibid., pp. 1308 f.

[86] *Am.* 289, 23.

[87] *Am.* 252, 5 ff.; 253, 32 ff.

the neighbourhood of Shechem, but lie, as far as we can identify them, in the plains to the north and west of the mountains of Samaria: Megiddo,[88] Shunem,[89] perhaps also Beth-Shan,[90] and Gezer.[91] If we remember, in addition, that for the whole of the mountain country from Jerusalem to the plain of Jezreel there is no evidence in the archives of Amenophis IV of a single city-state, it becomes even more difficult to avoid the conclusion that the whole large area must have been under the control of Labaya: not until it reached the plains did his advance meet with resistance he could not completely break down.[92] We have brought to light a contrast here between the plains and the mountains which clearly goes back to a different political structure: in the first, groups of city-states close together, in the second, an extensive territory under a single ruler. And this contrast is so well established that at least in the period illustrated by the archives of Amenophis IV, neither side could overcome the other, as long as the Egyptian overlord made no effective intervention on the side he favoured—that of the city-states. In the light of these facts the isolation of Jerusalem is particularly noticeable: it seems to have been the only city-state in the mountains of Judah and Samaria which throughout a long period made no attempt to extend its power over a wide region.[93]

The conclusion that a deep-seated rift existed between the political structure in the plains and that of the mountains, might perhaps be avoided by supposing that Labaya's kingdom was only a temporary creation and that before and af-

[88] *Am.* 244, 21 f.

[89] *Am.* 250, 42 f.; cf. *PJB*, xx (1924), pp. 34 ff.

[90] *Am.* 289, 19 f. (uncertain).

[91] *Am.* 253, 18 ff.; 254, 20 ff.

[92] Perhaps the lack of any letters from the group of cities on the inland edge of the coastal plain given on p. 191 was also a result of Labaya's advance.

[93] Whether there were any other towns in the mountains that were first destroyed by Labaya, and how many there were, we cannot say; but his successes over so wide an area make it unlikely that he found so many centres of resistance as in the plains.

ter his time the mountains were divided up into city-states like the plains. But is this likely to be the case? We certainly have evidence from the time of Amenophis III and IV, that the kingdom of Labaya having reached its greatest extent during his lifetime, was reduced soon after. But of the two events during this withdrawal that are attested by the archives of Amenophis IV, the first at least,[94] and possibly also the second,[95] concerned cities in the plains, and not the main part of the kingdom in the mountains. It cannot be proved from the archives that this main part lost its political unity and broke up into city-states. For the period before Labaya we may refer to our former conclusion that even in the time of Thutmose III the mountains south of the plain of Megiddo went their own way politically. It does not necessarily follow from this that the territorial divisions at that time were exactly the same as a hundred years later; Labaya's war of expansion must certainly have caused some disturbance of the existing political order.[96] But probably the political organization of the mountains took its own distinct form even in the time of Thutmose III, and when Labaya set up a single state of considerable size he was making no fundamental change in the state of affairs that had long existed there. During the whole period of Egyptian suzerainty there is no suggestion that the system of city-states ever spread throughout the mountains.

The situation seems to have been the same in Galilee. The city of Hazor (*Ḥḏr*) appears in the time of Thutmose III, and was perhaps still a simple city-state.[97] But the archives

[94] Shunem: *AO* 7098; cf. *PJB*, xx (1924), pp. 34 ff.

[95] Gitipadalla (site unknown): *Am.* 250, 11 ff. Recently identified by ALBRIGHT with *yett* on the western edge of the Samaritan mountains: *BASOR*, civ (1946), pp. 25 f.

[96] Labaya's own references to the status as vassals of his father and grandfather (*Am.* 253, 11 ff.) only shows that previously the Pharaohs were accepted as overlords in the mountains as well.

[97] SETHE, *Urkunden*, IV, p. 782, No. 32; references from the subsequent periods in BURCHARDT, *Die altkanaan. Fremdworte*, II, p. 37, No. 709. GARSTANG has made a convincing identification of the place, which has recently been shown by Egyptian execration

of Amenophis IV show that the prince of *Ḫazura* had recently begun to make large increases in his possessions and was carrying out in his own district a similar territorial policy to that of Labaya in the south: he broke away from Egyptian rule[98] and deprived other princes of their lands.[99] But in this case our information is not sufficient to tell us the exact extent of the territory he ruled. Nevertheless it is noteworthy that in Galilee also there was an attempt to bring large areas together under one ruler.

Our sources for the mountains east of Jordan are even more deficient; for example, hardly a single place is mentioned from the country between the Yarmuk and the Arnon later held by the Israelites. It is unlikely that they presented a picture essentially different from that in the mountainous parts of eastern Palestine. But without more exact information, we cannot hope to reconstruct the territorial divisions there during the centuries of Egyptian rule. We cannot even say for certain how far east Pharaoh's power extended.

But however unfortunate the gaps in our knowledge may be, they make no difference to the results we have obtained for the country west of Jordan. The contrast between the development of the plains and the mountains remains clear; nor does it appear that it decreased to any notable extent during the two centuries between the time of Amenophis IV and the end of Egyptian suzerainty in Palestine. The general features of the Egyptian method of government do not lead us to expect this, and as for the Pharaohs of the New Kingdom, they would have been very well pleased with any way of regaining and securing their possessions without too much expenditure of force. This was really possible only among the city-states of the plains, long accustomed to vassalage. This fact is confirmed by the only contemporary record known up

---

texts to have been a seat of government as early as the beginning of the second millennium B.C., with *tell waḳḳāṣ* (*tell el-ḳadaḥ*) south-west of Lake *ḥule* (*The Foundations of Bible History* [1931], pp. 381 ff.).

98 *Am.* 148, 41 ff.

99 *AO* 7094; cf. *PJB*, xx (1924), pp. 30 ff.

to now of the Egyptians' struggles for the possession of Palestine during these centuries—the record of an episode of the first campaign of Sethos I, which was found on a stele of this king in the American excavations at Beth-Shan.[100] This refers exclusively to the city-states of the Jordan depression: in a battle between *Btš3r* (Beth-shan, *tell el-ḥöṣn* near *bēsān*) and *Rḥb* (*tell eṣ-ṣārim* near *shēch riḥāb,* 4 km. south of *tell el-ḥöṣn*)[101] on one side, and *Ḥmt* (probably *tell el-ḥamme,* 9 km. south of *tell eṣ-ṣārim*)[102] and *Pḥr* (Pella, *ṭabḳat faḥl,* 7 km. east of *tell eṣ-ṣārim*)[103] on the other, Pharaoh intervened with part of his troops and imposed recognition of himself as overlord.[104] This document clearly reflects exactly the same territorial pattern as in the time of Thutmose III. We should not be surprised if von Calice is right in supposing that in the name of the spring Me-Nephtoah (*'ēn lifta*) near Jerusalem the name of Pharaoh Menephtah (*Mrj-n-Ptḥ*) is preserved.[105] Jerusalem appears in the archives of Amenophis IV as the only city-state in the southern mountains which remained a faithful vassal of Pharaoh, and it may have continued this policy afterwards, so that an Egyptian garrison remained there to perpetuate the name of its general.

Naturally the way in which territory was held may have changed in many details. But even if here and there a new city-state arose, or one came to an end, and if the extent of the larger states grew greater or less according to the circumstances, the fundamental difference between the plains and the mountains seems to have remained unaltered. Local ir-

[100] Cf. above, n. 29 and ALT, *K.S.*, I, pp. 251 ff.

[101] Other references in BURCHARDT, *Die altkanaan. Fremdworte,* II, p. 33, No. 628; for the identification of the site, ABEL, *RB,* N.S. 10 (1913), pp. 218 ff.

[102] BURCHARDT, op. cit., II, p. 35, No. 678.

[103] Cf. *PJB,* xx (1924), p. 32; xxii (1926), pp. 115 f.

[104] The description of the political situation before the first campaign of Setho I in LEPSIUS, *Denkmäler,* III, 128a is unfortunately not fully provided with geographical references; but cf. ED. MEYER, *Aegyptiaca for G. Ebers* (1897), pp. 75 f.

[105] *OLZ,* vi (1903), col. 224; cf. Jos. xv. 9; xviii. 15.

ruptions of one system into the area where the other was in force are only exceptions which clearly prove the rule. When we look back over our conclusions about the state of affairs before the Hyksos we can see that the essential point in the history of territorial divisions in Palestine from that time up to the end of Egyptian suzerainty is that the situation in the plains underwent a profound change, whereas that in the mountains in general continued unaffected. In the one, progress, in the other, reaction—so one might briefly sum up the whole process, at least if one can really describe the fragmentation of the plains into a multitude of city-states as progress, and the persistence in the mountains of large areas brought together under unified rule as reaction. In any case the different pace of political development in various parts of the country can be ascribed entirely to their different natural features.

What has been learnt so far about the history of settlement in Palestine fits the above picture. In and around the plains there are dozens of *tulūl,* the characteristically-shaped rubbish-heaps preserving the remains of walled settlements of an urban type. Many of them, on the evidence of their pottery, go back to the Middle Bronze Age, that is, to the first half of the second millennium B.C. In the mountains the *tulūl* are much rarer, and the oldest remains probably come mostly from the late Bronze Age and the early Iron Age, the second half of the second millennium. The actual settlement of the land seems to have lagged behind here, and this naturally retarded the political development as well. Perhaps large parts of the mountain ridges had not yet been cleared of their original trees and ploughed. However, I shall go no further in the question of the history of settlement here; its full answer must remain the task of the future archaeologists of the country.[106]

[106] Cf. ALT, 'Erwägungen über der Landnahme der Israeliten in Palästina', *PJB* xxxv (1939), pp. 8 f., pp. 28 f.; *K.S.*, I, pp. 126 f., pp. 144 f.

II. THE TERRITORIAL DIVISIONS OF PALESTINE AFTER THE ISRAELITE SETTLEMENT

A few generations after the end of Egyptian rule the political map of Palestine is completely changed: there were hardly more than half a dozen separate states in the country, including the area east of Jordan, which comes into the light of history for the first time. Only a complete shift of political power can explain this reversal of the situation. In this, the collapse of Egypt as a world power after Rameses III (shortly after 1200 B.C.) certainly played an important part.[107] Those states in Palestine which hitherto had remained on the side of the Pharaohs and used their authority to their own advantage, must have felt severely the loss of this support. But the withdrawal of the greatest foreign power to its own homeland is clearly not enough to explain the rise of new forms of political life and new territorial units. When native politics were left to develop in their own way, their obvious course was to preserve the state of affairs that had grown up in the country over many centuries: 'they persisted in dwelling in the land' is the comment of the very important first chapter of Judges on the inhabitants of many of the cities during the intervening period; and this expresses very exactly the prevailing tendency in their policy. The impetus towards a general re-ordering of the political organization of Palestine cannot therefore have come from them. This is confirmed by the fact that the new states were all named after tribes and peoples who had played no part in the earlier history of the country, and indeed had only just settled there—Philistines, Israelites, Judeans, Edomites, Moabites, Ammonites, Arameans. And the naming of states after their people also betrays a national consciousness which the earlier political for-

[107] The collapse of the Hittite Empire at approximately the same time could only indirectly affect the change in the political organization of Palestine.

mations, and the city-states in particular, never had and because of their structure could not have.

There is a very close connection between the national element in the make-up of the new states in Palestine, and the extent of their territory: they extend at least as far as men have settled who belong to the same people or tribe. This feature gives them a certain similarity to the larger territorial formations we noticed in the mountains as early as the period of Egyptian rule, and places them in apparently inexplicable contrast to the city-states of the plains. But the odd thing is that the new states were by no means restricted to the mountains, but also brought under their rule the areas where previously the system of city-states had prevailed. It will be worth while first to take a closer look at the final stage of the transformation, the swallowing-up of the city-principalities by the new larger states, since this clearly implies a most fundamental change in the territorial situation.

The encounter with the city-state system understandably took different forms and led to different results, according to whether a new community was built up from the beginning on land that belonged to the old city-states, or whether it advanced on to their domains at a later stage. The typical example of the first case is that of the Philistines in the coastal plains. The Old Testament shows them acting as a unit so often even in the centuries after their entry in the twelfth century, that we must accept as certain that they had a common political organization, even though its form cannot be exactly described. But another fact is just as certain, that the Philistine territory was divided at every period into city-states: Gaza, Ashkelon, Ashdod, Ekron, Gath.[108] Here, therefore, the change is limited to the superimposing on the

[108] Our sources show the existence of city-states—Gaza and Ashkelon at least—long before the entry of the Philistines (but see ALT, 'Ägyptische Tempel in Palästina', *ZDPV*, lxvii [1944], pp. 1 ff.; *K.S.*, I, pp. 216 ff.). We need not take into account here Philistine cities which we only meet occasionally as cities that were seats of government such as Gerar (Gen. xxvi. 1 ff.) and Ziklag (1 Sam. xxvii. 6).

city-state system of a higher form of political unit, covering a much wider area; and the later history of that part of the country, especially in Hellenistic times, shows that the essential features of the city-states were in fact retained with great tenacity throughout the process.

Unfortunately we do not know the course which the development took among the tribes who according to Egyptian records entered the country at the same time as the Philistines. We only know that one of these tribes, the *Ṯkr*, possessed the city of Dor (*el-burdsh* near *eṭ-ṭanṭūra*) on the coast south of Carmel, about 1100 B.C., and was under the rule of a prince.[109] Here also the old type of state persisted among the new inhabitants.[110] So we may presume the same to be true of all the members of this group, particularly as they apparently all settled in the plains, where the city-state system had been established for many years.[111] They presumably subjected the original aristocracy to their rule; but they made no alterations in the existing system, rather giving it a new lease of life. This is why the Old Testament never gives the names of these tribes. When the Israelites advanced against a district occupied by one of these tribes, they encountered only the individual city-states and had only to mention the names of the cities among which the country of the foreign tribe had been broken up.[112] It can be seen that it was where the division into city-states had been most fully developed under Egyptian rule that it was maintained most effectively afterwards and even imposed itself upon the new inhabitants.[113]

The kingdoms in the interior west of Jordan, i.e. Israel and

[109] The Journey of Wen-Amon, I, 8 ff., tr. in PRITCHARD, *Ancient Near Eastern Texts* (1955), pp. 25–29.

[110] There is as yet no earlier evidence for a city-state at Dor (cf. *BBLAK*, lxviii [1950], pp. 103 f.).

[111] Conjectures about the areas settled by individual tribes in ALBRIGHT, *BASOR*, xi (1923), pp. 8 f.

[112] Cf. especially 1 Kings iv. 10 f.

[113] I leave aside the insufficiently known history of the political organization of the Phoenician coast, particularly as the study of it would take us far beyond the northern border of Palestine.

Judah,[114] dealt quite differently with the city-states. This they could do because the nucleus of their kingdoms lay away from where the city-states were to be found, and because their advance into the lands previously ruled from the cities was not their actual entry, and did not take place at the same time, as in the case of the Philistines and related tribes. It was a secondary development of their power, occurring some time after the consolidation of a state in the area which they had settled. This explains why their encounter with the city-states did not result in the continuation of the old form of political life under a new aristocracy, but in their absorption, and thus in the virtual destruction of independent political activity on the part of the cities.[115] The cities only retained anything of their own distinct existence as small administrative units within the structure of a large kingdom: their role as independent states was ended. A new principle of political and territorial organization was here brought into effect with much greater thoroughness than by the Philistines, and it set aside at one blow a pattern that previous centuries had regarded as unalterable. The importance of this occurrence for the history of Palestine in general has not as yet been fully estimated.

The development in the case of the kingdom of Israel can be clearly seen from the records of the Old Testament. We possess on the one hand in a number of clear and precise verses in Judges i (with parallels in the Book of Joshua) a compilation showing the city-states which at the end of the time immediately preceding, or at the latest very shortly after, the rise of the kingdom of Israel under Saul (*c.* 1000

[114] I understand by Israel, here and in the following pages, the kingdom that for a time (under David and Solomon) was united under one person with the kingdom of Judah, but otherwise existed alongside it in complete independence; that is, the area from Dan in the north almost to Jerusalem in the south. Cf. *BWAT*, xiii (1913), pp. 18 f.; *PJB*, xxi (1925), pp. 100 ff.

[115] That the aristocracy of the cities they incorporated, accustomed to war and government, sought and could find new opportunities for the exercise of their talents within the framework of a larger kingdom, is a separate question that I shall not go into here.

B.C.) were claimed by the Israelites; but which had only partially been reduced to a condition of dependence, and were far from having been incorporated into Israelite territory.[116] The territorial ambitions displayed in this list are, by comparison with the later possessions of the kingdom of Israel, quite modest. In the north, admittedly, within or near the territory of the tribes of Manasseh, Zebulun, Asher and Naphtali, all the city-states that still existed are included, and a claim to them asserted.[117] But to the south of Carmel the whole coastal plain with the exception of Dor[118] remained untouched.[119] The author of these verses claims only the cities of the southern hill-country (Shephelah) from Aijalon[120] to Gezer[121] for the Israelite tribes.[122] With this we can compare the concise catalogue in 2 Sam. ii. 9 of the districts that were ready after Saul's death to acknowledge the continuation of his kingdom by his family, and can therefore be regarded with certainty as the hard core of the kingdom of Israel at the time it was taking shape. They are (*a*) Gilead, the area east of Jordan settled by Israelite elements; (*b*) Asher,[123] an Israelite tribe in Galilee; (*c*) Jezreel, which was only a city, but not an old city-state, although bounded by such on the east and west;[124] it was the centre

[116] For the literary analysis of Judges 1 cf. *PJB*, xxi (1925), p. 103 n. 4. That this catalogue presents the state of affairs under Saul at the latest is surely indisputable; but much in it would be even better explained if we may refer the document to an even earlier stage.

[117] Judges i. 27 f., 30, 31 f., 33.

[118] Judges i. 27.

[119] As far as we know, it lay at that time under Philistine domination: cf. the role of Aphek, 1 Sam. iv. 1 f., and the march of the Philistines to the north, 1 Sam. xxviii. 4–5, xxix. 1, 11. (But see ALT, *PJB*, xxxv [1939], p. 10, n. 3; *K.S.*, I, p. 128, n. 2.)

[120] Judges i. 35.

[121] Judges i. 29.

[122] Jerusalem (Judges i. 21) is not taken into account here, because it was not subsequently incorporated into the kingdom of Israel.

[123] According to the emended text.

[124] Judges i. 27.

of a district, and in fact presumably the capital of the Israelite tribe of Issachar;[125] (*d*) Ephraim, to be taken here in the wider sense, which besides the tribe of Ephraim includes Manasseh, and therefore the whole 'House of Joseph', once more an area long settled by the Israelites, and probably also Benjamin, Saul's own home, and likewise an Israelite tribe. This was at the time 'all Israel' as the conclusion of the list puts it. The statements of 2 Sam. ii. 9 and Judges i clearly supplement one another: so far as we can see the areas they describe nowhere overlap. The kingdom of Saul is simply the union of the Israelite tribes and their districts into one state, while the non-Israelite city-states remained outside or at least did not expect equal rights as part of the newly-founded kingdom.[126] A glance at the map will show that although the nature of the Israelite state provided a basis for national unity, it had not succeeded in rounding off the borders of its territory, and the strategical situation before Saul's last battle is a clear example of this. The Philistines had advanced right into the plain of Megiddo, and by setting up their camp at Shunem, they broke the link between the northern and southern tribes of Israel before a blow was struck.[127] If the kingdom of Israel was to guard permanently against this kind of crisis, it needed to renounce the stern ideal of national purity and concentrate on bringing about territorial unity, which could not be achieved on Saul's political principles.

As early as David's time, and in obvious connection with the completely different direction of his policies, which amount to the unification of the whole of Palestine under his rule, it is clear that this unavoidable change from a national to a territorial state of Israel was carried out. We possess no direct account of this; but when 2 Sam. xxiv. 7 summarily described the western limit of the kingdom as 'all the cities of the Hivites and Canaanites' this presupposes that the border in fact no longer lay where the districts previously settled by the Israelites came to an end, and that the adjacent city-states

[125] Jos. xix. 18.
[126] Cf. 2 Sam. iv. 2 f.; xxi. 2 ff.
[127] 1 Sam. xxviii. 4.

to the west, with their territory, had now been incorporated into the kingdom. It is most improbable that in the account of 2 Sam. xxiv matter might have been introduced at this point that expressed the conditions of a later period; for as we said, it was quite in accordance with the objects of David's policy to round off the shape of his territory by the inclusion in the kingdom of the city-states; and besides this, we possess from the time of Solomon, who was hardly likely to have exaggerated David's achievements, a most valuable document in 1 Kings v. 7–19a, which not only confirms our conclusions from 2 Sam. xxiv. 7 but also tells us the details of the extension of the territory. In the catalogue given there of the provincial officers 'over all Israel' and the areas under their authority, the districts settled by the Israelite tribes are once again clearly distinguishable, sometimes under the name of the tribe, sometimes called by the name of their chief towns or the seat of government.[128] But alongside them appear with the same duties and presumably with equal rights the domains of old city-states, mostly joined together in groups, and sometimes the very ones whose independence is stressed in Judges i, especially those in the southern Shephelah[129] and the line of cities from Dor on the sea as far as Beth-Shan in the Jordan depression in the north.[130] But there are some that are not dealt with at all in Judges i, and in particular the cities of the coastal plain south of Carmel.[131] The contrast of Judges i and 2 Sam. ii. 9 between the nation and the cities outside it has become a union within one state which is only given formal expression in the administrative division of the whole kingdom.[132] During the following period, as far as we know, the territory of the kingdom of Israel was never

[128] 1 Kings iv. 8, 13–19a.

[129] 1 Kings iv. 9; cf. Judges i. 35.

[130] 1 Kings iv. 11 f.; cf. Judges i. 27. Farther north the territorial plan given in 1 Kings iv is obviously less ambitious than the claims of Judges i, especially in the case of Asser (Judges i. 31).

[131] 1 Kings iv. 10.

[132] The details are more closely discussed in *BWAT*, xiii (1913), pp. 1 ff.: *PJB*, xxi (1925), pp. 100 ff., and by ALBRIGHT, *JPOS*, v (1925), pp. 25 ff.

extended beyond the limits it reached during the second stage of its development under David and Solomon. In the present context, therefore, this may be regarded as the last stage, notwithstanding the smaller or greater losses of territory the kingdom suffered during its later history. The incorporation of large parts of the old system of city-states is the most important event in the expansion of the Israelite state, founded originally on a much narrower basis. We can affirm here that this was also an internal revolution, from a state distinguished simply by nationality to a compact area within fixed territorial boundaries, and consequently without such a firm national unity. We cannot explore the further effects of this.

Before we turn to the question of the development of territorial divisions leading up to the original form of the kingdom of Israel before this second stage, we must take a look at the kingdom of Judah and its relationship to the city-state system. Unfortunately the sources do not provide such full information as in the case of Israel. Even Judges i provides hardly anything; its statement that the tribe of Judah took possession of only the mountains of southern Palestine and not the adjacent plain[133] is much too vague for our purpose, and does not even provide definite geographical information, because it is not quite clear to which the Shephelah, the hill-country between the mountains of Judah and the coastal plain, belonged. Moreover, it does not seem possible to distinguish between an earlier and a later stage in the establishment and expansion of the kingdom of Judah, as in the case of Israel. To all appearances the kingdom covered essentially the same area at the time of its foundation under David as afterwards, apart from much later enlargements and losses.[134] But that the kingdom of Judah incorporated into itself a number of city-states that had retained their inde-

[133] Judges i. 19.

[134] The essential features of these later changes, which have nothing more to do with the problem of the relationship of the Kingdoms to the city-states, are discussed in *PJB*, xxi (1925), pp. 107 ff.

pendence up to David's time, is indubitable. It was the cities of the hill-country just mentioned like Keilah and Lachish that met this fate.[135] One might certainly say that the increase in area of the state of Judah through this encroachment on the city-state system was in the long run not so important as that of the kingdom of Israel in the corresponding stage of the history of its territorial expansion. But for the whole process of change on the political map of Palestine it was very important that on its western border Judah should clear away such remnants of the former territorial pattern as had not already been removed by the Philistines. In the whole of the country west of Jordan there was no possibility from then on of the independent political existence of a single city-state. In the country east of Jordan, where in our study of the preceding period we found only the beginnings of the development of city-states, the same changes must have taken place.

We must return to the kingdoms of Israel and Judah. Only when we exclude the city-states as secondary elements incorporated into their territory later, do we come to the original nucleus, the land possessed by the Israelite tribes, whose union into a single political entity was the essential purpose of the formation of the state. The way in which the army was originally made up, for all that it was quickly outdated by the increasing use of mercenaries and chariot-mounted troops, makes it particularly clear how closely the new states were related to the old tribes: to summon the militia of the tribes to arms and lead them into the field to gain political ends was the first right and the first duty of the king. The reason the states of Israel are so called is that like the kingdoms of Edom and Moab, they bear the name of the tribe or group of tribes on whose military strength their existence depended. This very method of naming shows the immense contrast to the old city-states, where the possession of a single fortified city was the important factor even in the title of the prince.

[135] Cf. *PJB*, xxi (1925), p. 114.

But even though the power of the king of Israel and the king of Judah was based in the first place on their recognition by the tribes and their military support, the direct consequence of this is that for their part the kings had to respect the unity of the tribes and more especially their territorial rights. The tribes were older than the kingdoms: they had to be treated as having a right to exist in themselves, if the stability of the state was not to be imperilled by rash interference in the local affairs of the individual tribes it was composed of. So in the province-list of the kingdom of Israel in 1 Kings iv. 7 ff., each tribal district is designated as an administrative area in itself, regardless of whether it is as large a district as the 'House of Joseph' on Mount Ephraim[136] or as small as the neighbouring tribe of Benjamin.[137] Only in the colonized land east of Jordan could a different procedure be followed, and the division into provinces be made solely according to the lie of the land;[138] but even here, if I judge correctly, the old district of Gad is still set apart.[139] And in the same way I believe I have demonstrated elsewhere that for centuries after Judah was first divided into provinces those same small groups are kept distinct which previously enjoyed an independent political existence.[140] This conservatism is fully explained by the way in which both kingdoms came into being.

In these circumstances the provinces of Israel and Judah, so far as they are equivalent to the districts occupied by the tribes, are an important source for the territorial divisions before the formation of the state, and so ultimately for the course of the settlement itself. The results of the rapid development of the earlier period are as it were fossilized in them. I do not know, in fact, of a single case where any change was made in the territory of a tribe as such during the time of the kings. If the kings happened to alter the bounda-

[136] 1 Kings iv. 8.
[137] Ibid., iv. 18; cf. *BWAT*, xiii (1913), pp. 17 f.
[138] Ibid., v. 13 f.
[139] Ibid., v. 19a lxx; cf. *BWAT*, xiii (1913), p. 11.
[140] *PJB*, xxi (1925), pp. 113 ff.

ries of the provinces by annexation or for reasons of administrative convenience,[141] that was their affair, and no longer that of the tribes. On the whole, the changes in these boundaries do not seem to have been very great, nor is it surprising that the records of the division into provinces almost always take as their basis the same extent of the tribal districts as the other accounts of the tribal territories in the Old Testament, especially the descriptions of the boundaries in the Book of Joshua.[142]

Here we have found the key to what the territorial divisions of the time of the kings have to tell us about the settlement of the Israelites. Not that every acre of land that in this later period lay within the boundaries of the state and is presupposed or acknowledged to be the possession of one or other of the tribes, must actually have been claimed or settled previously by the tribe in question; for we have to take into account many increases in the area taken over or claimed. But the passages we examined in Judges i show that at least when the formation of the kingdoms was beginning, the territorial claims of the tribes were completely fixed, and that the sum of the districts settled and those that were claimed left no space unfilled. No one will deny the element of wishful thinking in the description of Judges; but even here the theory is based on reality and permits conclusions about earlier conditions.

We have now come to the end of our preparatory studies. Our task now is to understand the settlement of the Israelites as an event in the history of territorial divisions—an event which partly caused the alteration of the divisions of Palestine before their entry, into the new system under the kingdoms of Israel and Judah, and at least prepared the way for it.

[141] Cf. *PJB,* xxi (1925), pp. 112 ff.

[142] See for the differences and their causes, ibid., pp. 105 ff. Cf. also ALT, 'Das System der Stammesgrenzen im Buche Josua', *Sellin-Festschrift* (1927), pp. 13 ff.; *K.S.,* I, pp. 193 ff.

III. THE SETTLEMENT OF THE ISRAELITES IN PALESTINE

It has not yet been certainly decided which of the Israelite tribes already formed a unity when they entered Palestine, and which did not come into existence until after they had settled there, either by the union of formerly independent groups, or by the division of larger bodies. In discussing the history of the settlement in terms of territorial divisions, therefore, it is wise not to restrict ourselves to tracing the movement of the individual tribes that at a later stage, right up to the time of the formation of the states, come on the scene as units in themselves, for it is not really certain whether they were such at the time of their entry. Our investigation remains unaffected by these separate problems, if we make the basis of it the study of larger groups of tribes taken as a whole, i.e. those which were united either because they settled next to one another, or because they were united as son to mother by the relationship of their ancestors. One clear example of this sort of group is that formed by the sons of Rachel, Joseph (Ephraim and Machir or Manasseh) and Benjamin, who shared between them the whole of the area between the southern edge of the plain of Megiddo as far as just north of Jerusalem.[143] In the same way, to the south of Jerusalem, the tribe of Judah, with the tribes of Simeon, Caleb and Cain, etc., gradually being merged with it, must be seen as a unit on a higher level. The north provides the least opportunity of grouping the tribes together, for there the genealogical schema is only of partial use, and much of the history is obscure. We cannot deal with the country east of Jordan, because, as we said before, we have insufficient evidence for its territorial development in earlier times.[144]

How does the existence of three groups of tribes west of

[143] The area east of the Jordan, also colonized by them, does not come into consideration here.

[144] Cf., n. 4.

Jordan fit into the general history of territorial divisions in Palestine? Subsequent developments need not be further discussed, since we have shown in the previous section that the territories possessed by the tribes remained the same at the time when the kingdoms were being founded. But it becomes all the more necessary to ask whether this grouping together of the tribes was caused by the territorial formations of the previous period, or whether it came about, in complete independence of them, for reasons to be sought among the Israelite tribes themselves. No one can be in any doubt about the answer to be discovered in a comparison of Judges i and the related texts of the Old Testament with the other picture we drew, from non-Israelite sources, of the period of Egyptian rule. The resemblance is greater than one might suppose.

Let us look first at the gaps in the territorial possessions of the Israelite tribes, that is at the districts which lay like dividing walls between the different groups of tribes mentioned above. The principal one, in the north, is the line of city-states from Dor on the sea to Beth-Shan in the Jordan depression, which divides the territory of the Galilean tribes from that of the House of Joseph.[145] It is not new to us; we have come across almost every one of its members in the time of Thutmose III and later under Amenophis III and IV.[146] Admittedly Gen. xlix. 14 ff. and 2 Sam. ii. 9 show that there was one break in this rampart of cities that is not mentioned in Judges i: the tribe of Issachar had established itself very early in the region of the watershed between the plain of Megiddo and that of Beth-Shan, at Shunem and Jezreel. But a satisfactory explanation of this apparent disruption of the normal territorial pattern exists in non-Israelite records: the old city-state of Shunem[147] was destroyed in the time of Amenophis III by Labaya[148] and was not restored.[149] Issachar therefore occupied that part of the plain

[145] Judges i. 27; cf. 1 Kings iv. 12.

[146] Cf. p. 193.

[147] Reference in Sethe, *Urkunden,* IV, p. 782, No. 38.

[148] *Am.* 250, 41 ff.

[149] *AO* 7098; cf. *PJB,* xx (1924), pp. 34 ff.

where the system of city-states had already been broken into, and therefore is not an exception but merely confirms the rule. That Issachar was able to settle amongst the non-Israelite city-states only by renouncing her political independence, as is stated expressly in Gen. xlix. 15, and as Judges i confirms by its silence concerning the tribe, is the direct consequence of the nature of the locality.

In the same way the dividing line between the area settled by the Rachel tribes and the tribe of Judah with its associated groups, which is said in Judges i to consist of the city-states still remaining independent, from Gezer and Aijalon up to Jerusalem,[150] is known to us from a much earlier period in the archives of Amenophis IV.[151] We saw that here, under Egyptian rule, the system of city-states extended in the shape of a wedge from the coastal plain through the hill-country into the mountains and was continually fighting a desperate battle for existence against the differently organized powers round about. The conditions after the Israelite settlement show that this battle was eventually won by the city-states. Not until several centuries later did the expansion of the kingdoms of Israel and Judah rob them of their political independence.

Nevertheless the Old Testament tells of a large number of other cities in the mountains, which must have been conquered by the Israelite tribes, and which were apparently overcome at the very time of the settlement, or at least so soon afterwards that they could not be listed in the catalogue in Judges i of cities not yet conquered. This seems to be the case for the detailed accounts in the Book of Joshua, and for the short account in Judges, of successful battles against fortified cities. It can be taken for certain that these fortified cities were the most distant outposts of this political system in the mountains. Their isolated situation, far from the areas where the cities are found closely grouped together, explains why they could not maintain themselves, or at least

[150] Judges i. 21, 29, 35.
[151] See p. 196.

not for long, against Israelite pressure. To this extent one can say that the city-states system suffered territorial losses at the time of the Israelite occupation; but it affected only the outposts and scarcely touched the main body.

The previous political development of the areas of Israelite settlement west of the Jordan took place along different lines: we can recognize in them quite clearly the large territorial formations which were fighting for their independence from Egypt, perhaps under Thutmose III and certainly at the time of Amenophis III and IV, but quite separately from the city-states.[152] For instance, the territory settled by the Rachel tribes in the mountains of central Palestine is almost exactly the same as the furthest extent of Labaya's kingdom. We may recall that the Israelite tradition of the taking of this area lays great emphasis on the struggle for Shechem[153]—and it was Shechem which was the central point around which Labaya built up his kingdom. In Galilee the relation between the old and new states is also obvious. In the times of Amenophis III and IV we come across the prince of Hazor as the lord of an extensive kingdom.[154] Similarly in the Israelite tradition the destruction of Hazor clearly represents the decisive stage in the occupation of Galilee;[155] and it is indeed only natural, in a state of this sort, that its whole fate should be decided by the conquest of its capital.

For all the caution that the many gaps in our sources demand, we may thus sum up our account of the Israelite occupation of Palestine: basically, it was the occupation of those parts of the country which already formed large political units, and continued to do so afterwards, i.e. principally the mountains, which had been only slightly affected by the spread of the city-state system. These territories, as yet ill-organized politically, and probably still thinly populated, were least capable of resisting the advance of the Israelites, and offered them the best opportunity of settling down and

[152] See pp. 201 ff.
[153] Gen. xxxiv; Judges ix.
[154] See pp. 197 ff.
[155] Joshua xi; Judges iv.

gradually turning from their semi-nomadic way of life to an agricultural economy. In contrast to this, the city-state system established in the plains at first encountered the Israelite occupation only at its outlying points; and only a small part of it was destroyed immediately. Its final conquest was yet to come, when the Israelite states turned wholeheartedly to a policy of political expansion, at the beginning of the first millennium B.C.

Thus the history of territorial divisions in Palestine runs in an unbroken line from the pre-Israelite to the Israelite period. It is yet another example of the persistent survival of divisions based on the formation of the land. One might be tempted to make use of these conclusions to solve chronological problems. If the areas settled by the Israelite tribes correspond on the whole to the territories we found united as large states under Egyptian domination, then we might suppose that during the Egyptian period of the country's history it was perhaps the Israelites who ruled or at least shared political power in these areas. Are they perhaps to be equated—it has often been suggested, but never yet convincingly proved—with the *ḫabiru* who appear at the time of Amenophis III and IV as the strongest military support for the anti-Egyptian powers in the mountains of Palestine?[156] This question may be asked; but I must state expressly that the approach to the subject from the point of view of territorial divisions provides no sure way of answering it. On the contrary, it leads us to recognize the persistence of the same territorial relationships over hundreds of years, and from this point of view, whether the Israelite occupation was several generations earlier or later is a matter of indifference. But the often expressed view that if the occupation goes back as far as the period of Egyptian rule in Palestine some mention of their rule would appear in Israelite tradition is obviously unsound; for the areas settled by the Israelites in the mountains were apparently never so completely subjected to the Pharaohs as were the cities of the plains.

[156] Cf. ALT, 'Erwägungen', *PJB*, xxxv (1939), pp. 55 ff.; *K.S.*, I, pp. 168 ff.

On the other hand, from the study of the occupation in the light of the history of territorial divisions, a conclusion can be drawn about the history of Israel's cultural institutions. It was an advance when the necessity was recognized of relating the development of Israelite culture in the first centuries after the settlement to what excavations and other discoveries taught about the culture of city-states in Palestine during the second millennium. But now we see that the connection is not so close and must not be thought to have had an immediate and direct effect. The Israelites did not adopt the urban culture of Palestine as soon as they had occupied the country, but as it were dwelt at first before the city gates. This process in the history of their culture was completed, therefore, very slowly, and moreover something of the 'reactionary' tendency of the areas they settled must have long persisted in its effects. It is obvious that this was far from being a hindrance to the healthy development of the Israelite nation.

THE FORMATION OF THE ISRAELITE STATE IN PALESTINE

DIE STAATENBILDUNG DER ISRAELITEN IN PALÄSTINA
Reformationsprogramm der Universität Leipzig, 1930. The original version contained material which was later incorporated into Das Königtum in den Reichen Israel und Juda

At the same time as the last tribes of Israel were migrating from the southern wastelands into the mountain regions of Palestine, there also arrived a new element in the population of the plains: in the second half of the twelfth century B.C., warlike bands from the Aegean, including the Philistines, driven from their homeland by the revolutions of this period, forced their way to the south across Syria and finally established themselves in the lowlands of Palestine.[1] Although these incidents occurred simultaneously, however, there is no corresponding similarity in their effect, and one cannot fully understand the history of Palestine during the following centuries without first grasping the difference in the way of life and in the achievements of the two nations after they had settled in Palestine, and tracing it back to its more fundamental causes.

Among the Philistines and those who were associated with them in their migration, there still survived, basically unchanged, the political system which had existed in the plains of Palestine at least as early as the first half of the second millennium B.C. and which later came to full maturity under the domination of the Pharaohs: the system of dividing the country into a large number of small principalities each centred on a fortified town, and usually under the rule of a feudal lord. The new rulers entered into this long-established tradition, a step they took all the more readily since their own past history had not left them with any notably better principles of political organization. And for this reason also, it is

[1] For a detailed description of the probable course of their settlement and the form of government they adopted, see ALT, 'Ägyptische Tempel in Palästina', *ZDPV*, lxvii (1944), pp. 12 ff.; *K.S.*, I, pp. 225 ff.; 'Syrien and Palästina im Onomastikon des Amenope', *Schweiz. Theol. Umschau*, xx (1950), pp. 64 ff.; *K.S.*, I, pp. 238 ff.

not surprising that their government was very soon set up in its final form. The important factor is the replacement of the old ruling class by the new. The only change which the old system underwent as regards territorial boundaries was presumably when some feudal seat or other was destroyed, and its domain added to that of a neighbouring town; the individual administrative areas seem on average to have grown larger than the minute states of the previous period, and in some cases to have had new fortified capitals.[2] Thus the organizing principle which formed the basis of the whole system was hardly disturbed and we are justified in seeing in the little states of the Philistines and the other Aegean peoples in the plains of Palestine the heirs and successors to the early Canaanite system of city-states.[3]

The historical evidence does not, however, fit entirely into this simple formula. A distinctive form of political organization manifested itself, which was peculiar to the Philistines—and for that reason its influence was all the stronger, particularly in the generations which immediately followed their settlement in Palestine—and which cannot be easily attributed to their legacy from the Canaanites. In spite of their divisions, and the number of their city-states, they are regularly presented as working together whenever it furthered their political aims. As far as we can see, there was no example of this in the earlier history of the country. We have no indication of anything more than temporary alliances, in order to achieve a single political goal by combined military action, amongst

[2] Unfortunately there is no adequate material from an earlier period with which to compare the five Philistine cities of Gaza, Ashkelon, Ashod, Ekron, and Gath (cf. ALT, *ZDPV*, lxvii (1944), pp. 9 f.; *K.S.*, I, pp. 222 ff.; *Schweiz. Theol. Umschau*, xx (1950), pp. 64 ff.; *K.S.*, I, pp. 238 ff.). On the other hand, in the plains to the north (Sharon, Acco) great differences can be seen between records from the Egyptian period and the relevant Israelite documents (Judges i. 27 ff.; 1 Kings iv. 7 ff.) in regard to political centres; cf. *PFB*, xxiv (1928), pp. 53 ff.; xxv (1929), pp. 38 ff.

[3] Even during the rapid development of the Hellenistic state on the coast of Palestine the effects of this ancient system can still be seen.

the feudal lords in the pre-Philistine period.[4] However, since these prolonged alliances of forces across the frontiers of the individual states were not inherited from the previous inhabitants of Palestine, we must seek their historical root elsewhere, namely in the military constitution of the Philistines themselves. During their wars of migration, the collective nature of their every undertaking had been of vital importance, and even when they annexed Palestine they were to owe a great deal of their success to their strong cohesive unity. Naturally the other Aegean tribes had entered into the alliance during the nomadic period, or had individually founded similar organizations; after their occupation of Palestine, however, they seem to have rapidly fallen victim to the disunity effected by the system of tiny city-states which they adopted, so that in the Israelite tradition they are never again called by their tribal names and the only reference is to their cities. The Philistines, on the other hand, were able to preserve their combined organization for some time, and because of it were in a position to develop a political and military strength with a wide influence beyond the immediate area of their settlements. This would inevitably lead them to a position of political domination in Palestine, where the old Egyptian régime was now practically without influence. To this extent, they can actually be described as being the successors to the Pharaohs; even though their power was always confined to a far smaller area than had been that of the Egyptians previously, it was as a result much more effective. This brings us to consider a development which must have begun shortly after the annexation by the Philistines: a change seemed to take place apparently overnight from an Egyptian to a Philistine Palestine, whose development would be distinct and immune from foreign intrusion.

However, before we pursue further the question of the use the Philistines actually made of the possibility of creating an empire of the first rank, which was offered to them partly

[4] A general levy during the Pharaohs' campaigns such as we hear of occasionally in the Amarna letters (cf. especially *Am.* 201–6, KNUDTZON), was of course a quite different matter.

through their own native tradition, and partly by the situation which awaited them in their new home, we must first attempt to paint a similar picture of contemporary conditions among that section of the population in Palestine which was later to perform the historic function of disrupting the unity of the Philistines, namely the Israelites in the mountainous hinterland of the plains on which the Aegean peoples settled. There we find in almost every respect the exact opposite of what we have learned so far. For a start, the outward details of the immigration of the Israelites into Palestine were completely different; this was no single movement completed in a relatively short time, as it appears, I admit, in the later literary works of the Israelite tradition, particularly in the Book of Joshua. It was in fact a series of movements by single tribes and bands which may well have lasted for several centuries; and in the majority of cases they did not proceed by force of arms, so that although the accounts of individual military victories over older towns may well be correct, they insinuated themselves into thinly populated or even totally unpopulated districts where there was no chance of serious opposition. The result of this was that the tribes were not all established in one single compact territory, but were split up into several groups, whose lands were separated from one another by chains of non-Israelite townships.[5] The intermittent nature of the invasion, and the incomplete occupation which resulted from it, corresponded to the conditions under which the whole process was carried out, for the Israelites, who had been accustomed to a nomadic life under desert conditions, had none of the military superiority which had made possible the Aegean peoples' much swifter and more decisive victories over the existing population. Even in the later Israelite tradition, there are traces of the terror which was originally felt in the face of the Canaanite war chariots and city fortifications,[6] and it seems to be an exception rather

[5] Cf. ALT, 'Die Landnahme der Israeliten in Palästina' (1925); *K.S.*, I, pp. 89 ff.; 'Erwägungen über die Landnahme der Israeliten in Palästina', *PJB*, xxxv (1939), pp. 8 ff.; *K.S.*, I, pp. 126 ff.

[6] Compare with this the saga of the spies Num., xiii f.

than the rule to be able to tell, here and there, in the history of those early times, of the conquest of a township, either by cunning or by force.[7] There was from the start, therefore, for the Israelites, no question of attacking the well-populated and highly developed colonies of the plains of Palestine, with their numerous feudal states; in order to gain any foothold there, they were obliged to bow to the rule of foreign masters.[8] The occupation by the Israelites was limited to the mountain hinterland; only there could the tribes still find the vast, sparsely populated regions protected by few towns, which they needed for settling. Already the difference between them and the Aegeans was as great as it could be; these, as we saw, moved immediately into the older civilized regions, and took possession of its riches; on the other hand, the Israelite settlement in Palestine was really in undeveloped territory which was at first necessarily isolated from civilization. That this latter situation promised greater possibilities for the future is undeniable, a fact which will be proved by the further course of Israelite history. Immediately after the occupation it held the Israelites apart from the native Canaanite system, giving them time to develop their own civilization more vigorously in its new homeland, whereas the Aegean culture very quickly degenerated into that of the occupied country.[9] Naturally, the development of the Israelites proceeded more slowly because of this; they were unable after many generations to make up the earlier lead of

[7] It is of course still an open question whether each individual event (Jericho, Josh. vi; Ai, Josh. viii; Hazor, Josh. xi; Bethel, Judges i. 22 ff., etc.) were really as closely connected with the Israelite invasion as they are made to appear by the fusing and generalizing technique of the compilers of the sagas, who can only see the conquest of the country as the result of a battle fought from town to town.

[8] A historical example of the threat to the freedom of an Israelite group which settled in a plain is provided by the story of the tribe of Issachar (Gen. xlix. 14 f.).

[9] This is not disproved by the fact that the Philistines retained for centuries certain traces of their non-Canaanite origins, e.g. in the names they used. (Cf. *ZAW*, N.F. vi [1929], pp. 250 f.)

the lowlands and their rulers, not to mention overtaking them.

We must make careful note of the slow development in the organization of Israelite political life. There is no trace of any political constitution such as that which immediately resulted from the Aegean occupation in Palestine; they simply continued under the tribal constitution to which they had been accustomed when in the desert. Of course, the nomadic tribal constitution already contained some rudimentary functions of a national nature, and even if the Israelites had wanted to remain true to this constitution, when in a civilized country, the living conditions there made almost inevitable an increased emphasis on national functions. Even as regards their dealings with related tribes, the recognition or assertion of a claim to a defined territory required a conscious unity on the part of the members of a tribe.[10] Moreover, wherever the old towns remained in existence within, or near, the borders of one tribe, there sooner or later arose regulated relationships, friendly covenants, sometimes even incorporations of territory—legal contracts of one sort or another, which concerned and bound the people as a whole.[11] This ignores bitter entanglements with hostile neighbours against whose encroachments the able-bodied men of the tribe, and sometimes mercenaries as well, were recruited to be sent into the field.[12] For the moment we need not pursue further the question of whether or to what extent the tribe demanded duties of a national nature from its members, apart from the aforementioned military conscriptions, or claimed special privileges for itself as opposed to them;[13]

[10] The result of this bargaining between different tribes can be seen in the catalogue of the lands granted to each tribe in the Book of Joshua and in Judges i, which belong in all respects to the period before there was a unified state (cf. ALT, 'Das System der Stammesgrenzen im Buche Josua', *Sellin-Festschrift* [1927], pp. 13 ff.; *K.S.*, I, pp. 193 ff.).

[11] A treaty: Josh. ix; incorporation: Num. xxvi. 21 ff. (Cf. NOTH, *Das System der zwölf Stämme Israels* [1930], pp. 126 ff.)

[12] The national levy is taken for granted in all the early stories; for the employment of mercenaries, see Judges xi. 1 ff.

[13] The Israelite law of land ownership needs closer study to see

the examples given, dealing as they do with the tribe's self-assertion among its neighbours, show quite satisfactorily that the Israelites already regarded the constitution of the tribes in Palestine as adequate to obtain all their political needs, so long as there was no very serious threat to their existence from foreign powers. These activities of the tribe acting as a unity do not represent, however, any more than a first attempt at a national organization, and it does not seem as though the effect of life in Palestine was always in the direction of a greater consolidation and refinement of the political organization of the tribes. The opposed and diversified interests of the smaller genealogical and regional associations within the tribe itself tended to hinder this process, while the unequal balance between the factors deciding policy and political power, the aristocratic authority of the so-called Elders on one hand, and the democratic institution of the whole body of able-bodied men on the other, invariably led to difficulties, in the absence of a monarchical leader. It is significant, therefore, that even the Israelite tradition itself sees the real heroes of the period from the occupation in Palestine until the formation of the state, in men whose whole existence and activity lay outside the normal framework of the tribe. But in spite of the differences between the majority of these figures, the judges of the Book of Judges, there is one feature common to all of them: they did their warlike deeds to protect the Israelite territory against foreign encroachments, not by virtue of an authority given to them by their own tribe, or which was previously provided for in the constitution for special cases, but on the strength of the sudden appearance of a personal gift and power which was regarded in Israel simply as a charisma, a free gift of Yahweh to the individual, and which therefore swept the populace along with it.[14] It is, however, inherent

---

if the tribe possessed any kind of rights of possession over the property of one of its component families either in theory or in practice.

[14] Jepthah is a clear exception; he was entrusted as a mercenary by the elders of Gilead, that is, by the aristocratic delegates of the

in the nature of such charismatic leadership that it allowed no institutional consolidation, and, above all, that it could not be transferred to, or inherited by, another person. It ceased to exist after the death of the man who possessed it at any given time, if it had not already done so at the very moment when he returned victorious from his military and political task. Thus even the later compilers and authors of the old Book of Judges were unable to prevent in any way, in spite of their opportunity to impose a common pattern, the complete dissimilarity and independence of each other, as regards time and place, character and achievements, of these favourite characters of the tradition, from being quite obvious even today. Neither did these provide any durable basis for the formation of a state in the higher sense of the word. The only attempt of which we know, to found a kingdom by forcibly perpetuating the inheritance of one such leader, was that of Abimelech, the son of Gideon: but it was so poorly founded, and conceived on lines so remote from Israelite ideas and betraying such an overwhelmingly large Canaanite influence, that he could never have brought about an amalgamation and replacement of the Israelite system of tribes in a greater national structure comparable to the union of the Philistine towns.[15]

But although the independent political life of the tribes of Israel remained for the moment unchanged, it is important to note that there was at this time no lack of effective links which overcame the tribal barriers. I am thinking here

---

threatened Israelite territory, with the command of the troops who were to fight in its defence. (Judges xi. 1 ff.)

[15] Judges ix. The expansion of Abimelech's state was based not on an Israelite tribe, but on a Canaanite town, Shechem; it was later that he took control by force in Ophrah, Gideon's home, and other nearby towns. There is no question of his being accepted willingly, and even at Abimelech's death his dominions were only a few hours' journey across. This 'kingdom' could obviously never have become more than a brigand state, even if it had lasted some time; it completely lacked any national character, either Israelite or Canaanite. The story of an offer of kingship to Gideon by the Israelites (Judges viii. 22 ff.) is not historically acceptable.

not so much of the common interest aroused by external threats, which affected several tribes at once; for although these may indeed have led to temporary combined defensive measures, they soon lost their unifying power once the political situation had changed; and because of the vast area of Palestine colonized by the Israelites, and the very limited region actually threatened, it was rare that every tribe was affected at once.[16] More important, since the bond was more permanent, was the consciousness of the interrelationship of the tribes and of their alienation from their other neighbours. As Noth has thoroughly demonstrated in his book on the system of the twelve tribes of Israel, an established genealogical convention by which the state of affairs we are discussing was expressed, this fundamental consciousness rested on a historical basis of a religious nature, the unification of the tribes in the worship of the God Yahweh, which was not native to the civilized regions of Palestine, but which had been transplanted from the wilderness in the south. Here we can disregard the question of whether the origin of this alliance goes back as far as the later wanderings of the tribes in the desert, as is asserted by the story of Moses, or whether it first developed after the occupation in Palestine as we are given to believe by the tradition concerning Joshua,[17] and we need not go into the relationship between the common worship of Yahweh and the religious life peculiar to each individual tribe.[18] In the present context, it is much more important that we give full weight to the effective existence of

[16] This is shown particularly clearly in the song of Deborah (Judges v. 14 ff.), which concerns a conflict with the Canaanites in which an unusually large group of Israelite tribes quite clearly took part.

[17] Exod. xix. ff.; Josh. xxiv. The apparent contradiction between the two traditions seems to have been caused simply by the fact that the Moses saga, in accordance with the national character of the religion of Yahweh in historical times, takes all the tribes as being involved in the union from the start, while in reality the constitution of a complete federation of twelve tribes can only have come about in Palestine. See further NOTH, *Das System*, pp. 65 ff.

[18] I have given some indication concerning this in my essay on the God of the Fathers (1929), *K.S.*, I, pp. 1 ff.; tr. above pp. 3 ff.

an alliance of the tribes in the worship of Yahweh, at the time after the Israelites' settlement in Palestine, and above all of the fact that it took the form of the participation of all twelve tribes in the worship of a common sanctuary of Yahweh; i.e. it was a sacred bond similar to amphictyony which had already appeared in the early history of Greece and Italy as the normal form of permanent alliance between tribes in a similar undeveloped stage. One could hardly overestimate the importance of this union in the worship of Yahweh, and its regularly occurring festivals, in the awakening and preservation of the desire for unity among the tribes of Israel, and we must suppose that the national consciousness had its real roots here. Looking at the corresponding system in Greece and Italy, however, it must be stressed that such sacred alliances did not necessarily lead to any encroachment upon the individual political life of their participants, or develop any political institutions of their own to which the participants had automatically to subject themselves. So even the unity of the Israelite tribes in the worship of Yahweh did not apparently prevent the free control of their own private affairs, and as regards communal business, imposed a moral obligation rather than a political authority. Naturally, it is all the more difficult for us to ascertain what was the extent of its influence, but it is still worth noting that the charismatic leaders of the defensive campaigns against their hostile neighbours had a following which extended beyond their own tribe; for they came on behalf of Yahweh, who was not the God of a single tribe but of the whole federation of tribes, and, therefore, their appearance brought into being an authority binding not only within the narrow confines of their home life, but beyond. The one weakness was that, as far as we can see, no leader ever succeeded in achieving an alliance between all twelve tribes, and that this kind of leadership, because of its purely personal emphasis, was incapable of becoming a permanent institution. For these reasons, neither such a form of leadership, nor the sacral union between the tribes, could lead on to a national unification of the Israelites.

This imperfection in the political organization of the Israelites, in the period following their entry into Palestine, could only have constituted a temptation for the Philistines to assert in the Israelite domain, i.e. in the mountainous hinterland, that superiority which the possession of the country's lowlands had placed in their hands. This would not have been done in order to extend their possessions—their possessions in the lowlands were ostensibly quite sufficient for them—but rather with the intention of establishing their overlordship along the lines of the former dynasty of the Pharaohs, and with the practical aim of exploiting the husbandry and agriculture of the mountain regions by exacting tribute. They would be a ruling military class; the Israelites and Canaanites would be their subjects and produce the food—this is how the Philistines would have liked to see the distribution of functions throughout Palestine.[19] We have no precise data about how far and how quickly they were able to impose their will upon the Israelites and we would naturally make allowances for resistance and counter-attacks. But even the ancient Israelite tradition itself tells basically only of frustrated attempts at defence or revolt against Philistines so long as there was no organized Israelite state,[20] and there can be little doubt that at least the tribes in the mountain ranges west of Jordan and south of the plain of Megiddo were subjected to the rule of the Philistines. If, however, Galilee to the north, and what is even more probable, the eastern region across the Jordan, remained free,[21] this must have aggravated rather

[19] A forced levy of agricultural products: 1 Sam. xiv. 32; xxiii. 1; disarming and monopoly of iron: xiii. 19 ff.

[20] Especially in the story of the Ark of Yahweh, 1 Sam. iv (concerning the date of this cf. ROST, *Die Überlieferung von der Thronnachfolge Davids* [1926], pp. 36 ff.). The heroic actions against the Philistines which are celebrated in the story of Samson of Dan (Judges xv. f.), are at best pinpricks without any lasting effect, and the victory which a late story attributes to Samuel (1 Sam. vii) is scarcely historical.

[21] The isolated account of successful battles against the Philistines fought by the non-Israelite hero Shamgar (Judges iii. 31; cf. v. 6 and ALBRIGHT, *JPOS*, i [1921], pp. 55 ff.) from Beth-Anath in

than improved the situation, for the tribes there would have been even less prepared to send their conscripted forces to join those groups directly affected in an attempt at defence. What is more, the Philistines themselves saw to it that there was no combination of Israelite forces against their dominion. Their system of government was supported by the services of the professional army which they had possessed since their nomadic days, but which now was substantially strengthened by the addition of foreign soldiers and which, in the Israelite chronicles, is typically represented on the one hand by Goliath of Gath, and on the other by David of Bethlehem and his men.[22] These heavily armed infantrymen,[23] constantly ready for battle, formed an eminently suitable means of imposing and maintaining the rule of the Philistines in their extensive empire. Should it become necessary to break down more serious resistance, the whole body of available troops, Philistines and mercenaries alike, were sent into the field; from the start their superior weapons and training triumphed over the lightly armed and poorly trained enemy soldiers.[24] In more peaceful times, however, the establishment of permanent garrisons at key points,[25] and the dispatch of special

---

Galilee (Judges i. 33) naturally does not imply that the North remained permanently free from their rule. But the withdrawal of the family of Saul to the land east of Jordan after the disaster of Gilead shows that the Philistines did not come as far as that. (2 Sam. ii. 8 ff.)

[22] Goliath: 1 Sam. xvii. 4 ff. (his armour was practically all of bronze; only the iron point of his lance is a product of the iron age that had just begun); 2 Sam. xxi. 19; David: 1 Sam. xxii. 2; xxvii. 29 f.

[23] The Philistines do not seem to have made any serious use of chariots either during their migration (cf. the reliefs of Rameses III) or in the centuries that followed; the fantastic account of the secondary passage 1 Sam. xiii. 5 is contradicted by the silence of the older Israelite tradition (esp. xxix. 1 f.; but cf. 2 Sam. i. 6).

[24] 1 Sam. iv. 28; i. 4; xxix. 1 ff.

[25] 1 Sam. xiii. 3 (Gibeah), xxvii. 5 ff. (Ziklag); 2 Sam. xxiii. 14 (Bethlehem). The misfortunes of the tradition have left us here a description only of a small part of the total arrangements, but it is enough to reconstruct the system.

raiding parties to collect the tributes,[26] was sufficient to hold the subjected population in check. This was basically the same system of government as had existed previously under the Pharaohs, except with a more extensive disposal of military resources, and consequently, a greater effectiveness and a better prospect of its long and stable duration.

The extent to which the conquered people were oppressed by the rule of the Philistines can best be judged by the reaction it finally provoked. It caused—naturally against the wish of its participants—what neither the Israelites' entry into Palestine, nor their subsequent fortunes there, had been able to bring about; an organized state in the highest sense of the word. As a result the history, not only of this individual race, but of the whole country moved with surprising speed into a new phase. For this first alliance of Israelite powers in a nationally organized form proved to be strong enough to effect a complete reversal of the balance of political power in Palestine and in particular to overcome the domination of the Philistines. As regards the Israelites themselves, however, it involved them directly in a completely different manner and to a far greater degree in the course of the history of their country and the world than at the time of their emigration, imposing on them a new and unavoidable intercourse and participation in the life of the surrounding culture, from which they were unable to withdraw again by their own power. In view of its historical importance in this process, the formation of an Israelite state seems to me to be at least as worthy of special research as their occupation of Palestine, to which I have already devoted a study from one particular point of view.[27] In this case also, if I judge rightly, a particular approach is required by the present state of the

[26] 1 Sam. xiii. 16 ff. (Michmash and the towns round about); xxiii. 1 (Keilah). The Israelite tradition only recounts these incidents because they were successful attacks on Philistine patrols; their success was exceptional, and one can conclude that the general rule was different from the fact that they are mentioned.

[27] ALT, 'Die Landnahme der Israeliten in Palästina' (1925); *K.S.*, I, pp. 89 ff., tr. above, pp. 175 ff.

question. For while it is appropriate to explain the outward course of the development of the Israelite state, for the most part, from their extant tradition as far at least as it is adequate to the purpose, the problem of the inner structure of each form taken by the developing state is hardly ever even posed clearly, let alone satisfactorily solved. It seems, unfortunately, that many misjudgements made today about personalities and institutions in the history of the Israelite nation owe their existence to a failure to give adequate consideration to the principles of the national and political organizations to which men and affairs were subject at that period. I shall examine the formation of the Israelite state, therefore, drawing on previous research along these and similar lines,[28] from the particular point of view of the history of the constitution; the word 'constitution' is here taken, of course, in its broadest sense.

THE ORIGINAL FORM OF THE KINGDOM OF ISRAEL

We have established above that the formation of the Israelite state was by no means a process of uninterrupted natural growth, arising from internal impulses, which had previously lain dormant in the separate tribes and must sooner or later have grown to maturity. On the contrary: for a unified state to come into being at all, there had to be the powerful external impetus which arose from the rise of the Philistines to power in Palestine towards the end of the second millennium B.C. This gives us a much more suitable starting point from which to understand and explain the new organization. It seems at once proper to understand it as a

[28] I am thinking of writings such as those of CASPARI, esp. *Aufkommen und Krise des Israelitischen Königtums unter David* (1909) and *Thronbesteigungen und Thronfolge der israelitischen Könige* (1917), of M. WEBER's *Gesammelte Aufsätze zur Religionssoziologie*, III (1921), of PROCKSCH, *König und Prophet in Israel* (1924) and GALLING, *Die Israelitische Staatsverfassung in ihrer vorderorientalischen Umwelt* (1929)—to name only a few.

product of that reaction which had made the oppressive rule of the Philistines totter; and since in the violent action and reaction of a head-on clash between two powers, the direction taken by one was bound to be determined by the other, we must expect that the characteristics of the first Israelite state can for the most part be explained by their encounter with the Philistines, be it thought of as attack or defence. But however important it is to see things in the light of the contemporary historical situation, this method of approach can never adequately display the total structure of the political organism newly taking shape. For even if the Philistine oppression had been as severe as they wished, it could never have sufficed to arouse the Israelite reaction, far less to provoke it to such a fruitful development, if, once the foreign yoke had been laid on them in spite of their every effort to defend themselves, the Israelites had lacked the power to make a final attempt to cast it off. In view of the remarkable delay between the Philistine attack and the Israelite reaction the question of where the power was derived to produce the revolution remains urgent and inevitable.[29] And it is, of course, immediately clear that we can penetrate considerably deeper into the nature of the Israelite state by posing this question than by examining the interconnection between it and the Philistine system of government. The latter relationship offers us, for the most part only an external and superficial basis for explaining the formation and aims of the new political organization, but by inquiring into the forces which at this time were drawn together into a single effective impulse, we come to grips with the intrinsic element which underlay the development of the first Israelite state, and learn for the first time what this state possessed and what it lacked. Naturally we must first seek the sources of the

[29] Nothing in the extant tradition, as far as I can see, suggests that the successful Israelite revolt could have been inspired and encouraged by a weakening in the Philistine domination from some cause or other. It would seem improbable, if only because a weak pressure from outside could hardly have had a much more powerful effect on the Israelites.

powers which aided and gave shape to this process within the Israelites' own domain, and only support our explanation by the theory that these creative forces had their origin in other nations, and acted externally on the Israelites, if we fail to locate them among the Israelites. History usually makes a very cautious and economical use of such a procedure; it links new developments as closely as possible with the previous state of affairs in the immediate vicinity, and only looks beyond this when everything has been derived from it which can be utilized in the fashioning of the new situation. So our main question must be whether the rudimentary national functions which we studied above, in the life and activities of the Israelites in Palestine before the organized states came into being, surmounted the imperfection and disharmony which until then had been characteristic of them, and whether they were thus able to assist in the emergence of the new political organization. Did perhaps the old tribal groups still play a part and provide the framework in which the requirements of this altered situation could be satisfied? Or did the sacral alliance of the tribes come to bear the weight of the political change? Did the charismatic leadership of a single individual form the authority for the revolt of the whole people? Or did all these factors, which had previously only appeared separately, finally combine, and was it a direct result of this that a more highly developed state came into being? The logical advantage in method we gain by asking these questions is that they take us beyond the limit of a purely chronological viewpoint and make it possible for us to test and interpret the Israelite tradition of the first attempts to found a state, by comparing it with the results which we derived, without reference to this tradition, and the whole complex of problems it raises, from reliable witnesses to the political situation and institutions of the period previous to this.

To understand properly the very first Israelite national state, the kingdom of Israel under King Saul, it is particularly necessary to relate it in this way, on the one hand to the rule of the Philistines against which it turned, and on the other hand to the older political pattern within Israel itself, on which it was based. For the records available to us of its foundation and further history are so arranged that it is difficult to ascertain from them the specific nature of Saul's kingdom without supplementing the tradition by tracing its antecedents and its relationship to the contemporary scene. It consists almost exclusively of stories not of a strictly historical nature, which it has long been recognized must be divided, from the literary point of view, into at least two series of different ages. One of these series stands out particularly clearly from the confusion by virtue of the logical coherence with which the various incidents fit together; its logic is not, however, that of actual history, but takes for its premises demonstrably false conceptions of the situation before and at the time of the founding of the state, and moreover gives so much play to a factitious presentation of the history, in terms of an ideal view of the state based on theological principles, that it cannot claim to be accepted as a substantially true account of real course of events, even though there are traces of the use of older traditions. It stands at the distance of several centuries from the events with which it seeks to deal.[30] The other series, clearly distinguished from the first by numerous profound differences[31] and combined with it only later in a very inadequate manner, is markedly closer to the facts and seems to be so little affected by the theological trends of later times that one would very gladly refer to it as a historical source; but this too is no serious historical

[30] 1 Sam. vii. 3–17; viii. 1–22a; x. 18–25a; xii; xv. The reasons for treating this series of Deuteronomic stories as a separate literary entity have been so frequently and so thoroughly set out in recent commentaries on the Books of Samuel and in formal introductions to the Old Testament, that it is sufficient to refer to these works (cf. esp. NOTH, *Überlieferungsgeschichtliche Studien*, I [1943], pp. 98 [56] ff.). Older traditions seem to have been used in xv in particular; how far the author's basic picture of the state and the kingdom continued to be governed by the theory that underlay the institutions of the earlier period, is discussed below.

[31] They are dovetailed together by the redactor's additions 1 Sam. viii. 22b; x. 17, 25b–27; xi. 12–14.

work, but possesses all the characteristics of the saga, an art highly developed by the Israelites, to the extent that the accounts of Saul's ascendancy and early exploits are both separate entities and have little or no connection. Thus each individual part of these series must be first considered as an independent entity; then the question arises, what sort of meaning the compiler might have wished to express through the order which he himself imposed on the stories handed down to him. As is regularly the case in the composition of sagas, we can specify neither the date of origin of the individual stories, nor of their compilation into a series; it is very reasonable to suppose that at least the earliest arose not too long after the incidents they describe.[32] Neither of the series develops into a description of Saul's reign; the comprehensive older account we have just discussed closes with the very summary review of Saul's achievements and his family,[33] after having dealt with only two of his earliest cam-

[32] 1 Sam. ix. 1–10, 16; xi. 1–11, 15; xiii–xiv (with interpolations). The commentaries and introductions discuss in full the reasons for accepting that this series was originally independent. But they do not pay sufficient attention to the particular place occupied by each story within the series. But it seems clear to me that the story in Ch. ix. 1–10, 16, which reads as a unity, does not necessarily require any continuation and in any case is not provided with an appropriate continuation either by Ch. xi (as is usually held) or by Ch. xiii–xiv (as PROCKSCH suggests with some caution, *König*, p. 4, n. 1, following LOD's analysis of the sources). Similarly, the story of Ch. xi, which comes to a satisfactory conclusion, is as independent as the more highly elaborated account in Ch. xiii–xiv. The original independence of these three passages explains the slight contradictions between them; they can be regarded in the same way as the contradictions in the Yahwist account of prehistory, and there is no need to explain them by looking for further sources or by inversions (e.g. 13–14 before 11). A further discussion of these matters of literary criticism would be out of place here; cf. GRESSMANN, 'Die Schriften des Alten Testaments' in *Auswahl*, II, i (2nd ed., 1921), pp. 29 ff.; NOTH, *Über. Studien*. Details that are of importance for our historical picture of Saul's kingdom will be mentioned below.

[33] 1 Sam. xiv. 47 ff. The different views current about the literary origin of these verses originate simply from the fact that their explicit function as the conclusion of a distinct literary section has

paigns in minute detail; while the later version actually comes logically to an end with Saul's first exploit, since this action led to a misdeed which immediately deprived his kingdom of the right to exist.[34] There are nevertheless a few more details we can learn about Saul, from one further account which has been incorporated into the great collective work of Israelite history which begins with the entry of Israel into Palestine and ends with the fall of Jerusalem; this last literary source for the time of Saul is not, however, concerned with Saul nor his historical work, but concentrates from the beginning on David and follows his rise to power until the moment when he succeeds in founding a completely different type of state. Even this work is closer to legend than to genuine historical writing, especially in its first episodes, which take place in the immediate presence of Saul and because of this are important to us. Only towards the end, where the legacy of Saul's reign is dealt with, does it become more purely historical, and make it possible for us to draw certain valuable conclusions.[35]

With the traditional material in this condition, any attempt to reconstruct from the sources the outward course of the foundation of the kingdom of Israel and its subsequent history under King Saul would be pointless from the start. But the question with which we are concerned is an entirely different one: the inner structure of this first unified national state. The basic elements which stand out in individual accounts and collections of stories coincide far more than one would at first expect, considering the differences in their origins and contents. Of course, it does not necessarily follow from this

---

been too easily ignored; not enough trouble has been taken to ask what was the purpose of creating such a distinct section.

[34] 1 Sam. xv (victory over the Amalekites and the rejection of Saul), to which xvi. 1–13 (the anointing of David) and xxviii. 3 ff. (Saul and the Witch of Endor) are secondary additions.

[35] 1 Sam. xvi. 14–2 Sam. v. 25; viii (with some interpolations of a different origin). The aim of this writing is strongly emphasized in 2 Sam. v. 10–12; everything that follows can be easily recognized as supplementary material, probably from the hand of the author. (Cf. *ZAW*, xiii [1936], pp. 149 ff.)

that the harmonious features of the account in the tradition necessarily originate in the kingdom of Israel in its original form; their existence could also be explained if the tradition were based anachronistically on a later stage of the formation of the kingdom, when the original pattern had already been modified. This stage, of course, would necessarily have had to begin early enough, and last long enough, to influence the descriptions of the situations under Saul given by the early narrators as much as it influenced the later accounts. But anyone who seriously wished to defend this interpretation would first have to produce evidence that it was not in fact until later, in the period we can locate and for reasons we can understand, that the internal structure of the kingdom of Israel took the form attributed to it from the start of the tradition concerning Saul. Secondly, he would have to explain which were the other older elements of the national state which were ousted from their position by those which are presented in the stories as having been typical of the kingdom in its original form. This double proof is, however, unobtainable. For although it is certain that the inner constitution of the kingdom of Israel underwent profound changes in the course of its history, and indeed from its very earliest days, it was not these changes which gave rise to those features of its make-up with which the writers of the stories of Saul were preoccupied, without distinguishing older and more recent elements. We can say in advance, in fact, that for compelling reasons the kingdom of Israel became less and less able to remain within the framework which these authors attribute to its original form. Comparison with the modifications of the subsequent period inclines us to a considerable bias in favour of the authenticity of the features of the tradition on which the various accounts are in harmony. But we would fail to make full use of the evidence at our disposal if we cast no more than a backward glance, and try to evaluate the stories of Saul only by what can be inferred about the origins of the Israelite kingdom by working back from its later development. The other questions, the justification and necessity for which were explained at the beginning of this section, are at least as important to an inquiry beginning in the preceding period, and based on what we already know of the political institutions of the Israelites in the period before the founding of the kingdom and of the domination of the Philistines as the major incentive to the founding of the kingdom of Israel. Can its portrayal in the tradition be considered from this point of view as adequate to the historical facts and, consequently, as essentially authentic? And is the kingdom itself, therefore, in its original form, notwithstanding all its irrational features which are no more absent than in any other historical institution, the logically appropriate link between what had gone before and what was to follow? It is only when by attempting to work forwards, along the lines just laid down, and simultaneously backwards in time, that we will gain any clear picture of the structural features of the kingdom of Israel under Saul. It is, however, in accordance with the course of our investigation hitherto that we should first examine the important elements of the tradition simply by comparing the relationship of what it contains to the internal and external conditions under which the Israelites lived in the period before Saul, and to put aside for the present the question of their relationship with the subsequent development.

According to the stories of Saul no other element of political organization, among those which we found in effective operation among the Israelites during the period of history prior to the foundation of the national state, played such a decisive role in the rise of the kingdom of Israel as did the charismatic leadership. Saul's calling and endowment with special powers by Yahweh seems to have been throughout the main basis of his rise to power, and consequently of the birth of the new unified state. One of the later authors, on the basis of a wholly theological picture of the ideal state, condemns every human kingdom in Israel as an aberration from the kingdom of God, which he saw as the sole permissible kingdom, and originally the only one to exist.[36] When

[36] 1 Sam. viii. 7; x. 19. The ancient office of Judge (in the sense

he describes the first steps towards the establishment on Israelite soil of a kingdom of the type known throughout the rest of the world, he would much prefer to attribute the whole responsibility for this innovation to the action of the people, carried out not from necessity, but purely from a desire to imitate other nations.[37] But even he has to admit that Yahweh himself, be it only to punish the guilty, allowed the state to come into existence in the form they desired and virtually accomplished the change-over himself, by indicating the first king in the casting of a lot.[38] He himself is too dependent upon the basic ideas of the old tradition to turn his own opposing theory without modification into a historical picture; to this extent even the inherent contradiction in his own presentation is a convincing proof of the enduring effect of the historical reminiscence which he is combating. In the old stories, Saul's charismatic leadership is clearly revealed as a formative principle in the establishment of the kingdom of Israel. Where Saul's rise to power from the time he appeared to the time he becomes king is described without interruption, he seemed to display a sudden and fierce enthusiastic ecstasy which brought him the obedience of the tribes, military success against a hostile neighbouring race, and finally recognition as king.[39] And where, to go back even further, the very beginnings of Saul's career are dealt with, followed by the events leading up to his secret kingship which had still to wait for public proclamation and confirmation, there it was Yahweh himself who, purely from pity for these people oppressed by the Philistines, took the initiative and

of the Deuteronomic redactor of the Book of Judges), appears here as the highest honour permissible to a man in a theocracy.

[37] 1 Sam. viii. 5b. The theme of the discontent of the people with the way Samuel's sons carried out their duties occurs beside this but is not related to it and does not reappear (viii. 1–3, 5a).

[38] 1 Sam. viii. 7 ff.; x. 19 ff.; cf. xii. 13.

[39] 1 Sam. xi. It is typical of the abrupt style of this story, that it expresses the fact that Yahweh conducts the whole action, by the use of set phrases, but does nothing else to emphasize it (vs. 6 the Spirit of God on Saul, vs. 7 the fear of the Lord amongst the people).

through his prophet Samuel had the unsuspecting young Benjaminite chosen as deliverer from this distress and anointed.[40] From this, one can understand how a compiler can feel himself justified in placing these two stories in juxtaposition, although they do not agree in all details; he concentrated on tracing the direct line from Yahweh's designation of the charismatic leader to the acclamation with which the people later paid homage to him, and saw in this the fundamental element in the process by which the first Israelite nation-state was established.[41] It is obvious too that even the story of Saul's rejection by Yahweh assumes his vocation earlier.[42] Thus in the complex tradition concerning the beginning of the kingdom of Israel[43] only the story of Saul's first victory over the Philistines is to some extent unrelated to the otherwise very prominent fundamental idea of the charismatic leadership; so that even in this story the almost priestly traits with which the portrait of Saul is endowed should be taken as being influences or variations of that basic idea.[44] In the present connection we can disregard it quite

[40] 1 Sam. ix. 1–10, 16. Here the intervention of Yahweh is brought out much more strongly (God speaks to Samuel, ix. 16).

[41] The redactor did not feel obliged to do a great deal to bring the stories into harmony: the calling of Saul to assist in the struggle against the Philistines (ix. 16) and his attack on the Ammonites (xi. 1 f.), his seizure by the non-political enthusiasm of the ecstatic prophets (x. 5 f., 10 ff.) and his rapid action based on a fierce political anger (xi. 6 f.) occur together without any link or explanation. Even the introduction of Ch. xiii–xiv between these two stories would not make any difference.

[42] 1 Sam. xv. 1, 11, 17 ff.; cf. xiii. 7 ff.

[43] The stories of the rise of David are not relevant here; there Saul is simply the opponent of the new hero, and the Kingdom of Israel is a factor that is taken for granted, and does not need to be explained or described.

[44] 1 Sam. xiv. 17 ff. (the consultation of an oracle), 24 (a fast throughout the day of battle), 33 ff. (his concern for the correct ritual slaughter of the cattle taken as booty, and the building of the altar), 36 ff. (the consultation of an oracle and act of propitiation). Even if these features are attributed to the basic theme of Saul's charismatic leadership, it is still true that this is conceived quite differently than in ix. 1–10, 16 and in xi.

confidently, in that it is in no way connected, at least in its extant version, with the question of how the kingdom of Israel came into existence. Wherever it should be fitted in, it belongs outside the cycle formed by the other stories.

We have seen that the records of later generations, notwithstanding the different conceptions underlying each, all agree in making the charismatic leadership of Saul the real starting-point of the first Israelite state. In this they supply by the simplest means conceivable the principal necessity in the interpretation of a historical phenomenon of this type: they maintain continuity between the past and the new features which appear, and yet, on the other hand, make ample allowance for new and original developments. Among the many other attempts at political organization which we observed among the Israelites in Palestine before the founding of the nation-state, there is in fact no single one which can be said to have had such a profound effect on the basic structure of the kingdom of Israel as it came into being as had the charismatic leadership. It is clear that the predominant form of permanent political organization up to this time, the various constitutions of the individual tribes, played only a minor role in the formation of the state. We can in fact safely assume that it was the Israelite tribes as such that submitted themselves to Saul's leadership, and that Saul for his part had to respect their individuality.[45] But the kingdom of Israel even in its original form under Saul was no more a mere tribal state which had extended its influence under the old tribal constitution, than it was in its later stages.[46] The fundamental tendency, manifested from the

[45] It is not a cause for surprise that the older tradition no longer mentions this; even as early as this it concentrates entirely on the larger unity.

[46] At first sight the story of Saul's first battle against the Philistines, 1 Sam. xiii–xiv, might give the impression that at the beginning of his rise to power he had the forces only of a single tribe behind him, namely those of his own tribe Benjamin. But even if this impression were correct, it would only be a picture of a preparatory stage, rapidly superseded, and not to be thought of in terms of the establishment of a state, before the coming into being of the Kingdom of Israel in the proper sense.

beginning, is towards the organization of all the tribes under a centralized government, and only this explains the name adopted, which implies a decisive rejection of any attempt to unite the other tribes around one single group. However regrettable it may be for us not to be able to ascertain with complete certainty whether Saul was ever able to unify all the tribes of Israel in his kingdom—the extant traditions are simply inadequate for this[47]—it cannot prevent us from establishing the ideal pattern to which the kingdom of Israel in its very earliest form sought to attain, and to which in reality it did at least approach, namely a national state, in which the individual tribes had to be content with the role of ancillary members. Far from leading to a more advanced development of the ancient tribal constitutions, the organization of the tribes into a unified nation closed the way to their evolution into independent states; for although it left their traditional methods of dealing with their internal affairs undisturbed, it appropriated everything other than this to the new and greater national unity. Nevertheless, the tribal constitutions had a positive influence in the founding of the Israelite state. They were responsible for the fact that at the moment of its formation well-established political unities were in existence which only needed to be won over to its service; their very existence relieved the new nation of the necessity of building up its organization from scratch. Another important advantage was that the tribal constitutions could satisfy the normal internal requirements of individual tribes, as before; the new kingdom had therefore no need to con-

[47] The only list we possess of the tribes which belonged to the kingdom (2 Sam. ii. 9) refers explicitly to the time after the death of Saul and may only describe the remnant at that time, which would have to be extended towards Galilee in the north and Judah in the south to give a complete picture of the extent of Saul's kingdom. But in spite of all the arguments that can be adduced in its favour, it is not possible to give proof of the view that Judah and the South ever belonged to Saul's kingdom in the same sense as Benjamin and Ephraim; what the tradition has to tell of Saul's frequent appearance in Judah is explicable even supposing the connection was a great deal looser.

cern itself with these matters and could concentrate on applying itself to problems which concerned the whole nation. But precisely because this was the relationship between the tribes and the state in Israel from the very beginning, we are forced to conclude that the structure of the unified state did not stem directly from the ancient constitution of a tribe; the basis of the kingdom is too broad, and the fact that at the moment of its appearance it made considerable demands on the service of the individual tribes is of too great importance for this to be so. Only when we take into consideration the fact of a charismatic leadership does the picture take shape. On previous occasions the peculiar functions of the charismatic leadership had been to organize the Israelite forces in a concerted action, regardless of boundaries and individual tribal constitutions. It reveals at least some attempt to do what is the explicit intention in the case of Saul, to operate on a national scale, even though, as can be understood, this tendency was not equally powerful on every occasion; and the fundamental idea is always present, so that when these earlier leaders appear on the scene they do so, just like Saul, with a specific commission from Yahweh the God of the whole nation.[48] To this extent, then, the formation of the kingdom of Israel, with its conscious attempt to establish an authority wider than the individual constitutions of the tribes, introduced no fundamental new principle; it merely completed what had previously been implicit in the nature of the charismatic leadership.

Since the first Israelite state was national and not tribal in its nature, we are led at once to examine its historical relationship with the other organization which for a long time previously had given institutional expression to the unity of the Israelites, and which in fact we have found cause to believe was the source of the Israelite national conscious-

[48] I am thinking here, naturally, of the accounts given in the ancient stories of the Judges, not of the scheme provided by the redactor of the Book of Judges, in which the tendency of the charismatic leadership to include the whole nation becomes an uncritical generalization.

ness: the sacred federation of the twelve tribes in the worship of Yahweh at a common sanctuary. That a theoretical connection actually existed is of course almost certain, because even if the influence and authority of the old federation and the new state were not in actual fact coextensive, they were at least intended to be. But may the older organization not perhaps have contributed to the construction in a direct and practical way? The tradition never mentions this in plain terms, but that cannot be accepted as decisive by anyone who has a proper understanding of the kind of account we possess of Saul's rise to power on one hand, and, on the other hand, of the nature of the tribal federation which had preceded the unified state. And yet in the tradition concerning Saul there is no lack of details which can be made into a convincing testimony to a direct link between the foundation of his kingdom and the institutions of the ancient tribal federation. Thus it is with every justification that a recent author points to the remarkable similarity between Saul's drastic behaviour and language when he first called the whole of Israel to arms, and the no less drastic procedure when the whole federation of tribes was conscripted for military action against a rebellious member, of which an account exists in a story from the period prior to the founding of the state.[49] And did the Shrine of Gilgal owe its choice as the scene for the first act of homage of the tribes to Saul to the fact that it was at that particular time a central sanctuary for the federation?[50] There is, moreover, a great probability that

[49] 1 Sam. xi. 7; Judges xix. 29 f.; cf. NOTH, *Das System*, pp. 102, 109 f.

[50] 1 Sam. xi. 15. I consider it overwhelmingly probable that Gilgal near Jericho is referred to here (for another view, SELLIN, *Gilgal* [1917], pp. 17 ff.); in favour of this sanctuary is the fact that the traditions concerning it, which originally only refer to the tribe of Benjamin (Jos. i–x; cf. NOTH, *Das System*, p. 37, n. 2, and ALT, 'Josua', *ZAW*, Beiheft xlvi [1936], pp. 20 ff.; *K.S.*, I, pp. 183 ff.) have become national traditions, which suggests that it was important as a sanctuary for a much wider circle (cf. Amos iv. 4; v. 5; Hosea iv. 15; ix. 15). This could have come about in the period immediately before Saul, i.e. after the decline of Shiloh.

during the somewhat earlier period the Shrine of the Ark of Yahweh at Shiloh had once been a sanctuary of the whole federation.[51] Now at the time of Saul the successors of the priests of Shiloh served a sanctuary at Nob, which not only lay in the territory of the king, who ruled in nearby Gibeah, but was actually controlled by him.[52] Does this not also indicate an attempt to incorporate the remnants of the old institutions into the new organism? We may raise these questions, but we cannot answer them with any certainty. Yet even if they could be answered in the affirmative, and if there had been a conscious attempt at the beginning of the first Israelite national state to preserve a link with the old order of things in the tribal federation, this link would be of only secondary importance in comparison with the basic fact of Saul's charismatic leadership which took over the apparatus of the federation to forward its own historical mission, just as it had made use of the previous organization of the isolated tribes.

From what has been said it is sufficiently clear that the original form of the kingdom of Israel under Saul was formed entirely along the lines of those first moves towards political organization which had been in existence among the Israelites for a long time. It is also obvious that the more recent presentation of the facts is basically wrong in supposing it possible to discuss the Israelite state from the start as a mere imitation of the arrangements of other nations. But even so, there is a tiny grain of truth even in this error. For the nature of the new phenomenon can certainly not be adequately ex-

[51] SELLIN, *Geschichte des israelitisch-jüdischen Volkes*, I (1924), p. 102; NOTH, op. cit., pp. 94 ff. The even older centre of the federation of tribes at Shechem (NOTH, pp. 66 ff.) no longer plays any part in the time of Saul, or at least in the tradition concerning him.

[52] 1 Sam. xxi. 2 ff.; xxii. 6 ff. Because these passages belong to the series of stories dealing with the rise of David, the sanctuary of Nob is taken for granted, and the origin of its importance is not discussed; similarly, the future of this sanctuary after the priestly family of Shiloh had been exterminated by Saul remains a mystery. On the position of Nob near Gibeah, cf. *PJB*, xxi (1925), pp. 12 f.

plained as the sum total of the hereditary elements. This can be made clear perhaps if one considers the very earliest account of Saul's first military undertaking the campaign to rescue the town of Jabesh from the Ammonites, in the light of the results which we have obtained up to the present. Everything immediately falls into place: Saul's charismatic leadership, the military service of the tribes, the overwhelming success; up to this point one would think oneself simply confronted with a story from the Book of Judges, except perhaps that the circle of people who were borne along by the enthusiasm of the leader is wider here than elsewhere. But in the final terse sentences comes the unexpected twist: the victorious tribes bring Saul to their sanctuary and by their act of homage make him what no charismatic leader ever was before: the king of Israel.[53] And with this something new and of crucial importance, the acclamation of the people, was added to the designation of God which had always been sufficient by itself in the past. This finally completed the process by which the nation-state came into being and finished for ever all that had gone before. From this moment on, there existed by the tribes' own wish, a bond between Saul and themselves, which led from a military service carried out once to a recurrent and compulsory conscription, and from a leadership established for a single occasion to a permanent sovereign right, and so changed the single isolated case, based on a charismatic calling, into a permanent situation protected by fixed institutions. It can hardly be more than an accident that the tradition does not refer to this act and its effects on the constitution, by the expression 'covenant', which is usual for all such links between individuals or groups in the linguistic usage of the Israelites; for even if the word is missing the fact is undoubtedly there. This is shown particularly by the action of the tribes in paying homage not on the battlefield, but far away from it in a holy place, so that the whole procedure was under the guarantee and control of Yahweh, which was necessary to any 'covenant' in

[53] 1 Sam. xi. 1–11, 15.

the Israelite sense of the word. In addition to this, the accounts of Saul's rise to power reveal very clearly in other expressions that they are able and intend to differentiate between what Saul had become through the designation of Yahweh and the status he was given by the acclamation of the people; as the chosen of Yahweh he was merely called *nāgīd,* and it was the nation which conferred upon him the title of *melek,* 'king'.[54] A clear distinction is made between his divine ordination and his human rank. They are both essential constituents of the monarchy in Israel; just as without the previous designation of Yahweh, the acclamation of the people might never have taken place, so without the latter, the first might never have been sufficient to give the new organization the stability desirable in a growing state.[55] But the acclamation of the people does seem to have been a genuine novelty in the procedure, and the question arises, where this new feature came from, since unlike the initiative of Yahweh in choosing a charismatic leader, it is not foreshadowed in the old customs and institutions of the Israelites. What was it that now made the Israelites willing, as they had never been before, to accord to Saul a permanent authority over them? Historically there is only one answer to this question: it must have been the contemporary situation which produced this effect, or, to be more precise, the urgent need, in the existing circumstances, for a firm opposition to the Philistines, the importance of which for the formation of the kingdom of Israel has already been noticed in the beginning of this section. When Saul first appeared it was the

[54] 1 Sam. ix. 16; x. 1 (xiii. 14) by contrast with xi. 15. The religious aura of the word *nāgīd,* as opposed to the more profane *melek,* suggests that *nāgīd* can be taken as a passive participle, signifying that the charismatic leader was 'made known' by Yahweh. But this is a linguistic question that cannot be decided with certainty.

[55] Even in the historically impossible episode of the offering of the kingship to Gideon (Judges viii. 22 ff.) the sequence of events is the same: first the calling of the hero by Yahweh, then his victory in battle, and finally the idea of bestowing on him and his immediate descendants a permanent overlordship.

fact that here men were dealing not only with a sudden and acute danger, but with the chronic evil of a long-established system of foreign domination, which made the situation different from all the other threats which had been warded off by charismatic leaders. One single lucky blow was not enough to combat this; it was necessary above all, even if the Israelites desired nothing more than to win back their own freedom, to keep the available military forces in a permanent state of readiness; for the Philistines, because of their superior military techniques and organization, would naturally always try to maintain their domination in Palestine, even in the face of successful counter-attacks, by renewed offensives. The creation of a permanent unified supreme command over the levies of the Israelite tribes, in the hands of one man, was the least requirement if they were to make their final build-up for an attempt to shake off the Philistine rule with any prospect of success. But this very thing was the first objective, and almost the only significant purpose of the founding of the Israelite state, and especially of the monarchy. The king ruled the national army; his authority only really came into effect in camp and in battle and had hardly any function in peacetime. It was a kingship for the sole purpose of defence against the Philistines, and the idea of establishing a dominion over non-Israelite areas was far removed from it.[56]

At this point it was possible for the formation of the growing kingdom of Israel to be influenced to some extent by the examples of national institutions in other peoples. Such influences, of course, did not include the introduction of the

[56] Fierce isolated campaigns against neighbouring peoples who were organized as nation-states are certainly mentioned in the tradition concerning Saul (1 Sam. xi. 14, 47 f.), but by comparison with the decisive and continual confrontation with the Philistines (xiv. 52) they are no more than episodes and moreover can always be regarded simply as defensive campaigns. This is not so in the case of the campaign of extermination against the nomad tribe of the Amalekites (15) nor perhaps of some individual attacks on Canaanite towns (Gibeon: 2 Sam. xxi. 1 ff.; perhaps also Beeroth: 2 Sam. iv. 3 (cf. *PJB*, xxxv [1939], pp. 100 ff.).

principle of the monarchy amongst the Israelites; on the contrary, as we have seen, it was entirely native in its origin, arising from the fact that the earliest constitution of the Israelite state was simply a new form of the Israelite system of military conscription adapted to the needs of the situation and based on the long-developed concept of charismatic leadership. Nor were the Israelites and their first king able to incorporate suitable elements from the institutions of neighbouring states into the structure of their own kingdom; the course of the newly created state was already far too clearly prescribed by the circumstances of its origin, and the institutions of the neighbouring states within the view of the Israelites were too diverse for this to be possible. The states of the ancient Canaanite type, which spring immediately to the mind in this connection, are scarcely conceivable as models, for, as far as we can trace their development before and after the period when the first Israelite state was being formed, they possessed a completely different structure. Their military system was not based on popular conscription, but for the most part consisted only of a professional soldiery, few in number, and partly of aristocratic nature, ruling a population which was useless for fighting; accordingly a great majority of the people took no part in the formation of political purpose and action, and so power was accumulated in the hands of the upper classes, for whom the prince had to act as representative, if he were not equal to wresting the means of power from them.[57] Finally, there was an unmistakable tendency towards the formation of states of a very limited territorial extent, especially in Palestine.[58] All this is

[57] This weakness of the monarchy against the aristocracy in the small Canaanite city-states explains why in this final period before the setting up of the Israelite state some of them exchanged their monarchy for rule by their aristocracy (Shechem: Judges ix. 1 ff.; Succoth and Pnuel: Judges viii. 5 ff.; Gibeon: Josh. ix. 3 ff.; x. 2; 2 Sam. v. 6 ff.; Gezer: 1 Kings ix. 16). The history of the constitution of the Greek city-states in their early period provides an exact comparison.

[58] Cf. ALT, 'Die Landnahme der Israeliten in Palästina' (1925), pp. 11 ff.; *K.S.*, I, pp. 100 ff., tr. above pp. 175. The later develop-

in such marked contrast to what we have seen to be typical of the original form of the Israelite kingdom that we can scarcely speak of any genuine influence by the Canaanite institution. At the time of the formation of the Israelite state, moreover, the Canaanites in Palestine had almost played out their role of an independent political power, so there was not even any psychological incentive to borrow from them. It is more likely that the institutions of the Philistines, whose claim to power the kingdom of Israel was founded to resist, could have exercised a decisive influence; it was nothing new to attempt to pick up the secrets of power from a powerful enemy and to beat him with his own weapons by imitation of his techniques. But of course, as was shown in the introduction, the development of the Philistine state at the time of the occupation took such a peculiar form that to emulate it was utterly impossible for the Israelites; neither the city-states of the Canaanite type, which provided its original framework, nor their inclusion in one all-encompassing organization, which could be described as a state, could be artificially copied where the prerequisites for such a system were so completely lacking as among the Israelite tribes.[59] But in one other sphere, and indeed in that which, under the circumstances, was of the utmost importance in the conflict, namely in military affairs, there seems to me to be a direct influence on the kingdom of Israel, almost from the moment of its birth. At first mere conscripts from the tribes of Israel stood in opposition to the highly developed professional army of the Philistines; their union under a charismatic leader was the real power and originally the only power underlying the new kingdom. It is obvious that nothing decisive in the long run could be accomplished against such vastly

---

ment on the Phoenician coast of wider areas under unified rule (cf. especially the kingdom of Sidon) must be understood as an adaptation to the growth of large national states nearby.

[59] It is of little importance in the present context that we are almost totally ignorant of the organization of the Philistine federation, although we have clear evidence of its political and military effects outside its borders.

superior military power with these poorly equipped, inexperienced troops, who in any case could be spared from their own domestic agriculture only for a short time. Of course there may have been single victories won in isolated cases, if perhaps a strong Israelite force came across a Philistine party small in numbers and separated from the main body, and overcame it by sheer numbers;[60] but the Israelite army was far too unwieldy for guerilla warfare against superior numbers of raiding parties operating independently which would strike in several places simultaneously, and it could hardly chance a real pitched battle against the combined military forces of the Philistines.[61] It is wholly understandable, therefore, that Saul soon proceeded to supplement the army with troops who were better trained, and in particular, better adapted to guerilla warfare; the tradition tells how he gathered round himself a body of retainers permanently at his disposal, and led them in undertakings in which no part was played by the tribal conscripts.[62] This force is largely responsible for the fact that, as long as Saul reigned, the Philistines could to some extent be held back to the frontiers of the Israelite territories; this adoption of the enemy's techniques bore good fruit. It is equally significant, however, that with this professional force which could hardly have been recruited solely from people of his own nationality, and which in any case formed a parallel to the employment of mercenaries among the Philistines,[63] there came into the mili-

[60] The conflict described in 1 Sam. xiii–xiv, was of this nature.

[61] Saul's last battle against the Philistines, so fateful for him and for his kingdom (1 Sam. xxxi), is probably the only exception to the rule, not only in the tradition (since the battle against Goliath in 1 Sam. xvii must be regarded as unhistorical) but also as a matter of fact.

[62] The raising of these troops: 1 Sam. xiv. 52b.; their endowment with crown lands: xxii. 7; the military activity: xviii. 13, etc. David's pursuit by Saul, described in the tradition, must have been carried out largely, if not exclusively by these troops; whereas they are not expressly mentioned at Saul's last battle.

[63] After Saul's death, when these troops remained in the service of his family, it is quite clear that they were mercenaries (2 Sam. i. 12 ff.; this is the best example of the way in which battles of such

tary organization of the young kingdom of Israel an element which intensified its original unity, but later inevitably brought a dangerous internal tension into the organization of the state. Soon, we will have to discuss how this came about immediately after Saul's death; perhaps it is merely a result of the inadequacy of our extant tradition that we do not hear of conflicts between the king and the people during his own reign which could all too easily arise from the existence of an army which stood apart from the conscripted national forces and was bound by oath only to the person of the king himself.[64]

This adoption of the military institutions of their principal enemy, no matter how swiftly it may have occurred, marked a considerable departure from the original rigid conception of the army in the kingdom of Israel as a national levy; in this vitally important matter, and indeed in other respects, the original form of the kingdom shows distinctive features to which we would look in vain for analogies among the Philistines, and far less among the Canaanites. But this does not mean to say that it represents a complete novelty in the history of the formation of states in the region of Palestine. The real parallels to the internal structure of the young Israelite nation-state are to be found elsewhere: not in the plains of

---

regular troops were a kind of tournament [cf. EISSFELDT, *Nouvelle Clio* iii–iv (1951), pp. 110 ff.; iii, 1–2 (1952), pp. 55 ff.]; and 2 Sam. iv. 2 ff.). The tradition concerning Saul occasionally hints at the national character of the troops that followed him (1 Sam. xxiv. 3; xxvi. 2); but a figure such as that of the Edomite Doeg amongst Saul's 'slaves' suggests, and the appearance of Baanah and Rechab of Beeroth amongst the officers of Ishbaal's army (2 Sam. iv. 2 ff.) confirms that this mercenary force, here as everywhere, was international in composition. David's position as the harp-player, sword-bearer and officer of Saul was the same (1 Sam. xvi. 14 ff., etc.).

[64] The question arises whether the historical conflict between Saul and David had its roots not only in their personal struggle, but in the conflict between the body of mercenary retainers and the national levy; but the tradition does not provide the answer. Similarly, this conflict could underlie what later tradition describes in its own way as the rejection of Saul by Yahweh.

the west, where city-states, their origins far back in time, pursue their individual and widely divergent courses, but in the highlands to the east, on the far side of the Jordan, among those people in which the Israelites, in spite of their national consciousness, saw their closest relatives, and which from all appearances came only a few generations before the Israelites to occupy land and form states in the border areas of the settled agricultural regions near the Syrian-Arabian desert. Unfortunately, we are totally dependent on Israelite tradition for our knowledge of them, and consequently never see their tiny kingdoms in the process of development, but always as established powers which already existed when the Israelites entered civilized territory.[65] But even so it becomes quite evident that their kingdoms were just as far removed from the Canaanite pattern as was the kingdom of Israel in its original form. Edom, Moab, Ammon, Aram—in each case the name of these states shows, even more than their size and population, that they were based on national foundations, even if the limits of their territories did not always coincide with the area populated by those who bore their name.[66] The kingdom of Israel came on the scene as one of the last of this series of closely similar political structures,[67] and so played its own part in the sweeping change in the political map of Palestine which came to its conclusion in the tenth century B.C. From the purely chronological point of view, one might consider the much later development of the Isra-

[65] It is not an anachronism when the tradition accepts the presence of the new kingdoms in the southern part of the country east of Jordan, albeit mingled with the remains of the older system of city-states, during the period of the final Israelite drive into Palestine (Num. xx ff.) (cf. ALT, 'Emiter und Moabiter', *PJB*, xxxvi [1940], pp. 29 ff.; *K.S.*, I, pp. 203 ff.).

[66] In the case of the Aramaeans, their division into several smaller kingdoms caused them to be named after their principal town (cf. 2 Sam. x. 6, 8). But even there there was no question of city-states on the Canaanite model.

[67] The establishment in Palestine of the final form of Aramaean political organization in the shape of the kingdom of Damascus (1 Kings xi. 23 ff.) in the place of the smaller Aramaean kingdoms overcome by David (2 Sam. viii. 3 ff.), is more recent.

elite state as a mere imitation of the long-established nation-states east of the Jordan. But it is intrinsically improbable that the connection can be explained in such a mechanical way. In both cases we are dealing with related peoples, who were led from their common desert home by a similar route into the various parts of the civilized region of Palestine. If, as far as we can see, all these nations show in the formulation of the state traces of the same creative principles in operation, and if this is in fact a principle which was unknown to the previous inhabitants of the territory in which their new states were set up, then we should be able to recognize with greater confidence the consequences of a tendency which was common to all the new intruders, and which sooner or later, and according to individual circumstances, brought into being the same type of national structure, without one nation first having to learn from the others. The special case of the considerably later development of the Israelite state can be adequately explained by the fact that the Israelites were thrust far deeper into the area influenced by the ancient and completely dissimilar city-states of Palestine, and consequently had far less scope for the fulfilment of their political tendencies than their cousins east of the Jordan near the desert border.[68]

Although the original form of the kingdom of Israel was fundamentally the same as that of the neighbouring states to the east, this does not prevent the common pattern in the special internal and external circumstances of Israel from being developed in an independent direction. Everything that has been said previously about the peculiar development of earlier Israelite institutions, and the adoption of contemporary Philistine forms in the make-up of the Israelite kingdom, becomes extremely significant when we consider its distinctive features; for of course it is not to be supposed that all these elements played an identical part in the development of the

[68] Since the literary tradition has virtually nothing to tell about the rise of the national states east of the Jordan, their history can only be looked for from the results of archaeological investigation in the areas concerned.

kingdoms east of Jordan, and every disparity in the underlying causes at work necessarily resulted in a corresponding disparity in the resultant national structure. For it seems, moreover, according to the very fragmentary traditions on which we are dependent, that even in spite of the extensive similarities between their structure, there was still one important feature found only in the kingdoms east of the Jordan. Apart from the national principle on which their structure was based they were all without exception organized in a monarchy, yet we find that their kingdoms do not always appear to have had the hereditary form which was universal among the Canaanites, and which we can also presume to have existed among the Philistines and the other Aegean peoples in Palestine. On the contrary, in the only place in the Old Testament where the preservation of an authentic list of kings allows us to trace the development back to a very early period, in fact, perhaps, as far as the first formation of a national state, i.e. in the case of the Edomites, we also discover the remarkable fact that the title of 'king' was quite regularly passed on, for many generations, to men of completely different origins and that there is never any recognizable attempt to establish a dynasty;[69] it was only after David's suppression of their kingdom that the Edomites in their struggle for emancipation gave allegiance to a successor of the former king.[70] Elsewhere among the Ammonites and the Moabites we find the son's accession to his father's throne in isolated cases, but this also occurs only at the time of David, or later; so one may well ask whether dynastic continuity in a monarchy in these kingdoms was likewise a secondary development and replaced a more flexible form similar to that in Edom.[71] But even if we accept that before the birth of

[69] Gen. xxxvi. 31–39.

[70] 1 Kings xi. 14 ff. Cf. with this and with the list of Kings especially Ed. Meyer, *Die Israeliten und ihre Nachbarstämme* (1906), pp. 370 ff.

[71] Ammon: 2 Sam. x. 1 ff. (at the time of David); Moab: the inscription of king Mesa (9th century). The dynastic form of the monarchy in the Aramaean kingdom of Damascus (1 Kings xv. 19, etc.) is not strictly relevant to the present context, in view of the

the kingdom of Israel the dynastic form of monarchy had already been introduced into some of the states east of the Jordan, the list of Edomite kings still provides convincing evidence against the view that we should assume that this form existed throughout this group of peoples from the very beginning. In the case of the original form of the Israelite kingdom, therefore, we must first examine the tradition to discover whether or not the monarchy was thought of in dynastic terms. Now we know definitely of an attempt to hold the new Israelite state in allegiance to Saul's descendants after the disaster of his last battle against the Philistines. Abner, the leading figure of the whole clan,[72] brought Saul's son Ishbaal across the Jordan in safety from the Philistines who had regained their superiority, and there made him king over Israel in Mahanaim.[73] But for all that this action was planned and carried out as though to establish a dynasty, it is obvious that it is a complete departure from the procedure which had previously led to the founding of the kingdom. It is admittedly of little significance whether Ishbaal actually had his seat in Mahanaim or in Gibeah, like Saul; even Gibeah had not been a capital such as a more highly developed monarchy would have.[74] Much more to the point is the fact that he never appeared in the only place where according to the original concept the soldier-king of Israel could display the nature and value of his office: in the camp of the Israelite tribes and at their head in battle. Immedi-

---

later appearance of this kingdom in a quite different political situation.

[72] It is characteristic of Saul's military kingdom, that his relative Abner held the only office which to our knowledge had yet been separated from the decisive functions of the king (1 Sam. xiv. 50).

[73] 2 Sam. ii. 8 ff.

[74] It must of course be remembered that to all appearances Gibeah was not Saul's home, but the royal capital first chosen by him. The hereditary grave of his family was not there, but nearby (2 Sam. xiv; cf. Josh. xviii. 28). Saul's move to Gibeah must have been caused by the fact that this town had become, under the rule of the Philistines, a military and administrative centre for the whole area round about (cf. 1 Sam. xiii. 3).

ately after the disaster that overtook Saul when he last clashed with the Philistines, which was likewise a disaster for the army, Ishbaal—or Abner acting on his behalf—ought to have considered his most urgent task to be to gather an army together again, and lead it against the old enemy once more. Instead of this we see no more than occasional sorties across the Jordan by his raiding parties, unaccompanied by himself, not to do battle with the Philistines but to continue the ineffectual guerilla war against David and his mercenaries; thus he was wholly dependent on the military retainers of his own family which he inherited from his father, and which formed, as we have previously noted, a foreign element in the Israelite army.[75] It is self-evident that his kingship could win no popular support in this way and one might be inclined to consider his and Abner's political incompetence as wholly responsible for the failure of the whole experiment. But the trouble was much more deeply seated than this; the people had by no means yet accepted the idea of dynastic continuity in their national organization. The man to whom they had originally given lifelong authority to rule them had already been established as a charismatic leader, before the tribes paid homage to him: everything else was based on this in Saul's time. We do, however, learn from the early Israelite leaders that their charisma was inseparable from their own person and from their special task of saving the nation; and it was in no way regarded as transferable, let alone hereditary. There was no reason why Saul's case should have been any different simply because the tribes had subjected themselves permanently to his leadership, or because during his whole lifetime the fulfilment of his special charis-

[75] See above pp. 258 ff. The story in 2 Sam. ii. 12 ff. is relevant, but it would be a misunderstanding to suppose that the national levy was concerned in this battle between mercenaries. But we must not overlook the fact that our tradition concerning the period in question belongs exclusively to a work that purports only to describe David's rise to power, and is consequently not interested in any activities of Ishbaal's mercenaries against the Philistines, nor the fact that David at that time should in all probability be regarded as an ally of the Philistines.

matic task, the shaking off of the Philistine attempt to dominate Israel, was never definitely accomplished, in spite of all his successes. For his wide powers to be transferred to another member of his family was not, therefore, merely a matter of a private inheritance which came into effect automatically, but needed, in order to be valid, a repetition of the acts which had given the first impetus to Saul's own rise to power, that is, a new personal designation by Yahweh, and a new personal acclamation by the people. There is no mention of this in the case of Ishbaal; Abner, not the spontaneous will of the people, made him king, and there is a complete lack of any previous action by Yahweh to point him out and bring about his acclamation by the people. On the contrary, early tradition asserts that Saul's own charisma was displaced by 'an evil spirit from God' in the later years of his reign, and that this took away the full intrinsic authority, as it was conceived in the original constitution of the Israelite state, for his continuing to rule on the strength of the oath the people had once made to him.[76] Later accounts of Saul's rejection by Yahweh merely enlarge upon the same basic ideas and give even fewer grounds for attaching a royal dynasty to the person of the first king.[77] But even if this element in the tradition were no more than a later attempt to interpret the actual course of history, Abner's experiment with Ishbaal—and with Israel—still runs contrary to those imponderables which, only a few years before, had played such a decisive role in the establishment of the kingdom. For this reason, then, it is not beyond belief that Abner himself could have withdrawn from his experiment and pledged himself to draw the Israelites away from Ishbaal and on to the side of David, who was not of the House of

[76] 1 Sam. xvi. 14 ff. If Saul's power, here and in his later activities, appears to be crippled, this feature of the tradition may reflect the impression that must have been made amongst the Israelites when he no longer appeared as at first as the leader of the popular national levy, after he had raised his force of mercenaries and (presumably under Abner's leadership) left them to carry out his military tasks.

[77] 1 Sam. xv. 13, 7 ff.

Saul.[78] The attachment of a monarchy to a dynasty was not yet an established fact in the conscience of the people, and when a new man appeared who was a charismatic leader and seemed worthy of a homage and military service that Saul had been accorded, no one in Israel had any serious difficulty about dropping that earlier attitude of cautious expectation, abandoning the existing royal family and vesting all the authority of the infant nation in a new leader.[79] All the evidence implies that the idea of the dynasty was as foreign to the kingdom of Israel in its original form as it was to the kingdom of the Edomites, and I think that this probability will amount to a complete certainty, if we can go on to show that it was not until after many generations that the dynastic principle arose in the kingdom of Israel, under the pressure of the events of that later period, and that even then it never completely ousted the idea of a charismatic leadership, provided on each occasion by Yahweh, which had stood in the way of the establishment of a dynasty from the beginning.[80]

This is one more respect in which the kingdom of Israel shows its very elementary structure, comparatively little altered from the primitive forms of its historical origin. Its efforts were still all directed towards its pressing external affairs, and even there we have seen that it was merely an organization for national defence, making no attempt to dominate its neighbours outside its own national boundary. In internal affairs, it left everything except military matters to

[78] 2 Sam. iii. 12 ff. Abner's personal motives in this political volte-face do not concern us.

[79] Since the Israelites did not take the decisive step of supporting David until after the death of Abner and Ishbaal (2 Sam. v. 1 ff.), the point of view that governed their actions is not so obviously revealed in the course of events as one might wish. But since there were still sons of Saul alive (cf. 2 Sam. xxi. 7 f.) the dynastic principle could still have been invoked in their favour if it had carried any weight at all with the Israelites.

[80] Cf. ALT, 'Das Königtum in den Reichen Israel und Juda,' *VT*, i (1951), pp. 4 ff.; *K.S.*, II, pp. 118 ff. This idea must also have lain behind the troubled history of the monarchy in its early stages amongst the Edomites.

be managed by the older tribal groupings. It had not yet established a definite policy with regard to its monarchical leader; and it constantly gives the impression of being a transitional stage, of which one may well doubt whether it should count as the conclusion of the previous period, or the beginning of the following one. The Israelites were prevented from lingering at this intermediate stage by the general political situation in Palestine; after the disaster of Saul's defeat they had either to return to the conditions of the period before the national state, under the domination of the Philistines, or look forward to development of their new nationhood. History decided on the latter; a second completely different stage in the development of the Israelite state followed closely upon the first.

THE KINGDOM OF DAVID AND SOLOMON

Anyone who is used to noticing such things will realize immediately from the changed nature of the recorded tradition that the history of the Israelites moved into a new phase with David and Solomon. We have taken the accounts of Saul's early days as being essentially a form of historical saga: this explains how they can in fact grasp correctly internal motifs of the formation of the first Israelite state, while on the other hand disregarding almost completely the external relationship of events. The early accounts of David and Solomon which have come down to us are quite different in character. Of course the writing which described David's rise to power and from which we previously drew several features of our reconstruction of the original form taken by the kingdom of Israel, begins in the anecdotal style of heroic saga; but as it continues there is an increasingly marked change to a more continuous description which without digression leads the reader step by step to a picture of the further establishment of David's kingdom, with which it concludes.[81]

[81] See above p. 243.

A second work on the history of David, the excellent account of the complicated events which led to Solomon's inheriting power, takes the existence of the kingdom for granted, and confines itself to the question of the succession to the throne. But the very fact that it consciously subordinates the whole account to this one point of view shows that it is the creation of a genuine historian, who conceals rather than reveals his historical purpose, especially by his expert handling of a narrative style based on that of the saga in the arrangement of the individual scenes.[82] Both works, especially the latter, are quite close in time to the events they describe; only a few pieces originating elsewhere are inserted, and these are almost all of the same period.[83] Finally, in the single comprehensive description of the reign of Solomon which we possess, there are in fact elements in the style of the saga; the body of the work, however, which the author arranges, unlike all previous writings, not in chronological order, but according to subject matter, also consists of historical and in places even statistical or documentary material.[84] In this literary account there is reflected a tremendous heightening of the historical conscience of the Israelites. The highly developed traditional modes of expression of the saga were not apparently sufficient for the new experiences they had undergone since the time of David, and so for urgent reasons there blossomed among them with amazing swiftness a new species of historical style, the like of which could not be found in the whole of the ancient East, as Ed. Meyer especially has correctly pointed out on several occasions.[85] We should note in the present context that this

[82] 2 Sam. vii. 9–20; 1 Kings i–ii. In essentials I share the view of Rost, *Die Überlieferung*—even on 2 Sam. vii.

[83] 2 Sam. xxi–xxiv. For the passages which the author of the history of the succession found as separate complete stories and included in his own work, cf. Rost, op. cit., pp. 4 ff., 47 ff., 74 ff.

[84] 1 Kings iii–xi (excluding later interpolations, some of which are lengthy).

[85] *Die Israeliten und ihre Nachbarstämme*, pp. 478 ff.; *Sitzungsberichte der Berliner Akademie* (1930), pp. 67 f. It is unfortunate that Meyer, impressed by the apparently highly secular nature of

change of literary form in the writings we possess is associated not with the rise of the kingdom of Israel under Saul, but with its transformation by David. This agrees with the result of our historical investigation, as far as the description of the personal work of Saul is concerned; we saw how, in the first stage of the development of the national state, the early organization of Israelite life had such a powerful influence that the old way of recording folk-memories, in the form of a saga, could still be used and fulfil the needs of the time. But we are now faced with the problem of whether the second phase under David and Solomon was in its actual nature so far removed from the first that it could be responsible for bringing into being this new narrative form.[86]

Of course the far more historical character of the tradition concerning David and Solomon is a great help to us: in many cases we can take the relevant details directly from the ancient text with full confidence.[87] But this is not to say that we can hope to arrive at the correct composite picture of the

---

this historical text did not give full weight to the religious elements in the author's outlook and presentation. We should not be deceived by his apparent reticence, for it is at the decisive points in the story, as regards both form and content (in the history of the succession, in the introduction that sets the pattern for the whole story, 2 Sam. vii, at the turning point of the action, 2 Sam. xvii. 14b, and finally at the very end, 1 Kings ii. 45 f.) that his religious point of view breaks through, and governs the whole picture. Yet the difference from the older sagas, both in the religious outlook and in the way the story is presented, remains considerable.

[86] I cannot discuss at length the very important literary development, but I should like to point out that these new experiences could scarcely have called into being a new way of understanding and presenting history, if the Israelites had not been long accustomed to thinking historically under the influence of the religion of Yahweh, as a national religion. This is already clear in their saga tradition. (Cf. VON RAD, *Archiv für Kulturgeschichte*, xxxii [1944], pp. 1 ff.; *Gesammelte Studien zum Alten Testament* [1958], pp. 148 ff.)

[87] I do not make any use of the much more recent accounts in the Books of Chronicles, although they seem to me to be in urgent need of a new examination in regard to the picture they present of the state set up by David.

new political situation simply by reproducing our sources. For although these writings may set out a series of events, as do those on David, or give a succession of more static descriptions like those concerning Solomon, the author always had a definite purpose in mind, and consequently selected his material from what was available to him. It is quite understandable that there should be gaps, where none of the ancient authors had occasion to answer a question which seems important to us within the framework of the limited presentation he himself chose to give. Far more frequently, however, the three accounts dealing with David and Solomon are complementary, precisely because of the different manners in which their subjects are presented, and supply what is missing in the others. Moreover since each one deals with a particular time within the period,[88] one account will quite often show us a given aspect in its early stage, and another in its final development, so that we can study events and institutions as it were in growth. To this extent the difference between the lively progress of the stories of David, and the static description of Solomon's reign, to some degree due to the nature of things, has a particular value for us; it provides us with a means of control of the evidence from the more or less stabilized conditions of the later period, and we can work back from them and discover what it was in the first generation that formed the constituent elements of the new creation. But of course we will be equally obliged to draw our comparison in reverse—particularly in order to see what was in reality characteristic only of the intermediate and earlier stages, and must be omitted from a complete picture of the period. In short, our task is once again not to reproduce the sources, but to make an independent re-

[88] It is perhaps very probable that there is a considerable overlap in the periods dealt with by the account of David's rise to power and the history of the succession. This is suggested in particular by the connection between the list of David's measures against neighbouring states in the first account (2 Sam. viii.) and the fuller description of a war against the Ammonites in the latter (2 Sam. x.; xii. 26 ff.).

construction of the actual conditions and events. But this can be done only by taking into account, in addition to the express statements of the tradition, their complicated relationship with earlier, later and contemporary traditions, events and circumstances.

We must work back, therefore, from the circumstances of a new political organization to the stage that immediately preceded it, that is, to the original foundation of the kingdom of Israel and of Saul. This is necessary not only because it is required by the sources which tell of David's early career, but also from the methodological consideration we have set out in the previous section. When we work back to the picture we drew there of the early institutions of the kingdom, it provides a basis for our knowledge of what was retained, and especially what was changed in the next stage. Now of course the tradition leaves no doubt whatsoever about which part of the constitution of Saul's kingdom provided the stage for David's rise to power. His ascendancy was set in the context of the body of personal retainers, the professional soldiers which were developed by Israel's first military king, and which was the most suitable weapon in the vitally urgent battle against the domination of the Philistines, and consequently came to be regarded as indispensable.[89] Since this struggle not only went on, even immediately after Saul's disastrous defeat, but became of decisive importance for the existence of the young kingdom of Israel, one must accept at once that the process of historical selection followed a logical course, the placing at the head of the kingdom of Israel a notorious master of that specialized art of warfare in the person of David, Saul's former musician, armour-bearer, and commander. The essential military and technical prerequisite in bringing the war against the Philistines to a decisive and victorious conclusion—in order to achieve not only, as under Saul, a temporary and imperfect political equilibrium, but to bring about the final release of Palestine from their domination—was David's particular use and pre-eminently

[89] 1 Sam. xvi. 14 ff.; xviii. Cf. above pp. 258 ff.; 264.

skilful handling of the professional military force which belonged to him personally from his earliest days.[90] This of course inevitably means that neither the military nor, in consequence, the political organization of the kingdom of Israel could remain unchanged, if David was to be king. When the military retainers first appeared on the scene during Saul's reign, we had to admit that this was a dangerous foreign element in the organization of the kingdom, which was originally based only on the tribal armies, and Abner's experiment with Ishbaal and the mercenaries after Saul's death gave us practical proof that the continuation of the kingdom was immediately threatened, when the first king's heirs abandoned the national levy and finally depended exclusively on the professional soldiers. In spite of this the next stage of the history of the kingdom is linked to a single man, who because of previous experience is completely on the side of the cosmopolitan professional army. This implies a change in the basis on which the kingdom was founded, which, though it may not have been complete and permanent, was at any rate a fact, and was of decisive importance for the period immediately following. David's kingdom in Israel was as revolutionary as that of Saul before him. Saul proceeded by rapid steps from a military levy on a hitherto unknown scale, which he carried out in his function as a charismatic leader, through the proof of his worth in battle, to receive the homage and permanent submission of the national armed forces to his command. This could hardly be repeated by a political upstart who, like David, had a long career as a military leader at home and abroad behind him. Or to take a historical example from the time before the nation-state was formed, where indeed we found in our search for the earliest form of the kingdom the ancient patterns on which the new state was created: David may well have been a second Jephtah,

[90] There is no express statement in the very brief accounts we possess of David's decisive battles against the Philistines that he used mercenaries only (2 Sam. v. 17 ff.), but it is likely. This step, of course, was based not on military and technical grounds, but on political arguments which we shall discuss later.

who was also a mercenary leader abroad when the representatives of his country called him back and entrusted him with the command of the army; he was certainly not a second Gideon. Apparently the tradition concerning David realizes these dissimilarities and tries to conceal them to some extent. To this end it stresses in the description of David's service under Saul that he led Israel, that is his conscripted levies, in battle and won their especial affection,[91] and then when the emissaries from Israel offered him the vacant kingship, presents them as justifying their action on the grounds that David had already been the leader of the national levy under Saul and that Yahweh had designated him *nāgīd,* like Saul before him.[92] It is apparent that his kingship is intended at this point to follow the same pattern as Saul's as far as possible: a military monarch on national level, whose authority is in the end based on Yahweh's designation, can only prove his legitimacy by warlike deeds at the head of the national army, and can only attain complete recognition by the acclamation of the people. There is of course no cause to doubt that in the less-developed conditions at the time of Saul, an officer from the ranks of the professional army might have to command contingents from the national levy,[93] and it is quite credible that people would find justification for raising David to the rank of king of Israel by adapting his previous history, as far as it went, to accord with the prototype from the be-

[91] 1 Sam. xviii. 16; 'and Judah' after 'Israel' is an anachronistic addition from the point of view of the period when the two kingdoms were divided.

[92] 2 Sam. v. 1 f. This statement is prepared for by similar expressions from individuals in earlier stories in the same work (Abigail: 1 Sam. xxv. 30; Abner: 2 Sam. iii. 18); on the other hand it is accepted that the story of David's anointing by Samuel (1 Sam. xvi. 1 ff.) does not belong here.

[93] It should be noted that apart from Abner, who is only mentioned as being the commander of the levied national army (1 Sam. xiv. 50) there seems to have been no one in particular who was in command of the mercenaries. In the same way, a mercenary officer could have been put in command of a detachment of levied troops who were assisting his own force, for example in a comparatively unimportant engagement.

ginning of the kingdom. Without such fabrications the psychologically most important factor, their sense that the essential framework of the traditional order was preserved, could not be maintained in changed conditions.[94] Our insight into the historical necessity and importance of this fabrication, to which we must return later, should not, however, prevent us from admitting the fact that from the very beginning David's rise to power had a background other than that of the Israelite national army—even though its first stage came about through his extremely close personal relationship with the first king of Israel. Even at this stage, David's service under Saul was not the fulfilment of any sort of duty which Saul could exact from every one of his subjects because of the absolute power which he had been granted (not even if we accept that his home lay in the full sense within Saul's kingdom[95]); it was the result of a relationship of purely personal loyalty, into which in principle a foreigner could be drawn just as easily as a compatriot;[96] and after his break with Saul, David's story was carried on entirely outside the territory and framework of the Israelite state.

However unusual it may appear at first glance, it was David's rise to power outside Israel, in consequence of his following his own individual course of action, that brought the kingdom of Israel into his grasp after Saul's defeat, and the failure of Abner's experiment with Ishbaal. Already his appearance on the western and south-western borders of his home in Judah, at the head of a fast-growing troop of mercenaries which owed allegiance to him alone, and, like him, to no permanent state system, meant under the circumstances of the time the beginnings of a power which was not only of military significance, but which tended at least to assume

[94] The stress laid on this point of view, as well as other details in the account of David's rise to power, rather suggests the precise purpose of this work was to provide a historical justification for the handing over of the Israelite kingship to David.

[95] This is doubtful. Cf. above, n. 47.

[96] Cf. n. 63. Once he had entered Saul's service David severed his links with his family and became formally a slave of his Lord, in the same way as for example Doeg the Edomite.

political importance.[97] His entry into the service of the Philistine prince of Gath was another step in the same direction; for by receiving in feof the town of Ziklag, he attained the position of a small feudal prince, admittedly of course within the system of Philistine domination and by the acceptance of the duties of a vassal.[98] The next stage, however, led him much higher and at the same time much closer to the kingdom of Israel: his migration with his mercenary army to Hebron and his accession to the throne of Judah. It is most unfortunate that the only information we have on this occurrence is a few inadequate verses,[99] for with the establishment of the kingdom of Judah next to the kingdom of Israel the dualism between north and south which was already noticeable in the period before the kingdoms, was now hardened and intensified in an institutional form. It was never really broken down during the centuries to come, and was very seldom prevented by the overriding authority of a larger organization from having its full effect on the political life of the nation. It would be fortunate if we could learn directly from the traditions concerning the origin of the kingdom of Judah or from documents dealing with its activity in the period immediately following, what were its original distinguishing features in relation to the kingdom of Israel, a generation older. Only a few characteristic features can definitely be traced. Above all there is the fact that the new establishment was built entirely around David's person and the powerful position he had already attained, and so perhaps could never have come into being without him; the establishment

[97] 1 Sam. xxii. 2; xxiii ff.

[98] 1 Sam. xxvii; xxix f. It is characteristic of the Philistine system of government that in Ziklag and probably elsewhere in the foothills and in the plains (e.g. Gerar? Gen. xxvi. 1 ff.) they made use of the native system of city-states and made vassals of their dynastic princes, even handing over these functions to foreign mercenary soldiers; their policy in the mountains of Israel was different.

[99] 2 Sam. ii. 1–4a. The brevity of this account is explained by the fact referred to above, that the story of David's rise to power, to which it belongs, is primarily concerned with justifying the handing over of the Israelite kingship to David.

of himself and of his mercenaries in Hebron and the neighbouring towns was the starting-point for everything that followed. This fact forces its way into the foreground of the tradition before everything else. It is also obvious that the factor which played so large a part in the rise of the kingdom of Israel, the confrontation with the Philistines, had no place in the original conception of the kingdom of Judah. Apparently, in fact, to begin with it was loosely incorporated into the Philistine's system of government as a sort of vassal kingdom so long as it remained separated from Israel.[100] But in its early stages, the kingdom of Judah did not have any aggressive tendencies towards Israel either; at least we never hear of the army of Judah being conscripted to fight against Israel, but merely of occasional clashes between the mercenary troops of David and Ishbaal on Israelite ground.[101] In this connection, the underlying motive in the foundation of the kingdom of Judah seems to have been no more than that those who were separated from Israel by a band of Canaanite city-states stretching from Jerusalem to Gezer,[102] wanted to live a separate political life, after Saul's defeat had shown how unwise it was to depend on the kingdom of Israel. Seen from the point of view of its internal composition, the designation 'tribal state' fits the kingdom of Judah in its original form as little as it did the kingdom of Israel; for although its official name implies that the tribe of Judah, which lived between Jerusalem and Hebron, had a certain predominance, this may be derived only from the fact that the new state had a native-born Judean at its head. The removal of the political centre to the ancient Calebite city of Hebron shows that a larger area of the kingdom lay to the south, and that from the beginning it stretched as far as the southern limits of the civilized region of western Palestine in the plain of Beersheba.[103] This participation by groups from outside Judah,

[100] Cf. KAMPENHAUSEN, *ZAW*, vi (1886), pp. 43 ff.

[101] 2 Sam. ii. 12 ff.; cf. above, n. 75.

[102] Cf. ALT, 'Die Landnahme der Israeliten in Palästina' (1925), pp. 32 f.; *K.S.*, I, p. 123; tr. above pp. 175 ff.

[103] This view is supported in particular by David's earlier con-

who with the exception of Simeon did not even belong to the alliance of the twelve tribes of Israel, means that from henceforward the kingdom of Judah was similar in its composition to the kingdom of Israel, in spite of its smaller territorial boundaries; the chief intention in the case of the newer foundation was also that of the concentrating of a fairly large number of units into a wider political organization, and in this case too, it seems more than likely that the political organization consisted of an alliance of neighbouring groups which had already been present long previously in a sacral form and now reappeared in an altered and consolidated shape in keeping with the needs of the times.[104] Just as when Saul was accepted as king of Israel, the word 'covenant' would have been appropriate for the act that made David king of Judah, and the brief account undoubtedly refers to just such a thing when it tells how David originally established himself in Hebron with his soldiers, and how the men of Judah came there to anoint him king; the initiative of the one matches the initiative of the other, and together the two provide the mutual bond on which the body politic was based. On the other hand there was no mention of the initiative on Yahweh's part in every human action which strikes us so forcibly as the basic ideal factor in the kingdom of Israel in its original form. For the story that David consulted Yahweh by an oracle as to whether and to which place in the mountain region of Judah he should move his previous seat of Ziklag, may well have been intended by the narrator as a substitute for the missing spontaneous choice by Yahweh of the first king of Judah,[105]

---

nections with the districts in the south (1 Sam. xxiii. 13 ff.; 24–27, 30, esp. vss. 26 ff.).

[104] I suspect that the sacral centre of the group was the tree-sanctuary of Mamre near Hebron ('Der Gott der Väter' [1929], pp. 58 f.; *K.S.*, I, pp. 54 f., tr. above pp. 3 ff.); NOTH, *Über. Studien.*, pp. 106 f., correctly argues that it was a federation of six tribes. On the economic basis of this federation (their possessions were all in the Negeb; cf. 1 Sam. xxvii. 10; xxx. 14) I cannot say anything here.

[105] I do not think that this is a likely interpretation of 2 Sam. ii. 1. The special mention of David's question to Yahweh is simply

but still leaves the political initiative to David. This causes no surprise to us; it would now be too late to endow with charismatic leadership such as Saul's the commander of a mercenary army who had already attained the position of prince of a city, albeit under foreign domination. How important this situation is for the further development in Judah we will soon discover.

The strongest support would be given to the view we have just put forward, that this story is a fiction designed to make the historical facts fit a previously accepted theory, if in the following stage of David's rise to power when he came to be king of the kingdom of Israel reference is made to his earlier designation of Yahweh. The man to whom the tribes of Israel offered their orphan kingdom was no longer in the strict sense a political upstart, a *homo novus,* for not only had he possessed for a long time a military force of mercenaries, owing him personal loyalty, but had recently acquired control of the national levy of the kingdom of Judah, by virtue of a popular agreement, and it would be quite unhistorical to ignore completely the accumulation of power he controlled at this time, and try to trace a direct link, without any intermediate stages, between his acclamation as *melek* in Israel and a designation as *nāgīd* by Yahweh, which was supposed to have taken place during Saul's lifetime and to have been ratified by his successful leadership of Israel's army. We have already mentioned the psychological necessity of this fiction and I need not describe at length how appropriate it was to the intrinsic pattern of the kingdom of Israel in its original form which the tradition concerning Saul has revealed to us; that this ideal scheme can, apparently without difficulty, be transferred to a man who not only did not belong to Saul's tribe, but who had until the present moment lived in a state of feud with him, is an eloquent testimony to the lack of any idea of dynastic continuity in the Israelite conception of the monarchy to

---

meant to imply that Yahweh had also intended the intermediate Judean episode in David's political career, so that it becomes one more element in the demonstration of the legitimacy of David's rise to power.

which we have already drawn attention. But the ideal theory comes into conflict with historical reality when it is applied to David, because the simple and straightforward situation from which it has originally been derived no longer existed. Saul had become the military king of Israel by the designation of Yahweh and the acclamation of the people, no more and no less; the body of military retainers which he created for himself on a quite different principle was in plain contradiction to the fundamental self-sufficiency of the popular assembly and national army of Israel, and in practice could be tolerated only as long as the foreign military force was subordinate in numbers and effectiveness. But even when it attained a dangerous prominence, there was still one thing that could preserve unshaken the Israelite idea of the state, namely, the certainty that everyone, king and commoner, mercenary and conscript alike, was serving a unified and national political purpose. On the other hand, David no longer considered this single purpose to be the foundation laid down by past history, on which everything else had to be built, but regarded it at best as only one goal which had to be attained. For a start, the household guard of mercenaries that David brought with him was, as early as the time when he rose to be king of Judah, and still more when he was recognized as the king of Israel, a much more impressive body than the similar force that Saul or Ishbaal had possessed, and consequently lent a far greater degree of ascendancy to his military and political purposes from then on. But in addition to this, Israel was no longer alone in being subject to a king and in its claims upon him—even before Israel gave him allegiance, the new kingdom of Judah had already entered into an exactly similar relationship with him. In my opinion the difficulty of this complicated situation is never properly appreciated; it is only too easily avoided by supposing that immediately or as soon as possible after his accession to the throne of Israel, David must have fused the two kingdoms of Judah and Israel into a larger national unity, so that in this respect the situation under his rule, and ultimately under

Solomon, was fundamentally no different from that under Saul. We will in fact learn of individual features in the institutions of both reigns which confirm the existence of such a tendency. Before these features can be fully understood, however, we must point out the fact that the complete amalgamation of Israel and Judah into one unified state was carried out neither by David nor by Solomon, and was in fact not even contemplated by them. The evidence of the extant tradition, wherever it gives a precise account, leaves no real doubt on this point. But just as surely as in the earlier written sources, though more commonly in later literature, the word 'Israel' can occasionally be used in its original meaning, referring to the whole federation of the twelve tribes, as a name for the double kingdom of David and Solomon,[106] so, quite as often, this ideal usage is corrected in the course of the story to the more realistic expression 'Israel and Judah'. For example we read 'the anger of the Lord was kindled against Israel' at the beginning of the story of David's census of men liable for military service; but almost in the same breath, the idea with which Yahweh tempted the king is couched in the phrase 'go, number Israel and Judah',[107] 'Let Zadok and Nathan anoint Solomon king over Israel at Gihon', David decrees in the story of the succession to the throne; yet only a few sentences later he crowns his speech with the words 'I have appointed him to be *nāgīd* over Israel and Judah.'[108] But wherever the sources sound like official documents the two kingdoms are held distinctly separate. Thus we have this account of David's accession, immediately after the report of his being recognized as king of Israel; 'at Hebron he reigned over Judah seven years and six months; and at Jerusalem he

[106] E.g. in the accounts of David's war against the Ammonites, 2 Sam. x. 17; xi. 1. The expression takes no account of the inclusion of the states on the borders of Palestine in the larger Israelite empire.

[107] 2 Sam. xxiv. 1. The use of the name 'Israel' in the ideal sense may be caused here by the religious character of the first phrase.

[108] 1 Kings i. 34 f. We will deal later with the fact that the title *nāgīd* is misapplied to Judah here.

reigned over all Israel and Judah thirty-three years'.[109] The same thing appears even more clearly in reference to the reign of Solomon, in a statistical document which is incorporated in a rather mutilated form into the general history: a list of Solomon's provincial officers. 'Solomon had twelve officers over all Israel', runs the first introductory sentence; the following account, however, shows by details of the towns and territories of the individual administrative regions that by 'all Israel' only the old kingdom bearing this name is meant, and Judah is excluded, no matter whether the mention of one unnamed officer 'in the land of Judah', after the series of twelve officers 'over all Israel' who are presented by name, is looked upon as an original feature of the list, or as a secondary addition.[110] This phenomenon in the written tradition makes it constantly necessary, wherever in the period of David and Saul the name 'Israel' is mentioned, for the historian to note carefully whether it should be taken in the earlier ideal sense, to mean the whole nation, or whether it refers to the real but smaller political unit founded by Saul and taken over by David and Solomon, and excluding the kingdom of Judah. As we go on we shall have to make this decision in a number of important cases. But we can at least say this much on the strength of the documents cited, that in describing the history of the whole second stage of the formation of the Israelite state, we have to take into account the dualism of the kingdoms of Israel and Judah, in spite of their common subjection to David and Solomon, and that for this reason the king-

[109] 2 Sam. v. 5. It is important to notice here that 'Judah' occurs here beside the strongly emphasized expression 'all Israel'.

[110] 1 Kings iv. 7 ff. I believe I demonstrated that the twelve provinces of 'all Israel' excluded the territory of the kingdom of Judah in *Alttestamentlichen Studien zu R. Kittels, 60 Geburtstag* (1913), pp. 1 ff.; *K.S.*, II, pp. 76 ff. ALBRIGHT's attempt to show that there were Judaean areas in two of the Israelite provinces (*JPOS*, v [1925], pp. 25 ff.) I do not believe succeeded (cf. *PJB*, xxi [1925], pp. 100 ff.) and would perhaps not be maintained by him today, since he has felt obliged to make an important modification in his view (*ZAW*, N.F. iii [1926], p. 235).

dom of Israel can no longer be regarded as the self-contained unity which it had been under Saul.[111]

The way in which David received both royal titles in turn leaves no other constitutional development to be expected. When the representatives of Israel come to the king of Judah to make a 'covenant' with him—and here occurs the word which you might have hoped to find in the reports of other similar acts[112]—it is his and their own business and makes not the slightest difference to the special political relationship which had already existed for some time between David and Judah, unless the men of Judah could be made to give up their existing national organization and submit to being incorporated in the new agreement with Israel; and for this there is not the slightest evidence in the tradition. The Judeans, therefore, maintained their status as an individual state, and David continued as before as the recognized monarch of their kingdom—even when he also became king of Israel, without any assistance from the men of Judah. This is the typical form of a personal union between neighbouring states, and there is no lack of parallels in the ancient East.[113] The inevitable result is that the king whom they have in common never fully belongs to either of the kingdoms, and from his mediating position gains a superiority over both, which it would be far more difficult for him to acquire as ruler of a single kingdom. This effect was strengthened in David's case by the fact, already referred to, that he possessed in his mercenaries a domestic bodyguard owing alle-

[111] This fact naturally casts even more doubt on the commonly accepted view that Judah belonged completely to the kingdom of Israel under Saul (cf. above, n. 47); but to argue back from the dualism of the time of David and Solomon to the situation in the preceding period is no guarantee that the result will be historically correct.

[112] 2 Sam. v. 3. The Covenant was made in this case, as in the case of Saul (1 Sam. xi. 15) 'before Yahweh' (in Mamre?).

[113] A parallel from a neighbouring country and almost contemporary period is given by NOTH in an epigraphic document from central Syria in the first half of the eighth century B.C. (*ZDPV*, lii [1929], pp. 124 ff.).

giance to himself alone, before he ever became king, and the result was rapid and plain to see; he removed his capital from Hebron to Jerusalem, which, being neither Israelite nor Judean, was in a neutral position with respect to the two kingdoms. It lay on the border between the two, and had been a city-state of the early Canaanite type which had previously remained independent, and which he did not besiege and starve out with the national levy either of Judah or Israel, or both, but took by storm with his mercenaries, so that in future he could rule it in his own name, by right of conquest, as the 'City of David', without any interference from Israel or Judah.[114] The new constitutional situation could scarcely have had more obvious outward form. To his former double title, the king of Israel and Judah added a third, and once again by means of a personal union, and this was one which from its very origin lay completely outside the national framework of Israelite history:[115] from then on he lived within the administrative area of this third title, on his own personal estate, existing as it were on a higher plane outside the twin kingdoms of Israel and Judah. There is no doubt that David fully intended this third stage in his career, since it offered the best solution to the complications which had arisen in his affairs. This does not mean, however, that he saw it merely as a temporary stage, which would sooner or later be followed by a complete rearrangement of constitutional relationships, rather on the basis of a fusion of the three administrative areas, which at the moment existed independently. By mov-

[114] 2 Sam. v. 6 ff. I have examined the political significance of this action in an earlier essay (*ZDMG*, N.F. iv [1925], pp. 13 ff.) and only wish to add to what is given there the comment that the capture of Jerusalem by David, from the point of view of the history of that city, represents a forced change from a system of aristocratic government to the monarchical rule of a dynastic prince.

[115] If one includes Ziklag, a city-state which remained under the control of David and of the kings of Judah as his heirs, one has a system of political units of different kinds, two national kingdoms and two city-states, all under the control of a single ruler. But from the start Ziklag must have played a very subordinate role in this system (cf. NOTH, *ZDPV*, l [1927], p. 214, n. 3).

ing the Ark of Yahweh to his new residence, David shows his desire to form a closer, ideal link between this kingdom and the two others, especially with the kingdom of Israel.[116] The territorial separation of each state was not, however, lessened by this measure; for the sanctuary of the Ark at Jerusalem—whether it was a tent as in David's time, or a temple architecturally joined to the palace, as under Solomon—did not belong to the city-state, like the other sanctuaries still in use in the same territory, but was, if I may express it thus, a private temple for the royal house. This can be seen in particular from the king's rights to appoint priests and to arrange the disposal of revenues from the sanctuary.[117] From the modern point of view one might consider the fact that Jerusalem was not more firmly incorporated into the whole to have been a constructional weakness in the administrative system which David built up and Solomon inherited; but if this can in truth be called a constructional weakness, it is only the inevitable consequence of the other weakness that lay in the fact that the neighbouring kingdoms of Israel and Judah were not unified either, but held together merely by the principle of personal union. Neither David and Solomon themselves, nor their contemporaries, could ever have seen any fault in this disharmony between the parts of the king-

[116] 2 Sam. vi. When the author records that David gathered all the young men of 'Israel' to bring back the Ark (vs. 1), he can only be thinking of the kingdom of that name. It is doubtful whether Judah had the same close connection with the Ark as the Israelite tribes in the north. (Cf. Noth, *Oudtestamentische Studiën*, viii [1950], pp. 28 ff.).

[117] David carried out priestly functions when the Ark was brought back (2 Sam. vi. 18), and so did Solomon at the consecration of the Temple (1 Kings viii. 1 ff.); David at least from time to time gave priestly tasks to his own sons at the sanctuary of the Ark (2 Sam. viii. 18). This direct linking of the priesthood with the royal house does not appear later; but the professional priests at the sanctuary of the Ark owed their hereditary office down to the destruction of Solomon's Temple to the royal decree (they occur in the list of royal officers, 2 Sam. viii. 17; xx. 25; 1 Kings iv. 4, and Solomon's action in 1 Kings ii. 26 f.). The king disposed of the Temple income: 2 Kings xii. 5 ff.; xxii. 3 ff.

dom, and there must be some doubt as to whether it could have been at all possible, considering the basically different histories of the individual regions and the history of their alliance in particular, for a single man to have created a unified state from them so quickly. Once the administrative system had been constructed by David and taken over by Solomon, Jerusalem could only fulfil its function as a royal seat if it remained in the same constitutional position as before, a foreigner to its Israelite and Judean neighbours to the north and south. Only the king with his family and staff of officials and mercenary soldiers—or to use the Hebrew expression, with his slaves—moved into the city of the Jebusites, and established his seat amongst them; the free Israelites and Judeans could not and were not intended to follow him, but had to remain on the hereditary soil of their fatherland.[118]

But even Jerusalem did not by any means represent the final touch in the system of government David and Solomon were building up; further elements were added, and the more they multiplied, the more the standing of individual parts altered inevitably, with the change in the nature of the whole. We must recognize that each stage of this development came about with a compelling necessity. The alliance of the kingdoms of Israel and Judah under David's rule already represented an accumulation of power which was felt beyond their frontiers, and was bound to produce a reversal of the balance of political power in Palestine, if their neighbours to the east and west did not succeed in time in breaking down the newly formed bloc in the centre into the pieces from which it had been built up. It was obviously fortunate that no closer relationships or common interests existed between these neighbours, the Philistines and their adherents on the one hand, and the mountain kingdoms east of Jordan on the other; in

[118] I have explained elsewhere what this implies for the history of the building of Jerusalem (*PJB*, xxiv [1928], pp. 83 ff.); the opposite view of Procksch, that David's policy was necessarily one of 'making the Israelite element in his capital predominant' (*PJB*, xxvi [1930], p. 20), seems to me to lack historical foundation.

fact we have already had to mention the profound differences between these two groups of states.[119] For this reason, Israel's position between the two, which otherwise could quite easily have become dangerous, proved to be an advantage to David's newly created political unity. For the tradition contains not the slightest reference to a combined attack by all Israel's neighbours, nor even of a clash with the eastern states, before the decisive campaigns had been fought in the west.[120] These, however, or more precisely the challenge to the Philistines' claim to domination, must have begun immediately after David received the title of king in Israel, with the resulting fact that the Philistines immediately advanced into the region of Jerusalem, that is, into the border area between Judah and Israel, to cut communications between the two.[121] That they acted at once is probable not only on military grounds but also for political reasons. Up to this time, David, as king of Judah, had apparently been a vassal of the alliance of Philistine cities.[122] But once he had ascended the throne of Israel, it could be presumed that he would also take up that kingdom's traditional resistance to Philistine domination, which went back to its earliest origins, and that he would involve Judah in it.[123] This preventive campaign by the Philistines served only to bring the final crisis closer; they were defeated on repeated occasions, and lost for ever their hegemony in Palestine.[124] The importance

[119] Cf. above pp. 258 ff. The practical interests of these two groups were naturally different, in view of their different geographical situation.

[120] David seems to have maintained good relations with his neighbours to the east, as long as his forces were tied up in the west (cf. 2 Sam. x. 1 ff.).

[121] 2 Sam. v. 17 ff. In this section the material is ordered not chronologically, but according to its subject matter, so that the Philistine attack may have taken place before David took Jerusalem (vss. 6 ff.).

[122] More precisely of Achish, the prince of Gath.

[123] That agreements were made to this effect either before or at the time of David's elevation to the kingship of Israel is likely, even though the tradition is silent on the matter (but cf. 2 Sam. iii. 18).

[124] The account we possess unfortunately moves from the first

of this for the general course of the history of the country can be summed up in a few words; the balance of political power, which two centuries previously had shifted from Egypt to Philistia, was now advancing in the same geographical direction towards the interior of Palestine, from the plains into the mountains, and thus from the regions of the ancient and more or less exhausted Canaanite culture into the area peopled by the young nations out of the desert.[125] What is more important to us, however, is that with this sudden change, the original purpose in the founding of the kingdom of Israel was achieved and surpassed; their own subjection to the Philistines was not only ended, but turned into the subjection of the Philistines. Of course this was not dependence on the Israelites as such, but subjection to David's personal rule, which was later inherited by Solomon.[126] For after his victories over the Philistines David did not go so far as to deprive them of the traditional form of their own political life. The five city-states were allowed to remain in existence, so long as their feudal lords became his vassals and renounced any political ambition outside the boundaries of their own territories. He seems to have reduced their military forces, chiefly by taking their professional troops into his own service.[127] Throughout there is a repetition of what we saw

---

stages of the struggle (2 Sam. v. 17 ff.) directly to the ultimate political outcome (viii. 1); there must have been intermediate stages.

[125] The same historical movement from south to north can be traced even farther; from Thebes through the city of Rameses in the Nile Delta to Philistia, and from Jerusalem through Damascus to Nineveh and Babylon. That it had two separate stages in the limited area of Palestine is remarkable, and can only be explained by the proximity of two races and two cultures in that area (cf. also *ZDPV*, lii [1929], p. 19).

[126] This is what is meant at least by the subjugation of the Philistines by David in 2 Sam. viii. 1. For the reign of Solomon cf. 1 Kings ii. 40 ff. and the fact that none of his fortresses (ix. 15, 17 f.) lay on Philistine ground.

[127] This is particularly true if one follows the usual view that the Cherethites and Pelethites, who in the tradition concerning

when David took possession of Jerusalem. The person who benefited directly was once again the king himself, the only difference being that his own political power now extended much further, reaching beyond the Israelite national frontier. The only immediate apparent advantage from this by the kingdoms of Israel and Judah, which admittedly must not be underestimated, was that they were freed from the chronic threat of the Philistine's long-standing claims to dominate Palestine, so long as the latter remained subject to David and whoever should succeed him. There is, however, another factor which concerns both kingdoms much more directly and which at once resulted in a change in the internal structure at least of the kingdom of Israel. The hegemony of the Philistines not only extended as far as the interior of Israel and Judah, but from much earlier times had included the plains inhabited by the Canaanites and Aegean peoples, and its effect there had naturally been even more marked. Since the domination exercised by the Philistines had now passed into David's hands, he himself had to find for these people, neither Israelite nor Judean, who had previously been vassals or subjects of the Philistines, a place within his new empire, unless in the general change of rulers they should succeed in winning back their independence. The tradition makes no express reference to actions of a military or political nature performed by David with this in mind, but we do learn of the result achieved in David's reign as well as in Solomon's. The plains, with the exception of the five Philistine city-states and possibly the neighbouring regions which were directly dependent on them,[129] were not left in the condition of semi-

---

David's latter years appear as his main mercenary troops (2 Sam. viii. 18, 20, 23, etc.), came from Philistia. But cf. also 2 Sam. xv. 18 ff.

[128] Apart perhaps from the difficult final sentence of 2 Sam. viii. 1, whose text can hardly be corrected on the basis of 1 Chron. xviii. 1.

[129] I am thinking especially of the plain of Ono north of Philistia, which according to the annals of Sennacherib was still subject to Ashkelon in the year 701 B.C., and of the areas in the farthest south and south-west such as Gerar.

independent vassal states, but were incorporated, according to where they lay, into the kingdoms of Israel and Judah. In David's time, this is shown by the story of the census of the armies in 'Israel and Judah'; if the king's envoys travelled the whole of the western frontier of both kingdoms from Sidon in the north to Beersheba in the south through 'all the cities of the Hivites and Canaanites', this can only mean the towns of the western plains which, although neither Israelite nor Judean, were nevertheless equally obliged to provide troops and thus must have been allied to the kingdoms and possessed the same rights.[130] And this same situation is revealed even more clearly in Solomon's time in the list of officers who at that time governed the provinces of 'all Israel'; no less than four of these administrative regions belong by their location and by the fact that they are designated by the name of the city and not of the tribe, in the category of David's annexations in the area of the previous Philistine system of government.[131] Whether David had to take military measures to deal this political death-blow to the outmoded city-state system of the plains is uncertain, and of minor importance to us. One can hardly credit the individual towns with any means of serious defence once they had lost the support of the Philistine military resources. On the other hand it is important to know why David now proceeded to incorporate them into the kingdoms of Israel and Judah, instead of merely submitting the regions which he had acquired in one form or another to his own personal rule, as with Jerusalem. Were there perhaps historical claims which the king had to bear in mind when rearranging things in this area? I think that this was so. We know from a quite distinctive set of documents in the Old Testament that even before the formation of the Israelite

[130] 2 Sam. xxiv. 7.

[131] 1 Kings iv. 9–12. The districts named here, which are all in the plain, do not quite cover the same area as is referred to in 2 Sam. xxiv. 7, since they do not include the plain of Acco and Phoenician coast which lay directly to the north. But we know from 1 Kings ix. 11 ff. that the kingdom of Israel, as early as Solomon's reign, suffered a considerable territorial loss in this direction, which is reflected in this list.

state, there had developed a complete and, in the main, internally consistent system of territorial and political claims by the individual tribes to the areas remaining under foreign control on their borders, which was based on the idea that Israel had an exclusive right to the possession of Palestine.[132] David was now realizing these ancient claims by incorporating the annexed areas into the kingdoms of Israel and Judah, naturally with the exception of Philistia, so that Judah's desires were only very imperfectly fulfilled.[133] Israel, however, acquired practically everything that according to this theory she could possibly demand, from Sidon to Aijalon and Beth-shemesh, from the Mediterranean coast to the frontiers of the neighbouring states east of the Jordan. We must assume that this act of David's did much in the eyes of the Israelites to atone for the faults which they would have found in his policies. It also had the effect of rounding off the territory of the kingdom of Israel, which to its loss had still not come about during Saul's reign, whereas the kingdom of Judah had always possessed a compact shape.[134] Of course, on closer inspection one realizes that the situation created by David neither realized the old ideal, in the precise

[132] I am referring to the system of tribal boundaries in the Book of Joshua ('Das System der Stammesgrenzen im Buche Josua', *Sellin-Festschrift* [1927], pp. 13 ff.; *K.S.*, I, pp. 193 ff.) and the catalogue of towns not conquered by the tribes, but later made subject to Israel in Judges i. 19 (?), xxi. 27–35, which are both originally independent catalogues. The first unfortunately cannot be dated exactly, but the second clearly has in mind the situation created by David, and not quite maintained by Solomon.

[133] In the foothills between its own mountain homeland and the coastal plain Judah achieved only a very slight increase of territory. The new situation corresponds to the picture of Palestine that is envisaged by the Blessing and Curse of Noah: Shem (Israel and Judah) is lord of the land, and Japheth (the Philistines) the privileged sharer of the tents of Shem, while Canaan (the older population) is the slave of both (Gen. ix. 25 ff.).

[134] For this purpose the incorporation of the plains of Megiddo and Beth-shan was decisive (1 Kings iv. 12). Compare the strategic situation before Saul's last battle with the Philistines (1 Sam. xxviii. 4); ALT, 'Die Landnahme der Israeliten' (1925), pp. 26 f.; *K.S.*, I, p. 117, tr. above pp. 175 ff.

manner in which it was first conceived, nor had replaced it with a reality that was any better, but introduced into the kingdom of Israel stresses which it had never known in its original form. Until this time, these territorial claims had been the affair of the individual tribes, even though they were recognized by the other tribes and mutually guaranteed; David, however, as we can tell by working back from Solomon's list, did not join the annexed area to the tribes at all, but to the kingdom and formed out of them administrative areas which, having identical rights and responsibilities, stood alongside the tribal areas which were established on the same principles. This of course means a partial renunciation of the goal which would have been achieved if the old claims had been fulfilled, that is the penetration of every last remnant of foreign influence by Israelite men and laws. Now the national boundaries between Israelite and non-Israelite areas of settlement were disappearing, but only to spring up again as provincial boundaries and in this function serving once more to choke all intercourse and exchange of ideas. I would like to believe that it was genuine political insight that suggested this arrangement to David. If he considered that the time had come to combine the Israelites and non-Israelites into a single political body, it would have been clear to him that their mutual unfamiliarity could cause dangerous friction, if they were allowed to mingle among each other in a closer relationship within single provinces. Besides, the population resources of both parties were fully provided for by the land they already possessed, and they clung grimly to their lands; an exchange of population could be effected only with the surplus who had no possessions, and who had no national importance.[135] And should not the rights of the non-Israelites be respected just as much as those of the Israelite tribes? This was the state of affairs from then on. In the kingdom of Israel, Israelites and non-Israelites lived in union, and yet

[135] The obvious course would be the settlement of the mercenary troops; but we know that they were international in composition and consequently were not appropriate material for a national population policy.

segregated, segregated and yet united, and in future the kingdom only partially deserved its name since national unity disappeared as quickly as territorial unity increased. This was without doubt the profoundest change which occurred in the second stage of its existence; for while the other stresses with which David's whole life was burdened, within the two dualities Israel-Judah and Israel-Jerusalem, merely affected relations between the states, the duality of Israel and Canaan now became an internal problem, which the kingdom could avoid only by reverting from its new to its original form. The first serious consequences of the changes which had been introduced into the structure became noticeable as early as Saul's reign, and these were in the organization of the army. Apart from his mercenaries, David had only the conscripted armies of Israel and Judah at his disposal in time of war, and did very well with them, as his military successes show.[136] To these Solomon added a strong chariot corps, a weapon which until this time had been completely unknown to the Israelites, although characteristic of the Canaanites for some time. For this he could only recruit men and materials, vehicles and livestock from the areas which had been annexed, in so far as he did not actually draw them from foreign countries.[137] Naturally this corps had as little to do with the con-

[136] Uriah's announcement to David gives a full classification of David's army and a characteristic insight into its military conditions: 'The ark and Israel and Judah (i.e. the national levy of both kingdoms) live in booths; and my lord Joab and the servants of my lord (the king's mercenaries) are camping in the open field' (2 Sam. xi. 11). Note the distinction in the organization of the camp: the mercenaries are combat troops, always ready to strike; the levies are kept as a reserve for pitched battles.

[137] The outward reason for Solomon's creation of a chariot force was presumably the dispute which arose with the Aramaeans (1 Kings xi. 23 ff.–in which a battle can hardly have been avoided) who apparently made a greater use of chariots than the Philistines (cf. 2 Sam. viii. 4 and above, n. 23). The view expressed in the tradition, that Solomon recruited his chariot force exclusively from Israelites, is as little correct as the directly opposed view that he exacted forced labour only from the Canaanites in the kingdom (cf. below, n. 140).

scripted forces as had David's mercenary infantrymen. Thus the king's military power was increased at the expense of that of the Israelite nation and made the king's own forces even more independent of the national will.[138] And if we add the fact that the new strongholds in which Solomon posted the various divisions of his chariot corps were also built almost without exception in areas which had not previously belonged to Israel, indeed on the sites of the old Canaanite cities,[139] we begin to realize how in the kingdom of Israel the balance began to swing from the Israelite to the Canaanite side. It is the old superiority of the civilization of the plains over the mountains which was once more coming into play; its effect could hardly be ignored once the whole country was a national unity. Moreover the fact that Solomon, as far as we can see, was in other respects careful to distribute the rights and responsibilities of his subjects equally throughout the kingdom of Israel[140] may at all events have impeded and veiled the development which was under way. It was now impossible to stop it, however.

There was never any further incorporation of foreign territories into the kingdoms of Israel and Judah, although the earlier stages of David's career were followed by the subjection of the adjacent states east of the Jordan, so that his own and Solomon's system of government spread through the

[138] It is always possible that Solomon reduced the numbers of his professional infantry in favour of the chariot force, once it had completed its historical task against the Philistines. A supreme commander of the mercenaries such as is regularly named in the lists of David's officers, is never mentioned under Solomon, though admittedly no commander of the chariot force is either (1 Kings iv. 2 ff.).

[139] 1 Kings ix. 15, 17 ff. How far the architecture of Solomon's fortresses was influenced by the provision of facilities (stalls, etc.) for the chariot force, we begin to see from the results of the American excavations at Megiddo (cf. ALT, 'Megiddo im Übergang', *ZAW*, N.F. xix [1944], pp. 82 ff.; *K.S.*, I, pp. 271 ff.).

[140] For the provision of food this is shown by the list of officers in 1 Kings iv. 7 ff., for the forced labour by v. 27 and xi. 28, by contrast with the unhistorical assertion of ix. 21 (cf. above n. 137).

whole of Palestine as far as the edge of the wilderness, and thereby extended further than any native power of earlier times known to us, even the Philistines. In the course of these last great campaigns there must naturally have been just as many decisions about the boundaries in disputed territories to the advantage of Israel and Judah, but the actual areas settled by the hill tribes east of the Jordan were not disturbed. As far as we can see, they had never been the object of the territorial and political claims of the Israelites, who regarded them as the legitimate property of related nations, to which they felt as much respect was due as they expected from their neighbours towards their own possessions.[141] This explains why when David began to swallow up this whole series of mountain states from Edom in the south to the Arameans in the north, he did not join them politically to the kingdoms of Israel and Judah, but made each according to its circumstances either a vassal-state ruled by its previous king, and responsible only to himself, or removed the king and placed it directly under his own administration, as a subject-state, in his royal domain.[142] And yet these occurrences were of considerable importance to the internal history of the Israelite state. For the whole of Palestine was incorporated into a very

[141] The system of Israelite tribal boundaries in the Book of Joshua makes no provision for the land east of the Jordan (what apparently belongs there in Josh. xiii. is a later literary construction that does not record the original situation); similarly the list of towns not conquered in Judges i. can be expanded only by the addition of one verse preserved in Josh. xiii. 13, which refers to the east but covers only a very small area (it names two small Aramaic kingdoms, but no cities). The strongest evidence that the Israelites respected the ownership of the territory of their neighbours east of the Jordan is given by Num. xx. 14 ff. (Edom) and Judges xi. 21 ff. (Moab).

[142] 2 Sam. viii. 2 ff. gives only a very summary account of what took place. We can neither extract from it what led to military action in each case, nor can we obtain a clear picture of the individual details of the new political arrangements that were set up; other relevant passages such as 2 Sam. x. 1 ff.; xii. 30 f.; 1 Kings xi. 15 f. give valuable individual pictures but generalizations cannot be made from them (cf. ALT, 'Das Grossreich Davids', *ThLZ*, lxxv [1950], cols. 213–220; *K.S.*, I, pp. 66 ff.).

complicated system of dependencies, the only focal-point of which was the person of David and of Solomon after him,[143] and the authority of these rulers had spread considerably beyond the original alliances, which alone made a unified Palestinian system possible. Israel and Judah did actually still exist as the nucleus of the whole; David's battles were fought entirely by their armies, together with the mercenaries,[144] and it is easily understandable that the constitutional basis on which their relationship to the king was founded could not be withdrawn so long as their military support seemed necessary to the fulfilment of his ambitious political aims. The problem was, however, whether they would be equally willing to offer these services where the connection between the sacrifices they had to make and what they stood to gain was not so directly obvious. Suspicion is aroused at once by the fact, already mentioned, that the Israelites had no claims on the territory of their neighbours east of the Jordan such as they had had amongst the Philistines and Canaanites. From their own point of view, would they have thought it absolutely necessary that the eastern hill-states should be forced into David's administrative system by repeated attacks not only by the royal mercenaries, but by the national army of both the kingdoms—especially when this was done in a way which made it impossible for them to make a permanent and voluntary submission to this system? They would only have considered it necessary if the kingdoms of Israel and Judah had also feared a threat to their own safety from these neighbours. But there was no serious likelihood of this; once the whole of the country west of the Jordan was united under David's control, it represented a military force which could scarcely have been equalled by the eastern states, even if

[143] Admittedly, the gradual eating away of the Empire by the Aramaeans in the north-east had already begun under Solomon (1 Kings xi. 23 ff.), in a similar way to the losses suffered to the Phoenicians at about the same time in the north-west of the kingdom of Israel (ix. 11 ff.; cf. above, n. 131).

[144] See above, n. 136. There is nowhere any mention of levies from the border states taking part.

they had all joined in a combined action.[145] David himself, therefore, must have taken the initiative in making war on them, even though, clever statesman as he was, he may have held back his attack until the eastern states had shown him some provocation.[146] And he may not, of course, originally have intended such a wide extension of operations as necessarily resulted from the complicated interlocking of territories and kingdoms amongst these states.[147] This, however, made the military kingship which he exercised over the national army something quite different from Saul's defensive command, and his use of the levied army for this offensive was contrary to its original character as an organization of the country's armed forces merely for the purpose of national defence. All would have been well if the new conquests which were being made with the aid of the armies directly benefited the kingdoms of Israel and Judah as the annexations of the country west of the Jordan had done. But the political result was rather that the neighbouring states which were conquered and made subject to David in one way or another continued as before to be separated from Israel and Judah, and it is very difficult to decide how else they could have been dealt with. To send conscripted armies into the field time after time, perhaps year after year, for such a purpose made demands on the kingdoms which as time went by became increasingly difficult to fulfil. In short, the bow had been bent too far; however well it suited David personally to strive after a complete and perfect control over the whole of Palestine, it did not suit the individual interests of Israel and

[145] The military aid which individual Aramaean states provided for each other (2 Sam. viii. 5) or for the Ammonites (x. 6 ff.) was not for offensive purposes, but was intended as a defence against David's attacks.

[146] As in the case of the war against the Ammonites, 2 Sam. x, which gives the impression that it was the first of its kind.

[147] I am thinking especially of the subjection of the Aramaean states, not all of which even bordered on Israel. The summary in 2 Sam. viii, which is our only source for these matters, is not of its nature capable of casting any light on the underlying logic of the events that it describes.

Judah. Moreover, affairs proceeded so quickly under David's leadership that it would have been astonishing if the people of Israel and Judah had been capable of an inner adaptation to the new circumstances rapid enough to keep pace with the course of external events.

We must suppose, therefore, that it was precisely this tension which was the cause of the serious internal crisis which David's régime had to withstand even in his own lifetime, that is, the revolutions in Israel under Absalom and Sheba.[148] Naturally the tradition does not reveal as clear a connection as could be desired between these upheavals and Israel's disapproval of David's policy of conquering the land east of the Jordan; it concentrates solely on the question of succession to the throne, and for this reason, and also because of the special nature of the author's narrative style, places the leading personalities and the various motives for their actions so much to the fore that any interest in the motivation of the people's behaviour is lost as a result.[149] But chronologically there is nothing wrong with linking incidents together in this manner; the conquest of the states east of the Jordan must at least have been long under way when Israel rose up against David; and this is supported by the fact that it was Israel which revolted of its own accord, since its political structure was most affected by David's continual military and political offences against its neighbouring kingdoms.[150] The prevail-

[148] I cannot accept the attempt of CASPARI (*Aufkommen*) to attribute the whole crisis to motives of internal policy, and in particular to opposition to David on the part of the Israelite aristocracy on the grounds that the kingdom interfered with their ancient privileges.

[149] In the one introductory scene which is directly relevant here, where Absalom waylays Israelites coming to the royal court at Jerusalem with complaints and 'steals their hearts' (2 Sam. xv. 1 ff.), it is quite likely that these complaints were caused by alleged or real excessive demands in the matter of the military levy in the first place (cf. 2 Kings iv. 13). There is no evidence from this early period of the development of a royal court of appeal in matters of private legislation, as is often suggested.

[150] The chronology can be estimated approximately from the connection between 2 Sam. xvii. 27 and xii. 26 ff. (Ammon). It is

ing opinion is that the kingdom of Judah was also involved in the revolt under Absalom, and only the sequel under Sheba is considered to be a purely Israelite occurrence.[151] But the arguments on which this is based are not at all sound; from the start we cannot really suppose that the word 'Israel' or 'all Israel', the general name for the revolutionaries in the story, should be used first in the time of Absalom with the old ideal meaning which included Judah, then later under Sheba changed all at once into the new, more limited meaning, as a name for the kingdom which was constitutionally separated from Judah, especially as the author never indicates this change in meaning;[152] the usual conclusion that Absalom must have had the kingdom of Judah on his side since he gave the signal to revolt from Hebron, its former capital, takes for granted what first has to be proved.[153] Actually it can be seen clearly enough from the incidents between the revolutions of Absalom and Sheba that during the first uprising the Judeans remained neutral, which is not surprising, considering their exceptional position; their role in the later revolution under Sheba—and on David's side—is even more easily understood.[154] This brings the duality between

---

strange that the author does not mention any attempt on the part of the conquered border states to free themselves when there was a rebellion in Israel.

[151] Especially in SACHSSE, *Die Bedeutung des Namens Israel* (1922), pp. 85 ff.; cf. for the opposite view, B. LUTHER, ZAW, xxi (1901), pp. 25 ff.

[152] At the very least one should point out what is apparently the strongest piece of evidence for this view, that is, the advice of Hushai to Absalom, to call on 'all Israel from Dan to Beersheba' for the battle against David (2 Sam. xvii. 11). For the author is characterizing Hushai precisely by putting in his mouth a deliberate and theatrical exaggeration (cf. ROST, *Die Überlieferung*, pp. 125 f.).

[153] The author himself explains this action of Absalom credibly enough by saying that he considered David and the men of Jerusalem could best be deceived if Absalom did not go into Israel, but in the opposite direction towards Hebron. There is no mention of any act of allegiance to Absalom by the Judaeans during his stay in Hebron; the signal simply goes out from there to Israel.

[154] The decisive passage is 2 Sam. xix. 12 ff., where David sends

the two kingdoms into even sharper focus. Only the people of Israel rose against David, and by their behaviour showed how little they had departed from their original conception of the state and of the kingdom. They felt free to withdraw from the 'covenant' into which they had entered with David, immediately they felt that the king himself was no longer facing up to the responsibilities which he had assumed, or was exceeding the authority invested in him, and as soon as a new man appeared who seemed capable of restoring the kingdom to its former principles. Apparently it mattered little to the Israelites whether this new man belonged to the house of David or to the tribe of Saul; he might even have come from another region. Nor were they alarmed that neither Absalom nor Sheba was a charismatic leader like Saul; why should they not overlook this deficiency, since they had only been able to uphold the old ideal in this connection with a fabrication, when they had recognized David as king?[155] The real difference between the two revolutions was only that the first one was prepared long beforehand, and was intended exclusively as a change in the kingship, which would improve Israel's position without injuring the system of government which David would leave,[156] whereas the second, which

---

to Judah, after the end of Absalom's revolt, to abandon the neutrality they had shown up to then and to demonstrate to the Israelites, by giving the king a triumphal return, that everything remained as before in Judah. If Judah had taken part in the revolt that had just taken place, this would not in my view have been possible. The deeper reason why Judah did not take part has probably something to do with the obligation to provide troops for the national levy. It is likely that Judah did not provide levies, or provided fewer than Israel, for the campaign against the states in the northern part of the country east of Jordan, which were apparently the most dangerous and the most determined enemies.

[155] The absence of any mention of the designation of either Sheba or Absalom by Yahweh can be explained by the basic attitude of the author to what took place, even if this religious factor played any part in the way the Israelites thought about it.

[156] This aim is made clear in Ahitophel's advice to Absalom (2 Sam. xvii. 1 ff.) and explains the fact, which would be difficult to understand otherwise, that the first new man chosen by the

rose out of a momentary agitation, was directed almost more against Judah than against Israel, and, by renouncing Judah, also hoped to put an end to their personal union with him, and so finally to destroy the whole system.[157] Both attempts failed; in Absalom's revolt, David's mercenaries were enough to win a decisive victory over the army conscripted in Israel, and would also have been quite capable of suppressing the uprising under Sheba if David had not considered it politically advisable to join up with the army of Judah. Both incidents have more than a merely momentary importance, and were symptoms of a change in basic political principles. There is no need whatsoever to refer back to the beginnings of the growth of David's kingdom, but merely to remember the campaigns east of the Jordan, in which Israel, Judah and the mercenaries worked together, in order to make clear the whole difficulty caused by the change which had taken place. Israel which, had once spontaneously paid homage to David and which until recently had provided him with military support, was now held within his system of government by force of arms, and it is difficult to say which action in fact tore open the deeper political rifts; the reassertion of David's personal rule, aided only by the mercenaries, or the reassertion of the whole system with the help of Judah. But as we have seen, both formed part of the political structure from the beginning, and were in fact the two oldest powers which David created, and which he was now playing off against the third. The positive proof of their superiority which was now given dissuaded the Israelites from further attempts at revolt, and thus enabled the whole system of government to exist for another generation; the rift remained, however, in

---

Israelites should be no less than a son of David whom they were trying to overthrow. This dynastic approach will concern us later in another context.

[157] The revolt of Sheba, apparently directed only against David (2 Sam. xx. 1) is in reality Israel's answer to the special claims made by Judah in the exchange that immediately precedes it (xix. 43). Note that a generation later, when the personal union between Israel and Judah was finally removed, the same formula played a similar part (1 Kings xii. 16).

the foundations. It may have been in connection with this that Solomon renounced all further offensives and consciously prepared his whole kingdom for defence. He was no longer certain of the Israelite army, and was therefore more readily inclined to rely on the Canaanite chariots and fortresses. But this led him to enforce statutory labour on the Israelites, even for the construction of these fortresses; there was never any question of such a thing during David's reign, and certainly not under Saul. It was, apparently, intended as a duty to replace the military service which was no longer required and it is significant that it later gave rise to new conflicts between the monarch and the people, which led to the final break.[158]

In the final analysis it cannot be denied that the position of the kingdom of Israel in the political system, which should have been improved by the revolt against David, was worse under Solomon than it had been before. On the other hand, one should not assume that there had been a complete alteration of the system in favour of Judah and the border provinces. As always Israel still formed the nucleus of the whole, together with Judah and Jerusalem, now powerfully fortified, and the border provinces were still only loosely included by their various forms of dependence on the king. The best proof of this is Solomon's series of fortresses. The very loose network which they formed covered the whole of Israel and Judah, but nowhere encroached upon Philistia or the mountain states east of the Jordan; in the general defensive picture, these latter merely performed the function of a glacis in front of the inner line of fortresses, or politically speaking, had the role of buffer-states between the central

[158] 1 Kings v. 13; xi. 26 ff.; xii. 1 ff. (cf. above, n. 140). If the first of these passages speaks of the exacting of forced labour from 'all Israel', the setting we have attempted to describe makes it likely that the expression here also refers only to the kingdom of Israel, in contrast to the kingdom of Judah; there is no positive evidence that Judah shared in the forced labour under Solomon. The connection between the obligation of military service and labour on the building of fortresses is made particularly clear in 1 Kings xv. 22 (in the period after Solomon).

area of Solomon's domain and the independent kingdoms which lay beyond it.[159] It seems to me worthy of note, however, that within the higher executive staff of David and Solomon there was never any means of separating the mandates for Israel from the mandates for Judah.[160] As long as this arrangement persisted, it never led to any fundamental breakdown of the duality between the kingdoms; this still continued to exist even in the time of Solomon, when it really made itself felt for the first time since the revolt of Israel against David. But one can at least be certain that from the beginning to the end of the period, the principle of the personal union was strong enough to be able to create and maintain the institutions it called for, not only in connection with the king, the head of the whole system, but also within the higher official executive through which he worked, in spite of all the tension between individual kingdoms as a result of the constitution. It was not of course a desire of the nation as a whole which was manifesting itself in this way, but merely the superiority of the kings over their subjects. It is of course obvious that the international relationships which

[159] 1 Kings ix. 15, 17 f. Beyond the fortress of Hazor in eastern Galilee (for its site, cf. *PJB*, xxv [1929], pp. 48 f.) lay the conquered territory of the Aramaeans; beyond Megiddo the friendly kingdom of Tyre (see above, n. 131); beyond Beth-horon and Gezer, and beyond Baalath, much farther south (perhaps the Baalah of Josh. xv. 29) lay Philistia; beyond Thamar (south of the Dead Sea; cf. R. Hartmann, *ZDPV*, xxxvi [1913], pp. 110 f., Alt, *PJB*, xxx [1934], pp. 23 f.) lay Edom. The long eastern frontier between Hazor and Thamar is significantly not covered by fortresses, since the states east of the Jordan, stretching out beyond it, could provide a sufficient protection against the wilderness.

[160] Cf. the lists in 2 Sam. viii. 16 ff.; xx. 23 ff.; 1 Kings iv. 2 ff. When Joab's supreme command 'over the whole army' is described in 2 Sam. xx. 23, 'Israel' is an obvious addition, brought about by xx. 4 ff. (cf. xix. 14) and makes no difference to the unity of his command. The doubling of the office of secretary in 1 Kings iv. 3 has certainly got nothing to do with the two kingdoms—it was a family affair; two sons shared their father's office. A closer examination of these lists of officers is urgently needed (cf. Begrich, *ZAW*, N.F. xvii [1941], pp. 1 ff.).

were begun by David and continued by Solomon with such enthusiasm, should be considered from this exclusive point of view; neither Israel nor Judah could interrupt the kings in their diplomatic and mercantile undertakings, and whatever was gained from them benefited only the kings themselves and their courts.[161]

Thus the analysis of the various political phenomena during the reign of David and Solomon finally confirms what we had already realized when we studied their origins; it is a completely distinct self-contained stage in the political development not only of the Israelites but of the whole of Palestine, a construction with a varied basis and built of widely different materials, and which was as a result, in its final form and after all the changes it underwent, different from anything previous and anything which followed. From this we still have one last consequence to draw concerning the nature of the monarchy of David and Solomon, seen as the institution which crowned the whole structure and held it together. It was an amalgam of the popular monarchies of Israel and Judah, the city-state monarchies of Ziklag and Jerusalem, and in addition, directly or indirectly, of the popular monarchies of the eastern mountain states and the city-state monarchies of the Philistines; which category decided its nature? We have already been given a provisional answer to this question by the story of Israel's revolt under Absalom's leadership; the very kingdom which from its beginnings had a flexible form of monarchy based on the charismatic leadership, constantly regulated by Yahweh, wanted to transfer David's power to his son, when it rose against him.[162] When the handing over of higher power actually took place, it meant no less than a renunciation of the earlier freedom of

[161] Cf. 2 Sam. v. 11 ff.; viii. 9 ff. and especially 1 Kings v. 15 ff.; ix. 16, 26 ff.; x. 1 ff. I cannot describe the whole picture in detail here, and would only stress that Solomon's trading projects should be considered exclusively from the point of view of a royal monopoly of trade, of which there are many examples from the older empires of the ancient Near East (cf. ALT, 'Die Weisheit Salomos', *ThLZ*, xxvi (1951), cols. 139–44; *K.S.*, II., pp. 90 ff.).

[162] See above, n. 156.

Yahweh's designation and the acclamation of the people, in exchange for allegiance to the House of David on the part of Israel and of every other member of the system. And what the Israelites failed to achieve by rebellion, later came about by other means without their initiative when David included his son Solomon in a co-regency while he was still alive, and so assured his son's succession to the throne.[163] Of course there was no place here for the decisive element of an ideal charismatic monarchy which we found in the case of Saul, and which we saw applied fictitiously even in David's case; it was not Yahweh who chose Solomon as David's successor, but David who did it entirely of his own accord,[164] and in place of the acclamation of the assembly of the Israelite people there was that of the prince's partisans in Jerusalem. Even if the missing factors could have been formally supplied later by obtaining the approval of Israel (and naturally of Judah also),[165] the fact would still have remained that for the first time a king of Israel had disposed freely—and successfully too—of his throne. In this way the kingship over the whole of David's dominions was attached to a single dynasty. It must be admitted that this was the only arrangement that could cope with the practical necessities of the system. The simplest way to understand this is to imagine, for example, that David had died without deciding on his successor, and that the procedure in Israel had strictly followed the old idea, and that they had waited for the designation of a new king by Yahweh and then paid homage to him. We are able to say with great certainty how things would have developed in the meantime in David's dominions outside Israel. The city-state of Jerusalem could not have accepted Israel's choice

[163] 1 Kings i.

[164] It is a clumsy (and certainly intentional) misuse of an expression whose meaning had long been perfectly definite, when the author makes David say of Solomon 'I have appointed him to be *nāgīd* over Israel and Judah' (1 Kings i. 35); for only Yahweh could do so, and even he could only do so for Israel.

[165] It is not surprising that the author does not mention this. He is only interested in this context in the outcome of the rivalry between Solomon and his half-brother Adonijah.

for themselves if the new king of the neighbouring state had not been of the House of David. But according to the rights of conquest, Jerusalem belonged exclusively to David, and on the occasion of his death to his successors, as an inheritance, no matter what became of the rest of the kingdom as a whole. Thus there was in this case no question whatsoever of anything other than a dynastic monarchy.[166] It would have been very questionable whether the kingdom of Judah would also have recognized the new king of Israel, especially if he came from another tribe, as was to be expected.[167] The men of Judah had previously accepted David as king, without bothering about Israel. After the experiences of the rebellion of David's sons there was no reason why they should now accept a king imposed by Israel in whose election they had no influence at all. There was, therefore, a constant threat of the dissolution of the personal union between Israel and Judah. Moreover, no one will suppose that the mountain states in the west and the east, which had been dependent up to this time on David's own person, would be willing to enter into the same relationship with someone else. They were sure to break free. Finally, of course, there were David's mercenaries, the most important military force in the country. They would have been primarily at the disposal of David's descendants, just as Saul's mercenaries had previously been for Ishbaal, and would have been a great danger to a king of Israel who was not of the House of David. One can look at this hypothetical situation from whatever angle one will, but the result is always the same; only a dynastic succession could prevent the immediate collapse of the kingdom as a whole after David's death. It would not have been possible to re-

[166] This legal position was recognized hundreds of years later by the Assyrian king Sennacherib when he left Jerusalem to the descendants of David, while he took all Judah from them (cf. ALT, 'Die territorialgeschichtliche Bedeutung von Sancheribs Eingriff in Palästina', *PJB*, xxv [1930], pp. 80 ff.; *K.S.*, II, pp. 242 ff.).

[167] Even if Israel had chosen a son of David, other serious disagreements could have arisen. This is shown by Israel's support for Adonijah against Solomon before David designated Solomon (1 Kings i. 9).

turn to the ancient Israelite institution of a charismatic monarchy, that could be assumed by any chosen individual, even if the kingdom of Israel had had sufficient influence on the whole empire at the critical moment to be able to impose it. Within a single generation the course of history had superseded the fundamental internal structure of the Israelite state, and there is no doubt that this took place with the full knowledge of the participants. However, the ideal of kingship which the period produced found its expression in the new religious conception of an eternal covenant into which Yahweh entered with David, which guaranteed the undisturbed continuance of David's throne and house for ever,[168] and of a promise by Yahweh to David that he would accept his descendant and successor on the throne at any time as his own son.[169] If the first belief had legitimized the dynastic principle, so the second legitimized each king of the dynasty himself; the two together were quite sufficient to replace the old Israelite ideal of a choice carried out afresh on each occasion by Yahweh and the charismatic designation of a saviour for his people. This is the first appearance of the simple but highly creative historical origin of the expectation of the Messiah, which was later to show such an extensive development, for the Messiah was from the start none other than the descendant of David who in the relative or absolute end of future history would be the last king of his dynasty.[170]

[168] The wording of Yahweh's eternal covenant with David is first found in the so-called last words of David (2 Sam. xxiii. 5); they are dated early by PROCKSCH (*Alttestamentliche Studien zu R. Kittels, 60 Geburtstag*, pp. 112 ff.), and this does not seem to me to have been proved false by MOWINCKEL (*ZAW*, N.F. iv [1927], pp. 30 ff.). It is also contained in substance in the history of the succession (2 Sam. vii. 8 ff.). For the part played by this idea later cf. VON RAD, *Das Geschichtsbild des chronistischen Werkes* (1930), pp. 119 ff.

[169] 2 Sam. vii. 14. Hence the idea of the act of adoption in the ceremonial of the assumption of royal office by the later Davidic kings: Ps. ii. 7; Isa. ix. 5.

[170] In more recent studies of the Messianic expectation this indispensable point at which elements taken partly from foreign ideals

The first stage in the formation of the Israelite state, with Saul's founding of the kingdom of Israel, had brought about the penetration into the land west of the Jordan of the principle of national organization which had already been long established among the people in the mountains of the eastern borders of Palestine; the second, under David and Solomon, appeared to make an immediate departure from this principle, in the direction of a supra-national power which from the external point of view was purely a territorial system, but in its internal structure was based on personal allegiance.[171] Both the older and the more recently formed national states remained in existence as constitutionally separate powers; but they were now incorporated into a wider system of government, and the fate of the kingdom of Israel during this period shows us how little the various member-states could do against the tendencies of the overriding political leadership, even while they were actually trying to assert their traditional individuality. Now suppose the same tendencies had prevailed for a few more generations, and consider that perhaps, in course of time, other participant states might have failed in similar demonstrations of their internal opposition to the new system, just as Israel did. Would there not have come about a political unification which would finally have dispensed with national frontiers? And did not David or Solomon perhaps have this same aim in mind, even if they were intelligent enough not to wish to attain, by premature forcing, what would happen of its own accord? It is perhaps worthwhile to raise these questions and consider the possible lines of development they indicate. We must add at once that history gives a negative answer; the power which David and Solomon accumulated was actually far less than it may have seemed to them and to their contemporaries, and as a result, the immediate future did not lie with their system of

---

of kingship crystallize into a coherent idea is not given sufficient attention.

[171] If the different periods are separated according to this principle, the founding of the kingdom of Judah by David belongs basically to the first stage.

government, but in fact with the principle of the nation-state which they believed they had superseded. Even during Solomon's reign it was breaking down at the edge of the greater kingdom, and immediately after his death, when Israel broke loose from the throne of David, causing a breach of the centre, the whole system dissolved once more into the parts from which it had been constructed. Naturally in the light of what we have just learned, we cannot call this occurrence a split or division of the kingdom, as is customary. At first sight it is something of a far more limited nature, no more than the voluntary withdrawal of the kingdom of Israel from its form of personal union with the kingdom of Judah; a repetition, in fact, of what had already happened for a short period in the revolution led by Sheba, except that it had a more lasting effect.[172] Its direct consequences, however, were considerably more important, since Israel's action automatically brought with it the emancipation of all the border states from the domination of the House of David, so that the latter only remained in possession of the kingdom of Judah, apart from their personal property in Jerusalem and Ziklag. Thus at one blow, out of the system of government set up by David and Solomon, a system of more than half a dozen independent minor states sprang up in Palestine, and this system was maintained, basically unaltered, in spite of any variations, for a further two hundred years, until the Assyrians incorporated a large part of it into the provincial system of their universal empire.[173] History here has something very significant to say; it shows the empire created by David and Solomon with such amazing speed to be a swing of the political pendulum, which went far too far, beyond the prevailing inclinations and capabilities of the people of Palestine at the time, to make possible for it to stay longer, let alone permanently,

[172] The illuminating story of 1 Kings xii. describes this, and by 'Israel' and 'all Israel' invariably means only the kingdom of that name; Judah takes no part in the action, as is shown by the fact that it takes place in Shechem.

[173] Cf. *ZDPV*, lii (1929), pp. 220 ff.; *K.S.*, II, pp. 188 ff.; *PJB*, xxv (1930), pp. 80 ff.; *K.S.*, II, pp. 242 ff.

in this position, and it makes it apparent that actually only the principle of the nation-state, which was a very early, if not the earliest, type of political organization in the country, fulfilled the requirements of the peoples concerned and enabled some sort of balance to be set up between them. Under the circumstances it is not right to talk about a further stage in the formation of the states; the things that occurred after Solomon's death really constituted nothing more than a return to earliest conditions, in which each state built on whatever it had retained from the collapse of the whole empire.[174]

[174] The subsequent sections of the original essay were replaced by another article ('Das Königtum in den Reichen Israels und Juda', *VT*, i [1951], pp. 2–22; *K.S.*, II, pp. 116 ff.) dealing with the monarchy in the kingdoms of Israel and Judah, a translation of which follows.

THE MONARCHY IN THE KINGDOMS OF ISRAEL AND JUDAH

DAS KÖNIGTUM IN DEN REICHEN ISRAEL UND JUDA
Vetus Testamentum 1 (1951), pp. 2–22. E. J. Brill, Leiden

The monarchy was not, as is well known, part of the basic structure of the Israelite nation, nor did it succeed at a later period in attaining a permanent position as such, although it was the form of government under which the nation lived for centuries, and which had a decisive effect on its destiny. This is why the books of the law in the Old Testament normally make no reference to it even when they wish to present the existing law in comparatively full detail; what might perhaps have to be endured as the 'law of the king' (1 Sam. vii. 11 ff.) is distinguished in principle from what is recognized as the true law, given once for all by Yahweh to the federation of tribes. The Book of Deuteronomy might seek to treat the monarchy as part of a sacred constitution laid down there for the nation; but one has only to read the relevant passage (Deut. xvii. 14 ff.) to realize that this attempt did not succeed. For the monarchy is not presented there as an essential in the life of the nation as Yahweh desired it. It is seen as an additional feature which was optional, which could only be adopted if all kinds of precautions were taken to see that it did no damage, and which was unlikely to be accorded any function which was indispensable for the well-being of the nation. It must never be thought that the monarchy had the power in any way to alter or supersede the ancient law of God by its own legislation. The story of Naboth (1 Kings) makes it quite clear that even within the sphere of normal secular jurisdiction a royal court with professional judges was unable to overrule the judgement of a traditional local court. Despite the different views expressed about the monarchy in the oracles of the classical prophets, they clearly show that even at that time, several hundred years after its foundation, it had not yet managed to supersede the ancient, sacred ordinances in this preeminently important sphere of public life. It came into being too late, and the old order was by that time too firmly established, for the conflict between them to have any other result.

This disproportion between old and new is just as obvious in the relationship between the kingdom of Israel, and the federation of twelve tribes to which the name Israel had long been applied. One would have expected that a national state that came into being within that federation would have incorporated into itself all the members of the federation and them alone, and that its territory would accordingly have been approximately the same as the area settled by the tribes. But this is only true to any extent of the original form of the kingdom of Israel under king Saul (cf. 2 Sam. ii. 9) and at that period its name was appropriate. But as early as David's reign the situation was fundamentally altered; not only did he set up a kingdom of Judah alongside the kingdom of Israel, so making of one part of the twelve tribes a national state independent of the others, but added large areas with non-Israelite populations to both kingdoms, thus depriving them of their compact national unity (2 Sam. xxiv. 7; 1 Kings iv. 7 ff.). The personal union of the two kingdoms under his rule, and then under Solomon, cannot hide the fact that under this system the earlier organization of the federation of Israelite tribes has been abandoned, and the setting up by David of an empire stretching far beyond Palestine shows that in the second stage of its development the monarchy successfully carried out military and political ventures which of its very nature the ancient federation of tribes could never have contemplated (2 Sam. v. 6 ff.; viii). But even the collapse of this empire, which took place partly during the reign of Solomon (1 Kings xi. 23 ff.), and partly after his death, was not sufficient to restore the national basis of the kingdoms in Israel and Judah; not only did this continue to be impaired by the inclusion within both kingdoms of areas inhabited by foreign populations; after Israel had broken the personal union (1 Kings xii. 1 ff.), the dualism between the two kingdoms themselves led in the end to their separate existence under two different monarchies. It is understandable that the ruling house of David should always have regarded this latter step as an act of rebellion and disloyalty on the part of the kingdom of Israel (1 Kings xii. 19; Isa. vii. 17); on the other hand, during the whole period, up to the destruction of the kingdom of Israel by the Assyrians, which put an end to the dualism in this form, I can hardly think of a single passage which expressed any regret about it, or makes any appeal for it to be overcome, on the strength of the earlier unity of the federation of twelve tribes. It is as though the Israelites had come to terms with the fact that under the kings political life was taking quite a different course, varying considerably even from one kingdom to another. It is possible that despite the division of the nation into two separate states, the federation of tribes persisted at least in the form of an alliance based on the use of a common sanctuary, and played its part in keeping alive the Israelites' consciousness of unity beyond the boundaries of the kingdoms; the lack of any testimony to this does not seem to me, in view of the peculiar nature of the tradition found in the Old Testament, to be a convincing reason for supposing that this is not true. But whatever may be the case, the kind of state which came into being, and the monarchy as it developed in the kingdoms of Israel and Judah, continued to be markedly different in this respect from what had been demanded by the ideals of the ancient federation of tribes.

The separation of the two kingdoms, moreover, did not merely affect their external form, but reacted profoundly upon their internal structure, and in this respect gave rise to notable differences between them, which would be incomprehensible if one and the same preordained pattern had decided the course of political development in Israel and Judah. Although the ancient tradition concerning the rise to power of the first king of Israel, Saul, is very much of the nature of a saga, it shows clearly enough the original nature of his kingdom. It was closely related to an earlier feature of the life of the Israelite tribes, the charismatic leadership which appeared from time to time and which we meet, during the period before the formation of a national state, in the stories of the 'major judges' in the Book of Judges, and in part also in the stories of Moses and Joshua. It varies greatly from one individual to another and at that stage had no fixed institutional pattern. Just like the heroes of the past, the king of Israel, in the original conception, owed his authority exclusively to the fact that he was spontaneously called and endowed with charismatic powers by Yahweh (1 Sam. ix. 1–10, 16). The homage of the tribes that followed the first test of his powers (1 Sam. xi) signifies by contrast nothing more than a later ratification. As with the earlier judges, the authority imparted to the king of Israel empowered him originally only to summon together and command the army of the tribes to resist the claims of foreign neighbours against the territory and independence of Israel, which Yahweh, out of pity for his people, would not tolerate (1 Sam. ix. 16; x. 1 LXX). Campaigns of aggression lay outside his appointed task, and he had no concern with the internal politics of the tribes. In spite of these similarities, there are nevertheless certain essential differences between the kingdom of Israel in its original form, and the charismatic leadership that preceded it. Yahweh's commission to Saul is no longer restricted to the carrying out of a single defensive campaign against one particular hostile power such as the Philistines (cf. 1 Sam. ix. 16). He is to save Israel 'from the hand of their enemies round about' (1 Sam. x. 1 LXX), which can only be achieved by repeated campaigns in different areas as the occasion arises (e.g. 1 Sam. xi). Thus his recognition as king by tribes principally means that they place their military levy permanently at his disposal, as often as he calls it to arms for any compelling reason. Without such a constant state of preparedness they would have been unable to face with any hope of success what had become a chronic threat to their existence in Palestine. Thus the first Israelite state to be formed manifested an inherent and compelling tendency towards a permanent union of the whole nation, even though Saul was probably unable to bring it to full realization. The time was past when individual tribes or groups of tribes that were threatened could resist on their own under a charismatic leader with a correspondingly limited authority. But for the same reason, the charisma with which Yahweh endowed the king in order that he could fulfil the extensive task imposed upon him could not be allowed to exhaust itself in the first single blow against an enemy. Only if the charisma continued to give the king power to achieve the necessary success as the head of the army was it achieving its purpose, and only so long as this took place, demonstrating that the calling and endowment of the king by Yahweh was still in force, did his claim to lead the levy of the tribes still hold good. How seriously this was taken is shown by the story of the rejection of Saul, which certainly has some historical foundation (1 Sam. xv; cf. xvi. 14 f.). Thus he did not even retain his charisma until the end of his own life; far less could it have been handed down from him to his family, and when in spite of this Abner attempted after Saul's death to retain the office of king for one of his sons, without the designation of Yahweh or the acclamation of the people (2 Sam. ii. 8 f.), it is not surprising that this attempt to subvert the basic principles of the monarchy in Israel came to a very rapid end (2 Sam. iii–iv). Notwithstanding all this, it will not be denied that the monarchy in the kingdom of Israel originated in the charismatic leadership of the period before the founding of the state, and that at the beginning it did not depart very far from this inner structural principle. But on the other hand it is already evident in which direction it had to develop, sooner or later, beyond this basis, if it was to do justice to the task for which it was created. This task demanded that it should continually be in existence, and that fixed institutions should come into being which could last beyond the lifetime of any one king. This development would be bound to come into conflict with the flexibility of a charisma which was bestowed by Yahweh on one single individual, and could be withdrawn at any time, and would inevitably destroy it in the end.

This inevitable development, however, was to a considerable degree interrupted by the course of events in the period immediately following Saul, and its progress frustrated. For when the kingship of Israel passed into the hands of David immediately on its relinquishment by the family of Saul (2 Sam. v. 1 ff.) and from him to his son Solomon (1 Kings i), the kingdom of Israel was incorporated into a system of government much wider in its extent, and much more complicated in its internal structure, within which its specific features could scarcely be of much significance. In any case they would only be regarded as of any importance in so far as they could be reconciled with the purpose of the empire as a whole, or served to further them. Perhaps the simplest way of understanding this change in the situation is to compare the account of what took place when David became king of Israel with that of the handing on of the throne from David to Solomon. In the first story everything turns, exactly as in the case of Saul, on the designation by Yahweh and the acclamation by the tribes (2 Sam. v. 1 ff.); in the second, it is David who on his own authority designated his successor—even over the kingdom of Israel—and there is not even a mention of the consent of Yahweh or of the people (1 Kings i. 35; except by Benaiah i. 36 f.). But we must not overlook the fact that this latter scene takes place at the court of David and must accordingly be regarded in the first place as bearing witness merely to a view of the monarchy that had arisen there, at the seat of the central government of the whole empire. I will discuss this point of view later. We must certainly not suppose that the ideal of the charismatic kingdom had at the same time already been abandoned or forgotten outside Jerusalem, amongst the tribes in Israel. In fact, their attitude during the revolts against David shows that this was not the case; for in these crises in his authority it was the tribes of Israel that regularly provided the numerical support on which those who stirred up the revolts could most safely rely, regardless of whether, as in the case of Absalom (2 Sam. xv ff.), there was an attempt to transfer the throne before due time within the house of David, or whether, as in the case of Sheba (2 Sam. xx), it was intended to sever entirely the connection between the kingdom of Israel and David and his family. In both cases it is clear that the tribes of the kingdom of Israel acted from the conviction that their obligation of faithfulness and obedience to the reigning king ceased as soon as it became evident that for his part he was no longer carrying out the function bestowed on him according to the commission he had been given; it will be understood that the tradition, which is wholly on the side of David, does not say whether or not there was any suggestion that Absalom and Sheba had been called by Yahweh to take over the kingdom. As a result of the defeats inflicted during these revolts, the succession of Solomon to David was apparently accepted without resistance by the kingdom of Israel, although it was, as we have said, in fundamental contradiction to the Israelite conception of the monarchy; and in spite of all the grievances of his subjects concerning the way he fulfilled his office (1 Kings xi. 26 ff.), Solomon was acknowledged as king till the end of his life.

Immediately after his death, however, the original and distinctive features of the monarchy in the kingdom of Israel, which had lain more or less hidden for two generations, completely reasserted themselves, successfully caused the separation of this kingdom from the system of government set up under the family of David, by breaking the personal union that linked Israel to the neighbouring kingdoms (1 Kings xii. 1 ff.), and led in the course of the next half-century to the succession at the head of that state, once again ordering its affairs in its own way, of several kings who could be called true successors of Saul. According to the tradition, both Jeroboam I and Baasha were charismatic kings in the sense that they owed their position to the designation of Yahweh and the acclamation of the people (1 Kings xi. 29 ff.; xii. 20; xiv. 14; xv. 27), and perhaps Omri also belongs to this group, although as a result of the special circumstances under which he attained the throne (1 Kings xvi. 15 ff., 21 f.) the tradition does not give a sufficiently full account for us to determine this. The kings who occur between these, Nadab and Elah, in whose persons the families of Jeroboam and Baasha respectively attempted to retain the throne for themselves as an inheritance, had, by the ancient ideal standard, as little right to occupy the throne as Ishbaal, the son of Saul, at an earlier period. The reign of two years (in reality presumably only a few months of two consecutive calendar years in each case) which the tradition ascribes to them exactly as it does to Ishbaal (1 Kings xv. 25; xvi. 8; cf. 2 Sam. ii. 10), clearly represents nothing more than the interval which customarily occurred after the death of a legitimate king, before a true charismatic successor was designated by Yahweh and acknowledged by the people. In the nature of things, each newly designated ruler had then to take violent action against the illegitimate claims made to inherit the kingdom by the descendants of his last legitimate predecessor. Nor did he need to have any hesitation in taking the radical step of exterminating the family in question; his designation by Yahweh gave him the authority for this (1 Kings xiv. 10 f.). Thus one could call the kingdom of Israel, while its charismatic monarchy was still at this stage of development, a kingdom based on revolution by the will of God; every Israelite at that period had experienced at least twice the ascent of a newcomer over the ruin of his predecessor to the throne, and had recognized therein, be it with exultation or with horror, the carrying out of a decision made by Yahweh for his people; he himself, where circumstances allowed, would have had to play his part in carrying those decisions out, perhaps by military service (1 Kings xv. 27; xvi. 15 ff.). Moreover, every time such an upheaval took place, the monarchy passed from one tribe to another. Benjamin, Judah, Ephraim, and Issachar in turn provided a charismatic leader, as though Yahweh was constantly choosing the new king from a different place each time with the intention that the monarchy should not come to be firmly connected with any individual tribe. The same had been true earlier of the 'minor judges' mentioned in the Book of Judges, who had held the only office common to the whole of Israel in the period before the national state was founded (Judges x. 1–5; xii. 7–15), and also of the kings of the related Edomite tribes (Gen. xxxvi. 31–39), with which a much closer parallel is possible than with the kings of the Canaanite cities, which were quite differently governed, usually by an hereditary dynasty. There must also be a connection between this continuing flexibility in the charismatic monarchy and the facts, first, that a fixed seat for the kings of Israel grew up only gradually in Tirzah (1 Kings xiv. 17; xv. 23, 33, etc.; but cf. xii. 25), and secondly, that the sanctuaries which served the whole kingdom were set up at the beginning, apparently intentionally, in places like Bethel and Dan, which owing to their position on the furthermost borders of the kingdom could never be considered as a royal residence (1 Kings xii. 26 ff.). Thus well over a century after the time of its foundation, the institutions of the kingdom of Israel had not yet reached the final point of their development, and I have no doubt that the decisive reason for this delay, apart from the interruption in the course of events by the episode of David's empire, lay in the charismatic character of the monarchy, which militated against any continuing link between the occupant of the throne at any time and his successors.

A glance at the succession of kings in the period immediately following Omri suffices to show that from his reign there was a change. Instead of the loosely connected series of charismatic kings, of various origins, and certainly also of varied talents and authority (with non-charismatic sons inheriting the throne in the short intervals between them), which had been the rule up to that time, whole dynasties now ruled the kingdom, the first, the sons of Omri, providing three generations of kings who ruled for nearly half a century, and the second, the family of Jehu, four generations ruling for practically a whole century. How this sudden change took place is not immediately obvious from the tradition in the Old Testament, which for this particular period is much too closely restricted to accounts of external events. It is in any case a question which of its nature it is not possible to answer in full, for as always with such a process, especially when it takes place at so advanced a stage in the history of a state, it is necessary to take into account the complex interplay of many influences, which may very well come from more than one direction. It is possible that such pressures could come from within the kingdom itself, hardly, it is true, from the Israelite population, which presumably still held firm to their native ideal of a charismatic monarchy, but more probably from the Canaanite part of the population, whose aristocracy grew closer and closer to the kings as time went on, and acquainted them with the traditions and institutions of the previous Canaanite system of government with a dynastic monarchy as its nucleus. The close political alliance of the house of Omri with the dynasty of the Phoenician city of Tyre could only serve to strengthen from outside these Canaanite influences, once they had begun to make themselves felt within the kingdom (cf. 1 Kings xxi. 7). There is no way of knowing whether Israel received the same kind of stimulus from the strongest inland power amongst her neighbours, the Aramean kingdom of Damascus, due to the lack of any details of the form taken by the monarchy in that kingdom. On the other hand, if I am correct, the adoption and imitation of the organization of the strictly dynastic monarchy of the house of David by Omri and his descendants is an obvious and decisive influence behind this change. As soon as he came to the throne, after the destruction of the previous royal seat of Tirzah, Omri went on to found a completely new royal city on the hill of Samaria, which he had purchased (1 Kings xvi. 17f., 24; xxii. 39), and in my opinion it is virtually certain that he intended by this to create for the first time in the kingdom of Israel as close an equivalent as possible to David's royal city of Jerusalem. There was always of course the difference that the house of David ruled by right of conquest in the ancient city of the Jebusites, which David's mercenaries had taken by storm, while the reason for the unrestricted right of Omri and his successors to their new foundation was that they had bought the land where it was built. Moreover, excavations have shown that there had been no previous settlement there, so that it presented the possibility of a fully planned layout like the city of Solomon in Jerusalem. It was the latter, then, and not the city of David, which, from the architectural point of view at least, provided the real pattern for Omri's foundation. From the constitutional aspect, the parallel, or to use an expression that is historically more correct, the relationship of pattern and imitation between Jerusalem and Samaria is no less clear. For just as in the territory ruled by the house of David, the royal seat at Jerusalem always formed a separate city-state alongside the national state of Judah, so, from the time of Omri on, in the kingdom of Israel the new city of Samaria formed a distinct and separate political entity in the middle of the older state. Otherwise it would not be possible to explain why, after Jehu had already made himself king of Israel (2 Kings ix), he engaged in diplomatic correspondence with the aristocracy of the city of Samaria, as though they were a foreign power. He had already robbed them of their monarch, and now faced them with the decision whether they should carry on the independent government of their city-state under a king chosen by themselves from the previous ruling house, a procedure that would have led to a military conflict with the kingdom of Israel and its new king, or whether they would prefer to wipe out the remnants of the earlier dynasty and recognize him as their king. This would renew, under different circumstances, the personal union between the city-state of Samaria and the national state of Israel which had already lasted for several decades under the house of Omri (2 Kings x. 1 ff.). It is well known that the nobles of Samaria chose the second course, and this personal union between the city and the rest of the nation lasted until the fall of the kingdom of Israel. Isaiah still distinguishes in a single prophecy between 'Ephraim', the remnant of the kingdom of Israel after 732 B.C. and the 'inhabitants of Samaria', as two parallel and constitutionally separate entities, in the same way as the 'inhabitants of Jerusalem' and the 'men of Judah' are distinguished (Isa. ix. 8; cf. vii. 9; Micah i. 5; Isa. v. 3). This dualism, created by Omri and presumably further developed by his successors, was without question of decisive importance for the idea of a dynasty in the kingdom of Israel. It was self-evident that in the new city of Samaria, after the death of its founder, his authority should pass by law to no one but his descendants; and if the king of Samaria was also king of Israel it was virtually inevitable that the government of the kingdom of Israel should be included in the inheritance of the royal house, so long as affairs did not, as in the exceptional case of Jehu, reverse their normal course.

But although the true seat of the idea of a dynasty was in the new city-monarchy of Samaria, and was extended from there to the much older kingdom of Israel, its outward consequence, in the form of a succession of kings of Israel sprung from one family, does not mean that the Israelites were as completely converted to it either at once, or even in the course of the subsequent generation—as one can presume was the case with the Canaanites in the kingdom, who from the earliest times had been accustomed to such a system of government. In fact, the revolution of Jehu is a clear indication that the original Israelite idea of a charismatic monarchy still flourished and was powerful enough to reassert itself, if need be without and in opposition to Samaria. From the designation by Yahweh, and the acclamation of the people, to the extermination of the fallen royal house that had preceded him, everything that took place, as far as the kingdom of Israel was concerned (2 Kings ix), was basically the same as had been experienced by their ancestors from the time of Saul to that of Omri. One must suppose that this great event gave the threatened ideal of the charismatic king a new and enduring power over the minds of the Israelites, and that in consequence the most that was achieved under the dynasty of Jehu, even though the personal union of the kingdom with the very different city-state of Samaria remained in being, was a superficial reconciliation between the two different basic attitudes. Owing to the scarcity of evidence from the particularly sketchy tradition of this century, we have no way of telling what forms were created to express this reconciliation, or had already been created under the dynasty of Omri. (It might have been possible to transform the older idea of a charismatic authority bestowed on a single individual alone in the direction of an hereditary charisma, or to consider seriously the possibility of the personal charisma being bestowed on several members of the royal house in turn; cf. 2 Kings x. 30; xv. 12.) Even less is it possible to say how far any such compromise formulae may have penetrated beyond court circles, which undoubtedly had a primary interest in them, and beyond the royal ceremonial, to the mass of the population. But then, in the two centuries between the removal of the dynasty of Jehu and the destruction of the kingdom of Israel by the Assyrians, the veil is drawn aside once again, and it appears that even at that time the ideal of the charismatic kingship had not yet completely died out. Of course whether the usurpers who in turn took possession of the throne in Samaria at that period regarded themselves as kings with a personal calling from Yahweh in the old way, cannot be ascertained with certainty from the tradition concerning them, which takes the form merely of annals (2 Kings xv–xvii), although there is an historical probability that this was so. This makes the direct witness of the prophet Hosea, who lived at that time and actually commented in his prophecies on the coming and goings of the kings, of even greater importance for our purpose. But he still always judges them by the standard of the ancient ideal of the charismatic kingship, whether he is asserting that Yahweh gave them to the people and then took them away again, although it was only in his anger (Hosea xiii. 11), or whether, from another point of view, he is lamenting the fact that all this choosing of kings and princes has taken place without the knowledge and consent of Yahweh (Hosea viii. 4; cf. vii. 3 ff.; viii. 10; x. 3). Furthermore, the tension between the flexible charismatic kingship, and that which was bound to a dynasty, had obviously not yet been overcome. The latter had appeared too late, and was too alien in its background, for it completely supplanted the former; and how little Hosea himself regarded a dynasty as the permanent form of monarchy desired by Yahweh in Israel is shown by a prophecy from his early period concerning Yahweh's decision to overthrow the dynasty of Jehu (Hosea i. 4 f.). But his final and basic pronouncement on the monarchy was that it had to disappear from Israel altogether if the original relationship of love between Yahweh and Israel was ever to come into being again (Hosea iii. 4). With this final judgement Hosea comes very close to the sceptical provisions concerning the monarchy in the Book of Deuteronomy mentioned at the beginning of this essay, which I have no doubt originated in the same way as

Hosea's statements, in the views and experience of those who were acquainted with the monarchy in the kingdom of Israel (Deut. xvii. 14 ff.).

By contrast, the kingdom of Judah and of the associated city-state of Jerusalem presents, from the beginning to the end of a history lasting more than four hundred years, a much more unified and almost rigid picture. There is no sign of tension between a flexible, charismatic monarchy and one confined to a dynasty; the line of David carries on without interruption, though not without disturbance, from one generation to another. But even the disturbances that did occur make particularly clear the difference between Judah and the structure of the monarchy in Israel described above; though the accounts of these troubles are usually brief, they are always sufficient to refute the suspicion, which might otherwise arise, that these events could have been in any way influenced by the persistence in Judah and Jerusalem of a charismatic ideal of kingship similar to that in Israel. Whenever the removal by force of a reigning king of the house of David has to be described (revolts which did not have this result are not mentioned), it is never suggested that the initiative for this was taken by Yahweh. Nor is there any mention of a prophet or other man of God undertaking the designation of the new man selected by Yahweh. No city or district in the kingdom of Judah ever appears as the birthplace of a revolt, and one never hears that the population of the plains approved, even in retrospect, a rising begun elsewhere against the legitimate occupant of the throne, or joined it. It is Jerusalem alone where such disturbances always originated, and where for the most part they were enacted (2 Kings xi; xii. 21 f.; xiv. 19 [with a sequel in Lachish]; xxi. 23). If their leaders are mentioned at all, they are 'slaves of the king', that is, officials (2 Kings xxi. 21 f. [cf. xiv. 5]; xxi. 23)—apart from the case of the queen mother Athaliah, who on the death of her son the king, tried on her own account to exterminate the whole dynasty of David (2 Kings xi). Thus we are normally dealing only with palace revolutions, and we can only regret that, apart from the case of Athaliah, we have no way of knowing what political goal the leaders of these revolts had in mind. A large number of possibilities have to be considered, including the idea of a plan to weaken the power of the monarchy for the benefit of the aristocracy, though in view of the monarchical constitutions in force in perhaps every one of the neighbouring nations, this is not very probable (cf. Isa. vii. 6). On the other hand, the account we possess almost always describes in unambiguous terms the reaction aroused elsewhere in the kingdom of Judah by such revolutions at the court of David: as soon as the 'people of Judah', that is, that part of the population which had the power and the right to take part in political activity, heard that their legitimate king in Jerusalem had fallen victim to a mutiny of his 'slaves', they swarmed into the city and forded the ascent to the throne of the next descendant of David in line of inheritance (2 Kings xiv. 21; xxi. 24; cf. xxiii. 30). Judah played a similar part in the restoration of the legitimate Davidic monarchy when Athaliah was overthrown, and the words with which this story closes: 'So all the people of the land rejoiced; and the city was quiet' (2 Kings xi. 20a) gives an accurate picture of the situation which must regularly have arisen between Judah and Jerusalem as a result of such upheavals.

This conclusion, drawn from our first glance at the relevant passages, is surprising when one compares it with what we established above concerning the two forms of monarchy which existed side by side in the kingdom of Israel and in Samaria. For we found that in Israel in all probability the ideal of a charismatic kingship was very deep-rooted, and was kept alive amongst the Israelite population until the kingdom came to an end; while the attachment of the monarchy to a dynasty came about with the foundation of the city and the city-state of Samaria, and can reasonably be derived only from the conditions that obtained within this newly created entity. Now the city-state of Jerusalem was not of course the seat of a charismatic monarchy in the Israelite sense; we have not yet observed any trace of such a thing in the southern kingdom. Nevertheless, in the kingdom consisting of Judah and Jerusalem, linked together in a personal union since the time of David, it was the national state of Judah which, with astonishing consistency throughout the centuries, took repeated action against Jerusalem to preserve the link between the monarchy and the House of David. This attitude might seem more appropriate to the situation of the city-state of Jerusalem. In fact it is difficult to see how the tribe of Judah and the other tribes of the south, which together formed the kingdom of Judah, could themselves have developed this view of their monarchy, to which they obviously regarded themselves as permanently committed. Something may perhaps be due to the circumstance that some at least of these tribes had taken possession of what had previously been Canaanite cities, such as Hebron, Debir and Zephath, and as a result may have come under the surviving influence of the traditions and institutions of the dynastic city monarchies (Judges i. 10 ff.). Since Hebron was in fact the first royal seat in the kingdom of Judah, the possibility of such connections with the previous Canaanite period in the country's history is worth taking seriously, even though the excessively brief account of the foundation of the kingdom of Judah (2 Sam. 88. 1 ff.) provides no compelling evidence in this direction. We must not however forget that from the beginning the kingdom of Judah was clearly, in fact and by intention, something different from a Canaanite city-state, or a union of several such states. It was of considerably greater extent, and was based on the recognition of the king by the military levy of the 'men of Judah'. This last feature shows that the kingdom of Judah in its original form was much more closely related to the kingdom of Israel. No one doubts that at the moment of its foundation it was actually regarded as a counterpart to the latter, restoring the balance of political power. This makes it all the more remarkable that in the account of its origin there is no mention of the charismatic elements which are so clearly emphasized in the similar account of David's elevation to the throne of the kingdom of Israel (2 Sam. v. 1 ff.). What is recorded concerning Yahweh's part in bringing about David's decision to go up to Hebron is no sufficient substitute for the lack of any mention of a previous calling and bestowing of a charisma on David by Yahweh. Presumably, then, it must be conceded that in spite of a certain similarity, the kingdom of Judah did not possess from its origins exactly the same internal structure as the kingdom of Israel. Anyone who has formed an accurate picture of the personal background and history of David from the rich tradition dealing with his rise to be king of Judah (1 Sam. xvi–2 Sam. i) will also understand that in order to become king of Judah he had no need for the support of the charisma without which the kingship of Saul in Israel would have been unthinkable. But neither is there any suggestion, in the little we learn about the way the kingdom of Judah was founded, about any attachment of the monarchy to a dynasty; at that time it had perhaps not even been thought of, let alone laid down as a permanent rule.

But if the kingdom of Judah was so little advanced in its internal structure at first, it was as a result drawn all the more strongly into the further development of the whole system of government set up by David, and received from it distinct characteristics which would probably have remained foreign to it if it had gone on existing in isolation. To all appearances, the personal union set up by David with the city-state of Jerusalem which he got by conquest, had a much greater effect in this respect than the union with the kingdom of Israel, with which the Judeans, as is shown by the foundation of their kingdom and their attitude later on during the rebellions of Absalom and Sheba against David, lived in a relationship of unresolved tension. The end of the personal union between Judah and Israel immediately after the death of Solomon completely dissolved any political connection for which it may previously have been desired to prepare the way, and favoured the opposite tendencies which were also present. On the other hand, Judah remained constantly linked to the city-state of Jerusalem under the rule of the House of David, down to the invasion of Sennacherib in 701 B.C., and then, after a short interval, from the time of Manasseh onward. The transfer of the royal residence from Hebron to Jerusalem, carried out by David himself, gave the city-state an ascendancy over the rest of the kingdom which as a result of the growth and extension of the royal residence under Solomon and in later times grew even stronger. We never hear that the Judeans sought any alterations in this situation or demanded the return of their royal house to the territory of the kingdom of Judah. There is not even the least hint of a second residence of the House of David, be it in Hebron, or even merely in Bethlehem, and when a prophet from Judah, Micah, in connection with his struggle against the activities of the ruling class in Jerusalem, proclaims that the kingdom of David will one day be renewed from Bethlehem, and presumably, therefore, without any connection with the kingdom based on the city-state of Jerusalem, which was condemned to destruction (Micah v. 1 ff. [original text], cf. iii. 9 ff.), he is alone in his expectation of a radical end to the link between Judah and Jerusalem. At every period right down to the fall of the kingdom, the inhabitants of Judah as a whole, including their ruling class, had no other thought but that in the first place a member of the House of David must always occupy the throne, and that, secondly, this throne could only be located where David had finally set it up soon after the foundation of the kingdom, that is, outside the territory of Judah in Jerusalem. This tenacious loyalty of the Judeans to the arrangements laid down by their first king led to the result that disposition that may have been present amongst them towards a monarchy on a pattern peculiar to themselves was either prevented from developing any further, or was limited in its effect by the demands of the quite differently constituted monarchy of the city-state of Jerusalem. The latter, however, originated in a conquest of the city which had been carried out by David alone, with the support of his mercenaries and without any help from Judah or Israel. Thus it was inevitably bound to his dynasty, so long as the Jebusite population, which had not been removed, were not accorded the right to set up an independent political life of their own, either under a king from amongst themselves, or under the rule of their aristocracy. This, as anyone could foresee, would have occasioned the collapse of the whole system of government set up by David. The same fundamental danger threatened every time the throne changed hands later on, and for this reason alone it was a political necessity, obvious even to the Judeans, that the Davidic kings should always remain in Jerusalem, even though the seat of their kingdom lay as a result in a very remote part of the area they ruled. There was no particular need, then, for the adoption of traditions from the previous Jebusite kingdom, in establishing the dynastic form of the kingdom of David and his successors, first in Jerusalem and then in Judah, and in fact we do not know whether at the time of its conquest by David the city-state of Jerusalem still possessed a monarchic constitution, such that the institutions of its existing monarchy could be directly adopted. But there is no denying the possibility of such a continuity of ideas, which may have persisted throughout a period of rule by the Jebusite nobility in Jerusalem; it would simply be a question of providing more exact evidence that this continuity existed than has previously been possible on the basis of the few and ambiguous relevant texts (Melchizedek? Ps. cx. 4; cf. Gen. xiv. 18 ff.?).

From the historical point of view, then, we can adequately explain the early origin and the enduring effect of the idea of a dynasty in the kingdom of Judah, by the fact that from the very beginning there was a permanent link between the destinies of this kingdom and of the city-state of Jerusalem. The different nature of the original monarchy in Israel can then be seen to result from the fact that the link between the national state and a city-state, which decided the course of development in Judah, was lacking in Israel until the time of Omri. But this does not take into account all the known facts. During the reign of Solomon, the kingdom of Judah was not only joined in a personal union with Jerusalem and Israel, but was incorporated into a much larger empire, which at the time of its greatest extent reached 'from the Euphrates to the land of the Philistines and to the border of Egypt' (1 Kings v. 1=RSV. iv. 21). Even though this empire rapidly fell apart again, the brief climax of its power can hardly have passed by without leaving some trace in the very place where its ruling family remained in control, that is in Jerusalem and Judah. The continued existence of such an empire after the death of its founder was scarcely conceivable except through the inheritance of power by one of his family; the autocratic action of David in naming Solomon first as his co-regent and then as his successor (1 Kings i. 32 ff.), was fully appropriate to the needs of a system so entirely built around the occupant of the throne. Here, then, was an influence urging the necessity of attaching the kingdom to a dynasty, which was even stronger than that which arose from the particular situation of the city-state of Jerusalem; great and small causes worked together in the same direction. At the same time the brief existence of the empire of David and his family introduced into the ideal of the Davidic monarchy a factor of which there is no trace in the kingdom of Israel, but which under the house of David became a fixed part at least of the formulae in use at court. This was the tendency, occurring almost invariably in the empires of the ancient East, to extend the king's claims to authority to the whole world (Pss. ii. 8; lxxxii. 8; Zach. ix. 10). One might guess that the adoption of this outlook and these hopes came about in the time of Solomon; the main source from which they were drawn seems to have been the traditions of Egypt. In the first place, of course, this was a concern of the court, and therefore of Jerusalem; how far elements adopted from abroad were accepted amongst the mass of the people in the kingdom of Judah, with or without change, is difficult to tell.

Thus when we look closer at the kingdom of the house of David in Jerusalem and Judah, its essential features appear to grow steadily away from the basic charismatic character of the kingdom of Israel. The examination of the historical circumstances in which it took such a different form might well give the impression that by contrast with that charismatic kingdom it should be regarded as a purely secular phenomenon. If the succession to the throne in the house of David followed automatically the rules of the universally valid law of inheritance, where was there any room for the free initiative of Yahweh, which has to be effectively demonstrated in the kingdom of Israel as an indispensable precondition of the ascent to the throne of any legitimate king? But the monarchy of the House of David did not lack a religious and theological foundation; it was simply that this was different, and adapted to the special circumstances which, since the time of David, had come into being as a result of the prevalence of the idea of a dynasty, both in Jerusalem and in Judah. For this is the obvious significance of the conception of the eternal covenant which Yahweh made with David, which appears as early as the tradition concerning David himself, recurs later in the message of the prophets of Jerusalem and Judah, as well as in the historical books and in the psalms, and made legitimate the rule of the house of David for all time to come (2 Sam. vii. 8 ff.; xxiii. 5; Jer. xxxiii. 21; Ps. lxxxix. 3, 28; cf. Isa. lv. 3; 2 Chron. vi. 42). Through this covenant, the dynastic principle in the Davidic monarchy becomes a divine provision, through which Yahweh, by his own free decision, makes a single choice, valid for all time, and demands that it be permanently recognized by the subjects of the kingdom. The designation by Yahweh and the acclamation of the people, which we discovered were a basic element in the charismatic monarchy of the kingdom of Israel, are therefore present in a way; but the charismatic authority is not limited here, as in Israel, to the person and lifetime of one individual king chosen by Yahweh, but is bestowed as a permanent possession on the whole ruling house. However remote this conception may be from that which was accepted in the kingdom of Israel, one cannot say that it goes beyond the bounds of the views held by Israel concerning the pattern of Yahweh's plans and ordinances in covenants with men. It is true that the covenant with David can hardly be compared with the covenant at Sinai, in which Yahweh bound together the tribes in the higher unity of the people of Israel; in fact recent studies have correctly emphasized that for the prophets of Judah and Jerusalem, for whom the covenant with David is naturally of the first importance, the covenant of Sinai is much less significant. On the other hand, Yahweh's covenant with Levi forms a good analogy to that with David, even though in one case it is a whole tribe, and in the other only a single family which Yahweh sets in a special and permanent relationship to himself (Deut. xxxiii. 8 ff.; Jer. xxxiii. 21; Mal. ii. 4 ff.; Neh. xiii. 29; cf. Num. xxv. 12 f.). In both cases Yahweh's covenant signifies the permanent and therefore, of its nature, hereditary appointment of a greater or smaller group of men to a function in the life of the whole nation which henceforth was restricted to them alone.

But once this monarchy, linked to a dynasty, had been set up in principle by God, it was virtually inevitable that the ascent to the throne of individual members of the House of David in Jerusalem and Judah should not take place automatically, far less be treated as a purely secular event, but should be endowed with an elaborate ritual. In this Yahweh had to carry out the decisive act in which he himself designated the member of the royal house who was the legitimate heir as the man selected by him for the succession, and in which he bestowed upon him the necessary powers and abilities to carry out his royal office. Unfortunately this ritual is nowhere coherently described in the Old Testament; but most of the elements from which it was constructed are mentioned in one place or another. Only when Yahweh had adopted the heir to the throne as his son (2 Sam. vii. 14; Isa. ix. 5; Ps. ii. 7), determined his royal name in full (2 Sam. vii. 9; 1 Kings i. 47; Isa. ix. 5), granted him his first request (1 Kings iii. 5 ff.; Pss. ii. 8; xx. 5; xxi. 3, 5) and given him a sceptre (Isa. ix. 5; Ps. cx. 2) and crown (Ps. xxi. 3; 2 Kings xi. 12) could he legitimately begin to rule. There is no doubt that a good deal of this ritual was adopted from the traditions and institutions of the monarchy in the other kingdoms, in particular Egypt. But everything is closely related to the one central and specific idea of an inauguration, entirely depending on the decision of Yahweh, of the present heir to the throne into the exercise of an authority linked to his family since the time of David. The basic idea of the coronation ritual of Jerusalem and Judah is reflected by Isaiah when, to describe what is bestowed by Yahweh on each individual member of the House of David as he ascended the throne, he uses the term 'government', and in the list of official names of the king refers to him as 'prince' (governor) (Isa. ix. 5 f.), while he reserves the title of 'king' for Yahweh (Isa. vi. 5), from whose plenary authority this office is derived. Something similar is undoubtedly expressed by the author of the historical books of Chronicles, when he repeatedly refers to the kingdom and the throne of David as in fact the kingdom and the throne of Yahweh himself (1 Chron. xvii. 14; xxvii. 5; xxix. 23; 2 Chron. ix. 8; xiii. 8). However much the king may be raised above the people, the distance between Yahweh and the king is always kept. This makes it all the more difficult to suppose that the divine kingship of the ancient Near East, so frequently discussed nowadays, and which was allegedly universal, could have found acceptance within this circle of ideas, unless it were so thoroughly adapted as to be compatible with the strict subordination even of the kings of the House of David to Yahweh. On the other it is also certain that the expectation of the Messiah has its origin in this complex of ideas. It has nothing to do with the ideal of kingship in the kingdom of Israel described above; for the only expectation of a future ruler that could have been derived from this latter would have had to take the form of the elevation to the throne by Yahweh of another newcomer, such as he has often raised up in the past, out of any tribe which he should choose, to replace the existing kings, and perhaps of his endowment with even richer gifts (cf. Ps. lxxx. 18 f.?). On the other hand, the messianic expectation with which we are acquainted from the oracles of the prophets in the Old Testament is bound to the dynasty of David, even though a certain breach in the line of the dynasty may sometimes be anticipated (Isa. xi. 1; Micah v. 1). In any case, the future ruler, even in the so-called messianic prophecies, is in the first instance merely a member of the line of rulers in the succession of David, albeit one in whom this pattern of ideal kingship might be more perfectly realized than in his predecessors, as a result of the special fullness of charismatic gifts bestowed upon him (Isa. xi. 1 ff.); but this does not mean that he is in any sense the bringer of the longed-for time of salvation, independently of Yahweh. He is only a gift of Yahweh to that time, a gift which is differently represented by individual prophets according to their particular situation and task. Thus as an expectation which could always take on fresh elements, the ideal kingship of Jerusalem and Judah, as is well known, long survived the fall of the dynasty of David, and preserved something of its special characteristics not merely for later Judaism, but also for Christianity.

INDEX 1—AUTHORS

(Not including the editors of texts quoted in the Appendix to 'The God of the Fathers', pp. 67 ff.)

INDEX 2–SUBJECTS, PLACES AND PROPER NAMES

INDEX 3–SCRIPTURE REFERENCES

INDEX 4—GREEK AND SEMITIC GODS AND PROPER NAMES

(Not including references to the Appendix to the 'God of the Fathers')